This book offers a comprehensive overview of the structure, strategy, and methods of assessment of theoretical economics. Part I explains how economists theorize, and emphasizes the close relations between positive theory, the theory of rationality, and welfare economics. It clarifies the theoretical vision of economics that guides the construction of specific models. This vision sees economics as a "separate science," that is, as the application of a simple, unified, and complete theory spanning a distinct economic realm.

In part II, Professor Hausman defends the view that economic theory is "inexact," since its basic principles take account of only the few most important causes of economic phenomena. Economic theorizing consists largely of deducing the consequences of these principles in particular circumstances. Confidence in the implications of economic theory derives from confidence in its basic principles, not from testing their implications. Economic practice based on this methodology conflicts sharply with the positivist of Popperian methodological rules economists typically defend. But unlike many commentators, Hausman sees this conflict as revealing flaws in the methodology economists espouse rather than in the methodology they practice.

Part III links the conception of economics as a separate science to the fact that economic theories concern both the reasons and the causes of human actions, and it questions how empirically successful economics has been. Since market phenomena provide little evidence for or against economic theories, other data and hypotheses, especially including experimental studies of individual behavior, may contribute in important ways to economics.

With its authoritative appendix introducing relevant issues in philosophy of science, this book is a major addition to philosophy of economics and philosphy of social science.

The inexact and separate science of economics

The inexact and separate science of economics

Daniel M. Hausman

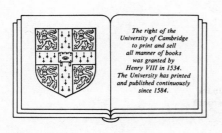

The right of the
University of Cambridge
to print and sell
all manner of books
was granted by
Henry VIII in 1534.
The University has printed
and published continuously
since 1584.

Cambridge University Press
Cambridge   New York   Port Chester
Melbourne   Sydney

Published by the Press Syndicate of the University of Cambridge
The Pitt Building, Trumpington Street, Cambridge CB2 1RP
40 West 20th Street, New York, NY 10011-4211, USA
10 Stamford Road, Oakleigh, Melbourne 3166, Australia

© Cambridge University Press 1992

First published 1992

Printed in Great Britain at the University Press, Cambridge

A cataloguing in publication record for this book is available from the British Library

Library of Congress cataloguing in publication data

ISBN 0 521 41501 2 hardback
ISBN 0 521 42523 9 paperback

JWA

Contents

Figures

For Cathy, Joshua, and David

Introduction

This book defends the old-fashioned view that the basic axioms of economics are "inexact" and that economics proceeds by deducing the consequences of these axioms in particular circumstances. The method of economics is deductive, and confidence in the implications of economics derives from confidence in its axioms rather than from testing their implications. In looking back two generations to this traditional methodological wisdom, I shall be defending economics and economists from common but unwarranted criticisms. I shall also be taking issue with the views defended in other recent monographs.[1] In my view many of the basic principles of economics can be regarded as inexact laws, and the methods of theory appraisal that economists employ in practice are scientifically acceptable.

But there is another aspect of economic methodology I shall not defend: the commitment to economics as a "separate science." To insist that any acceptable economic theory must, like current theory, aspire to capture the entire economic "realm" has no justification and leads, I shall argue, to stagnation. The keys to the methodological peculiarities of economics lie in its structure and strategy.

What is economics?

This book will be concerned only with contemporary microeconomic theory and general equilibrium theory. These theories are the best known of economic theories, the theories that have most influenced work in the other social sciences, and the theories which have been most discussed by philosophers, economists, and other social theorists.

In focusing on neoclassical economics, I am avoiding and begging questions about the definition and subject matter of economics. Phenomena do not come with the label "economic" attached to them.

---

[1] Blaug 1980a, Boland 1982b, 1986, 1989, Caldwell 1982, Klant 1984, Pheby 1988, Redman 1990, and Rosenberg forthcoming. My views are closest to those expressed in Stewart 1979.

On the contrary, theorists have had to decide what counts as an economic phenomenon. Like every other science, economics must define its object.

We are so accustomed to thinking about economies, that we often fail to notice how remarkable it is that there are such "things." As Marx points out with particular brilliance, market societies are strange human creations. Although they are constituted by the attitudes, actions, and artifacts of human beings, markets possess a very real objectivity, and they dominate the people whose actions perpetuate and constitute them. Although the "naturalness" of the domination of markets over human beings and the inevitability of market relations are, in Marx's view, illusory, there is nothing illusory about the domination itself.

The fact that these human activities and products so control human beings in market societies is part of what Marx means when he discusses "alienation." Consider the following story:

> A man was terribly down on his luck, out of work and desperate. He had only a few dollars left in his bank account. He decided to try prayer. He went down to his cash machine, got down on his knees, and prayed. Then he checked his balance and found that he was worth millions![2]

Whether this is a story of divine intervention or electronic failure, the picture of a man on his knees in front of a cash machine makes vivid the objectivity of market relations and the subjection of individual human beings to them.

Markets not only constrain the choices of individuals; they determine the fate of nations. Lester Thurow argues, for example, that in order to compete with Japan, the United States must increase its rate of investment (1980, pp. 96-7), otherwise it will suffer economic decline. What enforces this supposed necessity?

The world market. But what is that? What are markets? How do they work? How can they dominate a powerful nation of a quarter of a billion people? What are "economies"? What are the systems, norms, attitudes, and actions that economists study? What is "economics"? Attempts to answer these questions and to define economics are central to landmark works on economic methodology such as Mill's "On the Definition of Political Economy and the Method of Investigation Proper to It" (1836) and Lionel Robbins, *An Essay on the Nature and Significance of Economic Science* (1932, 1935).

Mill defines economics as "The science which traces the laws of such of the phenomena of society as arise from the combined operations of mankind for the production of wealth, in so far as those phenomena are

[2] This story was reported to me by students in a philosophy of science course I was teaching in 1979 at the University of Maryland.

not modified by the pursuit of any other object" (1836, p. 323). Such "substantive" definitions take economic phenomena to be linked to matters of wealth, but most also carry with them, as in Mill's words, commitments to a mode of explanation and a kind of theory.[3] Robbins, in contrast, offers a "formal" definition of economics as "the science which studies human behavior as a relationship between ends and scarce means which have alternative uses" (1932, p. 15). According to Robbins, economics is not concerned with production, exchange, distribution or consumption as such. It is instead concerned with an aspect of all human action. Although economists have not been able to draw the boundaries of their discipline in this way, they nevertheless like to think of their subject matter, as Robbins urges, as the consequences of rational choices in circumstances of scarcity. This vision has a determining influence on the questions theorists ask and the answers they are willing to accept. However, it is not the only possible vision of economics, and we shall see some of its limitations, but no alternatives will be explored here. *Indeed, to avoid unnecessary repetition, I shall usually omit the adjective "neoclassical" and just speak of "economics" when I am discussing neoclassical economics.* This is merely a convenience, not a covert attempt to denigrate other schools of economics or to define them out of existence.

Methodology and the problem of theory assessment

This is a book on economic methodology. But what is THAT? Just what might an investigation of economic methodology accomplish? There are at least four distinct answers.

First, investigators may simply want to know how the discipline of economics "works" now and how it has worked in the past. They may want to know answers to questions such as: How does one succeed as an economist? What character traits, stylistic preferences, or values are encouraged among economists? To what extent are the aims of economists bound up with the policy demands that are made of them? One may want to know the answers to these sociological and historical questions simply because one wants to understand the discipline, or one may have further aims, which answers to these questions may help one to achieve. One might want, for example, to learn how to get tenure in an economics department, to understand how empirical knowledge is possible, or to convict some group of economists of idiocy.

---

[3] Indeed Mill also defines economics in terms of the causal factors with which it is concerned. This dual specification in terms of causes and domains is crucial to the notion of economics as a separate science. The contrast between Mill and Robbins is thus less than it may appear, especially since the notion of a specifically economic "realm" has persisted. See section 6.4 below.

Second, one may study methodology to help assess aspects of economics from a practical or policy perspective. The questions which motivate such assessments are varied: What role should economics play in the curriculum of secondary schools or colleges? What role should economists play in policy-making? To what extent should other inquiries model themselves after economics? Philosophers are supposed to have a central role in such practical evaluation, which has not been sharply distinguished from philosophical inquiry (see Rorty 1979, p. 4).

The third reason for being interested in economic methodology is my reason. I would like to understand better how people manage to learn about the social world around them. By seeing how economists have succeeded – and failed – in acquiring such knowledge, one may be able to determine how best to study social phenomena: to what extent social inquiry ought to resemble inquiry in physics, how much humans can know about social phenomena, and what limits social inquiry encounters. Since such philosophical inquiry is in my view itself a kind of social inquiry, the whole project might appear absurd. I will defend it below in chapter 14.

Most of those who study economic methodology do so because they want to improve it or to help economists to practice it better. Just as economists may seek to improve monetary policy or the tax structure or compliance with the ideals of either, so students of economic methodology may seek to improve the way economic theories are generated and tested and the incentives that encourage economists to undertake certain kinds of study and to avoid others. Such ambitions make sense only if there is some way to determine whether one methodological rule is superior to another. Practical efforts to improve economic methodology will thus be heavily influenced by philosophical theories concerning knowledge acquisition. For one of the most important senses in which methodological norm N may be superior to norm M is if one is more likely to learn something if one follows N than if one follows M. The practical methodological implications of my views are drawn together and defended in chapter 14.

Many people regard economic methodology as concerned exclusively with the problem of theory *appraisal*, the problem of distinguishing good theorizing and good economic theories from bad theorizing and bad theories. Although theory appraisal is a central issue, about which I shall have a great deal to say, there are other philosophically interesting questions to ask about economic theory. One should also inquire about the *structure* of microeconomics and general equilibrium theory, about the *strategy* and *heuristics* that guide work in contemporary economics, about the *goals* of economic theorizing, and about the relations between economic theory and policy questions. As this book will show, these questions are crucial both in themselves and in order to understand the peculiarities of theory appraisal in economics. One should also ask more detailed questions that do not fall neatly under any of these general rubrics. Notice that many questions besides those related to theory appraisal are also normative. For example, to ask what the goals of economics are is to ask not only what they have been, but also what they ought to be.[4]

A reader's guide

The central problem of theory appraisal cannot be broached before one understands the content, structure, and strategy of economic theory as well as a good deal of philosophy of science. Yet readers would be impatient with so much introductory material. Accordingly I have placed the general discussion of philosophy of science in an appendix, which has been organized for easy use. I hope readers will find it a helpful reference. Those without any background in the philosophy of science may want to read it straight through before starting chapter 1.

Introductory material concerning economic theory could not be placed in a second appendix, for how one understands this material determines how well one grasps the structure and strategy of economics, which are the subject matter of part I. I think that the way in which the economic background is presented should be of value to students of economics and that it may even be of interest to trained theorists. Although the first four chapters contain many familiar analyses and can be skimmed by readers with a solid background in economics, they should not be skipped altogether, for they define the questions that the rest of the book attempts to answer, and they provide initial sketches of important philosophical distinctions. I urge readers not to skip sections 3.6, 3.7, and 4.6.

Chapter 1 focuses on the conception of rationality that is embodied in contemporary economics and is central to it. After presenting ordinal utility theory, I offer a critique of revealed preference theory and an introduction to expected utility theory. If one wants to understand economics, the theory of rationality is the place to begin.

Chapter 2 presents consumer choice theory and an example of a simple economic *model*, and it makes preliminary comments on the apparent empirical anomalies the theory faces. Its material is well-known, although

---

[4] It is not obvious how one should go about answering such questions, but rather than address explicitly such "metamethodological questions" – such questions concerning the methodology of the methodology of economics – I shall show how to answer them by doing methodology.

textbooks rarely develop the connections between specific models and fundamental theory so explicitly. Section 2.6 provides an illustration of "bootstrapping," a contemporary theory of confirmation discussed in section A.10.3, and it can be skipped by those who are not interested in confirmation theory.

Chapter 3 carries out the same tasks for the theory of the firm and for general equilibrium theory. In doing so, it pulls together the discussions of the first three chapters to offer a general sketch of the causal structure and basic principles of economics. It takes issue with the common view that general equilibrium theory is the fundamental theory of contemporary economics. Equilibrium theory, not general equilibrium theory, is fundamental.

Chapter 4 sketches the contemporary theory of economic welfare. It shows that welfare economics is an esoteric discipline, whose questions are determined more by equilibrium theory than by practical problems of economic welfare. In section 4.6 I explain why economists embrace perfect competition as a moral ideal. The argument I explore also explains why one finds among welfare economists a seemingly paradoxical combination of moral authority and moral agnosticism.

In the remaining three chapters of part I, I attempt to say more abstractly and precisely what economic theories and models are and to characterize their overall structure and strategy.

Chapter 5 is concerned with theories and models in economics. It surveys philosophical conceptions of theories and defends a common-sense view of theories as sets of lawlike statements that are systematically interconnected. Models are conceptual explorations without empirical commitments. They are definitions of predicates or kinds of systems. Models can be *used* to theorize, explain, or predict, when one offers "theoretical hypotheses" asserting that parts of the real world belong to the extension of the predicate a model defines.

Chapter 6 is one of the most important chapters in the book. It is concerned with the global strategy and structure of economic theory. After arguing that Thomas Kuhn's and Imre Lakatos' notions of "paradigm" and "research program" are misleading and not sufficiently detailed, I sketch the structure and strategy of economics as an inexact and separate science and comment on the role of abstract general equilibrium theories in this enterprise.

Chapter 7 concludes part I with an illustrative case study of Paul Samuelson's famous overlapping-generations model.

Part II, "Appraisal," focuses on problems of theory assessment. I develop my views in chapters 8 and 12, which are the most important chapters in this part. Chapters 9 to 11 are devoted to criticizing the views of others and may be skipped by those who are not interested in the views I criticize.

In **Chapter 8** I develop and defend the traditional conception that economics is an inexact science that investigates deductively the implications of assumptions that are known to be approximately true. I consider several interpretations of the problematic notion of inexactness or approximate truth and develop a concept of inexactness as vague implicit qualification. I explain how statements with vague implicit qualifications can be true and what conditions must be met if one is to have good reason to accept them. Chapter 8 also presents an interpretation of J. S. Mill's deductive method, which still appears to dominate methodological practice in economics.

This view of theory assessment was challenged and rejected several decades ago and has been replaced by more "positivistic" or "modernist" views of economic methodology, which are the subject of criticism in **chapter 9**. In developing and criticizing the views of Terence Hutchison, Paul Samuelson, Fritz Machlup, Milton Friedman, and Tjallings Koopmans, this chapter highlights the "methodological schizophrenia" of contemporary economics, in which methodological pronouncements and practice regularly contradict one another.

Chapter 10 criticizes Karl Popper's views on the philosophy of science, which have been particularly influential among writers on economic methodology. Popperian critics of economics are right to claim that economists seldom practice the falsificationism that many preach, but the problem is with the preaching, not with the practice: falsificationism is not a feasible methodology.

Chapter 11 turns to Popper's disciple and then critic, Imre Lakatos, whose influence on economic methodologists is second only to Popper's. Although Lakatos provides more resources with which to defend economics than Popper, his views are also inadequate and for a similar reason. Both Popper and Lakatos deny that one can judge how close to the truth or how likely to be true any scientific statement is. One is consequently unable to use such judgments either in engineering or in theoretical science. Popper and Lakatos are implicitly calling for a radical and destructive transformation of human practices.

Chapter 12 returns to Mill's inexact deductive method, as developed in chapter 8. I concede that it is too dogmatic, but I show how economics can be scientifically respectable, even though economists appear to conform to this method. The peculiarities of theory appraisal in economics follow more from the difficulties of testing in economics than from an aberrant view of confirmation. Chapter 12 considers some of the anomalies to which expected utility theory gives rise, to show how disconfirmation of basic principles of economics is possible and to expose the large and legitimate role that pragmatic factors play in theory appraisal in economics.

Chapter 13 concludes part II with a case study of the reactions of economists to experimental work on so-called "preference reversals." In this case the profession has not relied on an unacceptably dogmatic view of theory appraisal. Such dogmatism as there is (and there is some) stems from the commitment of economists to a vision of economics as a separate science.

Part III, "Conclusions," pulls together this long argument. In **chapter 14**, I defend the critical implications of chapter 12 against two further arguments that would justify dismissing anomalous experimental results, such as those concerning preference reversals. I then draw out some of the implications of my philosophical conclusions for the practice of economics, and defend the legitimacy of my "preaching" against criticisms such as those voiced most compellingly by Donald McCloskey.

In **chapter 15**, I summarize the argument and show that the methodological peculiarities of economics depend to a considerable extent on the fact that it is a social science. The fact that equilibrium theory includes a theory of rationality helps to explain why positive and normative economics are so intermingled, why economists are so strongly committed to their theory, and why they pursue such a distinctive strategy.

Although this book is an extended argument for a particular vision of economic methodology, it is also designed to serve as a reference work and an advanced textbook on economic methodology. It is written mainly for an audience of economists and graduate students in economics, but the issues with which it is concerned are also of interest to philosophers, other social scientists, and to policy-makers. The introductory material is designed to make the book accessible to these different audiences. I have tried to lay out a rich and coherent vision of the unique neoclassical theoretical enterprise, its special handicaps, and its brilliant, fascinating but unsuccessful strategies for overcoming them.

Sources and acknowledgments

When I began writing this book, almost four years ago, I thought I could pull together the methodological views I had expressed in *Capital, Profits, and Prices* (1981a) and in journal articles and produce a monograph in a few months. How wrong I was! In developing the extended argument of this book I changed my mind both about details and on many fundamental issues. I am gratified to be able to correct so many mistakes in previous works and am appalled that there were so many to correct.

Echoes of earlier works remain. The most distinct are to be found in chapters 5, 8, 9, 10, 12, and the appendix. The view presented in chapter 5 of theories and models is essentially that of chapter 3 of *Capital, Profits, and Prices*. The view of economics as employing an inexact deductive method receives a truncated exposition and defense in "John Stuart Mill's Philosophy of Economics" and chapter 7 of *Capital, Profits, and Prices*. "The Deductive Method" (1990a), which was drawn from early versions of chapters 8 and 12, is much closer to them in its content. Chapter 9 draws on "Economic Methodology and Philosophy of Science" (1988b) and "Economic Methodology in a Nutshell" (1989b). The discussion of Popper's views in chapter 10 follows my "An Appraisal of Popperian Methodology" (1988a). A version of chapter 13 entitled, "On Dogmatism in Economics: The Case of Preference Reversals," will be appearing late in 1991 in the *Journal of Socio-Economics*. The appendix incorporates material from the first half of the introduction to my *The Philosophy of Economics* (1984b).

My intellectual debts are heavy. I owe a great deal to Georg Aichholzer, Lorand Ambrus-Lakatos, Cristina Bicchieri, Jack Birner, Mark Blaug, Bruce Caldwell, Neil de Marchi, Ellery Eells, Berent Enç, Haskell Fain, Ronald Findlay, Ben Gales, Clark Glymour, Paula Gottlieb, Ed Green, Frank Hahn, Bert Hamminga, D. Wade Hands, Abraham Hirsch, Lester Hunt, Maarten Janssen, Mark Kaplan, Harold Kincaid, J.J. Klant, Maurice Lagueux, Isaac Levi, Andrew Levine, Uskali Mäki, Donald McCloskey, Michael McPherson, Roger Miller, Philippe Mongin, Karl Mueller, Robert Nadeau, Alan Nelson, Leland Neuberg, Bart Nooteboom, Benoit Pepin, Steven Rappaport, Alexander Rosenberg, Margaret Schabas, Julius Sensat, Teddy Seidenfeld, Elliott Sober, Hal Varian, E. Roy Weintraub, Leora Weizman, James Woodward, Andreas Wörgötte, and, most of all, Sidney Morgenbesser.

I am also indebted to students who have studied "Philosophy of Economics" with me at the University of Maryland, Carnegie Mellon University, Lawrence University, and the University of Wisconsin-Madison. They have forced me to be more lucid.

Paul Anderson, John Dreher, Merton Finkler, and Thomas Ryckman were kind enough to work through a partial early draft with me during the Summer of 1988 and to offer more good criticisms than I have been able to answer.

Neil de Marchi, Clark Glymour, Wade Hands, Abe Hirsch, Michael McPherson, and Alexander Rosenberg read large portions of the draft of May 1989 and made many helpful criticisms. The remarkable "Keklu" group at the University of Helsinki also worked through that version and, on a dark February evening in Helsinki, gave me hours of detailed and pointed criticism. Uskali Mäki is the organizer of this group, which at that time consisted of Visa Heinonen, Tarja Knuuttila, Katri Kosonen, Klaus Kultti, Markku Ollikainen, Mika Pantzar, Jukka-Pekka Piimies, Jorma Sappinen, and Suvi-Anne Siimes.

Bruce Caldwell, Lee Hansen, Michael McPherson, Roger Miller, Alexander Rosenberg, and several anonymous referees read the whole of the 1990 version of the manuscript and saved me from many errors. That version was used as a text for a course on the philosophy of economics at the University of Wisconsin, which I taught jointly with Roger Miller. I want to thank the students for putting up with a difficult text and helping me to improve the exposition. That version was also used in a graduate seminar on the philosophy of economics, and the participants (Evan Anderson, Mark Bauder, Ivan Gutierrez, Gregory Mougin, and Daniel Van Kley) were invaluable critics and advisors. Donald McCloskey helped with my style both through pointed criticism and through his splendid little book, *The Writing of Economics* (1987). Anne Rix provided expert copy-editing assistance.

I am also indebted to audiences at many universities, who have heard me politely and have corrected so many of my mistakes. The Wisconsin Alumni Research Foundation, administered by the Graduate School at the University of Wisconsin-Madison provided support during the Spring semester of 1989, when a large part of the manuscript was written. Lawrence University generously provided library and computing facilities. My family's healthy lack of interest in economic methodology has been a useful reminder that other things matter apart from how people can acquire knowledge of economic phenomena. They have helped to keep me sane. So many people have helped me on this material over so long a period that I am bound to have forgotten to thank someone who should be thanked.

Appleton, Wisconsin
February, 1991

Part I

Introduction, structure, and strategy

Part I provides an introductory account of microeconomics, general equilibrium theory, and welfare economics; links simple models (like those found in textbooks and easy applications) to fundamental theory, and explores the structure and strategy of economic theorizing. Although the first four chapters provide an introduction to microeconomics and welfare theory, their presentation is unlike a standard textbook. For I shall begin (chapter 1) with the theory of rationality that is implicit in economics and shall show how it ties together the theory of consumer choice (chapter 2), the theory of production and general equilibrium (chapter 3), and the normative theory of economic welfare (chapter 4). Building on the results of the first four chapters, chapters 5 and 6 will offer a general account of the structure and strategy of (neoclassical) economic theorizing, which I hope to make vivid with the case study in chapter 7. Only then, in part II, shall I turn to the problem of assessment.

The first four chapters raise a number of questions concerning economic theory that I try to answer later. I shall make a few specific criticisms of, for example, revealed preference theory and the iden- tification of individual welfare with the satisfaction of preferences, but in general I have tried to keep introduction and criticism separate. The many questions I shall raise concerning apparently odd features of economics are genuine, not rhetorical, and are not intended as veiled criticism. When I criticize microeconomics, as I shall later, particularly in part III, I will be forthright, and the criticism will not consist of pointing out superficial oddities.

1 Rationality and utility theory

Microeconomics portrays individual agents as choosing rationally. Many of the generalizations that it offers concerning how people do choose are also claims about how agents *ought rationally* to choose. This fact distinguishes economics from the natural sciences, whose particles do not choose and are not rational, and whose theories have no similar normative dimension. It might be objected that the normative plausibility of the view of rationality implicit in microeconomics is irrelevant to its empirical assessment, but see chapters 4, 12, and 15. Those familiar with the theory of rationality may want to skim this chapter, although the criticism of revealed-preference theory in section 1.3 may be of interest.

What is it to choose rationally? This is an old philosophical question, and not an easy one to answer (Resnik 1987). For there are many kinds of irrationality, and the notion of choice itself is problematic. Economists regard choice as arising from constraints, preferences (desires), and expectations (beliefs). Economists take preferences as givens and not themselves subject to rational appraisal. But choices and *sets* of beliefs and preferences may be rational or irrational depending on whether they are, in a sense to be discussed shortly, consistent. In ordinary language, we would not call someone who chooses to spend every possible waking moment calculating prime numbers rational. But in the economist's sense of "rational," Mr Number could qualify as entirely rational.

1.1 Rational preference and choice in conditions of certainty

The basic model of choice implicit in standard microeconomic theory and in many alternatives to it, takes an agent A's choice or action, to be the result of A's beliefs and A's desires or preferences. Choice is rational when it is determined by rational beliefs and preferences. Economists have had comparatively little to say about rational belief. Indeed, in many economic models, agents are taken to have perfect knowledge. But uncertainty cannot be avoided, and, in circumstances of uncertainty, something has to be said about the rationality of belief. Let us, however, defer discussing the rationality of belief (until 1.4 below) and begin with circumstances of complete certainty.

1.1.1   Rationally preferring and choosing options

In everyday language "preference" is taken to refer to a subjective state of individuals, which is reflected in their words and actions, while "choice" is ambiguous between subjective deliberation and its consequent action. For reasons I shall spell out below in section 1.3, *I shall take preferences to be subjective states for which choices, construed as actions, provide fallible evidence.*

The objects of preference and choice can be many different things. In consumer choice theory, they are bundles of commodities and services. In a more general context, an option is simply any object of preference or choice. It can be a gadget at the hardware store or a spouse. Since preferences for individual goods depend on what other goods one has (a compact disc is not much good without a compact disc player), the objects of preferences should in general be taken as complete descriptions of states of the world. But I shall sometimes simplify and speak of a preference for an orange rather than speaking each time of a preference for the status quo plus an orange.

Agents are taken to have rational preferences if their preferences are complete and transitive and to choose rationally if their preferences are rational and there is no feasible option that they prefer to the chosen option. An agent A's preferences are complete if for all options x and y, either A prefers x to y, or A prefers y to x, or A is indifferent between x and y. A's preferences are transitive if for all options x, y, and z, if A prefers x to y and y to z, then A prefers x to z; and if A is indifferent between x and y and y and z, then A is indifferent between x and z.

This view of rationality might be regarded as too weak, for economists typically take the existence of rational preferences as tantamount to the existence of a *utility function* and rational choice as utility maximization. But the existence of a real-valued utility function also requires that preferences be in a specific sense continuous (see section 1.2.1 below).

This notion of rationality has also appeared to many to be too demanding. Must an agent A be able to rank all feasible options, or is it enough that A be able to rank all the options that are available in the given context? Is full transitivity of preference and indifference necessary or is it enough that A's choices never form a cycle? Such possible weakenings of the standard theory of rationality have their own formal developments, and one can prove a variety of theorems relating these various conceptions to each other (see Sen 1971 and McClennen 1990, chapter 2). The details of these formal developments are not germane here, for most economic theory relies on the simple model of rationality above.

Moreover, as I shall explain in section 1.3, many economists have wanted to eliminate references to subjective preferences and to theorize instead in terms of choices only.

With these cautions in mind, let us then explore this first approximation, for, although the above definition or model of rationality is very simple, it is also powerful and, in some instances, confusing not only to critics of economics, but also to orthodox economists themselves. So some caution and patience here are essential.

1.1.2   Completeness and transitivity

Completeness states simply that individuals can compare all options. Some theorists prefer to talk about "comparability" of options or "connectedness" or "connexity" of preferences rather than completeness, but, whatever the label, what is meant is simple. Completeness is obviously an idealization, for most of us have no settled ranking of a myriad of options.[1] It is evident that, if asked whether one prefers x to y, one is often inclined to say, "I don't know" and sometimes, "I can't rank them." How would you have answered my five-year-old when he wanted to know whether one should prefer driving a backhoe to driving a payloader? My answer, which did not satisfy him, was "I don't know."

In defense of completeness one might argue that such difficulties are unimportant and would not apply in circumstances of complete certainty. But it seems unreasonable to stake one's defense of completeness on the assumption of certainty, since situations of certainty are exceptional.[2] For more on completeness and some reasons to question whether it should be regarded as a condition of rationality or even an acceptable empirical generalization about people's actual preferences, see section 12.4.3 below.

It is evident that a cunning experimenter could, with a sufficiently long and complicated series of choices among pairs of options, find intransitivities in everybody's preferences. But it seems to me that such blunders no more cast doubt on transitivity as a requirement of rationality

---

[1] The standard defense of completeness relies on an interpretation of preference as constructed out of choices and will be discussed below, p. 20.

[2] One can raise questions about whether completeness is required by rationality even under conditions of certainty. If asked which of my children I would prefer to be put to death, I might be unwilling to decide. But such difficulties are not as prevalent or threatening to the theory as the more humdrum ones that are ubiquitous in circumstances of uncertainty.

than do miscalculations cast doubt on arithmetic. In defense of transitivity, one can also argue that, if our preferences fail to be transitive, then others can make fools of us. Suppose for example that I prefer x to y and y to z and z to x, and that I start out possessing z. Then I should, in principle, be willing to pay a fee for each of the following three exchanges: trade z away for y, trade y away for x, and trade x away for z. I am then back where I started, except that I am poorer by the expense of the three fees. I have become a "money pump," and this argument is known as the money-pump argument. Intransitive preferences thus appear to be irrational (see Schick 1986 for a critical discussion of this argument).

1.1.3   Context independence

In situation 1, A faces a choice between x and y. Suppose A prefers x to y, and chooses x. With respect to these two options A's preferences are complete and (trivially) transitive. So it appears that A's choice is rational. In situation 2, A faces a choice between x, y, and z. Suppose that A prefers y to z, z to x, and y to x, and that A chooses y. In situation 2, A's preferences are complete and transitive, and A chooses the most preferred option. So A chooses rationally in situation 2, too. But the combined choices and preferences seem inconsistent.[3] One possibility is that A's tastes have changed, but suppose instead that A's preferences are *context dependent*. A's preference between x and y depends upon whether z is available, too. The standard theory of rationality implicitly rules out such context dependence, for it demands that A be able to weakly order the whole range of feasible options for all choice situations simultaneously. So, from the perspective of the standard theory, the choices and preferences in the two situations are indeed not rational. The possibility of constructing a revealed-preference ordering from choices, discussed in section 1.3 below, also depends on the assumption of context independence.

Is context independence a reasonable condition of rationality? I doubt that it is, but I shall not to try to decide the issue here. What is important to notice is that this requirement of context independence is hiding in the standard construal of rationality, and that it is in important ways more demanding than the requirement of completeness and transitivity of preference over the options available in any given context.

---

[3] One can defend the consistency of these choices by building dependence on the set of options into the definition of the particular options. The resulting theory would be much weaker than standard utility theory.

1.2   Ordinal utility functions

Completeness and transitivity together establish what is called a "weak ordering" of any finite set of preferences. In principle each agent A could write down a long list with those options that are most preferred at the top and those that are least preferred at the bottom. When A is indifferent between two options, they appear on the same line. Every option has exactly one place in this list. Thus, for example, if A prefers x to y and y to z and is indifferent between y and w, part of A's weak ordering would be:

x	1	200
y, w	0.75	13
z	0	12

One can then play a simple mathematical trick. One can assign numbers to each "row" in the ordering, with higher rows getting higher numbers. Either of the two assignments of numbers to rows, (1, 0.75, 0) or (200, 13, 12) will do just as well as the other. Such an assignment of numbers is what economists call an "ordinal utility function."

1.2.1   Continuity

When there are an infinite number of options one may be unable to play this trick. If A's preferences are not, in a specific sense *continuous*, then they may not be represented by a real-valued utility function. A's preferences are continuous if for every option x both the superior and inferior sets are closed.[4] It seems at first glance hard to justify making continuity a condition of rationality (Elster 1983, p. 8). For example, someone who ranks swordfish first by weight and then, in case of ties, by length would violate the continuity condition when ranking an infinite (non-denumerable) set of swordfish, but would not seem to be irrational. Yet, in defense of continuity, one might argue that it is needed only because of the

---

[4] The superior set for option x, $S(x)$, is the set of all options y such that A prefers y to x or A is indifferent between x and y. The inferior set of x, $I(x)$, is, similarly, the set of all options y such that A prefers x to y or A is indifferent between x and y. A set is closed if it includes its boundaries. See Debreu 1959, pp. 54–9, Harsanyi 1977b, p. 31, and Strasnick 1981. Lexicographic preferences like those in the swordfish example in the text violate continuity. If one were to draw a graph with swordfish length on the horizontal axis and weight on the vertical axis, with x marking the length and weight of a particular fish, the inferior set consists of everything beneath the point x and the horizontal line segment including x to the left of x, while the superior set consists of everything above x and the horizontal line including x to the right of x. Since the horizontal line including x bounds the superior and inferior sets, but is not wholly included in either, both are open.

mathematical idealization involved in the use of real numbers. Since complete and transitive preferences over any finite set will automatically be continuous, the continuity condition is arguably trivial.

The *ordinal representation theorem* states that, if an individual's preferences are complete, transitive, and continuous, then they may be represented by a continuous real-valued utility function (proved by Debreu 1959, pp. 54–9). The number assigned to each option tells us how highly ranked the option is – the higher the number, the more preferred the option. Such utility functions are called "ordinal" because the only non-arbitrary feature of the numbers is their order. Absolute magnitudes, sums, and differences are arbitrary.

1.2.2   Utility maximization

When economists say that individuals maximize utility, they are only saying that people do not rank any feasible option above the option they choose. Although the "utility" language was inherited from the utilitarians, some of whom thought of utility as a sensation with a certain intensity, duration, purity, or propinquity (Bentham 1789, chapter 4), there is no such implication in contemporary microeconomic theory. Good economists sometimes speak misleadingly of individuals as *aiming to* maximize utility or as *seeking* more utility, but they do not or should not mean that utility is an object of choice, some ultimately good thing that people want in addition to healthy children or better television. The theory of rational preference or choice specifies no distinctive aims that all people must embrace. Utility is just an index of preferences. An individual who is a utility maximizer just does what he or she most prefers. To say that individuals are utility maximizers says nothing about the nature of their preferences. *All it does is to connect preference and choice (or action* in a particularly simple way.) Rational individuals rank available alternatives and *choose* what they most *prefer*.

We can now offer a reasonably precise statement of what economists, philosophers, statisticians, and decision theorists call "utility theory" as a definition or model of rationality.

An agent A's **preferences** are **rational** if and only if:

   (1) A's preferences are complete,
   (2) A's preferences are transitive, and
   (3) A's preferences are continuous.

An agent A's **choices** are **rational** if and only if:

   (1) A's preferences are rational and
   (2) A prefers no option to the one A chooses.

What makes utility theory a normative theory is the fact that rationality is a normative notion. To define what rational preference and choice are, is *ipso facto* to say how one ought rationally to prefer and to choose. Utility theory may also be taken as a "positive" theory in which one not only defines rationality, but claims that people are rational in the sense defined. Utility theory, as a positive theory of preference and choice, is a crucial part of consumer choice theory.

Utility theory places no constraints on what individuals may want; it only requires consistency of preferences and that choices manifest preference. Utility theory has a much wider scope than economics. As is only appropriate in a theory of rationality, it says nothing specifically about commodities or services. It says nothing about people's aims, about whether they are acquisitive and self-interested or generous and other-worldly, about whether they are saints or sinners

1.3   Revealed-preference theory

In 1938 Paul Samuelson reformulated the positive theory of consumer choice so as to eliminate reliance on a subjective notion of preference. His motivation appears to have been philosophical. The sort of empiricism (appendix, pp. 283-4) prevalent in the 1930s made reference to subjective preferences methodologically suspect. Apart from some technicalities, Samuelson succeeded in showing that, if choices among commodity bundles satisfy a consistency condition, then a complete and transitive preference ranking can be constructed from the choices. Preferences can be taken as "revealed" by choices, and the empirical legitimacy of talk of preferences can be secured by thus reducing it to talk of observable choices. Samuelson was in this work mainly concerned with positive theory, not with the normative theory of rationality, but the two cannot be sharply separated. For further discussion of Samuelson's work on revealed preference, see section 9.2 below.

The basic idea of revealed-preference theory is that, if I choose option x, when I might have chosen option y instead, then option x is revealed to be preferred to option y. My choices are consistent if they satisfy the "weak axiom of revealed preference," WARP, which requires that, if x is revealed to be preferred to y, then y must not be revealed to be preferred to x. In the specific context of consumer choice theory, with which most revealed-preference theorists have been concerned, matters are somewhat more complicated. But, in either case, if choices satisfy the relevant consistency conditions, then one can construct a complete, transitive, and continuous revealed-preference ordering from them (Sen 1971, 1973).

So one might simplify the theory of rationality by maintaining that an agent A is rational if and only if A's choices satisfy WARP, or, in other words, that A is rational if and only if A never both chooses x when y is available and y when x is available.[5] One can now formulate the standard defense of completeness as a requirement of rationality. Since choice demonstrates preference, completeness follows trivially from the mere fact of choosing something: what one chooses is what one prefers. This violates ordinary usage. In ordinary speech it is not true that Peter prefers x to y if and only if Peter picks x when he might have had y instead. Peter may, for example, pick one can of soup from the super-market shelf rather than another without *preferring* the can he picks (Ullmann-Margalit and Morgenbesser 1977). One might say in response that the point here is not to capture ordinary usage. But using ordinary terms in unusual ways risks equivocation.

This defense of completeness remains problematic, for revealed prefer-ences will show intransitivities under conditions of risk and uncertainty that have nothing to do with irrationality. Suppose, for example, that an agent who prefers more money to less faces a series of choices among sealed jars containing hundreds of pennies, each of which contains a slightly different number of pennies. It is no requirement of *rationality* that one have complete and transitive preferences among these options, and one would expect the transitivity of revealed indifference to break down.

The revealed-preference simplification of utility theory faces four serious objections. First, it does not improve the empirical respectability of ordinal utility theory. Part of the reason is that the behaviorist objec-tions to ordinal utility theory were misconceived in the first place. But, in addition, the empirical advantages of revealed-preference theory are meager. For the fact that A chooses x when y is available and then chooses y when x is available does not show that A is irrational. A's tastes may have changed or A may be indifferent between x and y. To permit choice to reveal indifference, one must say something like: A is indifferent between x and y if and only if A is equally likely to choose x or y (Harsanyi 1977b, pp. 27–8). Judging whether an individual's choices satisfy the weak axiom of revealed preference and what preferen-ces they reveal thus requires in every case examining a long series of repeated choices to determine whether x or y is always chosen and thus preferred, whether the frequency of choosing x and y is close enough to equal to attribute indifference, or whether the individual violates WARP. And there is still the problem of determining whether the agent's tastes have changed. It is easier to ask people what they prefer

---

[5] This needs modifying to permit indifference to be rational. See two paragraphs below.

Second, consider strategic choices.[6] In a strategic situation I may choose an action x, even though I prefer y, in order to mislead others or to manipulate some choice mechanism. In his complacency at the prospect of being skinned alive and his shudders at the mention of the Briar Patch, Brer Rabbit falsely revealed to Brer Fox a preference not to be thrown in the Briar Patch.

Consider the so called prisoner's dilemma.[7] Individuals A and B may either cooperate (C) or not cooperate (NC). If A cooperates and B does not, this is the worst outcome for A and the best for B. Best for A and worst for B is cooperation by B with A not cooperating. Second worst for both is both not cooperating. Second best for both is both cooperating. Thus one has the situation depicted below:

		B	
		cooperate	don't cooperate
	cooperate	(2,2)	(4,1)
A			
	don't cooperate	(1,4)	(3,3)

The first number in each pair represents the ranking of the outcome by A, and the second represents the ranking of the outcome by B. If A and B cannot coordinate their actions (by, for example, punishing non-cooperation), A is better off not cooperating, no matter what B does, and B is better off not cooperating, no matter what A does. Yet the result of their both not cooperating is worse than if they both had cooperated. A and B might both cooperate for a variety of reasons (as people often do in such situations), and the revealed-preference theorist would be driven to misconstrue their preferences.[8]

Third, revealed-preference theory impoverishes both the normative theory of rationality and the empirical theory of choice. Whether one

---

[6] These are ruled out in circumstances of complete certainty, but no one attempts to defend revealed-preference theory with respect to circumstances of certainty alone.

[7] A version of the story that goes with the name runs as follows. A and B are caught attempting a burglary near the scene of a series of recent burglaries. The district attorney separates them and offers each a deal: if A confesses to the burglaries and agrees to testify against B and B does not confess, then A will get off with probation and B will get a long jail term and similarly if B confesses and A does not. If both confess (refuse to cooperate with each other), they will both get a moderately long jail term. If both refuse to confess (that is, they cooperate with one another), they will both get a brief jail term for attempted burglary.

[8] This discussion derives from Sen 1973, pp. 249–53. But if cooperating is irrational, should the revealed-preference approach be expected to elicit preferences? The prisoner's dilemma is a striking example of how individually rational action can lead to suboptimal outcomes. It can be used to model the economic concepts of market failures and externalities and will be discussed again later in chapter 4.

should impose completeness as a condition of rationality is a substantive question (see section 12.4.3 below), but it cannot even be broached within a revealed-preference approach. Nor can one ask whether individuals might sometimes choose (perhaps for moral reasons) something that they do not prefer (Sen 1977) or why they have changed their preferences (Hirschman 1985). The theory similarly makes the explanation of choice in terms of preference tautologous and empty.

Finally, there is something hypocritical about revealed-preference theory. For its sense and point remains parasitic on the subjective notion of preference that it supposedly eschews (Sen 1973, pp. 242-4). Economists are interested in choices, which are intentional human actions, not in reflex movements. But this distinction cannot be drawn in terms of revealed-preference theory. Since its purported empirical advantages are negligible and it impoverishes the theory of choice while presupposing the subjective notions it attempts to avoid, there is, I think, little to be said for revealed-preference theory.

1.4   Rationality and uncertainty: expected utility theory

The theory of rationality in circumstances of certainty, which is central to microeconomics, is a thin theory,[9] but it can be extended to cases of risk and uncertainty. Economists and decision theorists commonly speak of situations of *risk* when outcomes have known probabilities and of situations of *uncertainty* when the probabilities of the outcomes or even the range of the outcomes of actions are not known.[10] I shall treat these two cases together by allowing the probabilities mentioned below to be either known frequencies or subjective degrees of belief (A.10.2). This simplification begs the question of those who would argue that situations of uncertainty involve more radical ignorance and different principles of rational decision-making, but I shall later make some amends and pay heed to doubts about the existence of subjective probabilities.

When one does not know what the outcomes of actions will be, actions can be regarded as *lotteries* with outcomes as prizes. For example, suppose that the option of calling a plumber to fix a leaky pipe has three possible mutually exclusive and jointly exhaustive outcomes. Either one gets no

---

[9] But, as I shall argue, its ramifications for the structure of economics and the strategy of research remain vast.

[10] See Luce and Raiffa 1957, chapter 2. Since some Bayesians (A.10.2) deny that there are such things as objective probabilities, this definition is controversial. See Levi 1986, pp. 26-31.

answer, a refusal to help, or a repaired leak. The probabilities of these outcomes might be 0.7, 0.2, and 0.1 respectively. Suppose the option of calling a plumber matters to an agent only insofar as it has one of these consequences. It can then be represented as a lottery with three prizes that occur with the respective probabilities. In general one can represent lotteries as a pair $[R,P]$, where R is a set of mutually exclusive and jointly exhaustive outcomes or pay-offs, and P a probability measure defined on R. The lottery that pays off K with probability p and L with probability $(1 - p)$ can be denoted conveniently $[K,L,p]$. Since the choice of an action that leads with certainty to a particular outcome K can be represented as a "degenerate" lottery $[K,K,p]$ or $[K,X,1]$, one can conceive of preferences and choices as defined exclusively over the set of lotteries without loss of generality. This set includes lotteries such as bets on ball games, where there is no definite objective probability involved and where the "p" instead represents a subjective probability or a degree of belief. One should not be misled by the lottery terminology. One assumes away (via the "reduction postulate" below) the pleasures of gambling.

In offering a normative theory of decision-making under risk and uncertainty, one asserts as before that preferences (which are now preferences among lotteries) are complete, transitive, and continuous. In addition, one needs a "reduction postulate" relating compound and simple lotteries. Harsanyi calls it a "notational convention" (1977b, p. 24), and it serves as a criterion of identity for lotteries. For example, suppose Peter faces the following compound gamble: if a coin comes up heads, then he can roll a die and win $6 if the die comes up 6 and $1 otherwise. If the coin comes up tails, he draws from a deck of cards and loses $1 if he draws a heart. The reduction postulate says that this complex lottery, $[[\$6,\$1,1/6],[\$-1,\$0,1/4],1/2]$ is equivalent to the simple lottery, $[(\$6,1/12),(\$1,5/12),(\$-1,1/8),(\$0,3/8)]$. The reduction postulate implicitly rules out any preferences for gambling itself.

Second (and last![11]) one needs the so-called "independence" principle (which should not be confused with the context independence discussed above in section 1.1.3). The independence principle says that, if two lotteries differ only in one prize (which may itself be a lottery), then preferences between the two lotteries should be identical to preferences between the prizes.

---

[11] But the assumptions of ordinal utility theory, especially completeness and continuity, become more problematic in circumstances of risk and uncertainty.

Given completeness, transitivity, continuity, the reduction postulate, and the independence principle, it is possible to prove a (cardinal) representation theorem:[12]

If all of these claims are true of an agent's preferences, then those preferences may be represented by a utility function that possesses the expected utility property and is unique up to a positive affine transformation.

A utility function possesses the expected utility property if and only if the (expected) utility of any lottery is equal to the utilities of its outcomes multiplied by the probabilities of each, $U([K,L,p]) = pU(K)+(1-p)U(L)$. A positive affine transformation of an expected utility function U is a linear function $aU + b$, where a is a positive real number, and b is any real number. The representation theorem establishes that the expected utility of options for an agent whose preferences satisfy all the conditions is as measurable as temperature is on the centigrade or fahrenheit scales. The zero point and units in any expected utility scale are arbitrary, but nothing else about the scale is. Comparisons of utility *differences* are independent of the scale chosen. If $U(x) - U(y) > U(z) - U(w)$, and if U' is a positive affine transformation of U, then $U'(x) - U'(y) > U'(z) - U'(w)$.

As in the case of utility theory concerning choice under certainty, one relates choice to preference by asserting that individuals never prefer any feasible option to the one they choose. The utility of the chosen option is greater than or equal to the utility of any other feasible option.

If these axioms are true of an agent A, it is moreover in principle possible to determine both A's utility function and A's probability judgments by observing A's choices among lotteries. For example, suppose Marianne likes big fruits and prefers watermelon to oranges and oranges to grapes. Since the zero point and the units of her utility function are arbitrary, one can stipulate the values for utility of a watermelon, $U(W)$ and the utility of a grape, $U(G)$. Given the above axioms, for some probability p, Marianne will be indifferent between an orange for certain and a lottery that pays off a watermelon with probability p and a grape with probability $1-p$ (that is, the lottery [watermelon,grape,p]). The utility of an orange, $U(O)$ will then be $pU(W)+(1-p)U(G)$. The probability an agent attaches to an event E can be determined when one

[12] For an accessible presentation, see Harsanyi 1977b, chapter 3. Other proofs can be found in Herstein and Milnor 1953, Jensen 1967, and von Neumann and Morgenstern 1947.

knows the expected utility of a lottery that pays off a reward r_1 if E occurs and r_2 otherwise, where r_1 and r_2 have known (expected) utilities.[13]

The probabilities invoked in this elicitation process are personal, subjective probabilities, the degrees of belief of individuals; and the axioms for rational choice under conditions of uncertainty imply that these degrees of belief must satisfy the axioms of the probability calculus. Moreover, it can be shown that, if one's degrees of belief do not satisfy the axioms of the probability calculus, then one can be led to accept a series of bets on some chance event E leading to a certain loss whether E occurs or not. This demonstration is known as the "Dutch-Book Argument" (see Schick 1986 for critical discussion). Expected utility theory is thus not only a theory of rational preference and choice, but a theory of rational belief as well (A.10.2). Subjective probabilities may arise from knowledge of objective frequencies, or they may not. The formal theory of choice is itself silent on the origin and justification of probability judgments. Those who have made the most of this theory, the so-called personalist "Bayesian" philosophers and statisticians, are permissive about the grounds for these probability judgments.

In summary, expected utility theory, as a theory of rationality can be presented as follows:

An agent A's **preferences** are **rational** if and only if:

(1) A's preferences are complete,
(2) A's preferences are transitive,
(3) A's preferences are continuous,
(4) A is indifferent between options the reduction postulate identifies, and
(5) A's preferences satisfy the independence condition.

An agent A's **choices** are **rational** if and only if:

(1) A's preferences are rational and
(2) A prefers no option to the one A chooses.

Expected utility theory has been extremely controversial because, unlike ordinal utility theory, it can be applied to real choices, which inevitably involve risk and uncertainty. Consequently, one can study whether people actually choose the way expected utility theory says they should. Such investigations might only show that people fail to choose rationally, but results at odds with a theory of rationality cannot always be dismissed

---

[13] Given my short-cut description, it might appear that one could not *both* elicit probability judgments and a utility function. But one can – see Ramsey 1926.

so easily. Furthermore, theories of decision-making under circumstances of uncertainty can be used. They matter. Which theory one relies on can make an enormous difference in policy-making. Although the issues are highly theoretical, their resolution is deeply practical.

What are the issues? First of all, questions concerning completeness, context independence, and continuity become more troubling once uncertainty is admitted. When we are unable to rank options, is the uniquely rational response is to make various more or less arbitrary guesses (which is what many subjective probability "judgments" come down to) to compute expected utilities? Why should a rational agent's ranking of two lotteries K and L never be affected by the discovery of other options? Continuity implies that, if a rational individual J prefers $100 to $10 and $10 to slow fatal torture, then there is some probability p less than one such that the lottery that pays off $100 with probability p and slow fatal torture with probability $1 - p$ would be worth at least $10 to J. Is J irrational to refuse to pay $10 to play this lottery?

The new axioms are problematic, too. The reduction postulate seems indefensible, since there seems to be nothing irrational in preferring a compound lottery to the simple lottery to which it reduces, simply because one likes to gamble.[14] Although controversy concerning expected utility theory has focused on the independence condition, it actually seems at first glance easier to defend. In the case of indifference it serves as a substitution principle. If one is indifferent between options x and y, then substituting one for the other in a gamble should make no difference. When there is a strict preference, the independence principle seems to follow from considerations of dominance. Suppose, for example, that lotteries K and L involve flipping a coin. If the coin comes up heads, K has a better prize than L, while the prizes if they come up tails are the same. Then one can do no worse with K, and one may do better. On the basis of an argument like this one, Savage called a version of the independence principle the "sure-thing" principle (for a simple exposition see Friedman and Savage 1952, pp. 468-9).[15]

Yet many have found the independence condition unacceptable. For, as I shall illustrate in chapter 12, there are instances in which individuals not only seem to violate it, but in which the violations appear to be

---

[14] Perhaps one might take problems with the reduction postulate as narrowing the scope of expected utility theory: it is an account of rationality that applies in circumstances in which the reduction postulate holds and people do not have preferences for gambling itself.

[15] This reasoning supposes that one's choice of K rather than L does not affect the value of p, and does not necessarily carry over to the case where the prizes in the lotteries are themselves lotteries rather than definite outcomes.

rational. For the most part only faint echoes of the controversies concerning expected utility theory are heard within economics, since most economic models still assume that agents have perfect knowledge and employ only ordinal utility theory. I shall consequently say little about the literature examining expected utility theory and various alternatives to it. The challenges to expected utility theory raise interesting methodological issues about the role of evidence in economics, which I shall discuss in chapters 12 and 13 below, but I shall not attempt to resolve the deep problems concerning the nature of rationality touched on above. In any event, enough has now been said about rationality to enable me to show its central role in the theory of consumer choice (chapter 2), economic welfare (chapter 4), and in understanding the peculiarities of economic methodology (chapters 12, 13, and 15).

2 Demand and consumer choice

Although the theory of rationality developed in the first chapter is central to microeconomics, microeconomics is primarily a *positive* theory: a theory concerning actual choices and their consequences. In this chapter we will examine the microeconomic theory of consumer choice. Along the way we shall see examples of economic *models* and, in reflecting on the theory of consumer choice and the explanation of demand, many questions will arise concerning the structure of economic theory and whether the propositions of economic theory are in accord with the evidence. The material here should be familiar to economists, who may want to skip or skim this chapter.

2.1 Market demand for consumption goods

One of the central generalizations of economics is the law of demand, which can be oversimplified as: at higher prices, less of any commodity or service will be wanted. When the price of coffee increased, as it did dramatically in response to a Brazilian crop failure in 1975, consumers cut back on their purchases of coffee.

There are several obvious things to note about this generalization. First, it is not a mysterious or deeply theoretical claim. Its truth is obvious to any retailer who holds sales to eliminate excess inventory. Second, it is a generalization about markets, not about individuals. Third, the generalization appears to be inexact and vaguely stated. For example, in 1976, when coffee prices were high, demand for tea increased. With the larger demand for tea, the price of tea rose, so in 1976 one found *both* a higher price for tea and a larger demand for tea. This sort of "counterexample" shows that a more precise formulation is needed. The law of demand is in fact a *causal* claim: the dependence of quantity demanded on price is not only mathematical. Demand *causally depends upon* the price of x. There is an *asymmetry* here that is not represented by the mathematical relationship between price and quantity demanded.

How is one to make a generalization such as the law of demand more precise and serviceable? One might start by attempting to list the major factors that influence market demand:

1 Demand for any commodity or service depends on its price. As price increases (decreases) the quantity demanded decreases (increases).
2 Demand depends on the price of *substitutes*. For example, demand for tea is influenced not only by the price of tea, but by the price of coffee. Groups of commodities or services such as coffee and tea are called "substitutes" by economists. The quantity demanded is an *increasing* function of the price of substitutes.
3 Demand depends on the price of *complements*. For example, people want jam with bread and video cassettes with their VCR's. Such groups of commodities or services are called "complements" by economists. The quantity demanded is a *decreasing* function of the price of complements.
4 Demand causally depends on incomes and wealth. As the average income and wealth of buyers increases, people in societies such as ours typically want to buy more of most things.
5 Demand depends on tastes or fads. The frantic buying of Cabbage Patch Dolls several Christmases ago was prompted not by a decrease in their price or an increase in the price of toy trucks, but by a fad, a change in preferences.

With the help of these additional generalizations one can get a better grasp of market behavior, but, without further generalizations about the strength of these different causal factors, one has no way to predict even the direction of a change in demand in response to price changes. This aggregate theorizing is also *shallow*. All one has are generalizations from market behavior. One has no explanation for why these generalizations obtain, and one may reasonably doubt whether these generalizations themselves explain (see A.3) any market phenomena.

Empirical research can help flesh out these generalizations. With sufficient data, it is possible to estimate the magnitude of the change in demand with respect to changes in the price of x or changes in the prices of substitutes or complements. Large firms devote substantial resources to the empirical study of market behavior.

But market generalizations, rendered quantitative by empirical research and econometric manipulations of statistical data, are precarious. Fads are quirky. The introduction of new products can disrupt settled patterns of consumption. And, no matter how useful such work might be to firms who seek advice concerning how to price or package their products, it must be profoundly disappointing to economic theorists who aspire to imitate the great achievements of the natural sciences. For, apart from statistical techniques and empirical research methods, there is little theory here.

So those economists interested in theory – and not all economists are or should be theoretically inclined – have gone in another direction. Their research agenda has been to uncover "deeper" laws concerning human behavior to explain, systematize, and unify causal generalizations concerning market behavior. Just as Newton's theory of motion and gravitation accounts for (and corrects) Galileo's law of falling bodies or Kepler's laws of planetary motion, so a deeper theory of the economic behavior of individuals *might* account for and possibly correct generalizations concerning market behavior. Note that this strategic choice is neither inevitable nor guaranteed to succeed. More superficial and less unified theory is *ceteris paribus* worse than deeper and more unified theory, but a satisfactory deep theory may not be attainable.

2.2   The theory of consumer choice

The theory of consumer choice is supposed to explain the causal generalizations discussed above concerning market demand. It is made up of the following three "behavioral postulates" or "laws" (A.4):

1 (*Rationality*) Individuals are rational (they have complete, transitive, and continuous preferences and do not prefer any available (affordable) option to the one they choose).
2 (*Consumerism*)(1) The objects of every individual i's preferences are bundles of commodities consumed by i, (2) there are no interdependencies between the preferences of different individuals, and (3) up to some point of satiation (that is typically unattained), individuals prefer larger commodity bundles to smaller. Bundle y is larger than bundle x if y contains at least as much of every commodity or service as does x and more of some commodity or service. Consumerism implies self-interest.
3 (*Diminishing marginal rates of substitution*) For all individuals i and all commodities or services x and y, i is willing to exchange more of y for a unit of x as the amount of y i has increases relative to the amount of x i has.[1]

---

[1] See Hicks 1946, chapter 1. This is one case in which the mathematical statement is simpler. The third "law" states that agents' utility functions are strictly quasi-concave. I explain what this means below, p. 36.

In sections 1.1 and 1.2, I discussed the notion of rationality that is used here. Those sections can be taken as formulating a *definition* or *model* of rationality which is summarized on page 18. An individual *A* is rational if and only if *A*'s preferences are complete, transitive, and continuous, and *A* never prefers any available option to the option *A'* chooses. In the context of consumer choice theory, an available option is an affordable commodity bundle. Whether taken as normative or positive, utility theory has a much wider scope than economics. Consumerism, the second "law," brings utility theory to bear on economic behavior.[2] For want of a better term, I am using "consumerism" as a name for a cluster of claims. One might call it "non-satiation," but doing so would overemphasize just one element in the cluster. One might call it "self-interest," but doing so would not highlight the limitation of preferences to commodity bundles. One might call it "greed," but that would sound too pejorative. "Consumerism" seems the best compromise, although the label misleadingly suggests a preference for consumption over leisure.

Consumerism says that people typically want more of all commodities and services. As economists recognize, this claim is a caricature of human behavior. Like the other "laws," it might be defended as a reasonable first approximation, as the sort of harmless distortion of reality that is required for the construction of a manageable theory. One might argue that it captures a central causal "tendency" that is central specifically to economic behavior. Alternatively, one might argue that, given the presence of markets, non-satiation is not such a gross exaggeration after all. Since one can always sell one's seventeenth television and donate the money to a favorite charity, everybody should prefer a 17-TV bundle to a 16-TV bundle. The objection that selling a television is not costless in terms of time and hassle misses the mark, because, to the extent that it is correct, it is not the case that the 16-TV bundle differs from the 17-TV bundle *only* in the number of televisions. On the contrary, the 17-TV bundle arguably possesses less leisure. Whatever its virtues, this defense of consumerism has its theoretical costs, for the laws of consumer choice are supposed to form part of the explanation for why markets exist.[3] It is awkward to rely on a law whose truth depends upon the existence of the phenomenon to be explained.

---

[2] This is similar to Elster's distinction between rational man and economic man (1983, p. 10).
[3] As both Michael McPherson and Bruce Caldwell pointed out to me, this defense of consumerism has deeper problems, for consumerism is supposed to be a generalization about people's consumption preferences, and the possibility of exchange is irrelevant at the moment of consumption.

Consumerism implies that agents are self-interested, for their preferences are over bundles of goods and services, and the non-interdependence of preferences is designed to rule out commodities or services such as "food for starving Ethiopians." The satisfaction of the preferences of others must not be included, even implicitly, among the arguments of my utility function.[4] Consumerism identifies options with commodity bundles and implies that choices are based on nothing but essentially greed. Whereas utility theory is perfectly consistent with altruism, consumerism is not. It is consumerism that confines attention not only to "rational man" but to "economic man," who is motivated by materialist acquisitiveness. Consumerism precludes envy as well as altruism or even non-trivial sympathy. It is a libel on our species that is not seriously endorsed by even the most misanthropic economist. Obviously consumerism is not intended as the literal truth.

The "law" of diminishing marginal rates of substitution is the most difficult to state. The best way to grasp what it says is to use some old-fashioned language. Suppose that utility functions measured some quantity, such as pleasure, and that differences between the utilities of different alternatives were not arbitrary. Economists used to think of utility functions in this way, and expected utility to some extent justifies continuing to do so (see section 1.4 above and Ellsberg 1954). Such utility functions are called "cardinal" utility functions.

One can use the notion of cardinal utility to formulate a law of diminishing marginal utility. This law was independently discovered by several economists during the last century and was a cornerstone of the so-called "neoclassical" or "marginalist" revolution in economics. Given consumerism, if commodity bundle b' differs from bundle b only in containing more of some commodity x, then b' will be preferred to b. The law of diminishing marginal utility then offers the further generalization that the size of this (positive) increment in utility is a decreasing function of the amount of x already in commodity bundle b. As the apples from the tree keep falling in Peter's lap, each increases his utility, but the amount by which the 50th apple increases Peter's utility is less than the amount by which the 4th apple did so.

If one puts aside qualms or questions about cardinal utilities, one would surely judge the law of diminishing marginal utility to be a reasonable empirical generalization. It may not be universally true (see Karelis 1986), but it has a great deal of truth to it. It neatly explains the paradoxical fact that useful but plentiful goods, such as water, are often cheaper than relatively useless but scarce goods such as diamonds - a

---

[4] I am indebted to John Dreher for clarification of this point.

fact that bothered eighteenth- and early nineteenth-century economists considerably. But if, as in contemporary economics, utility functions are no more than a means of representing preference rankings, differences in utilities are arbitrary, and one cannot sensibly speak of diminishing marginal utility.

The law of diminishing marginal rates of substitution is Edgeworth's (1881) and Pareto's (1909, chapters 3 and 4) trick for formulating this generalization without commitment to cardinal utilities. The idea was rediscovered and popularized by J.R. Hicks and R.G. Allen (1934). Basically all that the "law" of diminishing marginal rates of substitution says is that an individual will be willing to trade away more of y to get a unit of x when he or she has little of x than when he or she has a great deal of x. Instead of looking at the utility increment provided by an additional unit of x as a function of the amount of x, we can look at the terms of exchange between x and other commodities. But the notion of marginal utility still seems to be lurking in the background as an explanation for diminishing marginal rates of substitution. The more x one has, the less x increases one's well-being and the less willing one is to part with other commodities in exchange for a unit of x.

Consumer choice theory portrays people as driven by rational greed (with diminishing marginal rates of substitution) and by nothing else, but one no more understands the theory merely by understanding its constituent "laws" than one understands quantum theory by grasping its laws. One needs to see how these behavioral postulates are used together and what simplifications and mathematical techniques are required to bring them to bear on actual phenomena. When we see how the theory of consumer choice accounts for market demand, we shall have a better sense of the theory. Even if the theory of consumer choice does account for market phenomena, it is a troubling theory, for it is hard to regard its basic claims as "laws" without the scare quotes. This problem lies at the heart of most methodological discussion concerning economics and will be discussed at length in part II.

In treating theories as sets of "laws" or "lawlike" statements, I am assuming the answer to a substantial question in contemporary philosophy of science: "What is a scientific theory?" (A.6). This view of scientific theories is defended in section 5.3 below.

2.3   Market demand and individual demand functions

Economists explain market demand in terms of individual demand. With given tastes and prices, each individual wants some quantity of x. Market demand for x is then the sum of individual demands. The market demand *function* (for x) is a mapping from prices, incomes, and tastes to amounts of x demanded. As in many elementary treatments, the discussion here will oversimplify and take market demand functions to be the sum of individual demand functions (for a careful treatment, see Friedman 1962b).

A more interesting step in the explanation of market demand is the derivation of *individual demand functions* from the general theory of consumer choice and from further statements concerning the institutional and epistemic (belief or knowledge) circumstances in which the choices of consumers are made. An individual demand function for some individual i and some commodity or service x states how much of x is demanded by i (as a flow per unit time) as a function of various (causal) variables, some of which may be left implicit. When economists treat i's demand for x as a function only of the price of x, they are not denying that demand depends on income, tastes, and other prices. When any of these other causal determinants of i's demand for x changes, the simple functional relationship between the price of x (p_x) and the quantity of x demanded by i (q_x^i) will shift. If in a particular application such changes are small or rare, it is handy to consider explicitly only the causal dependence of q_x^i on p_x.

Although the simplest treatments of demand in two-commodity models have special limitations, they permit a graphical treatment and are thus particularly easy to understand. Since they also illustrate central features of economic modeling and how fundamental theory is employed to derive and to explain useful economic generalizations, I shall focus in this chapter and the next on these simplest models.

2.4   The model of a simple consumption system

Using the theory of consumer choice to derive features of individual demand functions, economists often employ a simple *model* of consumer choice. I shall call this model, "a simple consumption system." This is my terminology.

A simple consumption system is supposed to model the behavior of some individual agent, A, faced with a choice between bundles of two commodities x and y in the context of a market economy. Obviously consumption possibilities always include many more than two commodities or services, but one might treat all commodities but one as a single abstract composite commodity. Let us suppose that Alice chooses a consumption bundle consisting of coffee (x) and "everything-else-Alice-consumes" (y). One then formulates the model of a simple consumption system as follows:

A quadruple $<A,x,y,I>$ is a simple consumption system if and only if:

1 A is an agent, x and y are kinds of commodities or services, and I is the agent's income.
2 A faces a choice over a convex set of bundles of commodities $(q_x,\ q_y)$, where q_x and q_y are non-negative real numbers representing quantities of x and y respectively.[5]
3 A's income, I, is a fixed amount known to A, and it is entirely spent on the purchase of a bundle $(q_x,\ q_y)$.
4 The prices of x and y, p_x and p_y, are fixed and known to A.
5 A's utility function is a strictly quasi-concave, increasing and differentiable function of q_x and q_y (or, alternatively A's indifference curves are continuous and convex to the origin).
6 A chooses the bundle $(q_x,\ q_y)$ that maximizes A's utility function subject to the constraint that $p_x q_x + p_y q_y \leq I$ (or the bundle (q_x,q_y) is on the highest attainable indifference curve).[6]

These six assumptions fall into three classes: (i) simplified specifications of the institutional and epistemic setting – fixed and known prices and income, (ii) restatements or specifications of the general "laws" of consumer choice theory (maximization of utility functions of a certain character), and (iii) further simplifications whose only point is to make the analysis as easy and determinate as possible – only two infinitely divisible commodities. Notice that the model is not an uninterpreted mathematical structure, but defines a quadruple of agent, commodities, and income.

(i) Institutional and epistemic assumptions. Although simplified, the specifications of the institutional and epistemic setting here are common in many economic models. By attributing perfect knowledge to individuals, one makes their beliefs match whatever the facts are and thereby avoids the problem that action depends on subjective belief (A.14.3). The assumption that the agent is a "price-taker" – that is, that the agent cannot knowingly influence prices – is common and is one of those defining what economists call "perfect competition." Introducing the possibility of bargaining would complicate the model and reduce its

---

5 There are some other technical conditions on consumption sets that I am leaving implicit. See Malinvaud 1972, pp. 21f.
6 Notice that the budget constraint: $p_x q_x + p_y q_y \leq I$, does not itself imply that (*ceteris paribus*) q_x is inversely related to p_x. Given no change in I or p_y, all one can infer is that q_x or q_y decreases as p_x increases. q_y is not and should not be included in the *ceteris paribus* clause because economists are concerned to explain quantities demanded (including q_y).

determinacy, since the outcome would also depend on bargaining power and skill.

(ii) Specifications of the "laws". The "laws" that make up the theory of consumer choice show themselves in mathematical disguise. Assumption 6 says that A chooses whatever commodity bundle maximizes A's utility, subject to the constraint that the value of A's consumption must not exceed A's income. This is a consequence of rationality and means nothing more than that: subject to the budget constraint, A chooses what A most prefers.

The utility function mentioned in assumptions 5 and 6 is an ordinal utility function and is definable only if A's preferences are complete, transitive, and continuous. Consumerism shows itself in this two-commodity model as the claim that A's utility is an increasing function of both q_x and q_y. Demanding that the utility function be differentiable is merely a mathematical convenience.[7] Finally to stipulate that the utility function must be strictly quasi-concave is to restate the law of diminishing marginal rates of substitution. Suppose that for any pair of bundles $b'[=(x',y')]$ and $b^*[=(x^*,y^*)]$, $U(b') \geq U(b^*)$. Then the function $U(b)$ is strictly quasi-concave if and only if for all b strictly between b' and b^* $U(b) > U(b^*)$ (Malinvaud 1972, p. 26). The alternative formulation of assumption 5 in terms of indifference curves will be discussed below.

(iii) Further simplifications in the model. Although the institutional and epistemic specifications and the restatements of the "laws" of the theory of consumer choice are problematic, what seems bizarre until one becomes accustomed to the habits of economists are the extreme simplifications – a convex consumption set containing only two commodities and all income spent. (A set is convex if a line between any two points in the set is entirely contained in the set. So, among other things, convexity implies infinite divisibility of commodities.) But such models are not silly. Some of these simplifications are avoidable and one can investigate whether they are likely to lead to significant error. At the cost of mathematical complexities and some indeterminacies, one can analyze consumer choice among lumpy commodities. Taking income as fixed separates decisions to consume from decisions to devote resources to increasing income. This separation seems a reasonable first approximation. When at the supermarket, people typically take their incomes as given.

---

[7] Since the difference between the (ordinal) utilities of two different commodity bundles is arbitrary, so is the derivative of an ordinal utility function. One must thus be careful to ignore the arbitrary consequences that may result from treating an ordinal function as differentiable.

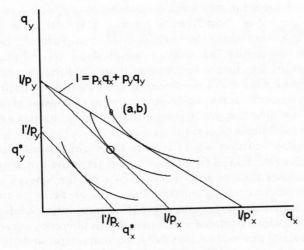

Figure 2.1. Individual consumption

2.5   Deriving individual demand

Let us now see how features of individual demand functions can be derived from the model of a simple consumption system. In principle it is possible to derive a demand function from a utility function, but, since economists never know the latter and since the exercise requires more complicated mathematics, I shall not show how it is done, although the next section gives some hints.

Since the commodity bundles among which A must choose consist of only two infinitely divisible commodities, the whole set of consumption possibilities may be represented by the portion of the $q_x - q_y$ plane bounded below and to the left by the lines $q_x = 0$ and $q_y = 0$ (see figure 2.1). Each point (a,b) in this quadrant represents a commodity bundle consisting of a units of commodity x and b units of commodity y. This is an instance of what economists call a "commodity space," and A's utility function assigns a utility (ranking) to each point. Given consumerism, if commodity bundle b_1 is northeast, or up and to the right of b_2, then A prefers commodity bundle b_1 to bundle b_2.

One can represent A's budget constraint (the line $p_x q_x + p_y q_y = I$) in this commodity space. It is a straight line with the slope $-p_x / p_y$ that intersects the q_x axis at I/p_x and the q_y axis at I/p_y. Since A cannot spend more than I and wants to move as far northeast as possible, A's consumption lies somewhere along the budget line.

To narrow this infinite set of consumption bundles to one, economists make use of the device of "indifference curves." Consider a set of commodity bundles among which the agent is indifferent. Such sets can be graphed in the commodity space. Since commodities are infinitely divisible and A's utility function is continuous, these "indifference curves" will be continuous. If (a',b') is northeast (or southwest) of (a,b), then (a',b') cannot lie on the same indifference curve as (a,b), and, given the transitivity of indifference, the indifference curve including (a,b) cannot intersect the indifference curve including (a',b').

To graph A's utility function would require three dimensions, but, since the actual values of the utility function (apart from the ordering) do not matter, one loses nothing in this regard by confining oneself to two dimensions. Instead of relying on the strict quasi-concavity of the utility function to draw inferences concerning A's consumption choice, one makes use of the closely related claim that A's indifference curves are convex to the origin, that is, that they have the shape represented in figure 2.1. The claim that A's indifference curves are everywhere convex to the origin, is, in fact, a good mathematical restatement of the law of diminishing marginal rates of substitution. For the absolute value of the marginal rate of substitution, given that A possesses commodity bundle (a,b), is the slope of the indifference curve passing through (a,b) at point (a,b). As q_x relative to q_y increases, the magnitude of the slope of the indifference curve increases ever more slowly. If q_y/q_x is small, a small amount of y sacrificed for a large amount of x keeps A on the same indifference curve.

The derivation and explanation of A's consumption choice is then simple. A does what he or she most prefers if and only if A chooses a bundle on the highest indifference curve that intersects the budget line. That indifference curve will be tangent to the budget line, except in the case of a so-called "corner solution." A corner solution obtains if the highest indifference curve intersects the budget line at one of the axes.

Suppose x were coffee and y were "$e-e$" (the everything-else composite commodity) and A were some particular person, Alice, then it looks as if one could explain why Alice buys 0.713 pounds of coffee (per week) in terms of institutional and epistemic givens: Alice's income, the price of coffee, some index price for e-e, and detailed knowledge of Alice's utility function or indifference curves. Such an interpretation is cogent, and, were one to possess the requisite knowledge, feasible. But economists never know enough about anybody's utility functions or indifference curves to make such quantitative applications.

So what explanatory application can the model of a simple consumption system have? Knowing little beyond what is stipulated in the assumptions of the model, economists would like to be able explain (or predict) *changes* in consumption as a consequence of changes in prices or income. But further assumptions about the shape of Alice's indifference curve are necessary. Almost anything is possible in general. A larger income may lead to a smaller demand for "inferior" goods and a price increase can even go with an increase in demand for "Giffen Goods."[8] Given indifference curves shaped like those in figure 2.1, which are reasonable in the case of many consumers and goods such as coffee, more definite conclusions can be reached. If income decreases to I' in figure 2.1 with no change in slope, Alice will consume less of *both* coffee and $e - e$. If the price of coffee decreases, then Alice will consume more coffee and less of $e - e$. Alice's demand for coffee is a decreasing function of the price of coffee, an increasing function of the price of substitutes, an increasing function of Alice's income, and causally depends upon Alice's preferences. Note that these claims compare equilibria. They do not address the dynamics of adjustment (see below p. 50).

Since market demand is the sum of individual demands, economists can explain the generalizations concerning market demand. And, moreover, just as one who sought to emulate Newton might have hoped, economists also have *corrections* for these market generalizations. The theory of consumer choice shows how those generalizations, including even the law of demand, can break down. It would be nice to have a quantitative account of market demand, and it would be nice to make use of a less idealized model than that of a simple consumption system, but the descent from the level of market generalization to supposed theoretical underpinnings appears to be a success.

2.6   Bootstrapping and evidential weakness

This highly qualitative derivation of market demand is, however, less satisfactory than I have suggested, not because science should always be quantitative, but because the data concerning market demand do not discriminate between this theoretical account and alternatives. As Gary Becker has shown (1962), completely random behavior could account for downward-sloping demand curves and the influence of income on demand; and habitual behavior could account for all of the market generalizations discussed above. So the theory of consumer choice is not

---

[8] The classic example concerned the Irish peasantry in the nineteenth century, who allegedly devoted so much of their income to potatoes that they were forced to consume less of more costly substitutes such as wheat when potatoes became more expensive. Whether or not there are empirical instances of this phenomenon of so-called "Giffen Goods" is, however, controversial.

strongly confirmed by its ability to explain the general facts concerning market demand.

To make this point more clearly, to illustrate how a quantitative theory could be much better confirmed, and to show how Glymour's notion of bootstrapping (A.10.3) can be applied, let us consider a hypothetical example of a simple consumption system in which we know Alice's utility function. In particular, let us suppose that $U = a + bq_xq_y$. One analytic technique for solving problems of constrained maximization (or minimization) is to form a special function combining the utility function and the budget constraint and to set the first derivatives of that function equal to zero. Provided that the second derivatives are negative at that point, utility will be maximized (see Henderson and Quandt 1971, pp. 404–7 and Samuelson 1947, p. 363). The function in this case will be:

$$V = a + bq_xq_y + d[I - p_xq_x - p_yq_y]$$

where d is called a Lagrange multiplier, whose interpretation need not trouble us here. The set of equations one uses to predict or to explain Alice's consumption choices is:

$$U = a + bq_xq_y \tag{i}$$
$$V'_x = 0 \tag{ii}$$
$$V'_y = 0 \tag{iii}$$
$$I = I^*; \quad p_x = p_x^*; \quad p_y = p_y^* \tag{iv}$$
$$V'_d = 0 \quad \text{(that is, } p_xq_x + p_yq_y = I) \tag{v}$$

where V'_x, V'_y and V'_d are the first partial derivatives of V with respect to x, y and d, and the starred quantities are specific observed values.

Suppose now that we do some experiments on Alice, giving her different incomes and observing her choices in the market when she faces various prices. In particular consider the following two experiments. In E_1 $I^* = 80$, $p_x^* = 1$, and $p_y^* = 1$, while in E_2 $I^* = 80$, $p_x^* = 1$, and $p_y^* = 2$. We carry out the experiment and observe that in E_1 Alice consumes 40 units of both x and y, while in E_2 Alice consumes 40 units of x and 20 units of y. These data provide a bootstrap confirmation of (ii) relative to the theory consisting of (i), (iii), (iv), and (v) and a bootstrap confirmation of (iii) relative to the theory consisting of (i), (ii), (iv), and (v). Moreover, relative to a theory consisting of (ii), (iii), (iv), (v) and a limitation on the functional form of U, these data provide a bootstrap confirmation of (i).

Let me demonstrate these claims. Given (iv) (the income and prices), (v), and (i), the Lagrange multiplier function in E_1 is $V = a + bq_xq_y + d[80 - q_x - q_y]$. Equation (ii) says then that $q_y = d/b$. From the experimental results $d = 40b$. Substituting $d = 40b$ and $q_x = q_y = 40$

into V'_y, one can deduce (iii), that $V'_y = 0$. Since this conclusion would not obtain regardless of the results of the experiment, we have a bootstrap confirmation of (iii) in E_1 relative to (i), (ii), (iv), and (v). (For example, if we observed that Alice chose 60 units of x and 20 of y, one could deduce that $d = 60b$ from (ii) and that $V'_y = -40$.) The deduction of (ii) from (i), (iii), and (iv) is just the same. The reader can check that the experimental results of E_2 also provide bootstrap confirmation of (ii) relative to (i), (iii), (iv), and (v) and of (iii) relative to (i), (ii), (iv), and (v).

Suppose now that our theory consists of (ii), (iii), (iv), and (v) and the claim (vi) that the utility function must be of the form $a_0 + a_1 q_x + a_2 q_y + a_3 q_x^2 + a_4 q_y^2 + a_5 q_x q_y + \ldots$ The function can have any finite number of terms, although the longer it is, the more data will be required for the bootstrap confirmation of (i) relative to (ii), (iii), (iv), (v), and this stipulation (vi) of the functional form. Since a great many functions can be approximated by functions of this form, this stipulation is not restrictive. Ignoring all the terms past the sixth for the purposes of illustration, (ii) and (iv) in E_1 tell us that $d = a_1 + 2a_3 q_x + a_5 q_y$, while (iii) and (iv) in E_1 tell us that $d = a_2 + 2a_4 q_y + a_5 q_x$. Combining and substituting the observed values of q_x and q_y, one gets the linear equation, $a_1 - a_2 + 80a_3 - 80a_4 = 0$. Carrying out the same operations in E_2, one derives the linear equation $2a_1 - a_2 + 160a_3 - 40a_4 = 0$. Given confirming data from additional experiments, it will be possible to deduce that $0 = a_1 = a_2 = a_3 = a_4$ and that $U = a_0 + a_5 q_x q_y$. Since the magnitudes of a and b are arbitrary, this constitutes a bootstrap confirmation of (i). If the postulated functional form of the utility function has more terms, more experiments will be needed in order to confirm (i).

Although fine as an illustration of bootstrapping, this example does not demonstrate that the theory of consumer choice is well confirmed, for the utility functions and the experiments are all fantasy. Economists do not attempt to determine the exact utility functions of individuals. Consumer choice theory is not empirically empty, but its content is small.

3 The theory of the firm and general equilibrium

Consumer choice theory purports to explain and to predict the demand "side" of markets, but an understanding of competitive economies also requires a theory of supply. And a theory is also needed concerning how the "forces" of supply and demand jointly determine economic outcomes. In this chapter I shall fill in these remaining pieces of positive microeconomic theory, before turning in chapter 4 to the normative theory of economic welfare. The material here – especially in the first four sections – should again be familiar to economists, but there are controversial claims in the last three sections, which should not be skipped.

3.1 Market supply of consumption goods and the theory of the firm

Just as market demand depends on prices, incomes, and tastes, so market supply depends on prices and technology. A higher price for x brings forth a larger supply; a lower price discourages supply.[1] Some copper mines, for example, were closed completely when the price of copper dropped in the 1970s. Higher prices of inputs either increase the price of output or decrease its supply. Improvements in technology can make it cheaper to produce something and will increase the supply of it at a given price.

As in the case of generalizations concerning demand, empirical work and statistical analysis can add a quantitative dimension; and the results can be of practical use. But, just as in the case of demand, economists seek deeper laws and more systematic explanation.

In theorizing about the supply of unproduced services, such as labor, the theory of consumer choice can itself be adapted, with quantity supplied depending on "consumer" choice between leisure, job amenities, resources, and consumption goods and services. But in theorizing about the supply of most consumer goods and services, one must

---

[1] At least when the seller is a firm. Higher prices do not (other things being equal) necessarily cause an increase in supply of productive services from individuals or households.

say something about the business firms that produce, transport, and market these goods.

The theory of the firm is made up of just three "laws":

1 The quantity of output in any production process is an increasing function of each of the inputs to the process, but within the range of the quantities of inputs normally used by the firm, the extent to which any given input d increases output, quantities of the other inputs held fixed, is a decreasing function of the quantity of d ("diminishing returns").[2]

2 If in the neighborhood of the equilibrium point, *all* of the inputs into production are increased or decreased in the same ratio, then output will increase or decrease in exactly that ratio (constant returns to scale).

3 Firms attempt to maximize net returns or "profits"[3] ("profit maximization").

Just as consumerism and the law of diminishing marginal utility state that utility increases at a decreasing rate when consumption increases, so the law of diminishing returns, or diminishing marginal productivity, states that the increase in output from an increase in the quantity of input d is a decreasing function of q_d. At extremely low levels of input d relative to the other inputs there may be increasing returns, and, with enough of any input, output can actually be reduced. Diminishing returns does not deny these facts; it merely claims that they do not obtain within the range of mixes of inputs found in actual firms. Just as in the case of marginal utility, one speaks of diminishing *marginal* productivity because it is claimed that the marginal product (the marginal increase in output due to an increase in the quantity of d as input) decreases, *not* that total product decreases.

The second "law," constant returns to scale, says that, if one doubles all inputs, one gets double the output. There is no conflict between constant returns to scale and diminishing returns, although the terminology might suggest otherwise. Constant returns to scale is a troubling

---

[2] It is sometimes said that, if the law of diminishing returns were not true, then all the world's food might be grown on one acre of land (Robbins 1935, chapter 4). But the law is not so indisputable. It asserts that marginal productivity is decreasing at the levels of inputs firms actually employ.

[3] There is some terminological difficulty here, since classical economists regarded interest as profits, while neoclassical economists regard profit as what is left after all costs, including the costs of capital ("normal" or "average" profits), are paid. Even though neoclassical economists, like their classical predecessors, see firms as attempting to maximize profits, economists now see profits in long-run competitive equilibrium as zero. Although it seems odd that firms should aim to maximize profits and on average get zero, the difficulty is only terminological. All that is meant is that in the long run firms do not get more than the average return on investment.

generalization. Some, such as Samuelson (1947, p. 84) regard it as a trivial definitional truth – whenever it appears not to hold, one invents some further input that has not been augmented enough or has been augmented too much. There is little evidence of its truth and no reason why it must be true, unless one is convinced that the economy is perpetually in equilibrium in a rather strong sense. If there were increasing or decreasing returns to scale, then, contrary to the assumption of equilibrium, firms would wish to be larger or smaller than they in fact were. It seems that constant returns to scale makes its appearance in economic models more because of its role in making such models coherent and mathematically tractable than because of economists' commitment to its truth. Perhaps it should not be regarded as a fundamental component of the theory of the firm.

The last of the "laws" – profit maximization – has been particularly controversial, but what it says seems from the armchair to be a reasonable approximation. There is, however, an important tension between this assumption concerning the motivation of firms and the claim that individuals are utility maximizers. What happens when, as is often the case, the preferences of managers and the higher profits of firms do not coincide? How can individuals be motivated so that firms will aim to maximize profits? Much work in agency theory is currently being done on this question (Fama 1980; Jensen and Meckling 1976; Williamson 1985).

By themselves, these three laws provide only the skeleton of the theory of the firm. As in consumer choice theory, one needs to see how these laws are used together and what sorts of simplifications and mathematical techniques are needed to bring them to bear on particular problems. Although the law of diminishing returns is relatively solid, the "laws" that make up the theory of the firm give rise to the same qualms (to be addressed in 8.1 and especially in 8.1.5 below) as do those of consumer choice theory.

3.2   Market supply and the supply function of a firm

Just as economists explain market demand in terms of individual demand, so they explain market supply in terms of the supply of individual firms, for the quantity supplied in most markets for consumer goods is the sum of the quantities supplied by various firms.

The interesting step is the derivation of supply functions of firms from the theory of the firm and from further statements concerning the institutional and epistemic circumstances in which production decisions are made. Some firms transport, distribute, or retail rather than produce, but, with a suitably abstract notion of production, all these activities can be regarded as production.

The supply function states how much of an output z is produced by firm F (as a flow per unit time) as a function of various (causal) variables. What is included among these causal variables depends on the extent of the interdependency among markets that is explicitly taken into account in the analysis, and depends on whether the firm is taken as operating in a competitive market, as a monopolist, or as a member of an oligopoly.

There are many complexities here and, as in the case of demand, I will confine my treatment to the simplest case.

3.3   The model of a simple competitive production system

In the most elementary use of the theory of the firm to explain supply, economists employ a simple *model* of the firm, which I shall call, "a simple competitive production system." This model, like the simple consumption system discussed above in section 2.2, illustrates many of the characteristic features of models in economics.

$<F,z,a,b>$ is *a simple competitive production system* if and only if:

1 F is a firm that produces and sells output z and uses inputs a and b to produce z.
2 F must decide how much of z to produce "in the short run" in which q_b is fixed as $q_b{}^*$.
3 $q_z = f(q_a, q_b)$, where f is continuous and differentiable and known to F, and the two first partial derivatives of f with respect to q_a and q_b are positive and the two second partial derivatives are negative.
4 The prices, p_z, p_a and p_b, are given and known to F.
5 F aims to maximize net returns: $p_z q_z - [p_a q_a + p_b q_b]$.

Only two of the laws of the theory of the firm are employed here: diminishing returns and profit maximization. Since the quantity of one of the inputs of production, b, is fixed, the scale is unchanging. The striking thought that one can think of factors that take a long time to adjust, as if they were fixed "in the short run" is due to Marshall (1930, book V, chapters 1–5; see also Boland 1982a). The institutional and epistemic assumptions mirror those made in the case of the simple consumption system. The firm is operating in a competitive market, where it cannot influence the price it must pay for inputs or the price it can get for its output. These prices are assumed to be known, which is assuming rather more than in the case of consumption, since production decisions are typically made much in advance of the sale of the product. This

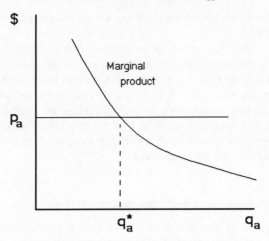

Figure 3.1(a). Marginal productivity

model leaves out capital, time, and uncertainty. It simplifies by assuming infinite divisibility (implicit in 3), one output, and only one variable input, a, into production.

3.4   Deriving a simple competitive firm's supply function

With the quantity of b fixed at some $q_b{}^*$, output is a function only of q_a, or, alternatively, one can regard the input requirements of a as a function of the level of output. One can thus think about a firm's decision-making technologically, with output determined by input, or economically, with the level of input determined by the level of output desired.

One can then graph the partial derivative of f with respect to q_a (with q_b fixed at $q_b{}^*$) or the derivative of the inverse function relating q_a to the desired level of q_z. In other words, one can consider the *marginal productivity* of a – the marginal difference in output owing to a marginal increment of a – as a function of q_a, or one can consider the marginal input requirements as a function of q_z. If one multiplies by p_z in the first case and p_a in the second, one can, as in figure 3.1(a), graph the relationship between q_a and the *value* of the marginal product of a and, as in figure 3.1(b), one can graph the relationship between *marginal cost* and q_z.

The marginal productivity curve will have a negative slope over the relevant range of input mixes: this is simply a restatement of the law of

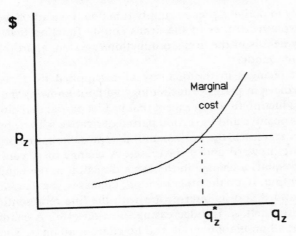

Figure 3.1(b). Marginal cost

diminishing returns. One can also indicate in figure 3.1(a) the fixed price firm F must pay per unit of a, p_a, as a horizontal line. Since F attempts to maximize profits and knows both p_a and the marginal productivity of a, the amount of input a employed will be q_a^*, and the level of output is then $f(q_a^*, q_b^*)$. If less of a than q_a^* is employed, then there are still profits to be made by increasing production, for an additional unit of a will result in an increment of output that is worth more than the cost of the additional input. If more than q_a^* is employed, then F is decreasing its profits by employing units of input that cost more than the value of output they produce.

In figure 3.1(b), the marginal cost curve (the marginal input requirements of a multiplied by p_a) must be upward sloping as a consequence of the law of diminishing returns. Just as one can represent the given p_a as a horizontal line in figure 3.1(a), so one can represent p_z as a horizontal line in figure 3.1(b). The intersection of the price and the marginal cost curves represents the profit maximizing output, q_z^*. If output is less than this, further net revenue can be obtained by producing more units, since their cost is less than their price. If more than q_z^* is produced, revenue is being lost on producing units that cost more than their price.

It is possible to derive a supply function from the production function ($q_z = f(q_a, q_b)$), the specifications of institutional and epistemic conditions, and the various simplifications. Moreover, such derivations may not be empty exercises (as they are in the case of demand), since firms may know their production functions. But, as in the case of demand, the object is not usually to derive a precise supply function. Instead the goal is to derive and explain features of the firm's supply function that do not depend on any details of the firm's production function, apart from those specified in the model.

One can predict changes in the quantity of z supplied by F as a consequence of changes in prices or technology without knowing much about the firm's production function except that its first partial derivative with respect to q_a is positive and its second partial derivative with respect to q_a negative. If p_z increases, the horizontal line representing this price in figure 3.1(b) shifts upward and q_z increases. A change in p_z causes (other things being equal) a change in the same direction in the equilibrium quantity of output. If, on the other hand, p_a increases, the marginal cost curve shifts upward and its intersection with the line representing the price of z is shifted left. q_z is a decreasing function of p_a. A change in p_b has no effect at all on *marginal* cost and no effect at all on q_z. Since a technological change will only be adopted by a profit maximizing firm if it lowers costs, technological changes which affect prices in the short run will tend to lower them. Economists are mainly concerned with properties of equilibria, not with the dynamics of adjustment.

Since market supply is the sum of the supplies of individual firms, economists can thus explain the generalizations concerning market supply sketched above. And, moreover, just as in the case of demand, they have learned how to refine these generalizations. For it is not the case that changes in input prices always affect supply. If the price change concerns a relatively fixed factor, then its influence on output will not register immediately. It would be nice to have a quantitative account of market supply, and indeed, with further information concerning the firm's production function, such a quantitative account would appear to be possible. It would also be nice to transcend such a simple model. But, again, as in the case of demand, the descent from the level of market generalization to supposed theoretical underpinnings seems a success.

3.5   Market equilibrium and supply and demand explanations

The above accounts treat quantity demanded and supplied as causally influenced by prices. In those theoretical explanations, one regards prices as givens that causally influence the behavior of consumers and firms. But, in a market economy, prices are not set by fiat; they arise as a consequence of the behavior of firms and households. Still needed is a theory of how market economies coordinate individual behavior, and not merely how, given that coordination, prices separately influence quantities supplied and demanded.

This basic explanatory task is not regarded as a task for micro-economics, but for general equilibrium theory instead.[4] But, short of doing general equilibrium theory, one can say still something about how prices are determined. Even if economies are characterized by general interdependence among markets, it may still sometimes be reasonable to focus on markets singly or in small groups. Such theorizing has been aptly called "partial equilibrium theory," for one is abstracting from the general interdependencies among markets.

A good explanation of price determination, whether in a particular market or in a whole economy, requires a well-articulated theory of how markets determine prices. No such theory exists. All economists have in the case of particular markets is essentially Adam Smith's story:

[When the quantity of a commodity] which is brought to market falls short of the effectual demand, all those who are willing to pay...[its natural price] cannot be supplied with the quantity which they want. Rather than want it altogether, some of them will be willing to give more. A competition will immediately begin among them, and the market price will rise more or less above the natural price, according as either the greatness of the deficiency, or the wealth and wanton luxury of the competitors, happen to animate more or less the eagerness of the competition. (1776, p. 56)

If at any given price there is an excess demand, competition among those who want the commodity or service will bid up the price until the excess demand is eliminated (see Arrow and Hahn 1971, chapters 11–13). Thus economists draw the famous graph shown in figure 3.2.[5] At any price above the equilibrium price p_e, such as p_o, there will be an excess supply, and competition among those who supply the commodity or service will lower the price. But economists do not have a detailed theory explaining how such competition among buyers or sellers determines prices. Indeed price competition is ruled out by a literal reading of simple models, such as those of a simple consumption system and of a competitive production system in which decision-makers are all price-takers. Nevertheless note that microeconomic theories of demand and supply can still have crucial roles to play *within* the implicit dynamics of price determination. Each price determines a supply and a demand as explained by the theories of consumer choice and of the firm. For example, a shift in demand as in the movement from D to D' causes a price shift. The new prices call forth new supplies and demands and the hypothetical process that begins

---

[4] There could be terminological misunderstanding here, for many regard general equilibrium theory as a part of microeconomics (or vice versa). See pp. 52–3 and footnote 7.
[5] Actually economists invert the axes and place quantities, which are the dependent variables, on the horizontal axis.

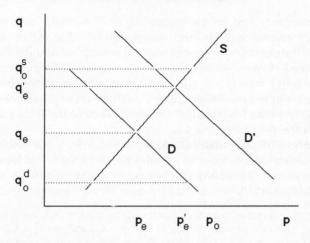

Figure 3.2. Supply and demand

with a change in some factor affecting supply or demand iterates until (partial) market equilibrium is restored. A market is in "equilibrium" when there is no excess demand or (unless the price goes to zero) excess supply. Little more is said about the real (processes) of equilibration within a single market, although there has been a good deal of discussion of hypothetical mechanisms such as Walras' "*tâtonnement*" and Edgeworth's "recontracting."

Such "comparative statics" supply and demand explanations can easily get confusing. Economists are, for example, often unjustifiably reluctant to regard them as causal, for economists are inclined to *distinguish* a comparison of equilibrium states from a dynamic and explicitly causal account. Instead of tracing the chain of consequences from some factor influencing supply or demand (such as a frost in Brazil that destroys its coffee crop), economists only attempt to say what price and quantity would be in equilibrium. Such partial equilibrium explanations thus differ from paradigm cases of causal explanation, since they abstract from the actual sequence of events and the causal relations in that sequence. There is no explicit mention of time ordering, which seems to many essential to a causal relation. In equilibrium, the supply and demand functions and the market institutions explain the equilibrium price and quantity, even though there is no explicit treatment of dynamic or temporal relations.

Although the distinction between dynamic and comparative statics accounts is important, both may be causal. The causal structure of comparative statics analysis is straightforward. In the background is an implicit temporal story in which the shift whose effects one is exploring precedes the establishment of a new equilibrium. In abstracting from the actual course of adjustment to the shock, one is assuming that the adjustment process has little effect on the final outcome. When this assumption is mistaken, one's explanation will be incorrect. But making such an assumption and then leaving the intermediate steps out does not make the explanation non-causal.

In the comparative statics account, the explanatory factors consist of the supply and demand *functions* and the unspecified market mechanisms. Supply and demand *functions*, unlike specific quantities supplied or demanded, can have a role in explaining prices if they are causally prior to the equilibrium prices and quantities they are supposed to explain. They will be causally prior to equilibrium prices whenever the causal factors which affect supply and demand for a given commodity or service, apart from its price, do not (to some degree of approximation) depend on its price or the quantity of it exchanged. Otherwise the demand curve or function will shift with each change in price. In a paradigm case of a supply and demand explanation, such as explanation for a coffee price increase in terms of a frost in Brazil, the various factors (other than the price of coffee) affecting supply and demand for coffee do not themselves depend appreciably on the price of coffee or the amount of it sold, and the explanation for the new higher price of coffee in terms of market mechanisms, the new coffee supply function, and the more or less unchanging coffee demand function makes perfectly good causal sense.[6]

3.6   Microeconomic theory

Although both problems and analytical techniques are usually more sophisticated than the simple examples above, this chapter and the last have set forth basically all there is to fundamental microeconomic theory. It consists in my view of seven laws:[7] those of the theory of consumer choice, those of the theory of the firm, and the assertion that markets "clear" or come quickly to equilibrium. Microeconomic models rarely include the assumption that markets are in equilibrium. Instead the existence of equilibrium is often *proven* from other assumptions, and indeed economists formulate their models in just the way they do in order to prove that an equilibrium obtains. But the claim that markets

---

[6] For more on the causal structure of supply and demand explanations, see Hausman 1990b. See also Friedman 1953b and Yeager 1969.

[7] Ten, if one counts the claim that individuals are rational as four rather than one.

clear is nevertheless a fundamental constituent of microeconomic theory and ought to be included in a careful restatement of the theory.

Yet there are disquieting aspects to the claim that microeconomic theory consists of these seven "laws." First, not all microeconomic models employ all of these laws, even when they are relevant to the explanatory tasks at hand. Not only are there models, such as the simple competitive production system above, that leave out laws (constant returns to scale in this case) that have no implications for the case at hand, but there are also microeconomic models that incorporate *contraries* to some of the fundamental laws of microeconomic theory. For there are models with satiation, models with increasing or decreasing returns to scale, models without profit maximization, even models without completeness, and models without transitivity (see p. 88 below). It is as if physicists sometimes supposed that force is proportional to acceleration and in other models took force to be proportional to acceleration squared.

This odd fact shows us that the behavioral postulates of microeconomics do not have the same status as fundamental natural laws. They are inexact and economists regard many as no more than useful first approximations, which theorists are free to supersede or reject in particular investigations. Some of the "laws," such as those of utility theory, diminishing marginal rates of substitution, and diminishing returns, are more central than others, and what makes some bit of theoretical work a part of economics is a commitment only to some disjunction of these seven "laws" and in particular to the more central ones. These facts raise difficult questions, which I shall address below in chapters 8 and 12. What sort of a science can economics be with only such basic generalizations?

A further problem with identifying microeconomic theory with these seven generalizations is that other claims, apart from "laws" also seem to be essential. For example, although these "laws" are also the core of general equilibrium theories, microeconomics remains distinct from general equilibrium theory.[8] What makes microeconomics microeconomics is not only these laws, but the sort of explanatory questions it is employed to answer. The focus of microeconomics, in contrast to general equilibrium theory, is on single markets or small groups of markets and thus

---

[8] See sections 3.7 and 6.7 below. Many economists regard general equilibrium theory as a part of microeconomics, but I think that the disagreement here is only terminological. Microeconomics and general equilibrium theory share the same theoretical vision, the same nomological apparatus, many of the same standard simplifications and mathematical devices, but they differ in the level and kind of aggregation they employ, in the extent of the interdependencies among markets that they consider, and in their theoretical ambitions.

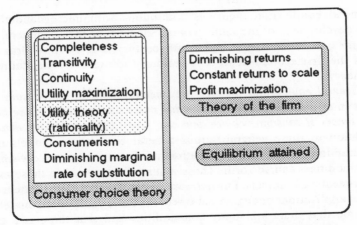

Figure 3.3. Equilibrium theory or the basic equilibrium model

on partial equilibrium. In order to distinguish microeconomics from its basic laws, which also form the core of general equilibrium theories, I shall say that these seven laws constitute "equilibrium theory" and shall take microeconomic theories to be particular augmentations and *specializations* of these laws. Figure 3.3 summarizes my view of *equilibrium theory* or *the basic equilibrium model* (on theories versus models see section 5.3 below). Both microeconomics (partial equilibrium models) and general equilibrium models are particular *augmentations* of the assumptions of the basic equilibrium model.

In addition to its laws and questions, microeconomics is also characterized by common simplifications. Households and firms are generally treated either as price-takers or as monopolists or monopsonists. Commodities are taken to be infinitely divisible. Economic agents are typically modeled as possessing perfect knowledge of all relevant data. The distinction between the "short run" in which some inputs are fixed and the "long run" in which all inputs can be adjusted is common. Although these simplifications are prevalent and characteristic of microeconomic models, they are less essential to it. It should also be stressed that economists are in no sense *committed* to them. They are not regarded as discoveries or theses of economics. One seeks to *relax* or to *avoid* such assumptions, not to maintain them in the face of opposition.

3.7   Microeconomics and general equilibrium theory

General equilibrium theory is supposed to explain how prices are determined and how market economies coordinate individual behavior.

General equilibrium theory is continuous with microeconomics and is a development of the same "laws." Some vague idea of general equilibrium goes back to the eighteenth century, but Leon Walras (1926) was the first economist to take seriously the task of elucidating such a theory.

General equilibrium theories are **augmentations** *of equilibrium theory, that is, of the seven laws that together make up the theory of the firm and the theory of consumer choice, plus the "law" that equilibrium obtains.* In addition to these generalizations general equilibrium models include assumptions concerning information, market structure, the divisibility of commodities, and so forth. These assumptions resemble those made in microeconomic models. Furthermore, general equilibrium models, unlike other applications or augmentations of the basic equilibrium model, often assume that there are many commodities and that there is a general interdependence among the markets in an economy. What distinguishes general equilibrium models from microeconomics are assumptions of this last kind and the apparent explanatory task of accounting for the operation of whole economies.

There are three different kinds of general equilibrium models. These are respectively (a) "small" general equilibrium models with few commodities and agents, (b) input-output models with dozens or hundreds of commodities, and (c) abstract general equilibrium models with no definite number of commodities or agents. I have made the distinction sound like a quantitative one, for it is easiest to remember the differences in this way, but what really distinguishes the models are their purposes and applications.

In attempting to address large-scale questions it can be helpful to employ highly aggregative general equilibrium models in which there are, for example, only two commodities – a consumption good and a capital good – only one unproduced input into production, labor, and only two kinds of agents, workers and capitalists. Such models are models of whole "toy" economies, and the interdependencies among the three markets for labor and the two commodities are treated with full generality. So they are general equilibrium models. But many of the complexities of the interdependencies among markets are assumed away by representing the myriad of actual commodities as merely one capital and one consumption good. When such simplified small general equilibrium models are clearly built around equilibrium theory (which in some macroeconomic work such as Keynes' is not the case) such models are similar in intention, although not in technique or object, to the partial equilibrium work characteristic of microeconomics.

The second kind of general equilibrium model is exemplified by input-output models.[9] By assuming, for example, that there are constant production coefficients and that demand will show special constancies, one can set up a model of an economy with perhaps a hundred different commodities and industries and, with the help of a computer, investigate how it operates. General equilibrium models of this sort are directed toward practical, predictive ends; and employ simplifications believed to be conducive toward achieving those ends. One might, for example, use input-output models to predict what effect a drop in oil prices will have on the cost of clothing.

The third sort of general equilibrium model is abstract and has proven to be puzzling and disturbing to many economists, since models of this kind appear to have little to do with real economies. Gerard Debreu in his classic *Theory of Value* states that his theory is concerned with the explanation of prices (1959, p. ix). Others as distinguished as Kenneth Arrow and Frank Hahn deny that general equilibrium theories are explanatory (1971, pp. vi–viii). Moreover, some prominent economists (Blaug, 1980a, 187–92) and philosophers (Rosenberg 1983) have argued that work in general equilibrium theory is not empirical science at all.

Theories of this third kind, which I shall call "abstract general equilibrium theories," place no limitations on the interdependence of markets or on the nature of production and demand, beyond those implicit in the "laws." When economists speak of general equilibrium theory, it is usually this abstract variety that they have in mind. Given the abstractness and lack of specification in abstract general equilibrium theory, many economists regard it as the fundamental theory of contemporary economics. As the previous discussion suggests, this seems a mistake. As suggested previously and defended in chapter 6, **equilibrium theory is the fundamental theory. General equilibrium theory is a particular application of the fundamental theory.**

What confuses matters is that applying equilibrium theory as the general equilibrium theorists do serves no clear explanatory or predictive purposes. Nor are these theorists attempting to develop a theory of a more specific subject matter within economics. Perhaps abstract general equilibrium theories may change, but current work lacks any clear explanatory or predictive purposes. For example, models of intertemporal general equilibrium commonly assume that agents have complete and accurate knowledge concerning the availability and prices of commodities

---

[9] Some might argue that input-output models are not really *equilibrium* models at all. For a good account of the practical utility of intermediate-sized general equilibrium models, see Whalley 1988. I am indebted to Merton Finkler here.

and concerning the production possibilities both in the present and the future! They also stipulate that there is a complete set of commodity futures markets on which present commodities and titles to future commodities of all kinds and dates can be freely exchanged (see Koopmans 1957, pp. 105–26; Malinvaud 1972, chapter 10, and Bliss 1975, chapter 3). Such assumptions render the model inapplicable to real economies, and there is little point or possibility of testing it. Furthermore, the fact that economic reality does not satisfy, even approximately, such fanciful assumptions leaves abstract general equilibrium theories with little predictive worth. So we face an interesting puzzle: given the falsity of stipulations such as perfect information, what is the point of abstract general equilibrium theories?

One further peculiarity of abstract general equilibrium theories is that they often take the form of existence proofs. One demonstrates that the axioms are sufficient conditions for the existence of an economic equilibrium. Abstract general equilibrium theories thus seem to have the form of explanatory arguments where the explanandum is the existence of an economic equilibrium. Yet construing general equilibrium theories as explanations of economic equilibria is implausible, since there is no fact of equilibrium to be explained.[10] These peculiar theories apparently lack explanatory power. What role can or should they play in a supposedly empirical science? In chapter 6 I shall venture answers to these questions.

[10] This is a controversial overstatement, since "new classical economists" believe that economies are in general equilibrium (Hoover 1988). Even if one does not accept their view (and I do not), it must be conceded that portions of economies may approximate equilibria. On rare and special occasions general equilibrium theories may be applicable and explanatory. But, if these theories have real importance, it is not for this exceptional applicability.

One's "welfare" is one's good or well-being. Economic welfare is that portion of the good or well-being of an individual that depends upon the goods and services with which economists are particularly concerned. The problems of economic welfare are multifarious. A broad social consensus supports providing minimum amounts of food, housing, medical care, and education to everyone. The highly inegalitarian distribution of income and other benefits in the United States seems unfair to some (liberals), while others (conservatives) may regard it as morally acceptable, or, like Robert Nozick (1974), they may insist that one should assess the processes that give rise to the distribution of benefits, not the distribution itself. Yet, in practice, conservatives would have trouble defending the actual distribution of benefits in this way, and Nozick does not do so. For it is difficult to believe that it could have arisen from a (fair) process that respected individual rights. As Lester Thurow has remarked (1980, pp. 201-2; 1975, chapter 3), the overall distribution of income in the United States is *much* more unequal than the distribution of income among fully employed white males, and it is hard to see how the contingencies that might legitimately give rise to income inequalities should cluster in women and Afro-Americans. And the distribution of wealth is even more unequal.

Although economists are important figures in debates concerning both the aims of welfare policies and, especially, the best means of implementing them, such issues largely *disappear* once one enters in to the realm of theoretical welfare economics. Why? What sorcery is at work? This chapter offers an answer. Since sections 2 to 5 lay out the basic tools and concepts of welfare economics (and complete the introductory economics presented in this book), economists may want to skip from section 1 directly to section 6.

4.1   Welfare and the satisfaction of preferences

From the perspective of equilibrium theory, welfare is the satisfaction of preferences. This implies not only that the only relevant perspective for assessing whether Sarah is better off is Sarah's own perspective, but also that what it is to be "better off" is to be understood in terms of Sarah's preferences. Income, food, housing, and education remain important, for they are the *objects* of preferences or the *means* of satisfying preferences. But needs have no special status. The panhandler who knows her neoclassical welfare theory tells no stories of how much she needs food or lodging. All that is relevant is that she prefers the handout. One might focus on income or wealth as indicators, but welfare in its theoretical purity is nothing but the satisfaction of preference.[1]

Is it plausible to take welfare to be the satisfaction of preferences? At the very least, one needs to screen out preferences based on ignorance. Falsely believing the cup to contain ordinary wine, Gertrude preferred to drink it. John Harsanyi has argued that one should also discount anti-social preferences, such as those of a sadist or a racist (1977a, p. 56). But, even after such screening or discounting is complete, why should we care about satisfying other people's preferences, unless we believe that doing so makes them better off according to *our* notions of what makes for a good life? The satisfaction of *my* preferences has an obvious claim on *me*, for like most people I believe that the things I prefer are generally good for me (see Sagoff 1986). But, unless I believe that what you prefer is good for you, satisfying your preferences has no claim on me. In response, one might argue either that there is no better way in practice of benefiting people than to attempt to satisfy their preferences or that respect for individual autonomy forbids employing my standards of what is good for others.[2]

To take welfare to be the satisfaction of preference may seem innocent, but its implications are large. For it aggravates the problem of interpersonal utility comparisons and makes it central to welfare economics. Lionel Robbins argued persuasively that there is no non-arbitrary way to compare one person's level or changes of preference satisfaction to another's (1935, chapter 6).[3] Formerly, in the late nineteenth and early

---

[1] For an interesting critique see Schwartz 1982, and for an even more interesting defense of an *informed* preference theory of well-being, see Griffin 1986. David Gauthier also builds a sophisticated theory of subjective value around expected utility theory (1986). Consider one of Schwartz's examples: Both my daughter and I need an operation and I prefer that she has it. Giving it to her satisfies my preferences, but seems to contribute to her welfare, not to mine. On issues concerning needs, see Braybrooke 1987, Griffin 1986, pp. 40f, and Rawls 1971, 1982.

[2] See Harsanyi 1977a, p. 55. But it should not be thought that concern for the satisfaction of the preferences of others is required by either democratic values or by obligations of mutual respect. An equal concern with everybody's welfare does not require that one equate welfare with preference satisfaction, and respect for the beliefs and wants of others does not require that one never criticize them.

[3] But there has recently been some work relating fairness to "envy-free" distributions (see Varian 1985 for a comprehensive bibliography).

twentieth centuries, economists argued that overall welfare would be maximized by equalizing incomes as much as was consistent with retaining incentives to produce. Citing diminishing marginal utility (see p. 32 above) of income, they argued that, for example, one hundred dollars contributes less to the well-being of someone with an income of $50,000 than to the well-being of someone with an income of $5,000. So a more equal distribution of income would increase total welfare, unless it greatly diminished incentives.

Whatever merits this argument may have if welfare is interpreted as material well-being, it has little force if welfare is interpreted as preference satisfaction (Cooter and Rappaport 1984). For, despite extensive argument by John Harsanyi to the contrary (esp. 1977b, chapter 3), there seems to be no non-arbitrary and ethically neutral way to defend the claim that $100 given to someone with an income of $50,000 satisfies fewer or less important preferences than $100 given to someone with an income of $5,000. Adopting a view similar to Arrow (1978), Harsanyi argued that there is, in effect, a single utility function that depends not only on the objects of choice, but on causal variables affecting and in effect identifying the chooser. Since psychological theory cannot specify this underlying utility function, people employ their empathic abilities to determine their "extended" preferences between, for example, being Norma with an extra cup of coffee or being Grover with one fewer pair of shoes (Harsanyi 1955, 1977a, and especially 1977b, chapter 4).[4]

In the view of most economists, one might judge *morally* that the preferences of the poor individual that could be satisfied with an extra $100 are more important than those which a rich person could satisfy with the extra $100, but this judgment depends on ethics, not science; and the ambition of theoretical welfare economics has been to rely on as few and as little controversial moral principles as possible. Recommending policies requires an evaluative commitment, but welfare economists have thought that claims about whether a redistribution makes a group better off should not depend on moral theory.[5] From time to time economists have made it sound as if some welfare recommendations presupposed no ethical views at all. But even recommending a Pareto improvement depends on an ethical premise (Sen 1970, chapter 5), and

---

[4] The awkward formulations are to alert or remind the reader that preferences must be defined over complete descriptions of the relevant alternatives. See p. 14 above. For a telling critique of this "mental shoehorn" tactic, see MacKay 1986. For further discussion of interpersonal comparisons, see Barrett and Hausman 1990 and Elster and Roemer 1991.

[5] In fact this judgment presupposes that well-being is the satisfaction of preferences, which is a substantive and, in my opinion, mistaken moral commitment. See sections 4.6, 15.3, and A.14.4 below.

the ethical premises thought to be required for interpersonal comparisons are not much more controversial.

4.2   Pareto efficiency, Pareto improvements, and market failures

If welfare is preference satisfaction, and the extent to which the preferences of different individuals are satisfied cannot be compared, how can one say anything substantial about economic welfare?

The welfare economist's answer lies in the notions of a "Pareto improvement" and of "Pareto efficiency" or "Pareto optimality." An economic state R is a Pareto improvement over an economic state S if and only if nobody prefers S to R and at least one person prefers R to S.[6] An economic state of affairs R is Pareto efficient or is a Pareto optimum if and only if there are no Pareto improvements over R. Given any feasible alternative S to R, someone prefers R to S. Notice that the Pareto concepts employed by economists are not well-defined if individuals do not have preference rankings. There is thus an intimate connection between the notions of rationality and welfare employed by economists.

The Pareto concepts do not permit very discriminating judgments. Suppose that there is a single consumption good, "bread," in some fixed quantity, and everybody prefers more rather than less of it. Then *every* distribution of bread that exhausts the bread supply is a Pareto optimum.[7] Moreover, R may be Pareto optimal and S may be suboptimal without R being a Pareto improvement over S. Suppose there are ten loaves of bread to distribute between A and B. The Pareto efficient distribution that gives seven loaves to A and three to B is not a Pareto improvement over the distribution that wastes two loaves and gives four to both A and B. Few economic states can be ranked as in terms of the relationship of a Pareto improvement. If R is a Pareto improvement over S, then *nobody* can prefer S. If everybody in R except for Sonya had triple the income in R as they would have in S, but Sonya had one penny less, then (assuming that Sonya for reason of that penny prefers S) R is not a Pareto improvement over S.[8]

---

[6] The notion of a Pareto improvement and of Pareto optimality often are phrased in terms of making people better or worse off, but these in turn are just a matter of individual preferences. The formulations in the text highlight this central fact.

[7] Note that a distribution of some commodity that exhausts its current supply is not necessarily (as in this case) Pareto efficient. If all the shoes produced in a given period are distributed to consumers, but Mary who has size 6 feet gets size 8 shoes, while Belinda who has size 8 feet gets size 6 shoes, then the outcome is obviously not a Pareto optimum.

[8] Although with just a tiny bit of redistribution R could be transformed into another state R' that might be a clear Pareto improvement over S. See pp. 63–4 below.

The Pareto notions have some real ethical appeal, for, other things being equal, it is better to make people better off, and the satisfaction of preferences surely has something to do with well-being.[9] But they have little bearing on questions of fairness. Economists often suggest that questions of economic welfare be factored into questions of efficiency (to which the Pareto concepts are pertinent) and questions of equity, upon which theoretical welfare economics has little to say (Okun 1975). This factoring is questionable, if for no other reason than the efficiency implications of perceptions of fairness (Hirsch 1976, pp. 131f).

Although one may question the normative appeal of preference satisfaction, and one may suggest that issues of equity are as important as questions of efficiency and not necessarily separable from them, at least the Pareto notions are coherent and clear. And they have some force, too. Recall the prisoner's dilemma presented above on p. 21. Although each of the players has a dominant strategy, the outcome is not Pareto optimal. One challenge economists have accepted is to study different institutional arrangements to see which lead to such suboptimal outcomes. Consider, for example, the prisoner's-dilemma-like situation created by a potential exchange transaction between Dick and Jane. Dick has a ball and Jane has a bat. Each values what he/she has, but would prefer to exchange. Exchanging is the "cooperative" solution, not-exchanging the suboptimal non-cooperative equilibrium, and the other two outcomes involve Dick or Jane winding up with both the ball and the bat. Property rights rule out the last two outcomes and thus enable the cooperative solution to arise voluntarily (Hardin 1988, chapter 3).

Perfectly competitive markets are in this regard "good" institutions, for the outcomes of interactions on them are Pareto efficient. But real market outcomes may be suboptimal, particularly in the case of *externalities*.[10] Externalities exist when the costs or benefits generated by an agent do not fully register as costs or benefits for that agent. Those who pollute the air or deplete the fish in a lake need not take the costs imposed on others into account in their private calculations of economic benefit. Nor can someone who builds a lighthouse collect from all those who benefit from it. One solution to the problems posed by externalities is a more refined assignment of property rights, so that either polluters will have to compensate those with a right to clean air or those who want clean air will have to pay those who would like to pollute not to do so.

---

[9] But the Pareto concepts lose their normative appeal if people's preferences reflect indoctrination or psychological foibles rather than what is of value to individuals. See sections 4.6 and 14.2.3.

[10] There are other sources of market failures, too, such as monopolies, which I shall not discuss.

As Ronald Coase proved (under some fairly restrictive assumptions), the same optimal amount of pollution will result with either assignment of rights (1960). Since the "transactions costs," the costs of finding the parties one needs to bargain with and striking and enforcing these bargains, are often prohibitive, better rights assignments do not solve all the problems. In many cases government provision of collective goods (such as lighthouses), government restrictions (such as hunting and fishing limits or limits on pollution), or government taxes or subsidies[11] can mitigate suboptimal outcomes.

But the scope of the Pareto concepts is very limited. Indeed it is almost always the case that there is somebody who would prefer that the government *not* intervene to build a dam or to save an endangered species. So even though externalities often lead to suboptimal outcomes, the feasible remedies are rarely true Pareto improvements. As sharp and clear as the Pareto concepts are, their scope is too limited. Economists have, however, increased their range and apparent force in three ways.

4.3   The two fundamental theorems of theoretical welfare economics

First, economists have proven two remarkable welfare theorems:

1 Every competitive general equilibrium is a Pareto optimum.
2 Every Pareto optimum can be obtained as a competitive general equilibrium given some distribution of initial endowments to economic agents.

"A competitive general equilibrium," is roughly an economic state in which the laws of equilibrium theory are true, and in which there are no market failures due to uncertainty, monopolies, externalities, and the like. The roughness here is only in my abbreviated description, not in the theorems. The first theorem might be called "the invisible hand theorem" after Adam Smith's famous claim that in pursuing one's own interest on a competitive market, one automatically winds up securing benefit to the public (1776, book IV, chapter 2, p. 423). It might be taken to provide a theoretical justification for a *laissez-faire* policy of leaving the market alone, but this would be a misunderstanding. For the assumptions which are sufficient to imply the existence of a Pareto-efficient general equilibrium are not satisfied in real economies. Indeed, interference with semi-competitive markets can sometimes bring about Pareto improvements (Lipsey and Lancaster 1956–7). Much of theoretical wel-

---

[11] Most economists regard taxes and subsidies as more efficient and ethically preferable to restrictions (or mandates), since they permit a greater range of individual choice.

fare economics is devoted to the study of "market failures" and of ways to overcome them.

Even if the market did provide a Pareto efficient outcome, it might be unfair. It is here (and also in relation to the possible role of markets in socialist planning) that the second theorem is so important. For it says that no Pareto optimal outcome (including those to the taste of the most egalitarian) is unattainable as a competitive equilibrium. Thus concerns about justice do not *necessarily* require interference with market transactions. It is sufficient to shift initial endowments by such means as taxation and education. Welfare economists can then focus on issues of market imperfection and problems of implementation.

4.4 Cost-benefit analysis

The second way in which welfare economists have extended the Pareto notions was hinted at before. Surely one can say that, if everybody's income in R were three times what it was in S, except Sonya's, who was a penny poorer, then R is an improvement, for Sonya *could be* compensated, and then one *would* have a Pareto improvement. In an example such as this one, R is a *potential Pareto improvement* over S, for the "winners" in R (compared to S) could compensate the losers and have some left over for themselves (Hicks 1939; Kaldor 1939; but see Samuelson 1950). Similarly public works, licensing, enforcement, taxation, and subsidies can sometimes be very good things, even if they are not unanimously wanted. One sense in which they can be good things is if they are potential Pareto improvements.

The notion of a potential Pareto improvement underlies cost-benefit analysis (Mishan 1971, 1981).[12] In theory (but *not* in practice), one asks the "winners" from each policy how much they would pay to institute the policy, and one asks the "losers" how much compensation they would require not to oppose implementing the policy. The policy with the largest net benefit is best, other things being equal. If everybody were to get an equal share of the net benefits, the policy with the largest net benefit would obviously be a Pareto improvement over the other alternatives. Since benefits and costs typically accrue to different individuals, cost-benefit analysis provides a means of making and utilizing interpersonal comparisons of willingness-to-pay (not of utility). In practice it is costly to ask people how much they would pay or how much compensation they would require, and their answers may not be truthful or accurate.

[12] Especially via the work of Richard Posner, the compensation criterion has had a major impact on legal theory. See Posner 1972, Baker 1975, Coase 1960, and Coleman 1984.

But economists have devised cunning methods of gleaning such information from data on prices and quantities traded. Much of cost-benefit analysis is devoted to devising, criticizing, and improving methods of imputing costs and benefits.

If cost-benefit analysis is taken to be a method for making social choices, rather than merely a technique for organizing information that is relevant to making social choices, it is easy to see why many are uneasy about it. Like the other Pareto criteria, it ignores questions of justice, and it does not even limit the sanctioned changes to those to which no one objects. For the compensation considered is only hypothetical. Some people win and some lose. Questions of fairness are obviously pressing in such circumstances. Moreover, there is a systematic bias in cost-benefit analysis against the preferences of the poor, for preferences in cost-benefit analysis are weighted with dollars, and the poor have fewer of these (Baker 1975). A poor person will (*ceteris paribus*) be willing to pay less for an improvement than will a rich man and will (*ceteris paribus*) require less compensation for a loss. Proponents have consequently explored ways of modifying cost-benefit analysis to compensate for possible injustices (Harburger 1978; Little 1957).

4.5   Arrow's theorem and social welfare theory

The last way in which economists have attempted to extend welfare economics is quite amazing. Since Pareto optimality gets one only a little way toward assessing social choices, why not think of it as merely one constraint on a "social welfare function" or "constitution" that will provide a social ranking of social options on the basis of individual rankings of these options. A society should have some way of deriving a ranking of alternatives from the ways in which individuals rank them. Let x, y, and z be social options. Suppose that the preferences of all individuals are complete and transitive and that social choices are consistent with an underlying social preference ranking that is also complete and transitive. In accordance with the notion of welfare as ordinal preference satisfaction, suppose further that one seeks some way of determining the social ranking of all pairs x and y that depends on nothing but the individual rankings of x and y. What else might one want of such an aggregation procedure?

Kenneth Arrow (1963, 1967) suggested that such a procedure should satisfy at least the following four conditions:

1 (*Pareto*) For all options x and y, if everybody prefers x to y, then x should be socially preferred to y. This so-called "weak Pareto prin-

ciple" is implied by favoring Pareto improvements, but demands even less.

2 (*Collective rationality*) The aggregation method should determine a social choice (derivable from an implicit complete and transitive social preference ordering) for all possible arrays of individual preferences.

3 (*Non-dictatorship*) There should be no dictator whose preferences are always decisive regardless of the preferences of others.

4 (*Independence of irrelevant alternatives*) The social choice between x and y should depend on individual rankings of x and y and on nothing else.

Arrow then proved the remarkable result that NO method of aggregating individual preferences into a social preference ordering satisfies these conditions!

This startling and fascinating theorem has given rise to a great deal of theoretical investigation. The controversial conclusion for welfare economics which seems correct to me is that the theoretical basis of economics is too impoverished to address the general questions of social welfare (Sen, esp. 1979a,b). It should not, in my view, have required Arrow's theorem to convince one that Arrow's independence of irrelevant alternatives condition is unacceptable – that one cannot decide whether policy x is better than policy y simply by examining individual ordinal preference rankings of x and y. There are other relevant facts, such as preference intensities, fairness, prior expectations, and rights. Economists may complain that their general theoretical perspective – equilibrium theory – does not help them to address these other questions, but they cannot reasonably claim that these other questions need not be addressed.

4.6   Rationality and benevolence: the moral authority of economists

There are crucial connections between positive economic theory and normative economic theories of rationality and of welfare. Making these explicit helps one to understand both theoretical welfare economics and the methodological peculiarities of positive economics to be discussed throughout the rest of this book.

Economists are often impatient with discussions of ethics. Concerning differences in basic values, Milton Friedman remarks that "men can ultimately only fight" (1953c, p. 5). Economists do not see themselves as moral philosophers, and they attempt to steer clear of controversial ethical commitments when doing theoretical welfare economics. Indeed economists have sometimes supposed that theoretical welfare economics was independent of all value judgments whatsoever. But economists cannot limit themselves to providing technical knowledge that may be relevant to the choice and implementation of policies (A.14.4). Moreover, as George Stigler has remarked, studying economics leads people to *value* private enterprise (1959). When economists address normative questions of economic welfare, they speak with at least an air of moral authority. They purport to know how to make life better. The solution to this paradox lies in the following argument.

Suppose (1) that one accepts the identification of individual well-being with the satisfaction of preferences and (2) that one accepts *the moral principle of minimal benevolence: other things being equal, it is a morally good thing if people are better off.* Then it is, other things being equal, a morally good thing to satisfy an individual's preferences. So (3) Pareto improvements are (other things being equal) moral improvements and Pareto optima are (other things being equal) morally desirable. Given (4) the first welfare theorem (that perfectly competitive equilibria are Pareto efficient), one can conclude (5) that, other things being equal, perfectly competitive equilibria are morally desirable and market imperfections that interfere with the achievement of competitive equilibria are morally undesirable. Note that this is a weak defense of *perfect competition*, it is not as it stands a defense of a policy of *laissez-faire*.

Premise (1) is a substantial, and, in my view, mistaken moral assertion. What makes it plausible for economists is their commitment to equilibrium theory as essentially the whole truth about the economic realm.[13] Equilibrium theory tells us that individuals have utility functions and thus that the Pareto concepts are well-defined. It also tells us that nothing matters to an individual except the satisfaction of preferences. The only possible notion of individual welfare or well-being is the satisfaction of preferences. Furthermore, given consumerism, individuals are motivated solely by the pursuit of more commodities and services.[14] Individuals seek goods for themselves rather than seeking status or the satisfaction of grudges. So they prefer the sorts of things on which individual welfare should depend. Moreover, these preferences for commodities and services are just givens. There is no niche for a theory of preference formation or manipulation, for "adaptive preferences" (Elster 1983), cognitive dissonance (see below pp. 259f), or other grounds for the criticism of

---

[13] This is an oversimplification. Economists are willing to consider supplementing equilibrium theory with further generalizations concerning beliefs, preferences, and constraints. I am here anticipating matters discussed below in sections 6.4 and 6.5.

[14] Insofar as individuals govern firms, they also seek maximum net returns. As noted before (p. 44), this introduces a theoretical tension. The "law" or behavioral postulate of maximizing net returns is designed to give determinacy to the theory of the firm, not to modify the account of individual motivation given jointly by rationality and consumerism.

actual preferences. All of this makes it easier to accept premise (1), that what people prefer is what is good for them.

Premise (2) is less problematic. Although moral theorists disagree on the content and legitimacy of the "other things being equal" clause and on the theory of individual well-being, virtually all would endorse minimal benevolence itself. Moral conclusions that require no moral premise other than minimal benevolence will thus be particularly secure.

The intermediate conclusion (3) then follows unproblematically, and, given the demonstration that perfectly competitive equilibria are Pareto efficient, the conclusion follows that such equilibria are, *ceteris paribus*, morally good and that market failures are, *ceteris paribus*, bad. This moral conclusion is highly theoretical, because real economies are not perfectly competitive and because of the "other things being equal" qualification. The conclusion is sufficiently abstract that both conservative defenders of *laissez-faire* and liberal defenders of activist government economic policy accept it.

What are the "other things" that are morally relevant? This question leads to ethical controversy, which many economists would like to avoid. A few are, to be sure, willing to make a case for their preferred economic policies on independent moral grounds. Milton Friedman (1962a), for example, argues for an unfettered market as the best defender of political freedoms. The protection of individual *rights* is also important to Friedman and to other economists. But many of these other moral commitments can be left in the background, for the sort of ideally competitive economy which minimal benevolence and equilibrium theory, via the first welfare theorem, show to be a moral ideal (other things being equal) also protects the individual rights and freedoms that have been of most importance to economists.

But the moral concerns of economists extend beyond freedom, rights, and benevolence to matters of justice, and Pareto optimal arrangements which protect individual rights and freedoms may show inequalities and apparent injustices. Among the "other things" that must be equal is justice, and a Pareto improvement that leads to distributional injustice is not necessarily morally desirable.[15] It is here that the second welfare theorem is so important. Given (6) the second welfare theorem, which says that all Pareto efficient states of affairs can be obtained as competitive general equilibria given the right initial distribution of endowments to

---

[15] Jon Elster suggests that some have taken the moral desirability of perfect competition, other things being equal, as an argument for the justice of market wages. "Since perfect competition is a desirable state, because of its efficiency properties, distribution according to marginal productivity also has normative force." (1989a, p. 229) But the inference does not go through because of the "other things being equal" clause.

individuals, one can conclude (although not validly): (7) other things being equal, perfectly competitive economies are morally desirable and Pareto improvements are moral improvements, and all other moral concerns can be satisfied by adjusting holdings without otherwise interfering in the market.

Let me then summarize this long argument:

1 Individual good = preference satisfaction (premise from equilibrium theory).
2 *Ceteris paribus* it is morally good to make people better off (premise: minimal benevolence).
3 *Ceteris paribus* Pareto improvements are moral improvements and Pareto optima are morally desirable (from 1 and 2, and the definitions of Pareto notions).
4 Competitive equilibria are Pareto efficient (premise: the first welfare theorem).
5 *Ceteris paribus* competitive equilibria are morally good and market failures are morally bad (from 3 and 4).
6 Given the right initial distribution every Pareto optimum can be obtained as a competitive equilibrium (premise: second welfare theorem). Thus
7 Other things being equal, competitive equilibria are morally good and market failures are morally bad, and all other moral concerns can be satisfied by adjusting the initial distribution (invalidly from 5 and 6).

The argument is not valid, because it contains the implicit premise that there is a Pareto efficient state of affairs that satisfies all other moral constraints. The second part of the argument is more oversimplified than the first, and there are many obvious objections that one might want to press. But enough has been said to make explicit how economists can speak with moral authority.

Whether defenders of *laissez-faire* or of extensive government intervention to address market failures, most economists share a moral commitment to the *ideal* of perfect competition. It is this commitment that gives point to the analysis of market failures (for why should they matter if market successes are not a good thing?). The fact that this commitment appears to presuppose nothing more controversial than minimal benevolence explains how economists can feel themselves possessed of moral authority, without the trouble of doing moral philosophy. The theoretical commitment to equilibrium theory and nothing more sets off a peculiarly economic domain of social life (see sections 6.3 and 12.7 below) and permits definite moral conclusions (apart from concerns about justice) that apparently rely on only the least controversial of moral premises. With one big step into the theoretical world of equilibrium theory, rationality, morality, and the "facts" of economic choice become tightly interlinked. These linkages not only explain the attractions of welfare economics, but they go a long way toward explaining the pervasive and deep commitment to equilibrium theory among contemporary economists.

This excursion into theoretical welfare economics reinforces the methodological point that equilibrium theory is absolutely central to the theoretical perspectives, problems, and projects of contemporary "orthodox" economists. It determines the questions asked and constrains the techniques employed to answer them. Without an appreciation of the vision inherent in equilibrium theory, welfare economics would be deeply puzzling. With such an appreciation, one can see it as a brilliant, but (in my view) unsuccessful attempt to address a set of pressing practical problems with a conceptual apparatus inadequate to the task.[16]

But how then is one to understand this commitment to equilibrium theory? What general sense can one make of neoclassical theorizing? We need to probe more deeply.

[16] For an interesting set of case studies showing how economists may in practice consider broader normative questions, see Johnson and Zerby 1973.

5 Models and theories in economics

Chapters 1-4 presented fundamental neoclassical theory – "equilibrium theory" – and explored how it is incorporated into partial and general equilibrium theories. The discussion showed how recourse to theory unifies and systematizes empirical generalizations, and it provided some of the flavor of theoretical work in microeconomics, general equilibrium theory, and welfare economics. We caught some glimpses of the challenging task of reformulating relevant parts of equilibrium theory, common simplifications, and specifications of the epistemological, institutional, and other circumstances so as to deduce enlightening theorems. We witnessed the significance and centrality of the theoretical enterprise of neoclassical economics.

But we did not comprehend that enterprise in a philosophically satisfying way, for nothing was said to connect the description of theoretical practice in microeconomics, general equilibrium theory, and welfare economics to general philosophical theses concerning the nature, role, and importance of theories in science. Indeed the discussion in the previous chapters has probably also been jarring to economists with its old-fashioned talk of laws and theories. For economists prefer to speak of "models" rather than "theories" and of "behavioral postulates" rather than "laws." Why? What are models and how are they related to theories? Should one not regard their central clauses or generalizations as laws?

My view of theories and models and of global theory structure in economics is controversial. I hope to show that it helps one to understand how economists theorize. This view is philosophically cogent and, I shall argue, enables one to describe theoretical practice in economics more compactly and intelligibly than do alternative philosophical accounts.

5.1   Logical positivism and the nature of scientific theory

Recent philosophical work concerning scientific theories either grows out of or reacts against the view of scientific theories developed by the logical positivists (A.1.1, A.6). According to the logical positivists, scientific theories are basically sets of *sentences*, which are closed under logical deduction. These sentences should be expressed in a formal language, such as the first-order predicate calculus. Sentences are syntactic objects, and their identity is independent of their interpretation. "$(x)(Fx \vee {\sim} Gx)$" is a sentence. Its logical notation is a precise way of saying "Everything is F or not G." If "F" is interpreted as the predicate "mortal" and "G" is interpreted as the predicated "human," then the interpreted sentence is true. If "F" is interpreted as "blue" and "G" as "red," then the interpreted sentence is false. Deducibility is a relationship between sentences, which is independent of their interpretation, and, by focusing on the sentences of which a theory is composed, one can investigate the deductive consequences of these sentences without semantic distraction.

Obviously scientific theories are not uninterpreted. There is always some "semantics," in particular, a standard interpretation, which consists of a specification of a domain for the variables (such as "x" in "$(x)(Fx \vee {\sim} Gx)$"), an assignment of "extensions" (sets of entities of which the predicates are true) to the predicates, of entities to constants, and of functions to function symbols. An interpretation constitutes a *model* of the theory if and only if it makes all the sentences come out true. A model is an ensemble of entities with various properties which a theory, when appropriately interpreted, is true of. Apart from its standard interpretation (under which the theory may or may not be true of some portion of the real world), there may be other interpretations and other models, which may be useful in the development and assessment of the theory. This logician's notion of a "model" is *not* what economists mean when they talk of models.

Since the sentences in physical theories often cannot be interpreted as making claims about observable things and properties, the semantics of such theories is philosophically problematic. The "correspondence rules" discussed by the logical positivists (A.7) are supposed to provide an interpretation of the sentences in a scientific theory that do not make claims about observables.

Alfred Mackay has provided a particularly nice illustration of this notion of theory and model in his book on Arrow's theorem (1980). Recall (pp. 64–5 above) that Arrow proved that there is no way to derive a social preference ordering from individual preference orderings, which satisfies the following four conditions:

1 It must provide some social preference ranking for any profile of individual preferences (collective rationality).

2 If everybody prefers social option x to y, then x must be socially preferred to y (weak Pareto principle).

3 There is no individual whose preferences are decisive over all options regardless of the preferences of others (non-dictatorship).

4 The social ranking of x and y must depend on nothing except the individual rankings of x and y (independence of irrelevant alternatives).

Arrow's proof, like all proofs, results from the syntax of the axioms, not their interpretation, and there may be alternative interpretations. MacKay (1980) proposed that one consider the problem of deriving an overall ranking of athletic performance in a multi-event athletic competition such as a decathlon on the basis of the ordering of accomplishments in individual events. Arrow's four conditions on social choice translate into the following four conditions on a multiathlon scoring system:

1 It must provide some overall ranking for any profile of finishes in individual athletic events (collective rationality).

2 If athlete x beats y in every event, then x must rank higher than y in the overall ranking (weak Pareto principle).

3 There is no individual event, the outcome of which is decisive regardless of how competitors perform in other events (non-dictatorship).

4 The overall ranking of athletes x and y must depend on nothing except how they rank in the individual events (independence of irrelevant alternatives).

When Arrow proved his theorem, he also proved that there is no system of multiathlon scoring that satisfies all these conditions.

Since Arrow's conditions cannot be simultaneously satisfied, their conjunction has no model, but there are, as we have seen, at least two significant and interesting interpretations. By separating syntax and semantics, one economizes on logical effort, and one can see precisely the formal identity of the distinct problems of scoring athletic events and making social choices. By seeing theories as syntactic objects and by formalizing them, one might, in the positivist's view, put logic to work, gain just such an economy of logical effort, and recognize the formal connections between distinct problems. How much improved might science be! An application to economics of the logical positivist's view of scientific theories can be found in Papandreou (1958, 1963).

5.2 Semantic and predicate views of theories

The positivists' syntactic view of scientific theories faces difficulties that has led philosophers such as Bas van Fraassen (1980) and Frederick

Suppe (1974, 1988) to propose in its stead a semantic view of theories. First, if one identifies a theory with a particular syntactic object (or with a class of syntactic objects with certain similarities of shapes or symbols), then any reformulation of a theory or even translation of a theory into a different language counts as a different theory. While there are ways around the objection, they undercut its appeal. Second, it is difficult to express scientific theories in formal languages and awkward, challenging, and time-consuming to do proofs in existing formal languages. Scientists do not waste their time this way. Third, one can argue, as Bas van Fraassen (1980) most effectively has, that the positivist emphasis on language is misplaced. One's focus should be on the content of scientific theories, on the models of which they are true, and on the relations among such models, not on the sentences used to express the theories. Indeed van Fraassen argues that some significant relations cannot be expressed within a syntactic view of theories (1980, p. 44). On grounds such as these, van Fraassen and Suppe urge us to regard scientific theories as the set of models of which the sentences in any particular formulation are true rather than as anything linguistic or sentential at all.

One might question whether the semantic view of theories differs more than linguistically from the syntactic view that it attempts to replace. What the logical positivists called the set of models of which a theory is true, the semantic theorists call "theories," and what the logical positivists called "theories," the semantic theorists call sets of sentences that are true of theories. But the relabeling is significant, because it redirects philosophical interest from sentences to things. There is also some question about whether one can accurately interpret "theories" in van Fraassen's and Suppe's sense as merely sets of models of which theories in the positivist's sense are true.[1] Apart from some awkwardness, which the semantic view shares with its predecessor and from some puzzles mentioned in the last footnote, I see nothing "wrong" with the semantic view of theories. But it does not fit the practice of economics as well as the alternative I prefer.

That third alternative is to regard scientific theories not as purely syntactic or purely semantic, but simply as a set of lawlike and interpreted *statements* (or as an equivalence class of such sets to allow one to count reformulations and restatements of theories as the same theories).

[1] If theories in the positivist sense are logically consistent, but not true in their standard interpretation, it is typically easy to find some alternative arbitrary interpretation that will specify a model. But the sets of models that constitute theories in Suppe's and van Fraassen's sense seem not to include such arbitrary concoctions. Instead they stress the ensembles of *possible* entities that may provide models in the positivist's sense. One reason why I am reluctant to accept this view of scientific theories is that it forces one immediately to confront confusing metaphysical questions concerning possible "worlds." I am indebted to Mark Bauder for help with these points.

Although my view might seem little different than that espoused by the logical positivists, it owes at least as much to a fourth view of scientific theories developed and defended by Patrick Suppes (1957, chapter 12), Joseph Sneed (1971), and Wolfgang Stegmueller (1976, 1979). Ronald Giere provides a useful simplified exposition of this fourth view in his *Understanding Scientific Reasoning* (1979 [1982]). Before saying more about my notions of theories and models, let us consider this fourth view.

In Suppes' view, scientific theories should be regarded as *predicates*. So they are linguistic entities, unlike the "theories" of the semantic theorists, but they are not *sentences*. The empirical claims of science consist of assertions that employ these predicates. Suppes argues that scientific theories are set-theoretic predicates, because he hopes to provide set-theoretical formal restatements of scientific theories. Since I am not concerned to formalize scientific theories, I shall not follow Suppes here. Other writers on economic methodology have provided formal reconstructions of economics modeled after the work of Suppes and, particularly, Sneed (see Händler 1980, Stegmueller, Balzer, and Spohn 1982, Hands 1985c, and Balzer and Hamminga 1989).

In Giere's simplified presentation (1979, chapter 5), scientific theories are definitions of predicates rather than predicates themselves. Newton's laws of motion and his law of gravitation define, for example, what Giere calls "a classical particle system." The predicate, "is a classical particle system," is true of something if and only if Newton's laws of motion and gravitation are true of it. The predicates which constitute scientific theories are not purely syntactic, for the terms in Newton's laws – body, force, distance, etc. – all have interpretations. But the interpretations of these terms do not determine (though they do constrain) the extension of the new predicate, that is, of the theory, in this sense of "theory." Reformulations of a theory in this sense that do not change its extension should not count as theory changes.

On Giere's view of scientific theories, the basic statements of what I have called "the basic equilibrium model" define a new predicate "is an economic equilibrium system" or a new kind of system, "an economic equilibrium system." An actual economy is an economic equilibrium system if and only if the laws of consumer choice theory and of the theory of the firm are true of it, and an equilibrium obtains. The simple consumption system of section 2.4 and the simple competitive production system of section 3.3 are explicitly formulated as such definitions.

On this view of scientific theories, there is no point in asking whether the claims of a theory are true or whether a theory provides reliable predictions. Predicates cannot be true or false or provide any predictions.

Definitions are trivially true, but also do not enable one to make any predictions.

Since science does more than provide definitions, the proposing of theories, in this view, is only one part of science. The other crucial part is proposing *theoretical hypotheses*, which assert that the new term is true of some actual system. Newton not only defined a classical particle system; he also offered the theoretical hypothesis that the solar system is a classical particle system. Economists do more than merely define an economic equilibrium system. In using microeconomic theory to explain or to predict, they also assert or imply that some actual economic objects, at least to some degree of approximation, constitute economic equilibrium systems.

This account of scientific theories idealizes, for in reality theorizing and modeling are not sharply separated, and there is often little point in attempting to pry them apart.[2] This account of scientific theories may also appear awkward, but much of the awkwardness can be avoided by an important terminological change. What Suppes, Sneed, Stegmueller, and Giere (in 1979) call a "theory," I shall call a "model." I shall then use the term "theory" for a set of connected lawlike assertions. Although terminological changes court confusion, this one is worth the risks, for it brings the language of this abstract discussion of scientific theories into close accord with the usage of economists and avoids the paradoxical denial that scientific theories make claims about the world.[3]

Economists use the term "model" in many ways (Machlup 1960, p. 569). Although some economic models are also models in other senses of the term, I know of none in theoretical economics which cannot be characterized as a predicate or as a definition of a predicate.[4] Taking models as definitions permits one to develop a cogent interpretation of economic models. Note that this sense of "model" is distinct from the logical positivist's notion. In their notion, a model is an interpretation of the sentences of a theory such that they all come out to be true. Models of the sort I am talking about, in contrast, are definitions and are constituted by sets of assumptions. They have nothing to do with the semantic interpretation of theories as sets of sentences. If the predicates

---

[2] Indeed the claim that they could be sharply separated would run afoul of Quine's critique of the analytic-synthetic distinction (appendix, p. 302).

[3] Suppes notes that scientists frequently use the term "model" as I shall to mean what Suppes means by "theory" (1957, p. 254). In the second edition of his *Understanding Scientific Reasoning* [1982], Giere changed his terminology in just the way I am recommending.

[4] Econometricians use the term "model" differently to contrast partially unspecified claims about some phenomena to fully specified "structures" (Marschak 1969). I shall not be concerned with the econometricians' notion of models.

models define have an extension – if actual systems satisfy these definitions – then with the proper interpretation of some "theory" in the logical positivist's sense – that is, of some set of sentences – the actual systems will be "models" in the positivist's sense of those sentences. But models in the sense of "model" specified here have no simple relation to models in the positivist's sense.[5]

Science consists not only of model making, but also of offering theoretical hypotheses that maintain that a model applies to the world. In defining a simple consumption system and offering the theoretical hypothesis that the quadruple consisting of Alice, coffee, the everything-else composite commodity, and Alice's income is a simple consumption system (pp. 34f), one is asserting that all the assumptions of the model are true of the relevant aspects of reality – that is, one is asserting that coffee is infinitely divisible, that Alice possesses a concave, increasing, and differentiable utility function, and so on.

From a theoretical hypothesis one infers what I call "closures" of the assumptions of the model (Hausman 1981a, pp. 47–8). The model Giere calls a "classical particle system" contains, for example, the assumption that any two bodies attract one another with a force inversely proportional to the square of the distance between them. Although the terms in the assumption are not uninterpreted, the assumption does not say what domain or system of entities it applies to. From the theoretical hypothesis that the solar system is a classical particle system, one can infer a closure of the assumption – that any two bodies in the solar system attract one another with a force inversely proportional to the square of the distance between them. In a closure of the assumption the domain is specified and in some cases the interpretation of the specific predicates in the assumption is sharpened. From a theoretical hypothesis one "recovers" the assumptions of the model as assertions about the world. A theoretical hypothesis entails closures of all the assumptions of the model. Closures of assumptions are genuine statements that are true or false.

For example, one might take the claims in chapter 1, that agent's preferences are complete, continuous, and transitive and that agents choose the option they most prefer, as providing a model of rationality. In doing so, one is just defining rationality. One is not saying that people's preferences are in fact complete, continuous, or transitive. One is not saying whether people are really utility maximizers. All one is doing is defining one notion of rationality. Having done only that, one has said nothing about the world, but, if the model is fecund, one has provided the means for making assertions about the world. One might, for example,

---

[5] I am indebted to Mark Bauder here.

discover that in certain domains people are not rational, or one might maintain that people are largely rational in certain sorts of decision-making activities. The latter claim is, of course, equivalent to saying that with respect to those decision-making activities people's preferences are complete, continuous, and transitive and they choose the option they most prefer. But formulating the model not only provides a useful abbreviation, it makes possible conceptual, logical, and mathematical explorations of the consequences of rationality so defined. Every model is, in a sense, a detour, but some models are very useful detours that greatly increase our conceptual resources.

The differences between models and theories can be displayed in the following table:

Models	Theories (Descriptions, explanations, predictions)
definitions of predicates, concepts, or systems	sets of lawlike assertions
trivially true or neither true nor false	true or false
point is conceptual exploration	point is to make claims about the world
assess mathematically or conceptually, untestable	assess empirically testable
consist of assumptions	consist of assertions

A model plus a *general* theoretical hypothesis asserting that the assumptions of the model are true of some portion of the world results in a theory. Some theoretical hypotheses, on the other hand, state that a particular real-world system, such as the solar system or the quadruple, < Alice, coffee, everything-else, Alice's income > belongs to the extension of the predicate defined by the model. When a theoretical hypothesis is such a singular statement, one might call the resulting set of closures of the assumptions of the model *an applied or restricted theory*. To say that New York stock brokers are rational is to offer an applied or restricted theory; one is asserting that the predicate defined in the model of rationality applies to a particular hunk of the world. Some restricted theories have much narrower scope than others, and indeed it may sometimes be misleading to speak of "theories."

Philosophers are sometimes attracted to the predicate view of theories (which I am calling "models"), because they are instrumentalists (A.2). They see the goal of theorizing not as discovering theoretical truths, but as discovering tools that enable one to predict and to control phenomena. From an instrumentalist perspective, one virtue of the predicate view of theories is that it permits one to avoid judging whether Newton's law of gravitation, for example, is a universal law. Instead one can merely judge, case by case, whether it is true of particular ensembles of bodies.

Although instrumentalists may thus make use of a predicate view of theories, they are mistaken if they think the view constitutes an argument for instrumentalism. Theoretical hypotheses need not be restricted to singular claims about individual systems. The closures of assumptions they imply may be general laws. Adopting a view of models as predicates or as definitions of predicates does not itself commit one to any thesis concerning the aims of science or whether general theoretical claims may be true.

Furthermore, instrumentalists are on dangerous ground if they tie their instrumentalism to a strategy of restricting the scope of generalizations. The methodological injunction to seek generalizations with broad scope is an important part of scientific practice. It explains, for example, why unsuccessful tests of a generalization are taken as casting doubt on the generalization rather than as merely revealing the limits to its scope. Without seeking broad scope and regarding successful generalizations as achieving it, how could scientists or engineers ever rely on laws in domains in which they have not been specifically tested?

In summary, models are definitions of kinds of systems, and they make no assertions. It is a category mistake to ask whether they are true or to attempt to test them. Their point lies in conceptual exploration and in providing the conceptual means for making claims that can be tested and can be said to be true or false. Theories are sets of systematically related lawlike statements. They do make true or false assertions about the world, and they can sometimes be tested. When one offers a general theoretical hypothesis asserting that something is the kind of system defined by a model, then one is enunciating a theory. The kind of assertion that results when one offers a theoretical hypothesis depends on the kind of theoretical hypothesis. A model may be used to state a general theory, to explain or to predict, or merely to state a fact about an individual.

5.3   Theories and models in economics

One might wonder what purpose this detour through the predicate view of theories has served. Since the activities of theorizing and of exploring models are constantly intertwined in fact, why bother with what I am calling "models," instead of considering theories directly?

Developing theoretical knowledge is not just discovering correlations among properties that are already understood. An absolutely crucial part of the scientific enterprise – a part that was underemphasized by the logical positivists – is the construction of new concepts, of new ways of classifying phenomena. Even extremely simple models, such as the model of a simple consumption system, provide such concepts.

Concepts or terms are important to empirical scientists only insofar as they may enable them to say informative things about the phenomena under study. But scientists may nevertheless wish partly to *separate* questions concerning their conceptual apparatus from questions concerning the extent to which that apparatus applies to the world. That is, they may sometimes wish to investigate the properties of models without worrying about whether those models depict or apply to any aspect of reality.

In defining a model of a simple consumption system and in proving that the individual's consumption will lie at the point of tangency between some indifference curve and the budget constraint, one is not making any claims about the world. Nor need theorists regard themselves as revealing mysterious hypothetical truths concerning hypothetical situations. They are merely constructing concepts and employing mathematics and logic to explore further properties which are implied by the definitions they have offered. Such model building and theorem proving does not presuppose that one believes that the particular model is of any use in understanding the world. An economist might, for example, be intrigued with a mathematical question or attempt to discredit certain assumptions by revealing their consequences.

Insofar as one is only working with a model, one can dismiss any questions about the realism of the assumptions one makes. But remember that the reason is that one is saying *nothing* about the world. The irrelevance of questions about the realism of the assumptions to the mathematical investigation of properties of models has nothing to do with any questions concerning the assessment of scientific theories. Empirical assessment is out of order simply because there is nothing to assess: no empirical claims have been made.[6] Insofar as one is only working with a model, one's efforts are purely conceptual or mathematical. One is only developing a complicated concept or definition.

---

[6] In this discussion I am thus not in any way joining in Friedman's (1953c) or Machlup's (1955) defenses of "unrealistic assumptions" discussed below in chapter 9.

Max Weber's "ideal types" can, I think, be construed as models in the sense presented here. In a famous passage, Weber introduces the notion of an ideal type as follows:

This conceptual pattern brings together certain relationships and events of historical life into a complex, which is conceived as an internally consistent system. Substantively, this construct in itself is like a utopia which has been arrived at by the analytical accentuation of certain elements of reality. Its relationship to the empirical data consists solely in the fact that where market-conditioned relationships of the type referred to by the abstract construct are discovered or suspected to exist in reality to some extent, we can make the *characteristic* features of this relationship pragmatically *clear* and *understandable* by reference to an *ideal-type*. This procedure can be indispensable for heuristic as well as expository purposes. The ideal typical concept will help to develop our skill in imputation in *research*: it *is* no "hypothesis" but it offers guidance to the construction of hypotheses. It is not a *description* of reality but it aims to give unambiguous means of expression to such a description....In its conceptual purity, this mental construct (*Gedankenbild*) cannot be found empirically anywhere in reality. It is a *utopia*. Historical research faces the task of determining in each individual case, the extent to which this ideal-construction approximates to or diverges from reality, to what extent for example, the economic structure of a certain city is to be classified as a "city-economy." (1904, p. 90)

Although Weber's ideal types fit my general characterization of models, they have special features, too. "Laws" play a lesser role than in models such as Giere's "classical particle system." What is important to Weber is not only more detail, but the specification of a sort of *system* or *entity*, not an abstract nomological structure. Most economists are less concerned with historical detail than was Weber and most are willing to use the term "model" sometimes much as Giere does. For example, most economists would find nothing strange or awkward in regarding continuity, completeness, transitivity, and utility maximization as a model of rationality. But economic models are generally definitions of (hypothetical) economies or markets, not of purely nomological concepts.

This observation may be of some general importance, for it suggests that the unit of theoretical analysis in economics is frequently not laws or theories but their *application* to particular ensembles of agents, markets, and institutions. Models are not themselves empirical applications, but they have the same structure. Economists are often concerned with developing applications of theory, not theory itself (section 6.4); and they are concerned with particular, albeit often stylized, circumstances. In these regards they are more like chemists than physicists (A.14).

Indeed, models in economics serve many purposes and are of many kinds. Models such as the simple consumption system of section 2.4 are crutches or pedagogical devices rather than conceptual innovations. Such models (which I have elsewhere called "special case" models (1981a, pp. 48–51)) simplify features of more general models and make them vivid. They are particularly useful for illustrating or evaluating more general models. "Model" is a particularly apt term for such constructions, because they resemble descriptions of the physical models that engineers build. Just as one can illustrate, develop, teach, and test claims about the properties of airplanes by means of scale models, so one can illustrate, develop, teach, and test features of theories and general models by means of special case models. But the use of special case models to assess theories and general models is controversial (Hempel 1965, p. 165; Popper 1968, pp. 442–56). For, unlike wind-tunnel tests on airplane models, for example, special case models do not provide us with occasions for the acquisition of new perceptual beliefs. They only help us to bring to bear the beliefs we already have.

The fact that theoretical economics is devoted to the exploration of models does not distinguish economics from other sciences. In theoretical work, *all* scientists attempt to exclude the complications of reality. As Galileo showed, the only good way to theorize is to develop models (1632, 1638). But, largely because of the possibility of creating simplified experimental circumstances, closures of assumptions in models in the natural sciences may often be regarded as truths of different degrees of universality. Model building in the natural sciences thus appears to be less distinct from empirical investigations.

In economics the problems of application are thornier. Even though models in economics need not be as abstract as those which characterize mainstream theorizing, they will never apply to economic reality cleanly. Insofar as one has any hopes for economic theory at all, there will always be some need to divorce conceptual development and empirical application. "Unrealistic" model-making is unavoidable for theoretically inclined economists.

The distinction between models and theories helps one to understand the attitude of economists toward what I called "equilibrium theory." Most are uncomfortable thinking of consumer choice theory, the theory of the firm, and the claim that equilibrium is attained as lawlike assertions that are either true or false. They prefer to think of these "laws" as "behavior postulates," as the most fundamental assumptions of the discipline, not as assertions. Given the obvious difficulties in regarding these claims as laws, one can sympathize with this attitude, and many economists are not committed to the truth of all these "behavioral postulates."

But questions of assessment must ultimately be faced. If economists did not believe that there was a great deal of truth to these "laws," if they only worked with "the basic equilibrium model" without any commitment to "equilibrium *theory*," then their practice would be mysterious. Unless one is to conclude that economists are uninterested in explaining or predicting economic phenomena, one must attribute to them either a commitment (much qualified and hedged) to the truth of the claims of equilibrium theory, or the conviction that the conclusions would still follow if the false assumptions were replaced with true ones (A.2).

As these last paragraphs and indeed the first four chapters suggest, it is unhelpful to regard neoclassical economics as a collection of separate and unconnected models or theories. Without understanding what unites and directs specific theoretical endeavors, one understands very little about economic theorizing. There are more global questions about theorizing in economics to which we now need to turn.

6   The structure and strategy of economics

Over the last two decades philosophers interested in scientific theory have been concerned not only to improve the logical empiricist's view of scientific theories, but to supplement it with accounts of the broader structures which shape individual theories and are in turn shaped by particular theoretical achievements. The best known of these accounts have been presented by Thomas Kuhn and Imre Lakatos.[1] Before offering my own abstract characterization of the structure and strategy of economic theorizing, let me consider whether their accounts can help with this task.

6.1   Disciplinary matrices

Although few philosophers of science are satisfied with his particular formulations,[2] Thomas Kuhn (1970) deserves credit for first devoting sustained attention to such "metatheoretical structures," which he initially called "paradigms," then "disciplinary matrices" (1970, Postscript, 1974). Disciplinary matrices are the constellation of beliefs, presumptions, heuristics, and values that tie together the theoretical efforts of practitioners of some discipline. When Kuhn speaks of a "discipline" or a "community," he has in mind specific theoretical enterprises which involve perhaps a few dozen scientists. But I shall not be stretching his remarks in an unusual way if I take them as applying to microeconomics as a whole.

In Kuhn's view, disciplinary matrices consist of four main components: (1) "symbolic generalizations," (2) metaphysical and heuristic commitments, (3) values, and (4) "exemplars." Symbolic generalizations

---

[1] Other philosophers have offered significant theories of global theory structure, but their work has had little influence in economics. Laudan's (1977) account should be of more interest to economists because of his emphasis on conceptual problems. See also Shapere 1974, 1984, 1985. Morgenbesser's distinctions between schemata and theories and between theories *of* a subject matter and theories *for* a discipline (1956, chapter 1) anticipate much of this later discussion.

[2] For criticism, see Scheffler 1967, Shapere 1964, and Suppe 1977. For an account of the ambiguities of the term, "paradigm," see Masterman 1970.

resemble fundamental laws. They are not merely empirical generalizations, but fundamental laws that often serve to define the terms they
employ. They are held tenaciously and are not easily revisable. The basic
claims of equilibrium theory are not quite symbolic generalizations in
Kuhn's sense, because economists are not firmly committed to all of
them. Indeed there are many microeconomic theories that assert the
contraries of some of its basic behavioral postulates.

The second component of a disciplinary matrix is metaphysical or
heuristic. Examples Kuhn provides include ontological claims such as
"heat is the kinetic energy of the constituent parts of bodies," and
preferred models, such as "the molecules of a gas behave like tiny elastic
billiard balls in random motion" (1970, p. 184). These metaphysical and
heuristic commitments set the standards for acceptable answers to questions. This aspect is of particular importance in understanding the simplifications economists employ in constructing economic models. In
studying economics, one learns the strategies for beating phenomena
into mathematically tractable shape. Without knowing these strategies,
one does not know economics. Furthermore, economists also have heuristic commitments against regarding aspects of human social life, such as
emotion, irrationality, or mistakes, as significant causal factors in
economics (see p. 66 above and sections 6.3–6.6 and 15.1 below). Heuristics are a crucial feature of economics.

Although Kuhn treats "exemplars" as a separate component of a
disciplinary matrix, it is useful to think of these as a further aspect of
the discipline's heuristics. One striking point Kuhn emphasizes is that
scientists mimic past achievements. There are few explicit rules for doing
science. Scientists instead imitate those whom they perceive to have made
major contributions. Past achievements not only lead to "symbolic generalizations" and the metaphysical or heuristic commitments that dominate a discipline, but they also determine a myriad of heuristic details.
The importance of problem solving in learning economics or physics is
solid evidence for the importance of exemplars.

Finally, by "values," Kuhn has in mind general commitments to
honesty, consistency, respect for data, simplicity, plausibility, precision,
problem solving, compatibility with other theories, and so forth. Kuhn's
most significant contribution concerning values is to point out that
individuals may differ in how they apply these values and that such
differences may contribute to scientific progress. The values of economic
theorists are distinctive in the weight given to mathematical elegance, in
the comparatively small attention given to experimentation, data gathering, and testing, and in the concern for policy relevance. I shall explore
later, particularly in chapters 12 and 15, whether these facts about
economics suggest a scientific failing.

Kuhn's account of disciplinary matrices provides a useful checklist of what to look for in examining the large-scale structures of economic theorizing, but economics does not fit his schema very well.[3] The role of the assumptions of the basic equilibrium model or of the fundamental laws of equilibrium theory is not well described in Kuhn's categories.

This fact might be taken as a criticism of economics, for Kuhn's purpose in characterizing disciplinary matrices was not only to describe scientific practices, but also to understand how larger-scale theoretical commitments contribute to the goals of science. If it could be shown that disciplinary matrices as described by Kuhn were necessary to successful cognitive enterprises, then one would have grounds to condemn microeconomics. But Kuhn never offers a normative defense of his account of disciplinary matrices, and nothing in his work provides a basis for criticizing economics. Furthermore, his account does not have enough structure to improve the general description of economic theory already offered.

6.2   Research programs

In highlighting larger-scale theoretical structures, Kuhn's *Structure of Scientific Revolutions* poses a serious challenge to the views of theory assessment defended by logical empiricists and by Karl Popper (see A.1). Committed as they are to disciplinary matrices, scientists do not, in Kuhn's view, confront theories with data that confirm or falsify them. In "normal science," scientists aim to solve the puzzles that arise in attempting to make reality fit the theory or disciplinary matrix, not to test theories. Kuhn singles out for criticism Popper's view that scientists should seek hard tests of theories and reject theories that fail the test:

As has repeatedly been emphasized before, no theory ever solves all the puzzles with which it is confronted at a given time; nor are the solutions already achieved often perfect. On the contrary, it is just the incompleteness and imperfection of the existing data-theory fit that, at any time, define many of the puzzles that characterize normal science. If any and every failure to fit were ground for theory rejection, all theories ought to be rejected at all times (1970, p. 146).

Lakatos attempts to defend a sophisticated Popperian view of theory assessment from this challenge. Crucial to his response to Kuhn is a novel account of scientific "research programs," which has been very influential in economics. Although Lakatos' views on large-scale theory structure are intertwined with his views of theory assessment, I shall

---

[3] For attempts to apply Kuhn's views to economics, see Baumberger 1977, Bronfenbrenner 1971, Coats 1969, Dillard 1978, Kunin and Weaver 1971, Stanfield 1974, and Worland 1972.

separate them and postpone discussing Lakatos' views on theory assessment until chapter 11.

In developing his alternative account of the global theoretical structure of developed sciences, Lakatos incorporates many elements from Kuhn's work, although Lakatos' account also owes a great deal to Popper's lectures on metaphysical research programs and to Lakatos' own earlier work on the philosophy of mathematics (1976). A *research program* for Lakatos consists of a series of theories that are linked to one another by *heuristics* and a common theoretical "core" (1970, pp. 48f). The heuristics that define a research program are of two kinds. The *negative heuristic* forbids those who work within the research program from tinkering with a group of propositions, which Lakatos calls "the hard core" of the research program. The hard core consists of fundamental laws, metaphysical presuppositions, or perhaps even non-law factual assertions. Lakatos' hard core is broader than Kuhn's symbolic generalizations, for Kuhn's metaphysical commitments and preferred analogies may also belong to the hard core. Lakatos, for example, regards Descartes' metaphysical view that the fundamental properties of all matter are mechanical or geometrical as the hard core of the Cartesian research program. Newton's three laws of dynamics and his law of gravitation constitute the hard core of the Newtonian research program (1970, p. 48). Writers on economic methodology have disagreed concerning what the hard core of neoclassical theory is.[4]

The other sort of heuristic that constitutes a research program, the "positive heuristic" consists of instructions about how to use the hard core to generate specific models and how to modify theories that face anomalies. Lakatos gives the misleading example of the way in which Newton first derived planetary orbits ignoring interplanetary gravitational forces and planetary volumes and then dealt successively with the complications left out of the initial derivations. Suggestions such as "think of bodies first as point masses" do belong to the positive heuristic of Newtonian dynamics, but the order of theoretical development in this

---

[4] Spiro Latsis, for example, argues that the hard core of the theory of the firm consists of four propositions:
   (i) Decision-makers have correct knowledge of the relevant features of their economic situation.
   (ii) Decision-makers *prefer* the best available alternative given their knowledge of the situation and of the means at their disposal.
   (iii) Given (i) and (ii), situations generate their internal "logic" and decision-makers *act appropriately to the logic of their situation.*
   (iv) Economic units and structures display stable, coordinated behavior. (1976, p. 22) (ii), (iii), and (iv) echo three "laws" of equilibrium theory: profit maximization, rationality, and equilibrium, while (i) seems a factual simplification or perhaps a heuristic decision about how to think about economic phenomena.

example is driven by the mathematical complications, rather than by the heuristics of Newtonian physics. Furthermore, the role of the positive heuristic is not only to guide the development of an initial testable empirical theory, but also to direct the improvement of already developed theories that confront anomalies. The positive heuristic of economics includes suggestions such as: "Think of choices as constrained maximization." "Make qualitative comparisons of equilibria." "Regard moral commitments as having no effect on behavior."

Although Lakatos plays down the role of what Kuhn calls "values" and says little about exemplars, his account of the global structure of theoretical science resembles Kuhn. With its more vivid and salient categories, it has, however, been more attractive to writers on economic methodology than has Kuhn's account (Blaug 1976), and, as we shall see later (11.2), Lakatos integrates his emphasis on heuristics into an account of scientific theory assessment.

It does not seem to me, however, that Lakatos' sketch of the structure of research programs helps one to understand or rationalize the structure and strategy of theoretical economics. Once one separates what Lakatos has to say about structure from what he has to say about assessment, one can see that the account of the structure of sciences is as thin as Kuhn's. Given the variety of propositions that may enter the "hard core" of a research program and the diversity of the suggestions that make up the positive heuristic, one scarcely enriches the description of enterprises such as microeconomics by applying Lakatos' categories.

Second, it is unclear how to fit economics into Lakatos' categories. The last footnote contains Latsis' description of the hard core of the theory of the firm. Leijonhufvud (1976, p. 71) and Blaug (1976, p. 162) claim that the hard core of pre-Keynesian neoclassical economics includes the claim that economies tend to converge to equilibrium. De Marchi (1976, p. 117) argues that Bertil Ohlin took the "mutual inter-dependence theory of pricing" as part of his hard core. Blaug regards the hard core of pre-Keynesian neoclassical economics as consisting of "weak versions of what is otherwise known as the 'assumptions' of competitive theory, namely rational economic calculations, constant tastes, independence of decision-making, perfect knowledge, perfect certainty, perfect mobility of factors, etc." (1976, p. 161). In an extended account, E. Roy Weintraub sees the hard core of the "neo-Walrasian research program" as consisting of six propositions (1985b, p. 109):

HC1. There exist economic agents.
HC2. Agents have preferences over outcomes.
HC3. Agents independently optimize subject to constraints.

HC4. Choices are made in interrelated markets.

HC5. Agents have full relevant knowledge.

HC6. Observable economic outcomes are coordinated, so they must be discussed with reference to equilibrium states.

These different accounts of the hard core of the theory of the firm, of pre-Keynesian neoclassical economics, and of neo-Walrasian economics are not necessarily inconsistent, since these might be regarded as separate research programs. But there are tensions between these different accounts, and the disputed questions do not seem to me to be useful ones. Attempting to apply Lakatos' view of the structure of research programs to economics creates unnecessary and unhelpful questions.

Furthermore, in attempting to make economics fit Lakatos' scheme, one must construe its hard core as extraordinarily weak, as, indeed, Weintraub in particular does. One cannot even specify that preferences are complete or transitive, for there are neo-Walrasian theoretical explorations which involve incomplete and intransitive preferences (McKenzie 1979, Mas-Collel 1974). The crucial fact that *most* neoclassical models embed the assumptions of equilibrium theory is cast into the shadows, while one worries fruitlessly about which are the real hard-core propositions. A Lakatosian reconstruction of the global theoretical structure of economics is thus, I contend, unenlightening. These criticisms will be developed further when I address Lakatos' views on theory assessment in chapter 11.

6.3   The structure of economics

Kuhn's and Lakatos' visions of disciplinary matrices and research programs do not provide any useful recipe for grasping the overall structure and strategy of contemporary economics. Let us see whether, assisted by the hints and questions that Kuhn and Lakatos provide, we can now provide a systematic philosophical overview.

Let us begin by listing salient features of the theoretical enterprise, which were discussed in previous chapters:

1 Theoretical work in economics takes the form of formulating models and investigating their properties mathematically (see 2.4 and 3.3). Models are definitions of complex predicates. Their axioms or assumptions fall into three main classes:

(a) Restatements of the core theory or model – that is, of the "laws" of the theory of consumer choice or of the theory of the firm. There is, however, considerable freedom here. Economists often construct models that contain as assumptions *contraries* to some of the "laws" of equilibrium theory.

(b) Standard simplifications concerning information, divisibility of commodities, existence of markets, the nature of competition, and the like.

(c) Specific assumptions concerning the sort of phenomena to which the particular model will be applied. Some of these may be accurately asserted of the initial institutional, epistemic, or physical conditions. Others may be extreme simplifications. The assumptions are made with an eye to the possibility of mathematical derivations, and they show many common features from model to model.

2 In applying equilibrium models for purposes of prediction or explanation, economists at least tacitly assert that the assumptions of their models are either approximately true or inessential (in the sense that the same implications would follow if the obviously false assumptions were replaced with true assumptions).[5]

3 Models in "positive" economics fall into two main classes: partial and general equilibrium models (3.6). In partial equilibrium models one ignores the general interdependence of economic phenomena and focuses on the markets for only a few (often just one) goods or services. These models are used not only for teaching economics, but in many practical applications. The "generality" of general equilibrium theories comes in gradations. Some highly simplified general equilibrium models with only a small number of commodities or services involve aggregation and, like partial equilibrium models, abstract from complicated interrelations among different markets. Input-output models include many commodities, but greatly simplify economic relations. Both simplified general equilibrium models and input-output models can be employed for predictive and explanatory purposes. Abstract general equilibrium models, on the other hand, permit consideration of the full range of economic interactions, but seem to be without predictive or explanatory use. Their function within the theoretical project needs further clarifying.

4 In attempting to explain or to predict economic phenomena, economists examine how economic equilibria shift in response to changes in

---

[5] See 5.3. With respect to explanation, this claim is hard to dispute. Showing that some phenomenon was to be expected given theory *T* does not explain why that phenomenon occurred unless *T* captures some relevant truths (A.3). If, on the other hand, the purposes of economics are construed as exclusively predictive, this claim might be challenged. It will be defended below in chapter 9 when I discuss Milton Friedman's methodological views.

initial conditions (3.5). This sort of inquiry is called "comparative statics," because it abstracts from the dynamics of adjustment processes. Comparative statics explanations and predictions are *causal.* One examines changes in equilibria as effects of differences in initial conditions. Many of the derived generalizations of economics, such as the law of demand, are causal generalizations.

5 Crucial to the basic equilibrium model is a definition of *rationality* (chapter 1), and the fact that economics is so often both a theory of how people do behave and of how they rationally *ought to* behave is a striking one. Its significance remains to be explored.

6 Equilibrium theory provides the "positive" or "descriptive" premises for a powerful argument in support of the conclusion that perfect competition is, other things being equal, a morally good thing (4.6). This argument is central to the standard policy perspectives of economists.

7 Equilibrium theory or the basic equilibrium model shapes the whole theoretical enterprise. Partial and general equilibrium models are augmentations of the basic model, and even normative theorizing shapes its questions and answers in terms of equilibrium theory. Macroeconomics has been to some extent independent of equilibrium theory, but this fact has been of deep concern to economists and much contemporary work is devoted to showing how macroeconomics may be derived from equilibrium theory. Equilibrium theorists seem hesitant about supplementing their theory with further behavioral generalizations, no matter how well confirmed.

This theoretical enterprise bears some resemblances to science as described by Kuhn and Lakatos, but the differences are significant, too. Let us see whether we can grasp the underlying vision.

6.4   The vision of economics as a separate science

Economics is governed by a coherent vision of its overall theoretical mission. I shall later argue that this vision is too confining, but my present purpose is not to pass judgment, but to characterize it and to show how it explains the major features of economics. Although the following theses are rarely explicitly stated, they are generally accepted and, much more than any generalities concerning paradigms and research programs, they define the global structure and strategy of economics.

1 Economics is defined in terms of the causal factors with which it is concerned, not in terms of a domain.

2 Economics has a distinct domain, in which its causal factors predominate.

3 The "laws" of the predominating causal factors are already reasonably well-known.

4 Thus, economic theory, which employs these laws, provides a unified, complete, but inexact account of its domain.

Moreover, as I shall explain in the next section, these theses about the structure of economics have definite implications concerning what sorts of theory modifications or qualifications are permissible. But first let me clarify and explain these theses.

(i) Economics is defined in terms of the causal factors with which it is concerned, not in terms of a domain.[6] As we saw in the introduction, John Stuart Mill defines economics as concerned with a particular domain. Yet, like Lionel Robbins, Mill emphasizes the causal factors with which economics is concerned. In Mill's view, "Political economy...[is concerned with] such of the phenomena of the social state as take place in consequence of the pursuit of wealth. It makes entire abstraction of every other human passion or motive, except those which may be regarded as perpetually antagonising principles to the desire of wealth, namely aversion to labour, and desire of the present enjoyment of costly indulgences." (1843, 6.9.3) Lionel Robbins' definition is less explicit about the causal factors and makes no reference to a particular domain. "Economics is the science which studies human behavior as a relationship between ends and scarce means which have alternative uses." (1932, p. 15) But it is the causal factors that constitute scarcity with which economics is concerned. Robbins' definition makes economics a study of an aspect of most human behavior rather than a study of a particular domain, and some economists, such as Becker (1976, 1981), have emphasized the relevance of economic theory to phenomena that have not been part of the traditional subject matter of economics.[7] But economics is more than utility theory, and few economists believe that the motivational "forces" with which it is mainly concerned (consumerism and profit maximization) are dominant in all domains of human behavior.

(ii) Economics has a distinct domain, in which its causal factors predominate. Mill makes a sophisticated case for this claim:

Notwithstanding the universal *consensus* of the social phenomena, whereby nothing which takes place in any part of the operations of society is without its share of influence on every other part...it is not the less true that different species of social facts are in the main dependent, immediately and in the first resort,

---

[6] For an intriguing discussion of the way in which scientific theories define their domains see Stegmueller 1976, pp. 93, 176-7.

[7] For an extreme example, see Fair 1978. Blinder 1974 is a parody.

on different kinds of causes; and therefore not only may with advantage, but must, be studied apart...(1843, 6.9.3)

Mill is not making the weak claim that some social phenomena depend principally on a limited number of causal factors. He is instead suggesting that a few causal factors are sufficient to account for the major features of a distinct domain of social phenomena. Here is a fuller statement:

There is, for example, one large class of social phenomena in which the immediately determining causes are principally those which act through the desire of wealth, and in which the psychological law mainly concerned is the familiar one that a greater gain is preferred to a smaller. ...By reasoning from that one law of human nature, and from the principal outward circumstances (whether universal or confined to particular states of society) which operate upon the human mind through that law, we may be enabled to explain and predict this portion of the phenomena of society, so far as they depend on that class of circumstances only, overlooking the influence of any other of the circumstances of society...A department of science may thus be constructed, which has received the name of Political Economy (1843, 6.9.3).

I do not know of any comparable modern defenses of the existence of an "economic realm," but what is taken to be obvious is not often defended. The substantive implications of this commitment to an economic domain are controversial. Since economics is defined by its causal factors, there can be an economic realm only if some domain of social life is dominated by the causal factors or "laws" with which economics is concerned.

Not all of what is called economics, even orthodox neoclassical economics, is concerned with the economic realm. Inquiries in game theory, for example, which shade into work in standard economics and are carried on by many of the same theorists, often relax the specific motivational assumptions which I called "consumerism."[8] The strategic interactions with which game theorists are concerned consequently need not lie within the specifically economic realm or domain. But to recognize that some of economics does not concern this domain does not imply that there is no economic realm or that economists are not concerned that their theory span this realm.

(iii) The "laws" of the predominating causal factors are already reasonably well-known. Mill and Robbins believe that they know the fundamental

---

[8] Recall that consumerism maintains that individuals are self-interested, that the sole objects of their preferences are commodity bundles, and that individual utility functions are independent.

mental causal factors, and indeed they take them to be platitudes such as "a greater gain is preferred to a smaller" (Mill 1843, 6.9.3) or "individuals can arrange their preferences in an order, and in fact do so" (Robbins 1935, p. 78). One might question whether most economists are committed to this thesis. Certainly no good Popperian, for example, could accept it. The detailed methodological discussions of chapters 8, 9, 12, 13, and 14 provide some evidence. Although economists may be uncomfortable with my bald formulation, very little work in microeconomics lacks apparent confidence that the fundamental principles have already been revealed. The extent to which economists have embraced Kuhn's views on normal science or Lakatos' claims about the negative heuristic of research programs as applicable to economics is evidence that economists believe that the predominating causal factors are already reasonably well-known. This fact has important implications for theory assessment in economics, which are explored in chapters 8 and 12.

(iv) Thus, economic theory provides a unified, complete but inexact account of its domain. Economic theories and models explore the implications of the laws of the major causes. Since an economic phenomenon is defined in terms of the causes with which economics is concerned, or, in other words, the laws that make up economic theory, economic theory thus provides an account of all economic phenomena. And, since economic causal factors predominate in the economic domain, the scope of economic theory is the entire economic domain. The theory provides a unified account of all of economics since the laws in the theory are themselves systematically interrelated in particular economic models and theories. The laws of separate subdomains of economics (such as consumer choice theory and the theory of the firm) are not united into a single theory only by arbitrary conjunction. In general equilibrium theories the "laws" of equilibrium theory work together.

Since the laws of the major causes are joined together within economic theory and are thought to be reasonably well-known, economic theory is regarded as *complete*. Economists recognize that causal factors left out of economic theory sometimes influence market phenomena. Everybody knows that. Economic theory is inexact. It is only supposed to be complete at a high level of abstraction or approximation. It is as if one wanted a theory of an economy as seen from a distance through a low-resolution telescope. Although economics is not merely imprecise, because minor "disturbing" causes occasionally cause anomalies even at a low resolution, one might reasonably hope that economics theory provides the whole "inexact truth" (chapter 8) concerning the economic realm.

(v) Implications. The thesis that economic theory provides a unified, complete, but inexact account of the economic realm, is pregnant with strategic implications. It implies that the explanatory task of economics is done when economic phenomena have been traced to the fundamental economic causal factors. Thus one finds economic theory "neither tracing back the circumstances which we do take into account to their possible origin in some other facts in the social state, nor making allowance for the manner in which any of these other circumstances may interfere with and counteract or modify the effect of the former" (Mill 1843, 6.9.3). Any attempt to explain the fundamental laws of economics is not a part of economics.[9]

Although Mill regards the formulation and pursuit of separate sciences as "preliminary" (1843, 6.9.4) to the development of an integrated social science, he holds that as things now stand no explanatory or predictive purposes of economists would be served by fusing economics with any other science.

All these operations, though many of them are really the result of a plurality of motives, are considered by political economy as flowing solely from the desire of wealth....This approximation has then to be corrected by making proper allowance for the effects of any impulses of a different description which can be shown to interfere with the result in any particular case. Only in a few of the most striking cases (such as the important one of the principle of population) are these corrections interpolated into the expositions of political economy itself; *the strictness of purely scientific arrangement being thereby somewhat departed from,* for the sake of practical utility [my emphasis]. (1843, 6.9.3)

The right approach is to deduce the consequences in the economic domain of the fundamental economic causes "once for all, and then allow for the effect of the modifying circumstances" which are "ever-varying" (1843, 6.9.3). The generalizations of psychologists and sociologists are not welcome in economic theorizing.

Furthermore, unlike in physics or biology, the search for fundamental laws is not a part of economics, for the fundamental principles are already reasonably well known and, in any case, come from outside. They are simple generalizations that are evident to introspection or everyday experience. Economists have work to do in refining them and in clarifying which of these generalizations are necessary to the explanation and prediction of economic phenomena, but economists are not engaged in

---

[9] One finds the same view expressed in the following definition of economics, offered by Mill's friend and methodological disciple, J. E. Cairnes. Political economy is defined by Cairnes "as the science which traces the phenomena of the production and distribution of wealth up to their causes, in the principles of human nature and the laws and events – physical, political, and social – of the external world" (1875, p. 71).

a search for laws. Unified and complete, economics is an inexact and separate science. The task of its practitioners is to apply the basic principles to particular problems.

Economics resembles individual theories such as Newtonian dynamics or Mendelian population genetics more closely than it resembles disciplines such as physics or biology. For an orthodox theorist, it is in effect a one-theory science. A perfected general equilibrium theory coupled with accurate descriptions of the significant circumstances would permit explanations and predictions of all economic phenomena. These explanations and predictions would not be exact, for there would be many "disturbing causes" (see 8.1 below). Other social forces affect economic outcomes, and generalizations concerning these other forces might occasionally be incorporated into specific economic models for particular purposes. But in the pure science of economics a single unified theory is refined and applied.

6.5   The strategy of the separate science of economics

What does this vision of economics as a separate science mean in practice? If one not only accepts this vision but also equilibrium theory itself, then one will take equilibrium theory as defining the causal factors with which economics is concerned. The domain of economics is then the realm of social phenomena in which those causal factors predominate. In particular:

Economic phenomena are the consequences of rational choices that are governed predominantly by some variant of consumerism and profit maximization. In other words, **economics studies the consequences of rational greed.**

The exact content of rationality can be left open. One can modify utility theory and still be doing economics. The nature of the predominant motivational "force" is also rather loose. One can do economics with satiation and with some interdependence among utilities. But agents seeking their own material welfare is what makes economies run, and theories which dethrone this motive cease to be economics. Economic theories may not portray agents as exploitable fools.

From the vision of equilibrium theory as the core of the separate science of economics, two central methodological rules follow, governing the use of additional behavioral generalizations in economic theorizing:

1 Generalizations about choice or other economic phenomena are *ad hoc* and should be avoided unless they are derivable from equilibrium

theory and further legitimate generalizations about preferences, beliefs, and non-economic constraints on choices.

2 Further generalizations about preferences, beliefs, and constraints are legitimate and may be incorporated into economic theories only if they do not threaten the central place of rational greed, the possibility of equilibrium, or the universal scope of economics.[10]

These are not the only methodological rules governing what generalizations can be added in the course of model and theory construction in economics. One might also, for example, insist that further generalizations be mathematically tractable. But these rules identify a distinctive theoretical strategy. Further generalizations concerning constraints, beliefs, and preferences are permissible, for these are the factors which, according to utility theory, govern choice. So one can add generalizations concerning time preference, as is common in theories of capital and interest, or about the extent to which economic agents believe economic theory, as the rational expectations theorists do. But additional generalizations about beliefs and preference must not dethrone consumerism or, to a lesser extent, profit maximization from their places as the dominant motives in the economic realm, and they must not make equilibrium impossible. The rules also express not merely the *preference* for *wide* scope that is characteristic of all science, but a *requirement* that fundamental theory retain *maximal* scope, that it span the entire domain.[11]

One sees these methodological rules at work especially in the reactions of economists to macroeconomic theories that lack explicit microfoundations. Keynes' claim that the marginal propensity to consume is less than one is by itself regarded as "*ad hoc*" (for example Leijonhufvud 1968, p. 187). It is legitimate only if it can/be shown to follow from equilibrium theory and generalizations about beliefs, preferences, and constraints, such as Modigliani's life-cycle hypothesis or Friedman's permanent income hypothesis (see Modigliani and Brumberg 1955, Ando and Modigliani 1963, and Friedman 1957). Modigliani's and Friedman's hypotheses about beliefs and preferences are not *ad hoc*, because they

---

[10] Those who prefer to think in terms of Lakatos' research programs, hard cores, and heuristics will read these rules, with some justification, as the negative heuristic of neoclassical economics. But as I have already insisted, there is more to the core of microeconomics than the "hard core" implicit in these rules. Moreover, as I pointed out above (p. 92), there is respected theoretical work that is hard to separate sharply from economics in which the motivational supremacy of consumerism is not respected.

[11] One can provide some defense for this requirement on grounds that are independent of a preference for a separate science of economics. For generalizations that are not linked to equilibrium theory may, like some of the generalizations of Keynesianism, not be robust to changes in the environment and consequently, as Lucas so forcefully argued (1976), they may be a precarious basis for policy.

do not threaten the explanatory unity of equilibrium theory. Generalizations about wage or price stickiness have been criticized as *ad hoc* on the same grounds (Olson 1984, p. 299). Similarly, defenders of the rational expectations hypothesis have called the attribution of adaptive expectations to individuals *ad hoc*, since the failure to use relevant information, which adaptive expectations implies, conflicts with rational greed (Begg 1982, pp. 26, 29).[12]

6.6 Methodological individualism, rational choice, and the separate science of economics

The only general methodological principle governing economics and the other social sciences for which one finds much *explicit* argument is methodological individualism – the insistence that explanatory laws in economics concern features of individual human beings (see A.14.2, esp. p. 322, Hayek 1952 and Sensat 1988). The demands of methodological individualism are much looser and less specific than the rules presented in the previous sections. For example, Keynes' "*ad hoc*" generalization that the marginal propensity to consume is less than one was cited approvingly by John Watkins in an article defending methodological individualism (1953). Notice that the prohibition against using *ad hoc* generalizations also seems to apply at more theoretical "levels" than does methodological individualism, which is only intended as a constraint on ultimate, or "rock-bottom" laws. Although consistent with some formulations of methodological individualism, the strategy of economic theorizing is more specific and more closely tied to equilibrium theory.

One should also mention the intermediate methodological demand that all economic explanations must be in terms of the rational choices of individuals.[13] In some ways this demand is more stringent than methodological individualism, which does not forbid explanations in terms of individual irrationality. But the insistence on rational choice models is also more permissive than some versions of methodological individualism, since rational choice explanations permit references to institutional facts among the constraints on individual choices. The

---

[12] D. W. Hands argues that accusations of *ad hoc*ness by economists should be construed in a Lakatosian way: *ad hoc* claims are those which are not in accord with the positive heuristic of a research program (1988; see also section 11.2 below). He is right, but the reference to Lakatos is too unspecific. The relevant parts of the "positive heuristic" are the two rules above.

[13] "If an institution or a social process can be accounted for in terms of the rational actions of individuals, then and only then can we say that it has been 'explained.'" (Coleman 1986, p. 1) I return to this view in the concluding chapter.

limitation to rational choice explanations is implicit in the insistence on the separate science of economics and helps to explain why economists will accept some modifications and reject others. For example, to insist that further generalizations may only concern beliefs, preferences, and constraints follows from the methodological preference for rational choice explanations. But to insist on rational choice explanations is much weaker than insisting on the primacy of acquisitive preferences, the possibility of equilibrium, and on maximal scope.

Implicit in the theoretical practice of economics are the requirements that all economic explanations employ some subset of equilibrium theory and that they eschew additional behavioral postulates unless they have wide scope and are compatible with rational choice explanation, consumerism, and equilibrium. The only justification for these restrictions is the fruitfulness of insisting on them. I am unconvinced that these methodological constraints have been that fruitful. In my view, not even methodological individualism or the insistence on rational choice models is justifiable. If unfamiliar forms of explanations can be well tested and can command empirical support, they should be pursued. Economic theory has not been successful enough to justify theoretical or methodological purism.

Within a vision of economics as a separate science, the features we have seen in this chapter and the preceding ones fall into place. Apart from the general scientific virtues of abstract model-making, this activity is exactly what one would expect of a discipline devoted to applying a single theory with only inexact implications. Partial equilibrium theorizing is a practical compromise: general equilibrium theorizing, if only feasible, would get things right. Since equilibrium theory captures the fundamental causes of economic phenomena and the nature of individual rationality, normative thinking about economic welfare is properly cast in its terms. Later when we consider questions about assessment of microeconomics and the nature of progress in economics, this portrait of economics as a separate science will, I hope, seem even more enlightening. For, as I shall argue in part II, this view of the structure and strategy of economics, rather than any mistake about theory assessment, is the source of the dogmatism in contemporary economics.

6.7   The function of abstract general equilibrium theories

I have not yet explained where abstract general equilibrium theorizing fits in a separate economic science. Recall that I argued that *equilibrium theory, not general equilibrium theory, is the central economic theory.* General equilibrium theory is one application of equilibrium theory, and one's understanding of neoclassical economics should not turn on the interpretation of general equilibrium theory, no matter how puzzling or interesting it may be.

Since abstract general equilibrium theories seem to have no explanatory or predictive implications, many have wondered what good they are. Why has so much effort been devoted to proving the existence of general equilibrium in completely unrealistic circumstances? What role do abstract general equilibrium theories have in economics?

These are difficult questions upon which leading theorists disagree (see Coddington 1975). Some believe, mistakenly (as argued at greater length in chapter 7 of my 1981a), that general equilibrium theories serve to explain prices (Debreu 1959, p. ix; Malinvaud 1972, p. 242). C. J. Bliss denies that abstract general equilibrium theories "represent reality," but claims that they are a good point of departure and a good guide to which concepts are fundamental (1975, p. 301). Bliss's view is somewhat misleading. When uneasy about how unrealistic their models are, economists are often tempted to say that their models only provide a "logic" of economic phenomena or that they are merely "bags of tools" into which one dips when convenient. These claims have a certain truth to them, which I have tried to capture by distinguishing equilibrium theory from its applications and distinguishing between models and theories. But these claims do not resolve problems of theory assessment. If an economic theory is only a logic, a tool, or a guide, one still needs to ask whether it is a *good* logic or a *good* tool or a *good* guide. And to tell whether a theory is a good guide, one has to be able to apply it.

One can, however, interpret Bliss and others as arguing only that general equilibrium theory may be of heuristic value (see Green 1981). For example, in extending proofs of atemporal general equilibrium to proofs of intertemporal general equilibrium, economists hit upon the idea of regarding the same "good" (such as a loaf of bread) as a different commodity depending on the *date* or *place* at which it exists. In this way proofs of atemporal general equilibrium could be reinterpreted to be proofs of intertemporal general equilibrium. But, quite apart from the role of this construct in such existence proofs, distinguishing commodities by place and date has proven helpful in practical theorizing. Although heuristics is a complicated subject, one can show that general equilibrium theories have been of heuristic value merely by showing that they have in fact helped in developing valuable empirical economic theories.

Yet it seems to me that the existence proofs that general equilibrium theories provide also have an important role. Weintraub argues that the existence proofs show us that the "hard core" of economics, which includes the claim that there are equilibrium states, is consistent, and that without such proofs the general research strategy of economics would be futile (1985a, 1985b, esp. chapter 7). But the consistency of the "hard core" propositions or of the "laws" of equilibrium theory (which embody these propositions) can be established in simple models and does not require the sophisticated mathematical work of the past four decades.

My views are closest to those expressed by Kenneth Arrow and Frank Hahn. They concede that general equilibrium theories have little directly to say about real economies, but argue that the theories answer important theoretical questions (1971, pp. vi–viii). Arrow and Hahn point out that, ever since Adam Smith, economists have believed that self-interested voluntary exchanges in favorable conditions lead to coherent and efficient economic organization. Yet previous economic theories could not explain how this order could come about. Economic theorists might doubt whether their theoretical framework captures the crucial features of the economy. In developing equilibrium theory, will one eventually be able to explain how self-interested individual action within particular institutional constraints leads to coherent economic order? Do economists really have a grip on the central economic regularities? Can equilibrium theory ever become a successful separate economic science?

Suppose one believes, as many economists do, that the existence of some sort of equilibrium is one of the crucial *explananda* which a general economic theory ought to account for. In employing equilibrium theory to prove the existence of equilibria under various highly simplified conditions, the abstract general equilibrium theorists give one *some* reason to believe that equilibrium theory can accomplish this central explanatory task and thus some reason to believe that equilibrium theory can be made to function as an adequate general economic theory.[14]

The abstract general equilibrium theorists have demonstrated that, were the world much simpler, one could use the "laws" of equilibrium theory to explain how economies work. If one regards the resemblances between the defined worlds of the models and actual economies as

---

[14] Notice that economists are not merely trying to show that the existence of equilibrium is consistent with prior beliefs. The "explanation" of an equilibrium of a possible economy needs to be distinguished both from explaining "How possibly?" in the sense of Hempel and Dray and from any discussions of the feasibility of economic equilibria. Hempel's and Dray's view is that sometimes things happen contrary to our expectations which need explaining (away) (see Hempel, 1965, pp. 428–30, Dray 1957, p. 158f). Nor, despite Hahn's claims (1973, p. 324), are abstract general equilibrium theorists concerned with whether a competitive equilibrium is feasible in practice. One does not need all this theory to know that real semi-competitive capitalism does not regularly achieve full employment. If one did need general equilibrium theories for the purpose, they would not help anyway, since the existence proofs that the theories provide generally show only what conditions are sufficient for competitive equilibria, not what conditions are necessary.

significant, these demonstrations give one reason to believe, in Mill's words (1843, 6.3.1), that economists know the laws of the "greater causes" of economic phenomena. Economists thus have reason to believe that they are on the right track. Proofs of the existence of general equilibrium provide theoretical reassurance, rather than explanations or predictions. Abstract general equilibrium theories may also help economists to improve current economic theories. By progressively weakening and complicating the stipulations used to demonstrate the existence of equilibria, one comes closer to being able to apply the theory to real economies.

But such theoretical reassurance is to be had only if it focuses on the existence proofs and turns a blind eye on the rest of abstract general equilibrium theory. For, in addition to addressing questions concerning existence, theorists have also considered the *uniqueness* and *stability* of the general equilibria of simplified hypothetical economies. And these results have generally been negative (Arrow and Hahn 1971, chapters 9–13). Without making assumptions that are known to be false of actual economies,[15] one cannot prove that equilibria will be unique or stable. And the instabilities and multiplicity of equilibria cannot be cured easily by filling in or stipulating more details about the hypothetical simplified economies. In these applications of equilibrium theory there are, as it were, no empty "slots" into which one can place more information. The fact that one cannot explain *which* equilibrium obtains in these simplified economies suggests that equilibrium theory is incomplete and needs to be supplemented with additional "laws," which, when conjoined with information of the sort that the laws would deem relevant, would be able to explain why an economy is in one equilibrium rather than another. The existence proofs suggest that equilibrium theory may provide the nomological structure of a successful separate science, but the failures to prove uniqueness and stability suggest the opposite. This latter suggestion is, however, weaker, for there are many ways to apply the laws of equilibrium theory; and it may be that an explicitly dynamic application could solve the problems that current general equilibrium theories cannot solve.

Having now done what I can to make clear in general terms the structure and strategy of neoclassical economic theory, the stage is set for a consideration of the vital problems of theory assessment. But before turning to them, a case study may help make these general claims clearer.

---

[15] Such as the assumption that every two commodities are gross substitutes for each other (Arrow and Hahn 1971, pp. 221–7). Commodities x and y are gross substitutes if more of y is consumed whenever the price of x increases.

7   Overlapping generations: a case study

In this chapter I shall present a case study to illustrate and clarify the notions of theory and of model developed above and to make more concrete the general claims in chapter 6 concerning the character of the neoclassical theoretical enterprise. I shall focus on a celebrated paper by Paul Samuelson, "An Exact Consumption-Loan Model of Interest with or without the Social Contrivance of Money," and on some of the discussion and applications it spawned. I selected this case study for several reasons.

First, this paper is regarded as a significant contribution to contemporary theoretical economics. It was published in 1958 in the *Journal of Political Economy* by a leading economist (later a Nobel laureate) and attracted the attention of other major theorists. Although even Samuelson himself thinks it deficient in some regards (1960, pp. 82–3), it is much cited.

Second, although largely a paper in "positive theory," normative issues intrude in interesting ways. This overt concern with normative issues is *not* characteristic of all papers in theoretical economics, but it illustrates the frequent interplay between positive and normative in economics. Samuelson's paper is not perfectly representative of contemporary economics. For work within neoclassical economics is diverse, including inquiries into econometric techniques, heavily statistical empirical studies, abstract mathematical theorem-proving, cost-benefit analyses, studies of rationality and game theory, and so forth. There is no clear sense in which any essay could be "representative." Samuelson's essay is at most representative of one kind of theoretical endeavor.

Third, "An Exact Consumption-Loan Model" illustrates strikingly the power and pitfalls of abstract model making in theoretical economics. We shall see how easy it is to get carried away by fictions.

Fourth, despite some intricacies in the details, little mathematical competence is required to follow the argument.

Finally, Samuelson's essay vividly exemplifies the properties of economic theorizing that I have emphasized. Although I contend that the Samuelson paper is *in this regard* typical, there is a great deal of diversity in the theoretical literature, and less favorable cases can be found. I am presenting the case not to *demonstrate* the correctness of my views, but to illustrate them.

The problem Samuelson addresses is the following: Suppose individuals want to save for their old age, when they cannot produce anything, and there is nothing imperishable that they can lay by. All people can do is to strike a bargain with younger workers to support them later in exchange for some current consideration. In a world of endlessly overlapping generations of workers and retirees, what will the pattern of interest rates be? To isolate the effect of this desire to provide for one's old age, from the effects of technological productivity, of subjective preference for present consumption over future consumption, and of expectations of improving or worsening economic circumstances (Böhm-Bawerk 1888; Kuenne 1971, pp. 25-34), Samuelson either assumes these other factors away or includes no assumption about them at all.

7.1   The basic model

1 Life has three periods. In the first two periods workers each produce one unit of a single completely perishable output – call it "chocolate." In the third period of their lives retired workers produce no chocolate at all and consume only what younger producers transfer to them.
2 All individuals have concave and increasing utility functions for consumption of chocolate in all three periods of their lives. As they mature, their tastes (and utility functions) do not change.
3 Productive activities take place in a closed competitive market economy. Nobody is a net creditor or debtor. Markets clear.

Let R_t be the "discount rate" that prevails in period t for chocolate available in period $t+1$. A contract in period t to provide one unit of chocolate in period $t+1$ will not in general exchange for one unit of chocolate in period t, although in some circumstances it might. Instead it will, by definition, exchange for R_t units. $R_t =_{def}$ the value in period t of one unit of output in period $t+1$ divided by the value in period t of one unit of output in period t. $R_t = 1/(1+i_t)$, where i_t is the one period rate of interest in period t. For, if the rate of interest is zero, $R_t = 1$. If the rate of interest is 100% ($i_t = 1$), then the value in period t of a unit of output in the next period is one half the value of a unit of output in period t and so forth.

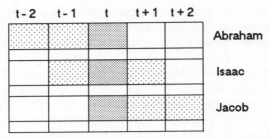

Figure 7.1. Overlapping generations

Consider a person, Jacob, born in period t, as in figure 7.1. C_1, C_2, and C_3 are the amounts of chocolate consumed by Jacob in the first, second, and third periods of his life, which occupies periods t, $t+1$, and $t+2$ of the history of this economy. The value of Jacob's consumption in the first period of his life (period t) in terms of chocolate in period t is simply C_1. The value in period t of Jacob's consumption in the second period of his life (period $t+1$) is $C_2 R_t$, and the value in period t of Jacob's consumption in retirement (period $t+2$) is $C_3 R_t R_{t+1}$. So Jacob faces the budget equation:

$$C_1 + C_2 R_t + C_3 R_t R_{t+1} = 1 + R_t$$

The left-hand side of the equation is the total value in period t of Jacob's lifetime consumption, while the right hand side is the total value in period t of Jacob's lifetime production, which consists of one unit of output in each of periods t and $t+1$, with the latter multiplied by the discount factor R_t to get its value in period t.

It is more convenient to work with each individual's *net savings* in each period – that is the amount of chocolate produced (zero or one units) minus the amount consumed. So Jacob's net savings in period t, S_1, the first period of his working life is $1 - C_1$. Similarly $S_2 = 1 - C_2$ and $S_3 = -C_3$. In terms of savings, the budget condition becomes:

$$S_1 + S_2 R_t + S_3 R_t R_{t+1} = 0 \tag{1}$$

It is important to keep in mind that Jacob's consumption or savings in the three periods of his life depend on the two discount rates R_t and R_{t+1}. For Jacob, like all individuals, decides on that lifetime pattern of consumption that maximizes his utility, and that pattern will depend on what the terms of trade are between output in the different periods. Indeed Samuelson always explicitly notes this dependence of savings on discount rates in his more detailed notation.

The condition that markets clear provides a second equation. Let B_t be the number of Jacobs first entering the labor force in period t. So in period t there are B_t Jacobs, B_{t-1} people in the second period of their lives (Isaacs) and B_{t-2} retirees (Abrahams). Since markets clear, one has the equation:

$$B_t S_1(R_t, R_{t+1}) + B_{t-1} S_2(R_{t-1}, R_t) + B_{t-2} S_3(R_{t-2}, R_{t-1}) = 0 \qquad (2)$$

The savings decision of those entering the work force in period t depends on R_t and R_{t+1}, while the savings decision of those born in the preceding periods depends on the discount rates they will encounter in their lives as indicated. Knowing the utility functions one could determine the savings if one knew the discount rates, but one has four unknowns and only two equations. If one adds the further equation stating that the market must clear in period $t-1$ (or period $t+1$), one picks up one equation, but one picks up another unknown, too. Without further constraints, there is no way to determine the discount rates or the rates of interest.

7.2   Stationary and constant growth cases

One drastic way to get some determinacy is to consider the case of an unchanging economy with a constant population, B and a constant discount rate, R. Equations 1 and 2 become:

$$S_1 + S_2 R + S_3 R^2 = 0 \quad \text{and} \qquad (1s)$$
$$BS_1 + BS_2 + BS_3 = 0 \qquad (2s)$$

Without considering the dependence of savings on the discount rate, one can see by inspection that one solution (and there are others!) is $R = 1$ or $i = 0$. Given that Samuelson has placed no constraints at all on the extent to which individuals might prefer present to future consumption, this is, as Samuelson notes, a remarkable result. The terms of trade across periods are entirely equal. In every period t, individuals can secure exactly x units of the consumption good in a future period by surrendering x units of the consumption good in period t.

Suppose now that, instead of a stationary population, population is growing at some constant exponential rate such that $B_{t+1} = (1+m)B_t$. Suppose, as in the stationary case, that the rate of interest is constant through time. Equations 1 and 2 now become:

$$S_1 + RS_2 + R^2 S_3 = 0 \quad \text{and} \qquad (1e)$$
$$B_t S_1 + [B_t/(1+m)]S_2 + [B_t/(1+m)^2]S_3 = 0 \qquad (2e)$$

One can see that one solution (and again there are others!) is $R = 1/(1+m)$ or $i = m$. Samuelson thus proves the following theorem:

Every geometrically growing consumption-loan economy has an equilibrium market rate of interest exactly equal to its biological percentage growth rate. (p. 472)

The stationary case is just a special case of an economy growing geometrically with a zero percentage growth rate. Having found this result, one might have expected Samuelson to consider whether equations (1e) and (2e) have other roots and to consider which of these are economically relevant, and eventually he does just this. But first his discussion takes two interesting turns.

7.3   "Hump-saving" and social welfare

First Samuelson addresses the question of whether the biological interest rate maximizes the "lifetime (ordinal) well-being of a representative person, subject to the resources available to him (and to every other representative man) over his lifetime" (p. 472). (The answer is that it does.) Why would one ask this question here? One answer is that this is one way to determine whether this solution to these equations is economically relevant. Since individuals are attempting to maximize their (ordinal) utility, one would expect a market rate of interest to arise that permits them to do just that. But this expectation need not always be met. A second reason, which is at least as important, is that Samuelson has an abiding interest in the welfare properties of competitive markets (which I attempted to explain above in section 4.6). He wants to know how well they would perform in hypothetical circumstances such as those envisioned. Note, however, how constrained the welfare question is by prior theoretical commitments.

Second, Samuelson considers whether there is some "common-sense market explanation of this (to me at least) astonishing result" (p. 473). It might appear that he is inquiring whether this particular mathematical solution to equations (1e) and (2e) makes economic sense. But consider what he actually says:

1 Samuelson first suggests that in a growing population workers outnumber retirees, so retirees can live better than in a stationary economy and this surplus shows up as a positive rate of interest. But, as Samuelson himself points out, this suggestion says nothing about how market interactions might give rise to this result.

2 Samuelson argues that, since there are more Jacobs than Isaacs, the Isaacs have more bargaining power and do not have to bribe the Jacobs so much to support them during their retirement period.

3 Although the second remark is superficially plausible, it implies that Isaacs are turning over goods to Jacobs in exchange for an agreement that Jacobs will support them later. But Samuelson points out that, if there is no time preference, consumption should be equal in every period in the stationary case, so Isaacs are not turning over goods to Jacobs.

4 In fact, within the institutional constraints specified, the mathematical solution $i = m$ is economically impossible. Samuelson suggests that we consider the two-period case where individuals work the first period then retire. Although one can derive the same mathematical solution, $i = m$, voluntary savings is here obviously impossible. Non-retirees have nobody with whom they can exchange who can support them in the next period. In the three (and n) period case, however, Isaacs can make repayable loans to Jacobs. An extension of the two-period argument does, however, show that it is economically impossible (in the model as described) for representative workers to save in the first period of their lives.[1] For there is nobody who can repay consumption foregone in the first period with additional consumption later. Indeed in a numerical example of a stationary population economy with completely symmetrical preferences for present as compared to future consumption, Jacobs consume more than they produce and the free-market rate of interest that arises is strongly negative – approximately $-2/3$. Isaacs are giving up x units of consumption to the Jacobs in exchange for a retirement income of only $x/3$.

5 So two conclusions emerge. The biological interest rate is not an economically relevant solution to the model and, whatever the economically relevant solution is, it is suboptimal (given the infinite time horizon). The invisible hand fails. The free market here leaves everybody worse off than they could have been.

This expository order, which is abbreviated and slightly altered in the retelling here, is curious. Why make arguments for the economic plausibility of mathematical solutions that cannot arise through market transactions, except, perhaps, to anticipate objections that are bound to occur

---

[1] Individual first period workers may, of course, arrange exchanges with other first period workers. All the argument shows is that there can be on average or in total no first-period savings.

to readers?[2] The (theoretical) normative relevance of the discussion also seems central. A large part of what makes the puzzle Samuelson poses interesting is the strong presumption that free markets are efficient.[3] The (positive) theoretical question, "What's going on here?" gets its interest from these normative concerns.

Samuelson himself argues that the model is instructive in five respects:

1 It shows what interest rates *would be implied* if they were determined only by the desire to save for retirement.
2 It shows that zero or negative interest rates are in no sense logically contradictory.
3 It helps to isolate the effects of other causal influences on interest rates such as technological productivity, innovations, time preference, government action, or uncertainty.
4 "It points up a fundamental and intrinsic deficiency in a free pricing system, namely, that free pricing gets you on the Pareto-efficiency frontier but by itself has no tendency to get you to positions on the frontier that are ethically optimal in terms of a social welfare function; only by social collusions – of tax, expenditure, fiat, or other type – can an ethical observer hope to end up where he wants to be." (p. 479)
5 It gives one a new perspective on the importance of money as a store of wealth. For money now appears to be a sort of social compact that makes up for the perishability of goods.

The remainder of Samuelson's essay is devoted largely to the fourth and fifth respects in which the model is supposed to be instructive. The causal questions concerning the effect on interest rates of the desire to save are dropped rather than answered. Samuelson points out that, if individuals can make some sort of compact whereby current workers support retirees in return for support from workers-to-be when the current workers are themselves retired, then (assuming an infinite horizon) everybody is better off and the biological interest rate can be attained. The contrivance of money has this effect, for even though (by assumption) goods do not keep, money may keep (even if paper crumbles and coins corrode). By purchasing consumption goods from producers, retirees

---

[2] There is a good deal more to be said in answer to this and other questions than I shall say here. What Donald McCloskey calls "the rhetoric of economics" (pp. 265f below) is an interesting subject indeed. It seems evident that Samuelson is not only anticipating objections but also teasing the reader. He clearly wants the reader to appreciate the puzzles he has formulated.

[3] Although the free-market solution is far inferior when confronted with an infinite horizon, it is Pareto optimal for any finite time horizon. For the biological interest rate arrangement with S_1 greater than zero leaves the last generation of workers (who will starve in retirement) worse off during their productive years than does the free-market solution with S_1 negative.

can pass on to them claims for the consumption goods which can be cashed in later. This feature of money is remarkable, but not miraculous, for it depends, as Samuelson reminds us, on each generation agreeing to accept the greenbacks of the previous generations. Notice how peculiar this concern with issues 4 and 5 is. Why should one care about a "deficiency in a free pricing system" that only appears in an infinite-generation hypothetical economy?[4] What makes this issue important is that it shows that perfectly competitive equilibria are not always Pareto optimal and are thus not always desirable (other things being equal) on the grounds of minimal benevolence (p. 68 above). Anything that shakes the status of perfect competition as a moral ideal (*ceteris paribus*) shakes the stance of welfare economics and thus commands attention. The issues about optimality are abstract theoretical questions, which are not them-selves normative. But their importance and interest flow directly from their role in the normative argument for the moral desirability of perfect competition.

7.4   On the reception and influence of Samuelson's model

The history of the influence of Samuelson's essay and of the critical reactions to it are as interesting as the essay itself. In the immediate aftermath of its publication there were two substantial critical discussions by Abba Lerner (1959a,b) and William Meckling (1960a,b). Both alleged that Samuelson made mistakes in his positive analysis, but both were in fact motivated by normative or ideological concerns. The point and motivation of both Meckling's and Lerner's remarks are almost purely normative, although, as in the case of Samuelson's original essay, most of Meckling's and much of Lerner's comments concern positive theoreti-cal economics.

7.4.1   Objection from the "right": Samuelson is subversive

Meckling, from the "right," made four criticisms. First, and most impor-tantly, he maintains that Samuelson misspecified his model. In the station-ary case, in place of (2s) $S_1 + S_2 + S_3 = 0$ (dividing by B), Meckling argues

---

[4] Although, as argued in chapter 6, I find Lakatos' models of theory development in mathematics and the natural sciences too coarse-grained to help one to understand economics, one can see Samuelson's result as akin to the sort of "refutation" that, in Lakatos' view, spurs work in informal mathematics. Samuelson establishes a counter-example to the claim that all competitive equilibria without externalities are Pareto optimal. One might then try to sort the responses to Samuelson's counterexample in terms of Lakatos' classification of strategies as "monster-barring" (1976, p. 86) or "exception-barring" (1976, pp. 24–30) (see Meckling's response discussed below) or "lemma incorporation" (1976, pp. 33–42). See also Weintraub 1985b.

that Samuelson should have specified (2s') $S_1 = RS_3$. ((2s') is derived from (2s) and (1s) $S_1 + RS_2 + R^2 S_3$.) For, if one assumes, as Meckling does, that there can be no social contract, then retired Abrahams can only consume what they loaned last year to Isaacs (plus – or minus – interest). Meckling simply rules out the possibility of a social contract. So a zero interest rate or a unitary discount factor can obtain only when the individual utility functions lead individuals to be willing to offer and accept zero interest loans.

Second, Meckling insists on the fact that, in any *finite* economy, the competitive equilibrium, with its negative interest rate, will be Pareto optimal. The Samuelson biological interest rate "cheats" the young in the last period who transfer goods to the old and receive nothing in return (1960a, p. 75).

Third, Meckling objects that Samuelson does not consider the incentive effects of a biological interest rate, "Whether they choose more leisure or less, the terms of trade between work and leisure will be altered by the social contract – a fact which makes $R = 1$ even less appealing" (1960a, p. 75). Samuelson has, in Meckling's view, abstracted from a factor that is central to the determination of interest rates.

Finally, in his "Rejoinder," Meckling argues that a zero interest rate in a stationary economy (or a biological interest rate in a growing one) "would *not* persist. Individuals entering the third year of life have *nothing* of value to offer to individuals entering the first and second years of life....the zero-interest-rate equilibrium can prevail only if the sheriff is retained on a permanent basis." (1960b, pp. 83–4)

One need not interpret Meckling's criticisms as primarily normative or ideological, for, unlike Lerner, he is not explicitly offering normative criticisms. But the combination of (a) a clear mistake in Meckling's last criticism, (b) the puzzling accusation that an economist of Samuelson's abilities has overlooked incentive effects (which do not in any case necessarily support Meckling's preference for an unconstrained competitive market), and (c) a vague defense of the unattractive optimality of a non-monetary negative-interest-rate competitive equilibrium are jointly a strong indication that what bothers Meckling is the implication in Samuelson's essay that perfectly competitive equilibrium is not necessarily morally desirable (other things being equal). Indeed, in a gentle way, Samuelson notes this feature of Meckling's essay when he begins his response by telling an anecdote of a former teacher of his who complained about a talk of Samuelson's, "Well, it wasn't so much what Samuelson said as what I knew he was thinking."(1960, p. 76)

Meckling's technical criticisms are that Samuelson has misspecified his model and that, even given the presence of fiat money, the biological interest rate could not be sustained by the market. Is it a mistake to use (2s) $S_1 + S_2 + S_3 = 0$ rather than (2s') $S_1 = RS_3$? *If* one rules out a social contract and insists that the consumption of Abrahams must come from repayment of their loans last year to Isaacs, then Meckling's equation is the correct one to include and $R = 1$ is not a general solution. But the whole point of Samuelson's article is that it is possible for the young to transfer goods to the old and to be compensated in turn later on by individuals who are not yet born.

Is this possibility a market possibility? Not, of course, without fiat money or a social contract. But, once a society with fiat money is functioning, the old buy goods from the young, who hold the money and in turn use it to purchase goods from the young of the next generations. Although one could not *get into* this state without a social contract, this state can, as Samuelson argues (1960, p. 80), be maintained by *laissez-faire*.

Not so, Meckling argues, because, as Samuelson suggests (1958, p. 482), the young would have an incentive to repudiate the currency. Why should they care that the current old supported the old of a previous generation? Only the sheriff (or a moral sheriff within) can keep the system going. But this objection and Meckling's view seem mistaken in two regards. First, each individual agent in a competitive economy, who (of course) takes the currency as an institutional given, has an incentive to sell some of his or her consumption goods and to save the money (see Cass and Yaari 1966, p. 362). Only as a *group* do one-year-olds have any incentive to repudiate the currency. But since the young individuals want there to be an institutional arrangement to provide for their own old age and since the fiat money system accomplishes this better than the non-monetary market solution, it is hard to see how the group of one-year-olds will manage to solve their collective-action problem in order that they can myopically and self-destructively repudiate the currency.[5] If the sheriff is needed to avoid short-sightedness in this regard, the sheriff is no less necessary in the non-monetary competitive equilibrium to prevent Isaacs from reneging on their debts to retired Abrahams.

So there is no economic mistake in Samuelson's model. On the contrary, the model that Meckling prefers prevents one from noticing that there

---

[5] Except in the last period of a finite model. If there is a known end-point in time, then the social contract or fiat money system unravels in the same way as a finite iterated prisoner's dilemma game. For it would be in the self interest of the young in the last period to repudiate the currency. Since the young in the period before can anticipate this, it would be in their self-interest not to accept the currency of the old in that period, and so forth. The soundness of such apparently persuasive "backwards-induction" arguments is, however, in dispute (see Binmore 1987, 1988, Kreps *et al.* 1982, and Pettit and Sugden 1989).

are biological interest rate equilibria and that these are sustainable by market processes (though not attainable by them). There is no principled way to avoid facing the "unpleasant fact" that, without political interference, markets would work badly in the hypothetical circumstances envisioned by Samuelson. But why should such a hypothetical result be regarded as "a fundamental and intrinsic deficiency of a free pricing system"? Because, as I have argued, the demonstration of the Pareto optimality of perfect competition is central to welfare economics.[6]

Meckling's normative or ideological concern about this seems exaggerated. Although the fact that non-monetary competitive equilibria in infinite economies may not be Pareto optimal may be uncomfortable (as is the fact that in finite economies the non-monetary competitive equilibria may be unattractive) these results have been shown to obtain only in fanciful circumstances. It would be no great virtue of competitive markets if they functioned splendidly in such unreal circumstances. Nor have they been shown to have any great deficiency if they perform poorly in those circumstances. Secondly, markets only work well given that the coercive apparatus of the state (or some moral substitute) enforces contracts and protects property rights. It is unclear that appreciably more state interference is needed to maintain a biological rate of interest.

7.4.2   Objection from the left: against the pretence of individual savings

Abba Lerner objects to Samuelson's essay from the left. Although he, too, offers a technical criticism of Samuelson's essay, his concerns are openly normative. Assuming similar and interpersonally comparable utility functions and ignoring incentive effects, welfare will be maximized with equal consumption by individuals of each generation. If there is no time preference, then this welfare maximum is attainable by taxing those who are earning and giving the proceeds to those who are not. In a growing economy, this welfare maximum is not attainable by the market. One should think of social security as a tax and gift program, not as "saving for the future," which in Samuelson's model, in which nothing can be saved, is simply impossible. Samuelson, in Lerner's view, is confused about this feature of his model and mistaken in holding that the biological interest rate is optimal. On the contrary, it leads to wasteful scrimping by the young and wasteful overconsumption by the old.

---

[6] There are some other reasons, too, which I discuss briefly at the end of this chapter.

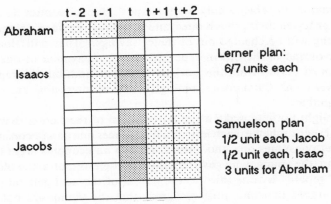

Figure 7.2. Samuelson's and Lerner's plans

Lerner's formal objection, like Meckling's, is off the mark. Samuelson demonstrates this neatly in a two-generation example with a population doubling every generation. Under "the Samuelson plan" each individual consumes half of his one-unit first-period output and "saves" the rest. This "savings," which is the consumption of the retirees (who are half as numerous), thus leads to a second-period consumption of a full unit and a lifetime consumption of one and a half units. Under "the Lerner plan," in contrast, individuals "save" one-third of their first-period one-unit output, and consumption in both periods is two-thirds of a unit, for a lifetime total of one and a third units. So, baring time preference, everybody is better off under Samuelson's plan.

But this result seems paradoxical. For first, as Lerner points out, Samuelson's plan offers everybody more *goods*, when exactly the same amount is produced. Second, as Samuelson points out, everybody is better off under his plan, yet (assuming interpersonal comparability of utility), the total utility in every period is larger in Lerner's plan. But, as illustrated in figure 7.2, the contradiction is only apparent, because in the Lerner plan, with an exponential growth rate, the greater utility of the many young in any given period outweighs the lesser utility of the less numerous old in that period. Samuelson's plan offers everybody more lifetime consumption, because in each period, more is given to a less numerous group; and, since there is no end to time, there is never a moment of reckoning.

Although these remarks resolve all suspicion of mathematical contradiction, they do not, in Lerner's view, acquit Samuelson of a normative mistake. For Samuelson has, in Lerner's view, given the right answer to the wrong question. His biological interest rate avoids the fraudulence of a chain letter scheme only by its infinity. But economies do come to an end or lessen their growth rates, and consequently during some period the young will be cheated out of their "savings." They will "loan" half of their output to the old in expectation of a repayment of one unit of output next period from the workers of that period, but the repayment will never come. Samuelson's biological rate of interest is thus ethically unacceptable.

But might not one make a similar criticism of the Lerner plan? After all, in Lerner's scheme, each individual produces one unit of consumption good but consumes one and a third. If such an economy were to come to an end, the young, who gave one-third of their output to the old would not be "repaid" by one-third of the output of the next generation. But, Lerner argues that one must recognize that the young are not *saving*. They are not making loans to the old that the next generation repays. On the contrary, there has been a social decision to provide pensions, and the young are being taxed to do so:

Yet there is no larceny in the Lerner plan because no individual is *promised* a refund of his tax, let alone interest. The tax-and-pension is nothing but a device by which today's pensioners are maintained out of today's social product, which is, of course, produced by today's workers. (1959b, p. 524)

Notice how intermingled are issues of positive and normative in economics!

7.4.3   Later influence

So the discussion concluded in 1960. Although Samuelson's "Exact Consumption-Loan Model" is obviously an impressive theoretical performance, bubbling with brilliance, one might question whether anything of empirical significance was accomplished. Circumstances such as those stipulated in the model do not exist, and no argument was given to believe that Samuelson identified a causal factor that continues to affect interest rates in the presence of durable goods and net technological productivity. Can one "add-up" the "forces" of positive time-preference, productivity, and the desire to save for one's retirement into a better theory of interest? Indeed Samuelson himself seemed to lose interest in the empirical questions with which he began. Apart from its technical innovations, the main contribution of the paper seems to be the demonstration that competitive markets can fail to achieve optimal outcomes in infinite economies and that money resembles a social contract.

The model taught conceptual rather than empirical lessons. Although empirical questions about the determinants of the rate of interest and about the properties of various social security schemes may have driven the inquiry, it is hard to see how any were answered by it.

It is unclear what one learns from the model. The participants in the discussion achieved some recognition of the oddities of infinite horizons and of the possibility not only of suboptimal non-monetary market equilibria in the context of infinite horizons, but of the unattractiveness of Pareto-optimal competitive equilibria in finite-generation overlapping-generations models. The model provides a neat account of one function that fiat money can play in a world without durable goods, but it is hard to see how to apply the model to address empirical questions.

But the history of overlapping-generations models had in 1960 scarcely begun. In this later history, the interplay between positive and normative is less striking and more variegated, and, in the remainder of this case study, I am mainly concerned to illustrate how Samuelson's analytical construction came to have a life of its own and how strongly theoretical development in economics is dictated by the commitment to equilibrium theory. Note that this is not a history involving theory choice or replacement in the sense (whatever it may be) in which economists faced a choice between classical and neoclassical theory or between cardinal and ordinal utility theory. It is a history instead of differing developments of a particular analytical device, both to incorporate further complexities into the model and to employ variants of the model to address very different questions.[7]

In 1965 Peter Diamond succeeded in incorporating durable goods and production possibilities into a two-generation overlapping-generations model. He explored whether a competitive market solution is necessarily efficient in such a context (it isn't) and considered the utility effects of government debt. A year later, Cass and Yaari explore other equilibrium rates of interest besides those discussed by Samuelson and argue that, if one incorporates durable goods into the model, then severe inefficiencies[8] can be expected, which cannot be alleviated by any privately run

---

[7] As Malinvaud (1987) points out, the history ought to begin with Allais' *Economie et Intérêt* (1947), which introduces essentially the same analytical construction. Allais' presentation was not nearly so influential as Samuelson's, and the affinities between Samuelson's model and Allais was not noticed for decades, even by those who had worked through the details of Allais' complex model.

[8] The inefficiencies that Cass and Yaari are concerned with are not mere failures of Pareto optimality but cases where not all of the consumption goods produced are consumed. For criticism of the way Cass and Yaari present the issues see Asimakopulos 1967. Cass and Yaari show that the sort of inefficiencies they are concerned with can arise in finite as well as infinite models.

financial intermediary. These models are as abstract and unrealistic as Samuelson's, and inferences concerning real economic phenomena are still precarious.

Although the inquiries suggested by Samuelson's essay and its extension by Diamond and by Cass and Yaari continue (Shell 1971, Gale 1973, Cass, Okuno, and Zilcha 1980, Okuno and Zilcha 1983, Esteban 1986), Samuelson's device of overlapping generations has come to be employed in other ways that are important to the "new classical" or "rational expectations" school of macroeconomics (see Begg 1982, Carter and Maddock 1984, Hoover 1988, and Minford and Peel 1983 for overviews of this school). Samuelson's overlapping-generations model is particularly congenial to the new classical school, because it is already implicitly a rational expectations model. Decisions to borrow and lend depend on expectations about what future generations will do and about what they will expect about the still more distant future. Results are obtained by assuming that everybody expects what actually occurs. As Samuelson notes in reaction to Meckling, different sets of expectations can justify themselves (1960, p. 83). But the overlapping-generations models in contemporary macroeconomics owe little to Samuelson apart from the general overlapping-generations framework.

I shall comment briefly on only three of the many applications of overlapping-generations models in contemporary macroeconomics. The first is illustrated by Robert Barro's essay, "Are Government Bonds Net Wealth?" (1974). In this essay Barro utilizes an overlapping-generations model in an argument that government bonds do not represent any addition to private wealth because of the anticipated tax liabilities required to retire the debt.[9] Although Barro uses a two-generation overlapping-generations model and acknowledges Samuelson's essay, he is indebted to Samuelson's model only for the general idea of overlapping generations. In Barro's model there is no problem of retirement income, and both generations have a certain endowment or output. Indeed the older generation makes a bequest to the younger, which adjusts almost perfectly to the amount of government·debt. Barro is not concerned with what determines the rate of interest or with the functions of money. The model does not rely on an infinite horizon and is, despite its abstractions, more empirically persuasive than Samuelson's.

More interesting in the context of this book is Neil Wallace's use of an overlapping-generations model to explain how fiat money (money

___

[9] As Roger Miller pointed out to me, one might question whether it is sane, let alone "rational" to expect the federal debt to be retired. But Barro was writing several years before Reaganomics.

that is inconvertible and of no intrinsic use) can have value.[10] Wallace argues,

In order to pursue the notion that fiat money facilitates exchange, one must abandon the costless multilateral market clearing implicit in the Walrasian (or Arrow-Debreu) general equilibrium model. Since exchange works perfectly in that model, there can be no role for a device that is supposed to facilitate exchange. In order to get a theory of fiat money, one must generalize the Walrasian model by including in its some sort of *friction*, something that will inhibit the operation of markets. On that there is agreement.

But what sort of friction? On that there is no agreement, which is to say that there is no widely accepted theory of fiat money. I will try to alter this situation by arguing that the friction in Samuelson's 1958 consumption loan model, *overlapping generations* gives rise to the best available model of fiat money. (1980b, p. 50)

Although Samuelson's essay does contain a suggestion of how fiat money may have value, Wallace's question is not Samuelson's. Wallace like Barro gives members of both generations of his two-generation overlapping-generations models endowments of their own and is unconcerned with the problems of "hump" savings and with the hypothetical and normative issues that occupy Samuelson, Lerner, and Meckling. Wallace also offers what seems to me to be a premature empirical application of this abstract model to analyze the effect of credit controls (1980a).

Although Wallace's account of fiat money has received serious criticism (see especially Tobin 1980, Hahn 1980, 1982, and McCallum 1983), it has been influential (see, for example, Sargent 1987). Indeed Cass and Shell argue that regardless of whether one endorses Wallace's particular model, dynamic and disaggregative theorizing is unavoidable in theories of money, government debt, or intertemporal allocation. And, Cass and Shell argue, the only manageable framework for such theorizing is the overlapping-generations model (1980, p. 260). Although McCallum is critical of Wallace's specific theory (since it finds no place for the function of money as a medium of exchange), he too is a defender of the use of overlapping-generations models in monetary theory.

But, as McCallum correctly points out, there is no necessary connection between the use of overlapping-generations models and new classical economics. There is some affinity, since overlapping-generations models typically include rational expectations and since the infinity of such models permits theorists to offer a theory in which fiat money can have value without imputing mistakes to individuals or making money an

---

[10] 1980b. For a somewhat more accessible exposition, see McCallum 1983.

argument in the utility functions. But despite these affinities, there is no necessary connection.

And indeed Geanakoplos and Polemarchakis (1986) deploy overlapping generations models to vindicate the consistency of Keynes' view that "animal spirits," that is, expectations of future economic performance can have a dramatic effect on current economic activity. For the same infinity that Wallace relies on to find a value for fiat money, also introduces indeterminacies. Current prices can depend on prices expected next period which in turn depend on expectations then about the prices for the period after, and so on forever. In one of Geanakoplos and Polemarchakis's models there is a two-dimensional continuum of possible equilibrium paths depending on initial nominal wages and price expectations.

The appeal of the overlapping-generations framework is that it provides a relatively tractable way to address the effects of the future on the present. It enables one to study an economy that is in competitive equilibrium with heterogeneous individuals who are changing over time. Yet the heterogeneity results from the effects of aging on an underlying homogeneity of taste and ability. The temporal constraints on the relations among different agents introduces complexities and frictions in a non-arbitrary way. Yet it seems to me that caution is still advisable: the large body of economic modeling that employs Samuelson's construction continues to be nearly as remote from empirical applicability as Samuelson's original model was.

7.5 Concluding remarks: on the grip of neoclassical modeling

Samuelson's inquiry appears at first glance to rely very little on equilibrium theory. He does, to be sure, make use of consumer choice theory in discussing optimality properties of the biological interest rate and in deriving the market rate of interest in the numerical example he works through. But the derivation of the biological interest rate and the demonstration of its economic untenability require little theory. Yet an inquiry such as Samuelson's would be inconceivable without equilibrium theory in the background. For his task is precisely to discover how equilibrium theory may be extended to account for the hypothetical phenomena with which he is concerned and to investigate whether the usual normative implications continue to hold. He has no interest in bringing to bear potentially relevant sociological or psychological generalizations or in modifying or augmenting the "laws" of economics. Nor do theorists such as Barro, Wallace, or Geanakoplos and Polemarchakis (as different as they are in other regards) question equilibrium theory or attempt to introduce new behavioral generalizations about individuals. Their inquiries are driven by their commitment to equilibrium theory and to the puzzles that derive from that commitment.

From what does this commitment derive? In discussing Samuelson's "Exact Consumption-Loan Model," I have emphasized the centrality of equilibrium theory to the normative attitudes of economists. Although this factor is an important one, it is only one among many. Equilibrium theory is also captivating because it permits a separate science of economics – that is, because it holds out the possibility of a single unified theory providing (apart from possible further specifications of beliefs and preferences) the whole truth about a distinct "economic" sphere of social life. There is moreover a remarkable aesthetic appeal in the thought that order and prosperity could come virtually on their own from the selfish enterprises of individuals. Furthermore, commitment to this model tells economists what questions to ask and how to answer them. Such commitment permits elegant mathematical theory development and spares economists the confusions and hard work of other social theorists who have to seek sometimes almost blindly for significant causal factors.

Conceptual and mathematical exercises such as Samuelson's "Exact Consumption-Loan Model" would appear bizarre without an appreciation of economics as a separate science with equilibrium models at its core. This is, to be sure, only one sort of economics – indeed only one sort of orthodox neoclassical economics, which consists of a great variety of different kinds of work. But this case study has, I hope, done its job of illustrating how the global theory structure of neoclassical economics shapes particular theoretical endeavors.

Part II

Theory assessment

Part I distinguished models and theories and clarified the importance of model construction in theoretical economics. It thus helps defuse superficial criticisms of microeconomics and postpones questions of empirical assessment. But economics only provides knowledge of economies if it consists of valuable *theories* as well as of elegant *models*. In part II, I turn to the central problems of theory assessment, canvas the traditional solutions to them, and offer my own resolutions.

When one thinks of economic methodology, the first questions that come to mind are questions of appraisal. Is equilibrium theory a good theory? What sort of confidence should economists place in it? Do economists behave as good scientists should? Are standards for appraising social theories the same as those which apply to the theories of the natural sciences? When one focuses on economics, these questions seem particularly pressing, for economic theory strongly resembles theories in the natural sciences, except in predictive success. One of the most striking problems of theory appraisal in economics is that equilibrium theory is full of "laws" that are, if taken literally, false, and further false assertions are made when the theory is applied to specific problems. Do these facts show that there is something fundamentally wrong with economics?

I shall try to show that the answers to these questions lie in the peculiarities of the structure and strategy of economic theory discussed in part I and in the complexities of economic phenomena rather than in problems of confirmation theory. I shall argue that one can sensibly regard economists as employing an unremarkable, indeed platitudinous, theory of confirmation in their appraisals of economics. Although their appraisals seem too favorable, their overconfidence does not result from an erroneous view of theory assessment. It comes instead from methodological and substantive commitments to equilibrium theory as a "separate science" as discussed above in chapter 6.

8   Inexactness in economic theory

The standard view of theory appraisal is the so-called "hypothetico-deductive" or "HD" method, which is presented in the introductory chapters of countless economic textbooks (see A.10.1). Stripped to its bare bones, the HD method consists of four steps:

1 *Formulate* a hypothesis.
2 *Deduce* a prediction from the hypothesis and other statements.
3 *Test* the prediction.
4 *Evaluate* the hypothesis on the basis of the test results.

The inexactness of the basic "laws" of equilibrium theory and the many consequent failures of particular applications makes the fourth step difficult. Given how many interferences there may be, economists have little basis for increased confidence in an hypothesis when things are as predicted, and they have little basis for lessened confidence when things are not as predicted. How can economists learn from experience? Similar difficulties arise when one thinks of assessment in terms of Bayesian (A.10.2) or bootstrapping (A.10.3) approaches, but for now let us stick with the familiar HD method.

One solution is offered by the view of theory appraisal in economics that dominated methodological discussion until the 1940s and that still appears to dominate methodological practice. This view dates back at least to David Ricardo's time. It was first explicitly enunciated in the 1830s and 1840s by John Stuart Mill (1836, 1843) and Nassau Senior (1836).[1] I shall focus on Mill's more sophisticated discussions.

Mill's economics, which derived from Ricardo (1817), posed problems of assessment resembling those posed by modern economics. For its basic claims such as "Individuals seek more wealth," are not true universal generalizations, and its predictions were often incorrect. Mill was both a Ricardian economist and an empiricist, but his economics seems

---

[1] See Hollander 1985, pp. 142-9 for a discussion of the differences between Mill and Senior's methodological positions.

not to measure up to empiricist standards for knowledge.[2] The implications of Ricardian economics were not strenuously tested, and they appeared to be consistently disconfirmed (de Marchi 1970). For example, Ricardo's theory incorrectly predicted that the share of national income paid as rent would increase. How could Mill reconcile his confidence in economics and his empiricism?

In Mill's view (1836, 1843, book VI), the basic premises of economics are either introspectively established psychological claims, such as "People seek more wealth," or experimentally confirmed technical claims, such as the law of diminishing returns. Mill believes that these established premises state accurately how specific *causal factors* operate. They are statements of *tendencies* and are *inexact* rather than universal generalizations. In formulating them, vague *ceteris paribus* qualifications will be unavoidable.[3] Economics explores the consequences of these established, but inexact, premises. Since so much is left out of economic theory, these consequences will not always obtain.

Mill regards economics as an inexact science. Economists know the major causes of economic phenomena, but there are many "interferences" or "disturbing causes." The confidence of economists in this science is based on confirmation of its basic "laws," not on confirmations of their economic implications. In Mill's terminology, the method of economics, the way it establishes its conclusions, is "deductive" or "*a priori*."

This view solves the problem of the inapplicability of the HD method by denying that the grounds for accepting or rejecting economic theories are the successes or failures of their economic predictions. Theorists rely instead on other empirical evidence, which requires further clarification.

Not only were Mill's views adopted by followers such as J. E. Cairnes (1875) and early neoclassical methodologists such as John Neville Keynes (1917; 1st. edn 1891), but, if one updates the language and the economic theory, one has the view to which most economists (regardless of what they may *say* in methodological discussion) still *apparently* subscribe.

In the so-called "neoclassical revolution" of the last quarter of the nineteenth century, both economic theory and its methodology changed. For neoclassical theory (particularly in its Austrian or Walrasian forms), focuses on individual decision-making and short-run micro effects, unlike classical economics which was more concerned with social classes and long-run issues of growth and distribution. Despite these differences, which were emphasized by authors such as Frank Knight (1935b, 1940),

---

[2] For some questions about whether Mill's views of economic methodology were truly empiricist, see Hollander 1985 and Hirsch forthcoming.
[3] Mill does not use this last terminology in his methodological discussions, but he does sometimes do so in his economics. See footnote 11 below.

Ludwig von Mises (1949, 1978, 1981), and Lionel Robbins (1935), neo-classical economists agreed with Mill that the basic premises of economics are well-justified, and that empirical failures do not cast them into doubt. In defending this view, Lionel Robbins explicitly notes this long tradition (1935, p. 121), and provides the following exaggerated but persuasive formulation of essentially Mill's view:

The propositions of economic theory, like all scientific theory, are obviously deductions from a series of postulates...The main postulate of the theory of value is the fact that individuals can arrange their preferences in an order, and in fact do so. The main postulate of the theory of production is the fact that there are [sic] more than one factor of production. The main postulate of the theory of dynamics is the fact that we are not certain regarding future scarcities. These are not postulates the existence of whose counterpart in reality admits of extensive dispute once their nature is fully realised. We do not need controlled experiments to establish their validity: they are so much the stuff of our everyday experience that they have only to be stated to be recognised as obvious (1935, pp. 78-9).

Although this traditional notion of a deductive or *a priori* method seems intuitively appealing, it is far from clear. What exactly is the "deductive method" or the "method *a priori*?" Why is it particularly apt for inexact sciences? What makes sciences "inexact?" What are the major sorts of inexactness in economics? Can inexact claims be true? How can one use evidence to support or dispute them? How does the method *a priori* relate to contemporary views of theory appraisal? Can one rationally defend microeconomics by employing this method? This is a formidable list of questions.

8.1   What is an inexact science?

In "On the Definition of Political Economy and the Method of Investigation Proper to It," (1836), Mill argues that political economy is a science of "tendencies," that its claims are "true in the abstract" and would be true in the concrete were it not for disturbing causes. What can he mean?

When Mill returns to these issues in his *A System of Logic* (1843), his language is a little different and a little clearer. He maintains that in an inexact science

the only laws as yet accurately ascertained are those of the causes which affect the phenomenon in all cases, and in considerable degree; while others which affect it in some cases only, or, if in all, only in a slight degree, have not been sufficiently ascertained and studied to enable us to lay down their laws, still less to deduce the completed law of the phenomenon, by compounding the effects of the greater with those of the minor causes. (1843, 6.3.1)

Mill cites the science of tides as an example. Scientists know the laws of the greater causes, the gravitational attraction of the sun and the moon, but they are ignorant of the laws of minor causes, such as the configuration of the shore and ocean bottom. One might suggest (as I believe) that there are no exact sciences, although in some cases for some purposes the inexactness of a science might be negligible. But Mill disagrees. He believes that astronomy is an exact science, "because its phenomena have been brought under laws comprehending the whole of the causes by which the phenomena are influenced...and assigning to each of those causes the share of the effect which really belongs to it." (1843, 6.3.1)

Mill relies heavily on an analogy between motives and forces, and, when he speaks of "compounding the effects" of causes, he has in mind the vector addition of forces in mechanics. One can capture what Mill means by "compounding effects" by thinking of the combination of laws within a theory (or of assumptions within a model) from which consequences may be deduced.

When Mill talks about an "inexact science," he is not concerned merely with inaccuracy in the *predictions* of a science. Even if knowledge of relevant causal factors were complete, one might still be unable to make accurate predictions because of difficulties in learning the initial conditions or because of computational limitations. Mill is concerned with inexactness *within theories* – within the set of lawlike statements that constitutes a theory (see 5.3 above).

Moreover, Mill is not mainly concerned with rough empirical generalizations such as "Birds fly" or "Trees shed their leaves in winter," that express patterns in the data and for which one seeks explanations.[4] In Mill's view the *"empirical laws"* of the social sciences are typically just rough generalizations (compare Rescher 1970, pp. 164–7):

All propositions which can be framed respecting the actions of human beings *as ordinarily classified, or as classified according to any kind of outward indications,* are merely approximate. We can only say, Most persons of a particular age, profession, country, or rank in society have such and such qualities...[my emphasis] (1843, 3.23.3)

---

[4] A good example of such an empirical generalization in economics is the claim that the share of national income paid as wages is roughly constant over time. Although there has been considerable dispute about whether this constancy was real, nobody regards the generalization as explaining anything. It is rather a (disputed) fact in need of explanation.

Rough generalizations are false and lack explanatory power.[5]

Although rough generalizations are in a sense the raw material for theorizing, they do not play a role in theories themselves. In Mill's view, the explanatory or causal laws of inexact sciences are not rough generalizations. Causal laws are not mere correlations among features of human action as these are ordinarily classified. Tendencies are the causal powers underlying the genuine regularities that inexact laws express (see Cartwright 1989, chapters 4 and 5). Thus Mill writes:

there is no reason that it [the science of human nature] should not be as much a science as Tidology is...

But in order to give a genuinely scientific character to the study, it is indispensable that these approximate generalisations, which in themselves would amount only to the lowest kind of empirical laws, should be connected deductively with the other laws of nature from which they result. ...In other words, the science of Human Nature may be said to exist in proportion as the approximate truths which compose a practical knowledge of mankind can be exhibited as corollaries from the universal laws of human nature of which they rest, whereby the proper limits of those approximate truths would be shown, and we should be enabled to deduce others for any new state of circumstances, in anticipation of specific experience. (1843, 6.3.2)

The "science of Human Nature" is an inexact science, insofar as its rough empirical laws can be connected deductively to genuine universal laws of human nature. The generalizations concerning market demand and supply discussed in chapters 2 and 3 are empirical laws, while the "laws" of equilibrium theory from which they can be derived might be regarded as "universal laws of human nature."

Since economists, in Mill's view, know only the laws of the "greater causes" of the phenomena, they are unable to infer invariably and

---

[5] One might wonder whether microeconomic theory might enable economists to explain phenomena, such as the empirical "laws" of market supply and demand, despite the absence of (true) laws. Most philosophical models of explanation rule out this possibility, but these models may be mistaken. Any account of how false statements can be explanatory must distinguish those false statements that are (in certain contexts) explanatory from those which are not. To defend the view that microeconomics contains explanatory rough generalizations, one would presumably need to stress that the generalizations of microeconomics appear to be lawlike and not *ad hoc*, that they are reliable in certain domains, that one can often explain why they break down, and so forth. By stressing and clarifying such virtues, one might be able to vindicate the claim that, although false, these claims are nevertheless explanatory. But the same virtues enable one to make a case that these generalizations are qualified laws. I think it makes more sense to proceed as I do in the text and to show how apparently false statements might still be regarded as laws. Since everything asserted by a proponent of a no-law view of explanation can also be said in terms of an analysis of inexact, but genuine laws, there seems to be no good reason to face the philosophical task of formulating an account of explanations involving false generalizations.

precisely what actually occurs. Economics is in this way an *inexact science*. This inability is a consequence of inexactness *within* the theory, not merely of faulty data or mathematical limitations. Economics employs *inexact laws* and thus *inexact theories*. Equilibrium theory certainly seems to be in some sense inexact. One might say that its "laws" possess *inexact truth*. They are not literally true, but there is a good deal of truth to them. But what exactly is inexactness? How should one analyze this inexactness and make precise the idea that economists possess true causal laws that capture only the behavior of the most important causes of economic phenomena?

There are at least four ways in which one might attempt to analyze inexactness or the notion of a "tendency." These are not mutually exclusive, and some may be combined with one another:

1 Inexact laws are approximate. They are true within some margin of error.
2 Inexact laws are probabilistic or statistical. Instead of stating how human beings always behave, economic laws state how they usually behave.
3 Inexact laws make counterfactual assertions about how things *would be* in the absence of interferences.
4 Inexact laws are qualified with vague *ceteris paribus* clauses.

Like J. N. Keynes (1917), I prefer the last interpretation, but the counterfactual view seems most faithful to Mill. The differences between the counterfactual and vague qualification interpretations are, however, slight.

8.1.1   Inexactness as approximation

Sometimes lawlike claims are made that are not true as stated, but which can be made true by specifying a margin of error in a certain domain. If the claims of special relativity theory are true, then the claims of Newtonian mechanics are in this sense approximately true in most macroscopic domains. Provided that one is dealing with bodies that move slowly compared to the speed of light, the predictions one makes using Newtonian theory are correct within a small margin of error. By limiting the scope of Newton's mechanics and slightly "smearing" what it says, one can regard it as literally true.

Mill, however, does not interpret the laws of inexact sciences as true within a margin of error, and very little of the inexactness of economic generalizations is a matter of approximation in this sense. The difficulties with the claim that firms are profit maximizers are not resolved by making the weaker claim that the actions of firms are always within some neighborhood surrounding the profit-maximizing action.

8.1.2 Inexactness as probabilistic

Why not interpret the "laws" of equilibrium theory as probabilistic claims? People's preferences are not always transitive, but the frequency of intransitive preferences in circumstances of economic choice is low. Satiation is not impossible, only unusual.

There is little support in Mill's writing for this construal, and economists have seldom explicitly defended it. Why? The main alternative interpretations of probabilistic claims are to regard them as assertions about frequencies or as expressions of degrees of belief. The latter is not appropriate as a reconstruction of what the basic "laws" of equilibrium theory *assert*. People may have various degrees of belief in these propositions, but the propositions themselves are not assertions concerning degrees of belief. On the other hand, in attempting a frequentist interpretation, it is not clear what elements of chance or randomness are involved or what reference sets one is referring to.[6] These claims are also not stated in an explicitly statistical or probabilistic form; they merely appear to have counterexamples. One may, if one wishes, regard their merely statistical validity as the validity of merely statistical generalizations. But without more probabilistic structure, this is only to admit that these generalizations are not universally true.

8.1.3 Inexactness as counterfactual

Like many others (Schumpeter 1954, pp. 1049–50n or Gibbard and Varian 1978, esp. pp. 673ff), Mill sometimes explains the inexactness of economic laws by arguing that these "laws" state how things *would be*, *were* certain conditions met. They do not describe actual regularities. When the hypothetical conditions implicit in the laws are not met, things may not be the way the laws say they would be. This counterfactual view of the inexact "laws" of economics is especially pronounced in Mill's "On the Definition of Political Economy...," but as de Marchi (1986) has persuasively argued, it is also his view in book VI of *A System of Logic.* Here is one of the clearest formulations:

The conclusions of Political Economy, consequently, like those of geometry, are only true, as the common phrase is, *in the abstract...*

[6] Recently many philosophers have defended a view of probability as a sort of *propensity* (for interpretations of probability, see Kyburg 1970, esp. pp. 46–50). Such an interpretation would assimilate the probabilistic view of tendencies to either the counterfactual or *ceteris paribus* views to be discussed in the next two subsections.

They would be true without qualification, only in a case which is purely imaginary. In proportion as the actual facts recede from the hypothesis, he [the economist] must allow a corresponding deviation from the strict letter of his conclusion; otherwise it will be true only of things such as he has arbitrarily supposed, not of such things as really exist. That which is true in the abstract, is always true in the concrete with proper *allowances*. (1836, pp. 326-37)

These claims are ambiguous, for Mill may be asserting only that economists generally propose only models, and are thus not making assertions about economies at all. On this interpretation, these remarks would not address the question of what empirical content or worth inexact claims have. On the other hand, Mill may be suggesting that economic theories make modal or counterfactual assertions, that they are accounts of the relationships obtaining between possible entities in possible circumstances. (Such a view can naturally be connected to the semantic view of theories developed by Suppe and van Fraassen and discussed in section 5.2 above.) Economic theories themselves are not true (without "allowances") of anything real.

One must be careful to distinguish between "unrealistic" assumptions in models, which are used for conceptual exploration, and "unrealistic" assertions in theories, predictions, and explanations, which are used to say how things would be in certain possible states of affairs. Otherwise the ubiquity of model making in economics would demonstrate that economists are constantly making counterfactual claims. For example, one might be inclined to say, "What could Samuelson be talking about except a possible state of affairs in which no goods can be stored, yet individuals still wish to save for retirement?" But Samuelson may only be exploring the mathematical implications of a particular definition. He need not be interpreted as offering metaphysical assertions about possible economies. Insofar as the "laws" of equilibrium theory are taken to be merely the assumptions of the fundamental equilibrium model, the problem of inexactness – of understanding how apparently false *assertions* can nevertheless have explanatory and predictive worth – does not arise. The mere use of models does not imply that one is making modal claims.

Much of Mill's discussion is consistent with the view that the laws of inexact sciences are modal claims (see, for example, 1843, 6.9.2). R. P. Anschutz (1953, pp. 85-96, 118, 167) and Neil de Marchi (1986) believe that this modal interpretation of inexact laws is Mill's settled view. Indeed the following passage seems conclusively to show that Mill preferred a modal view over the implicit-qualification view to be discussed in the next subsection:

To accommodate the expression of the law to the real phenomena, we must say, not that the object moves, but that it *tends* to move, in the direction and with the velocity specified. We might, indeed, guard our expression in a different mode, by saying that the body moves in that manner unless prevented, or except in so far as prevented, by some counteracting cause, but the body does not only move in that manner unless counteracted; it *tends* to move in that manner even when counteracted; it still exerts in the original direction the same energy of movement as if its first impulse had been undisturbed, and produces, by that energy, an exactly equivalent quantity of effect. (1843, 3.10.5)

Although Mill finds this modal view consistent with his empiricism (see footnote 9), I have my doubts, for the confirmation of claims about possible worlds is puzzling. In any event, since the intuitions that support the modal view can for the most part be accommodated by the *ceteris paribus* qualification view, I shall focus my attention on it.

8.1.4   Some remarks on idealizations

The modal view of inexact laws and theories should be distinguished from the related claim that economics involves *ideal* entities, circumstances, or generalizations. Shapere (1969, esp. pp. 140–1) has argued that an entity or property is ideal if scientists find it useful to mention it in stating their theories, even though its existence is conclusively ruled out by well-established scientific theories. This is too limited. First, there is no reason to insist that well-established scientific theories do the ruling out. For example, the existence of markets now for titles to all commodities and services for the whole future of the universe is not ruled out by science, but it is ruled out by accepted knowledge with no less epistemic weight. Thus (*pace* Rosenberg 1976, p. 133), one cannot use Shapere's view to deny that economic theories contain idealizations.

Second, not every claim that is known to be false counts as an idealization, no matter how useful it might be in theory development. The claim that crocodiles have feathers is not an idealization. For idealizations also involve exaggerating some actual property toward some limit.[7] In the class of quantitative relations idealization can be a matter of taking some small quantity to be zero, some large quantity to be infinite, or some quantities that are almost equal to be exactly equal. These limiting exaggerations also have a *point*. They allow one in theorizing to escape from the "mess" of reality. Idealization permits interconnected phenomena to be treated as isolated, and it cuts off (in theory) the effects

---

[7] See Brzeziński *et al.* 1990, Cartwright 1989, chapter 5, Krajewski 1977, Kuipers 1987, Mäki forthcoming b, Nowak 1972, 1980.

of subsidiary causes.[8] Idealizations can thus be successively relaxed and the complications from which idealizations permit one to abstract successively tackled. As Mill's remarks on geometry show, he believes that idealization has a legitimate role to play in science and that statements involving idealizations are confirmable and may be counterfactually true.[9]

An idealization is a literally false exaggeration that serves an abstractive or isolating theoretical purpose. Although this account of idealizations is consistent with both counterfactual and vague qualification construals of inexactness, it fits the counterfactual view most comfortably. A good idealization can be regarded as correctly stating how things would be were friction zero rather than small or were people perfectly rational rather than prone to err. The modal interpretation of purported (inexact) laws is one attempt to explain how statements that are thus literally false can nevertheless be regarded as laws. The modal view asserts, for example, that the derivation of the ideal gas laws shows how a collection of such non-existent point particles *would* behave. According to the modal view, the antecedent of the ideal gas law is satisfied by some possible gas, not by any real gas.

8.1.5 Inexactness as vague qualification

Much of what one would like to say in terms of a counterfactual construal of inexact laws can be restated in terms of a vague implicit qualification view and vice versa. Indeed, if one is willing to talk of possible worlds, the implicit qualification view entails the counterfactual view. If a generalization is true, with qualifications, in this world, it is true in that possible world in which those qualifications are always met. Indeed one

---

[8] In a fascinating unpublished paper, Uskali Mäki argues that idealizations are one method of achieving *isolation*, which is the more fundamental notion. What is crucial about modeling, in Mäki's view, is that models achieve a form of conceptual isolation by means of idealizations and "omissions." Isolations for the purpose of focusing on the essential features of a phenomenon carry, Mäki suggests, an implicit commitment to a strong form of realism.

[9] Mill 1843, 2.5.2 and 2.5.4. Consider the following remarks, "Those who employ this argument to show that geometrical axioms cannot be proved by induction, show themselves unfamiliar with a common and perfectly valid mode of inductive proof – proof by approximation. Though experience furnishes us with no lines so unimpeachably straight that two of them are incapable of enclosing the smallest space, it presents us with gradations of lines possessing less and less either of breadth or of flexure, of which series the straight line of the definition is the ideal limit. And observation shows that just as much, and as nearly, as the straight lines of experience approximate to having no breadth or flexure, so much and so nearly does the space-enclosing power of any two of them approach to zero. The inference that if they had no breadth or flexure at all, they would enclose no space at all, is a correct inductive inference from these facts..." (1843, 2.5.4, p. 153n). Jukka-Pekka Piimies called my attention to this passage and provided invaluable help with the argument in this section.

might question whether the two views are really alternatives, for it may be that one should analyze *ceteris paribus* clauses in terms of counterfactuals (or *vice versa*). Although these philosophical problems cannot ultimately be avoided, they can, I think, be avoided in this discussion.[10]

According to the vague qualification view, one should regard the "laws" of inexact sciences as carrying with them implicit *ceteris paribus* clauses. This interpretation is consistent with Mill's empiricism and much of what he writes about inexact sciences.[11] To assert that people's preferences are transitive or that the marginal utility of commodities is a diminishing function of the quantity possessed is to make a qualified claim. A change in tastes, for example, falsifies neither, since changes in tastes are ruled out by implicit *ceteris paribus* clauses. When Mill speaks of the "psychological law" "that a greater gain is preferred to a smaller," he is not claiming that people always prefer greater gains, but that this is a major motivational "force." One should regard economists as telling us how real agents behave in the absence of various complications. The models that economists construct are intended to analyze the predominant factors that operate (although modified and sometimes counteracted by disturbing causes) in real economic behavior. (Much more will be said about *ceteris paribus* clauses below.)

The *ceteris paribus* clauses that render laws inexact are imprecise and ineliminable and thus problematic. Is it sensible to regard statements so vaguely qualified as laws (see 9.1 and Hutchison 1938, pp. 40f)? Not all appeals to *ceteris paribus* qualifications to explain away apparent disconfirmations are legitimate: it is certainly not the case that, *ceteris paribus*, we are all immortal or that dogs have six legs. One who regards the laws of inexact sciences as vaguely qualified claims must distinguish legitimate from illegitimate uses of ineliminable *ceteris paribus* clauses. What do sentences with *ceteris paribus* clauses mean, and when, if ever, can they be true? When is one justified in regarding them as laws?

8.2   The meaning or truth conditions of qualified laws

Economic laws are qualified with *ceteris paribus* clauses in two different ways. In partial equilibrium theories and practical work, it is common practice to consider separately the effects of different causal factors. As

---

[10] I do not know whether one can provide an intelligible and plausible philosophical construal of science without bringing in counterfactuals somewhere, as in fact I implicitly do in the discussion of the pragmatics and semantics of *ceteris paribus* clauses.

[11] See also John Neville Keynes 1917, pp. 217–21. In at least one passage Mill explicitly treats an economic generalization as carrying a *ceteris paribus* qualification, "The cost of production of the fruits of the earth increases, *caeteris paribus*, with every increase of the demand." (1871, book IV, chapter 2, section 2, p. 702)

discussed in section 2.1, for example, demand for widgets depends on the price of widgets, other prices, income, and tastes. Yet one may want to consider demand for widgets as a function (*ceteris paribus*) of the price of widgets only. Here the constituents of the *ceteris paribus* clause are precisely those factors that economic theory *itself* identifies as other causal determinants of demand for widgets. Such *ceteris paribus* qualifications are of philosophical interest in the analysis of the causal structure of partial equilibrium explanations, but the meaning and justification of "laws" with only such qualifications is relatively unproblematic. Provided that one takes for granted fundamental economic theory, the term "*ceteris paribus*" can be replaced with a list of specific causal factors, the effects of which are considered separately (Hausman 1989c, 1990b). Although the *ceteris paribus* clauses attached to derivative laws introduce no *additional* vagueness, they inherit the vague qualifications attached to the fundamental "laws" of equilibrium theory.

The *ceteris paribus* laws I am concerned with in this section and the next are more problematic. Fundamental economic theory considers only some of the causes of economic phenomena. The basic claims of economics are true only under various not fully specified conditions. Without specifying the disturbing causes, can one still make substantive claims concerning the "greater" economic causes. What precisely is a vague *ceteris paribus* clause? What does it mean to say that "*Ceteris paribus* people's preferences are transitive"? What must the world be like if such a claim is true?

The same sentence can be used to say different things in different contexts. Following Stalnaker (1972, pp. 380–97), let us distinguish the *meaning* of a sentence – the context-invariant interpretation of the sentence – from its *content* – the proposition expressed by the sentence – which may vary in different contexts. "I'm confused by this book" has a single *meaning*, but its *content* depends on who utters it and when it is uttered. Stalnaker suggests that one should regard the meaning of a sentence as a function from contexts to contents or propositions. The meaning of a sentence determines a content in a given context.

Adapting this terminology, I suggest that *ceteris paribus* clauses have one *meaning* – "other things being equal," which in different contexts picks out different *propositions* or *properties*.[12] The context – especially the economist's background understanding – determines what the "other things" are and what it is for them to be "equal." Although the phrase, "*ceteris paribus*," has an invariant meaning, its content, the *property* or

---

[12] Sometimes it is natural to take *ceteris paribus* clauses as functions from contexts to propositions, but when they are part of the antecedent of quantified generalizations, they are functions from contexts to open sentences or properties.

proposition it picks out, varies from context to context. So, for example, in the simpler case of the precise *ceteris paribus* clauses of partial equilibrium analyses, the term, "*ceteris paribus*" might pick out the proposition "Other prices, tastes and incomes do not change."

The phrase "*ceteris paribus*" need not determine a property or proposition in every context. Sometimes in uttering a sentence containing such a clause, one fails to express any proposition. Does the sentence, "*Ceteris paribus* all dogs have six legs," have any definite content? Does it express any proposition at all? Moreover, the properties *ceteris paribus* clauses pick out in different uses may vary greatly in clarity and precision. At one extreme are examples such as those in supply and demand explanations or in some laws of physics such as Coulomb's law.[13] For example, the "holding other inputs constant" clause in the law of diminishing returns is a sort of *ceteris paribus* clause and does not have a precise extension, but it is not completely vague, either. Although there are formal difficulties with vague predicates, such predicates abound in science and ordinary language, and we cannot do without them.

What proposition does a vaguely qualified law, such as "*Ceteris paribus* people's preferences are transitive*" express? Suppose that the logical form of such a law is "*Ceteris paribus* everything that is an F is a G*" where "F" and "G" are predicates with definite extensions.[14] Consider first the unqualified generalization, "Everything that is an F is a G." Logicians interpret sentences with this form to mean that there is nothing in the extension of the predicate F that is not in the extension of the predicate G. (Recall that the extension of a predicate is the set of all things of which the predicate is true.)

In the case of qualified generalizations such as "*Ceteris paribus* everything that is an F is a G," some things that belong to the extension of F do not belong to the extension of G – otherwise the qualification

---

[13] Coulomb's Law says that in the absence of other *forces*, or other forces being equal, any two bodies with like charges q_1 and q_2 separated by distance r will repel one another with a force proportional to $q_1 \cdot q_2 / r^2$. The phrases, "in the absence of other forces" or "other forces being equal" are *ceteris paribus* clauses, although they have a more precise *meaning* (and less variable *content*) than do the words "*ceteris paribus*" in an assertion such as "Heavy bodies will, *ceteris paribus*, fall when dropped" (Mill's own example – 1836, p. 338).

[14] It has been argued that the form of the "neoclassical maximization" hypothesis is more complicated, "There is something that everyone maximizes." See Boland 1981, Caldwell 1983 and Mongin 1986a. The account offered in this section can be extended to laws with a logical form involving "mixed quantification" such as this. If, for example, the unqualified form of the maximization hypothesis is $(x)(Ax \rightarrow (\exists y)Mxy)$, then the qualified form might be $(x)(Cx \rightarrow (Ax \rightarrow (\exists y)Mxy))$, where "$Ax$" is "$x$ is an agent," "Mxy" is x maximizes y, "$\exists$" is the existential quantifier ("there is"), and "C" is the predicate picked out by the *ceteris paribus* clause in the context.

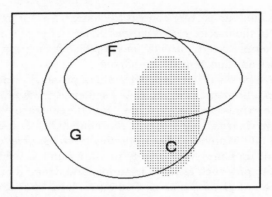

Figure 8.1. Inexact generalization

would be unnecessary.[15] In my view "*Ceteris paribus* everything that is an F is a G" is a true universal statement if and only if in the given context the *ceteris paribus* clause picks out a property – call it "C" – and everything that is both C and F is G. If one considers only the interior of region C in figure 8.1, one sees that all of region F contained there (that is, the intersection of regions F and C) lies within region G. In offering a qualified generalization, one is only asserting that, once the qualifications are met, all of region F lies within region G. The predicate C belongs in the antecedent of the law, although it may be awkward to state the law in this form. I have drawn C with an array of dots only to suggest that one does not *know* precisely what the extension of the *ceteris paribus* predicate is and not to suggest that it does not have a definite extension – which it must have if the qualified claim is truly to be a law. In committing oneself to a law qualified with a *ceteris paribus* clause, one envisions that the imprecision in the extension of the predicate one is picking out will diminish without limit as one's scientific knowledge increases.

Thus to believe that, *ceteris paribus*, everybody's preferences are transitive is to believe that anything that satisfies the *ceteris paribus* condition and is a human being has transitive preferences. One need not be disturbed by intransitive preferences caused by, for example, changes in tastes, because such counterexamples to the unqualified generalization lie outside region C. In my analysis, sentences qualified with *ceteris*

---

[15] It might be the case, although I can think of no example, that the unqualified generalization was *accidentally* true, but only the qualified generalization was a true law.

paribus clauses may be laws. A sentence with the form, "*Ceteris paribus* everything that is an F is a G' is a law just in case the *ceteris paribus* clause determines a property C in the given context, and it is a law that everything that is C and F is also G.

The phrase, *ceteris paribus*, may be used in other ways. In offering a rough generalization, such as "Birds fly," one need not believe that there is any set of conditions that, conjoined with being a bird, is sufficient for flying.[16] One might simply believe that there is a high frequency of flying among birds. Indeed, scientists may sometimes believe that the true law will not involve the current predicates "F" or "G" at all. One may regard a rough generalization, "F's are generally G's" as having some predictive force, even though one expects it to be superseded in the course of further inquiry. My analysis is not intended to deny these truths, nor am I taking any position concerning whether there are prob-abilistic or statistical laws. All I am claiming is that when one takes an inexact generalization to be an explanatory law, one supposes that the *ceteris paribus* clause picks out some predicate that, when added to the antecedent of the unqualified generalization, makes it an exact law.[17]

Suppose one has two qualified laws: (a) *Ceteris paribus* everything that is an F is a G and (b) *Ceteris paribus* everything that is an A is a B. From these two laws one can apparently deduce (c) *Ceteris paribus* everything that is an A and an F is a B and a G. But caution is required, for the properties picked out in the three occurrences of the phrase "*ceteris paribus*" will not generally be the same. The qualification in (c) will usually include *all* the qualifications in both (a) and (b). Matters are, however, still more complicated. Consequences such as (c) can only be drawn reliably when one has what Mill calls "mechanical phenomena" (1843, 3.6.1 and 3.6.2). In mechanical phenomena the effect of two causal factors acting simultaneously is the same as the total effect of each acting separately. Each factor continues to "operate" no matter what other causes are operating (3.10.5, Cartwright 1983, pp. 44–73). When one has such "mechanical phenomena" the causal factor captured in the qualified law is responsible for a "tendency" in the phenomena that is present whenever the causal factor is.

When one is not dealing with causal factors that are in this way independent or when one simply does not know how various causal factors will interact, one may still use laws qualified with *ceteris paribus* clauses. Qualified laws dealing with non-mechanical phenomena will,

---

[16] I owe some of the examples to Sidney Morgenbesser, who helped me a great deal with these issues.

[17] The discussion of this point in my 1981a, p. 127 is mistaken.

however, be more provisional and will have a more restricted scope. They may apply only when there are no appreciable interfering factors (Elster 1989a, p. 216). Even if the basic generalizations of equilibrium theory are qualified laws, they will not help one to understand real economies with their inevitable disturbing causes, unless economic phenomena are mechanical phenomena. Mill simply asserts that economic phenomena are mechanical, that the basic economic causal factors continue to act as component forces in the total complicated effect (1843, 6.7.1). Such a supposition is implicit in most applications of economic models. Its only justification is success. For an illustration of how Mill treats economic phenomena as mechanical, see his discussion of the combined effects on rents, profits, and wages of an increase in capital and labor and of technological change (1871, book IV, chapter III).

Is my suggestion that one should regard inexact laws as qualified with vague *ceteris paribus* clauses sensible? Since scientists do not know exactly what property a *ceteris paribus* clause picks out, why regard it as picking out any property at all? Why regard generalizations such as the basic "laws" of equilibrium theory as true or false? One can recognize that they may guide research and help economists to interpret data without regarding them as lawlike assertions or assessing their truth. If a theorist believes that *in a certain domain* the interferences inadequately denoted by the implicit *ceteris paribus* clause are absent, he or she can regard the generalization *in that domain* as a restricted law.[18] But the theorist need not regard the unrestricted generalization as true or false. The unrestricted generalizations may be taken merely as assumptions in models and only restricted generalizations asserted. To regard inexact general "laws" as thus *schematic* is tempting. It highlights the elusiveness of *ceteris paribus* clauses, which I have perhaps understated, and it emphasizes that scientists regard inexact "laws" differently when they use them to give explanations than when they rely on them in doing speculative research.

These qualms about regarding inexact generalizations as qualified laws do not challenge the position I have defended. There is nothing in my account that demands that one judge all sentences that contain *ceteris paribus* clauses to be true or false. It may be that the justification conditions (to be discussed in the next section) are satisfied in certain domains, while in others they are not. For example, if forced to judge the truth of the general lawlike statement that, *ceteris paribus*, *all* agents prefer more commodities to fewer, one might have to decide that it is false. But in domains such as those consisting of market behavior, one

---

[18] See Morgenbesser 1956, chapters 1, 2 on "virtual laws" and Levi and Morgenbesser 1964.

might be justified in regarding restricted versions of this claim as laws. It might be best to regard the unrestricted "law" as merely a general assumption in an implicit model (of "economic man"?) and not as an assertion to be judged true or false.

Theorists use basic economic "laws" to try to explain economic phenomena. They cannot regard them as mere assumptions, but must take them as expressing some truth, however rough (see A.3). Otherwise their attempts to use them to explain economic phenomena would be incomprehensible. So at some point, with respect to some domains, economists must construe the assumptions of the basic equilibrium models as qualified lawlike assertions.

Countenancing qualified laws forthrightly, one need not make invidious comparisons between the natural sciences and social sciences. One finds instead gradations of inexactness. Scientists strive for exactness, but possessing, as they typically do (whether in economics or physics), only qualified generalizations, they nevertheless have learned something about their particular subject matter and can explain some of the phenomena in the domain.

8.3   The justification of inexact laws

It is not enough to explain how qualified generalizations can be laws. One also needs to consider when, if ever, *one has reason to believe* that a qualified generalization is indeed a law. Standard theories of confirmation are of little help, since scientists do not know precisely what the extension of the *ceteris paribus* predicate is – that is, what the size and location of region C in figure 8.1 is. When is one justified in regarding a statement with a vague *ceteris paribus* clause as a law?

When one is able to do controlled experiments, these difficulties may not be pressing, although they do not disappear altogether. For, even without knowing what the disturbances are, one may be able to arrange two circumstances so that one can be fairly confident that little differs between them except whether F obtains. If G then obtains just in case F does, we have evidence for a lawful connection between them. But there are, of course, anomalies even in controlled experiments, and the failures of the "law" in less controlled circumstances would still demand explanation. So the possibility of carrying out controlled experiments (which is severely circumscribed in economics) is only a partial cure for the problems of justification.

I suggest that one is justified in regarding a counterfactual claim with a vague antecedent or a statement with a vague *ceteris paribus* clause as a law only when four necessary conditions (lawlikeness, reliability, refinability, and excusability) are met:[19]

First, the statement must be *lawlike*. It must be the sort of statement which would be a law if it were true. It does not make much a sense to say of a particular piece of fruit that, *ceteris paribus*, it is a pear. *Ceteris paribus* clauses attach to purported laws. As explained in A.4, the notion of lawlikeness is philosophically perplexing, but the philosophical problems are oddly untroubling in practice. Scientists and lay people are usually able uncontroversially to distinguish lawlike from non-lawlike claims.

Second, the *ceteris paribus* law must be *reliable*. In some class of cases, after ignoring the *ceteris paribus* clause or allowing for *specific* interferences, the scientist should rarely need to explain away apparent disconfirmations. Reliability is a statistical requirement. A generalization such as "*ceteris paribus* all F's are G's" is reliable only if (perhaps after making allowances for specific interferences) almost all F's are G's.[20] The evidence for reliability will typically be sample frequencies.

The reliability condition is either empty or unsatisfiable unless one places constraints on the class of cases in which the generalization is supposed to be reliable. "All roses are yellow" is highly reliable if tested in the class of yellow roses or in the class of roses my mother likes best. "Bodies fall when dropped" is highly unreliable if tested in the class of cases in which its *ceteris paribus* condition is not satisfied. The class of cases in which the generalization should be reliable is the domain of application for the generalization, and it should be sampled in some unbiased way. I do not know whether there is a great deal to be said in an abstract way about what are appropriate specifications of domains of scientific investigation.

Third, one does not have good reason to regard a qualified claim as a law unless it is *refinable*. If scientists add specific qualifications, the generalization (stripped of its *ceteris paribus* clause) should become more reliable or reliable in a larger domain. Theorists may not be interested

---

[19] As Harold Kincaid points out (1989), domain-specific knowledge may lead one to believe that the *ceteris paribus* conditions are met, in which case, one is able to test the unqualified generalization. He also notes that investigations of the robustness of a claim, of how little dependent it is on precise initial conditions, may undercut excuses for predictive failure that rest on supposed failure of the *ceteris paribus* condition or make us confident that an inexact generalization is a law. The four necessary conditions I mention are designed to complement various other requirements on confirmation.

[20] When Mill speaks of economics as capturing the "greater causes" of its phenomena, he seems to have in mind the case in which one can simply ignore the interferences and still have a reliable generalization. Given my notion of reliability, in contrast, one could regard Galileo's law of falling bodies as reliable, even if one lived in a molasses world in which virtually nothing fell with a constant acceleration.

in actually refining the generalization. The uncomplicated original claim may be more convenient. Refinability only demands that scientists *can* make the generalization more reliable.[21] The refinability condition does *not* demand that theorists can *completely* replace the *ceteris paribus* qualification with specific provisos.

It might appear that refinability is a trivial condition. Suppose that in a particular experiment, E, the generalization, stripped of its *ceteris paribus* qualification, fails. Simply appending the specific proviso "except in experiment E" makes the generalization more reliable. To have some teeth, refinability must demand that the modifications or qualifications of the theory that make it more reliable not be *ad hoc* in this way. But stating this requirement merely restates the problem, for it is not easy to characterize in any general or abstract way which theory modifications are *ad hoc* (see pp. 195–6).

Finally, no one is justified in regarding a statement with a *ceteris paribus* clause as a law unless it is *excusable*. One should not invoke the *ceteris paribus* clause blindly. One should know which interferences are important and should usually be able to justify relying on the *ceteris paribus* clause as an excuse (see Rescher 1970, p. 172). The excusability condition differs from both the reliability and refinability conditions, because it does not demand good statistical results. Unlike the refinability condition it is also unconcerned with modifying generalizations. Instead, the excusability condition demands that, after scientists have done their tests and have identified those cases in which the generalization is not reliable, they be able to cite the interfering factors except possibly in a few anomalous cases. It should not seem a miracle that the generalization "works" sometimes and fails others.

Again there is a danger of trivialization. To cite an interference is not just to cite any arbitrary feature of a circumstance in which the generalization fails. It is to cite a "causal factor" and thus shows a commitment to a lawful connection between the factor cited and the failure of the generalization. To explain away anomalies in terms of interferences is to make a claim that can be tested in other circumstances in which these "interferences" are present.

In my view, one may regard a generalization as a law even though it would, but for its qualifications, face disconfirmation, only if it is lawlike, reliable, refinable, and excusable. These conditions need filling in, since I am offering no account of lawlikeness, of theory assessment in general, of how to specify domains of application, of how to distinguish *ad hoc*

---

[21] In the case of probabilistic laws, the refinability condition demands that with the addition of further provisos $\Pr(G/F)$ gets closer to r, the true probability, which will differ from one.

theory modifications, or of how to determine whether interferences cited are truly "disturbing causes." As pressing and difficult as these philosophical problems are, they are usually not serious difficulties for practicing scientists, or if they are, they are detailed difficulties that involve specific features of particular theories and tests. So the account offered here, despite such large loose ends, is not empty. This account should also be integrated into the general confirmation theories presented in A.10.

The lawlikeness, reliability, refinability and excusability conditions seem plausible. Not only are they a reasonable formulation of the implicit criteria by which scientists and laymen assess the legitimacy of invoking *ceteris paribus* clauses to explain away apparent disconfirmation, but they are also rationally defensible. Since one does not know precisely which predicate C the *ceteris paribus* clause picks out in a given context, the lawlike statement "Everything that is C and F is G" is unavoidably vague. One cannot directly look for phenomena that are C and F that one suspects may not be G as well. Unless there is a strong probabilistic connection between F and G (perhaps given some *specific* qualification), there seems to be little reason to believe that such a law exists. Furthermore, if there is such a law, then it must be the case that, with more explicit (and non-*ad hoc*) qualifications, the probabilistic connection between F and G must grow stronger.[22] Finally, if scientists could not generally explain away cases in which something is both an F and not a G in terms of specific disturbing causes, then what reason could they have to believe that everything that is C and F is also G? Unless these four conditions are met, one cannot reasonably regard vaguely qualified generalizations as laws.

8.4   The deductive method

Even inexact causal laws are going to be hard to come by when dealing with complicated phenomena, such as those encountered by the social scientist. But the method by which advanced sciences study complex phenomena, which Mill calls "the deductive method" or "the method *a priori*," offers a partial solution. Mill describes the deductive method and defends its necessity as follows:

When an effect depends on a concurrence of causes, these causes must be studied one at a time, and their laws separately investigated, if we wish, through the causes, to obtain the power of either predicting or controlling the effect; since

---

[22] Although, if the law is not deterministic, this probability will have a definite bound less than one.

the law of the effect is compounded of the laws of all the causes which determine it. (1843, 6.9.3)

If, for example, one wants to "obtain the power of predicting or controlling" an effect such as projectile motion through understanding its causes, one needs to investigate separately the separate causal factors (gravity, momentum, friction) and their laws. This notion of "compounding of the laws of all the causes" is crucial to Mill's methodological views and is a matter of *deducing* the consequences of the concurrence of a plurality of causes.

By a deductive method Mill does *not* mean the hypothetico-deductive method, which he calls "hypothetical method" and which he criticizes, when it fails to prove its conclusions inductively (1843, 3.14.4–5). In insisting on the need for a deductive method, Mill is also not primarily concerned with how laws and theories are *discovered*. In discussing Whewell's views, for example, Mill makes clear that his methods of induction serve to justify scientific claims, although they may also serve as methods of discovery (1843, 3.9.6). Mill is not maintaining that what distinguishes the deductive method is that one creates hypotheses rather than derives them from evidence. Quite the contrary, the deductive method is in part an account of how one can *derive* economic laws from inductive evidence of a different kind (see A.9).

Mill's deductive method consists of three stages (1843, 3.11). In the first, one establishes laws by *induction*. Whether induction functions here as a method of discovery does not matter. First, for example, scientists interested in tides induce the laws of mechanics and of gravitation, or borrow the results of the inductions of others. Good evidence for these laws comes from diverse sources, but little or none of it concerns complex phenomena such as tides.[23] Second, they deduce the laws of tides from these fundamental laws and specifications of the relevant circumstances. Third, scientists must verify the deductive results. But notice that they are not testing the basic laws, just their (inexact) lawlike consequences concerning the tides. Since in this case many causal factors are left out, one does not know without testing how accurate or reliable the theory of tides is. The more complex the phenomena, the less one can study it directly and the more one needs to develop one's science deductively on the basis of laws that are independently established. It is important to stress that for Mill induction and deduction are *not* contraries. What is opposed to deduction is experimentation (1843, 2.4.5). Deductive

---

[23] Mill argues that the verification of derived laws provides additional confirmation to the inductively established laws upon which they are based, but the possibility of disconfirmation is not even considered, and the evidential weight of such results is slight (1843, 3.11.3).

justification is ultimately inductive! The evidence that supports (inductively) the premises of a deductive argument is the (inductive) basis for one's belief in the argument's conclusions (1843, 2.3.3).

To make clearer the basic idea, let me give two further illustrations. Suppose *W* is sick, and we would like to know whether penicillin will help cure *W* (compare this to Mill's own example, 1843, 3.10.6). The empirical *a posteriori* method, or, as Mill calls it, the method of specific experience, would have us inquire whether others with symptoms resembling *W*'s recovered more often or more rapidly when given penicillin. The method *a priori* in contrast would have us draw upon our knowledge of the causes of *W*'s symptoms and upon our knowledge of the operation of penicillin to decide whether penicillin will help cure *W*. Both methods are "empirical" and involve testing. The difference is that the former attempts to use experiment or observation to learn about the complex phenomenon directly, while the latter employs observation or experiment to study the relevant component causal factors. Similarly, one could determine empirically the range of an artillery piece directed at different angles with different charges, wind conditions, and atmospheric pressure. Or one could make use of the law of inertia, Galileo's law of falling bodies, and experimentally determined laws of air resistance and explosive force to calculate the range. The latter deductive method is, in Mill's view, the method of all advanced sciences. But deductive conclusions should be checked by the method of specific experience, whose results can also be useful in themselves.

Presented in conjunction with examples like those in the previous paragraph, the deductive method seems unobjectionable. The evidence concerning the correctness of Galileo's law or the law of inertia that can be garnered from controlled experiments is of higher quality than that provided by observations of the range of artillery pieces, so the application of these laws to complex phenomena test these laws only slightly. The laws do not say what will inevitably happen, but only what *would* happen in the absence of other causal factors or what will happen *ceteris paribus*.

But the application of the deductive method to economics is problematic, because, especially in contrast to the example of determining the range of the artillery piece, causal factors that are known to be significant are left out of the story. The inexactness is no longer negligible. Indeed Mill criticizes members of the "school of Bentham" (especially, by implication, his father, James Mill) for analogous "geometrical" theorizing about government. James Mill argued for representative government on the ground that individuals pursue their own interests and rulers in non-representative governments will not have the same interests as those of the governed (1820). This account is, in the view of the younger Mill, not only empirically inadequate, but methodologically flawed, for it focuses on only one admittedly important causal factor and ignores many others. J.S. Mill writes:

They would have applied, and did apply, their principles with innumerable allowances. But it is not allowances that are wanted....It is unphilosophical to construct a science out of a few of the agencies by which the phenomena are determined, and leave the rest to the routine of practice or the sagacity of conjecture. We either ought not to pretend to scientific forms, or we ought to study all the determining agencies equally, and endeavour, so far as it can be done, to include all of them within the pale of the science; else we shall infallibly bestow a disproportionate attention upon those which our theory takes into account, while we misestimate the rest, and probably underrate their importance. That the deductions should be from the whole and not from a part only of the laws of nature that are concerned, would be desirable even if those omitted were so insignificant in comparison with the others, that they might, for most purposes and on most occasions, be left out of the account. (1843, 6.8.3)

But when it comes to economics, Mill apparently recommends just the methodological practice that he condemns in the remarks just quoted. For the correct method of including all of the "determining agencies" "within the pale of the science" is not feasible. Economists must set their sights lower and aim only at a *hypothetical* science of *tendencies* which is, in Mill's view, generally "insufficient for prediction" yet "most valuable for guidance." (6.9.2) Since in political economy "the immediately determining causes are principally those which act through the desire of wealth..."(1843, 6.9.3), one can separate the subject matter of political economy from other social phenomena and theorize about political economy as if the desire for wealth were virtually the only relevant causal factor.

Mill defends this sort of partial deductive method, that so closely resembles the geometrical method of his father he criticized just a few pages earlier, as follows:

The motive which suggests the separation of this portion of the social phenomena from the rest, and the creation of a distinct branch of science relating to them, is, that they do *mainly* depend, at least in the first resort, on one class of circumstances only; and that even when other circumstances interfere, the ascertainment of the effect due to the one class of circumstances alone is a sufficiently intricate and difficult business to make it expedient to perform it once for all, and then allow for the effect of the modifying circumstances; especially as certain fixed combinations of the former are apt to recur often, in conjunction with ever-varying circumstances of the latter class. (1843, 6.9.3)

The defenses Mill offers for employing this partial or inexact deductive method thus seem to be (1) practical – that there is no alternative, (2) metaphysical – that, although the results are only hypothetical, the same causal influences persist even when there are other disturbing causes, and (3) pragmatic – that this is an efficient way of theorizing and that more order can be found this way than in any other.[24]

In the case of economics, theorists first borrow basic "laws" from the natural sciences or psychology, which Mill regards as an introspective experimental science. One tests the fundamental laws upon which economics is constructed on *other* phenomena where there are fewer disturbing causes. Then theorists develop economics deductively. Verification is essential, but not in order to test the basic laws; they are already established and could hardly be cast in doubt by the empirical vicissitudes of a deduction from a partial set of causes. Mill is unclear about whether verification is necessary in order to regard the deductively derived laws as economic laws at all, or whether verification merely determines the economic applicability or usefulness of these laws.[25]

The deductive development of economics is not a matter of proving theorems with nothing but established laws and true descriptions of the relevant circumstances as premises. The premises of the deductions also include stipulations and auxiliary hypotheses that are often poorly established and not infrequently known to be false. Contrary to Samuelson's assumptions, some goods keep and some people support their old parents without any expectations of a *quid pro quo* from members of the next generation. Furthermore, the implicit *ceteris paribus* qualifications in the fundamental lawlike claims themselves complicate matters, for the theorems will carry complex qualifications compounded of the qualifications on all the laws.

The messiness of the "deduction" in the inexact deductive method as it is applied in economics is not necessarily a fatal handicap when one is attempting to discover or generate theories. One task of the weakest sort of logic of discovery is to lay bare the reasoning which makes

[24] Surely much the same argument could have been given by Mill's father in his own defense. There is an irony here in the fact that recent extensions of neoclassical economic models to political phenomena recapitulate (although more subtly) the account of political behavior presented by James Mill. See for example Buchanan 1975, 1979.

[25] Compare 1836, pp. 325–6 and 1843, 3.9.3 and 6.9.1 and see de Marchi (1986) and Hirsch (forthcoming). Indeed, Mill writes, "To verify the hypothesis itself *a posteriori*, that is, to examine whether the facts of any actual case are in accordance with it, is no part of the business of science at all, but of the *application* of science." (1836, p. 325) It is not clear from the text of Mill's writings whether Mill regarded the deductive method as a distinctive method of theory appraisal or whether he regarded it as the implementation of standard inductive methods when theorizing about complex phenomena. See chapter 12.

plausible first attempts at scientific theories, and deduction from some-what plausible premises does make what is deduced plausible (Nooteboom 1986). If an economic claim can be shown to follow from more fundamental generalizations and auxiliary hypotheses, which are reasonable approximations, one has reason to take that claim seriously. Principles such as Say's Law were embraced by economists on such grounds.

It might be argued that the partial deductive method can do no more than to help make economic hypotheses plausible. For, as Mill notes, the deduced implications must themselves be confirmed, and it might be contended that whether or not they are confirmed, the fact that they were deduced from inductively established laws (and various simplifications) seems irrelevant. Either way our confidence in the implications would depend on the extent to which they were confirmed. One might thus be inclined to conclude that the deductive method is only really valuable when it cannot be used.[26]

But this dismissal of the inexact deductive method would be unjustified. There are degrees of confirmation and degrees of belief. An economist's confidence in generalizations such as those concerning market demand and supply may be rationally increased by showing that they can be derived from the inexact fundamental laws of the theory of consumer choice and specifications of relevant circumstances. The general strategy of developing models that incorporate the laws of equilibrium theory provides the implications of those models with a certain credibility in advance of specific testing. Furthermore, when deciding whether to attribute anomalous data to some disturbing cause or to a fundamental inadequacy in the theory itself, the deductive method turns out to be crucial. I will return to this point at length below in chapter 12.

To sharpen the discussion, let us then formulate a schema expressing the broad outlines of the deductive, or *a priori* method, as it may have been conceived by Mill to apply to economics. Later, in chapter 12, qualifications will be needed, but at this point a bold formulation will provide a useful focus.

1 *Borrow* proven (*ceteris paribus*) laws concerning the operation of relevant causal factors.
2 *Deduce* from these laws and statements of initial conditions, sim-plifications, etc., predictions concerning relevant phenomena.
3 *Test* the predictions.

---

[26] I suggested this in a confused discussion of these points (1981b, p. 383). In that discussion I did not remember that one employs the deductive method to justify the implications of the inductively derived fundamental laws, not to justify those laws themselves.

4 If the predictions are correct, then regard the whole amalgam as confirmed. If the predictions are not correct, then *judge* (a) whether there is any mistake in the deduction, (b) what sort of interferences occurred, (c) how central the borrowed laws are (how major the causal factors they identify are, and whether the set of borrowed laws should be expanded or contracted).

This method should be called the **inexact** method *a priori*, because the true deductive method relies only on facts and causes, not on simplifications, and one is supposed to include *all* the causes. The inexact deductive method, to which economics is condemned, cheats and omits significant causal factors. I have left out of the summary formulation the "proving" of the laws concerning relevant causal factors, which Mill takes to be the first step of the deductive method, because I want to focus on the tasks of economists, who are concerned with applying psychological and technical laws, not with establishing them. Formulating the deductive method in this way also helps to make absolutely clear how this method differs from the hypothetico-deductive method. The differences are in step 1, where one begins with proven (but inexact) laws rather than mere hypotheses to be tested, and in step 4. Since the laws are already established, they are not open to question in the judgment step. Apart from discovering logical errors in the deduction, all that is open to assessment are the sufficiency and accuracy of the other premises and the extent of the "coverage" provided by the borrowed laws.

Knowing (as Mill maintains) that individuals seek wealth (and leisure and "the present enjoyment of costly indulgences") economists investigate deductively what follows from these tendencies in various situations given other plausible assumptions and simplifications. The deductive method is needed for all sciences in which there is a complexity of causal factors. In inexact sciences the implications of theory will only agree with the results of experiment approximately for the most part.

In disciplines such as economics the correspondence between the data and the implications of theory is rough, and complete failures are frequent. Since economic phenomena are the effects of numerous causes, many of which the theory does not encompass, one can expect nothing better. Yet, with only this sort of evidence, how could economists rationally commit themselves to these theories? What good reason do they have to accept them? Mill believes that one cannot answer these questions by attempting to apply the HD method directly and considering how well the claims of economic theory are confirmed by observations of economic phenomena. Only the deductive method renders commitment to the (inexact) truth of economic theory justifiable.

8.5 Qualms

Having thus offered (a) an interpretation of the inexactness of the "laws" of economics, whether they be fundamental or derived, (b) an account of how one may rationally become convinced that generalizations are inexact laws, despite apparently disconfirming evidence, and finally (c) a construal of how one can rationally have indirect inductive grounds for accepting claims about economies by showing them to be deductive implications of premises that include fundamental laws of equilibrium theory, all that remains – so it seems – is to consider how justified various portions of economics are. Do the fundamental "laws" satisfy the lawlikeness, reliability, refinability, and excusability conditions? Are they really well established? What is one to say about the credibility of the simplifications that are needed to deduce economic conclusions? To what extent are these conclusions indeed justified?

To offer a fully satisfactory answer to these questions is beyond my competence, for to do so would require detailed knowledge of the success of particular applications of equilibrium theory. In some contexts, it seems to me uncontroversial that the propositions of equilibrium theory employed do satisfy the above conditions, and that the simplifications used can be given an analogous defense.[27] In my *Capital, Profits, and Prices* (1981a), I raised serious questions about whether the laws of equilibrium theory satisfied the excusability condition (p. 134). Economists show little concern to explain empirical anomalies. The reasons lie, I think, in their commitment to equilibrium theory as a separate

---

[27] In my (1981a, p. 142), I suggested that it was legitimate to employ a simplification – a literally false non-nomological claim – in an explanation or prediction only if the following four conditions were satisfied:

1 *Confirmation condition.* One needs the simplification not only to derive the statement of what is to be explained or predicted, but to derive other testable consequences, most of which can be confirmed.

2 *No-accident condition.* One can understand why, even though one has no reason to believe the simplification is true, one can use it in explanations and predictions and meet the confirmation condition.

3 *Sensitivity condition.* If one replaces the simplification with a (true) specification or with another simplification which is more realistic or a better approximation, one is able to explain or predict more phenomena or to predict under a more refined description or within a smaller margin of error.

4 *Convergence condition.* In those circumstances in which the simplification is a better approximation, one is able to explain or predict the phenomena under a more refined description or within a smaller margin of error.

These justification conditions are, I suggest, implicit in the way scientists assess explanatory arguments. They are reasonable criteria for judging whether the falsity in simplifications is irrelevant to the conclusions one derives with their help. I do not develop these criteria with care in this manuscript, for, unlike in my 1981a, I am not concerned with the empirical appraisal of a specific theory.

science and in the pragmatic virtues of equilibrium theory discussed below in section 12.4.2. In my view, questions about whether it is reasonable to regard the postulates of equilibrium theory as inexact laws should be regarded as questions about the scope of these postulates and ultimately about the strategy of economic theorizing.

But there is no point in asking to what extent equilibrium theory satisfies the conditions that should be imposed on inexact sciences, if the use of inexact propositions and of the deductive method are scientifically illegitimate. And during the past half century both economists and philosophers have made just this charge. During this period, most of those concerned with economic methodology have found something fishy or even fraudulent in Mill's and Robbins' tolerant attitude toward inexact fundamental laws and their frequently disconfirmed consequences. For it seems that, in Mill's and Robbins' view, evidence can only confirm economic theory or show that there is some disturbing cause. There seems to be no real possibility of empirical criticism and, thus, no real empirical justification for the theory. In the judgment step, no judgment of the laws themselves is permitted.

Mill's inexact method *a priori* has been subject to (a) logical, (b) methodological, and (c) practical criticisms. The logical criticism (a) is directed to inexact laws themselves, and maintains that statements that are vaguely qualified with *ceteris paribus* clauses are scientifically illegitimate, because they are too vague, untestable, or not conclusively refutable by empirical testing. The account above of the truth and justification conditions for vaguely qualified statements provides part of the answer to this logical criticism, which will be completed when we consider in chapter 10 whether the logical requirement of falsifiability can justifiably be imposed on scientific claims.

The methodological criticism (b) maintains that the rules implicit in the deductive method are unacceptably dogmatic. In particular it may plausibly be alleged that one ought not to regard the basic laws as proven or to refuse ever to regard unfavorable test results as disconfirming them. This criticism will be considered in chapter 12, where I shall also discuss the practical criticism.

The practical criticism (c) alleges that, by regarding apparent disconfirmations as inevitably the result of some disturbing cause, the inexact method *a priori* winds up justifying theories that cannot be of any practical use. For policy purposes we need to know what *will* happen, not what *would* happen in the absence of disturbing causes.

These are serious criticisms, and indeed, since the early 1940s, the only defenses of the traditional view of justification in economics have been J. Watkins' (1953), J. Melitz's (1965), I.M.W. Stewart's (1979), mine, and those of the Austrian school (Dolan 1976). Beginning in the 1930s, there was a dramatic revolution in theorizing about economic methodology, which led to a repudiation of the inexact deductive method in precept, although apparently not in practice. From what is now the orthodox contemporary perspective, the view of theory assessment in economics that I have developed in this chapter appears reactionary and wrong-headed.

In the next three chapters I shall consider contemporary alternatives to the deductive method, their philosophical underpinnings, and the theoretical basis for the criticisms of the deductive method. I shall point out the inadequacies in these alternatives and in their philosophical roots before returning in chapter 12 to the specific criticisms of Mill's inexact method *a priori*. There I shall show how to resolve the conflict that has arisen between methodological practice (which still appears to adhere to the deductive method) and methodological precept (which is typically positivistic or Popperian in character) not by preaching better methodology to the practicing economist, but by preaching better preaching to the methodologist.

9   Methodological revolution

Although there had been challenges to the "abstract" deductive method in the nineteenth century by members of the so-called "historical school," who defended a view of economics as normative and historically bounded,[1] the first real change in accepted views of theory assessment in economics occurred in the 1930s. In this chapter I shall examine this revolution in the methodological self-conception of the economics profession. In chapters 10 and 11 I shall then explore criticisms and alternatives that derive from the work of Popper and Lakatos. Unlike the previous chapters, this chapter and the next two will be largely critical. They attempt to show what is wrong with the alternatives to the inexact deductive method. The objections to the method *a priori* are best answered by showing constructively in chapter 12 what role empirical criticism should have in economics.

I argue in this chapter and the next two that *both* the criticisms and defenses of economics in contemporary methodological writings are misconceived, because both depend on faulty views of the nature of science. These views are either reminiscent of the early logical positivists or of Karl Popper,[2] or they depend on the more sophisticated views of the later logical empiricists. In criticizing the philosophical presuppositions of recent controversies concerning economic theory, I shall also point out the striking methodological *schizophrenia* that is characteristic of contemporary economics, whereby methodological doctrine and practice regularly contradict one another. This schizophrenia is a symptom of the unsound philosophical premises underlying contemporary economic methodology, and it shows the importance of transcending the terms of current debate.

[1] Knies 1853, Roscher 1874, Schmoller 1888, 1898. See also Menger's critique (1883).
[2] It is hard to say how much direct intellectual influence there was. Those who made the most important "positivist" changes in economic theory, such as Hicks and Allen (1934), Robbins (1935, chapter 6), or Samuelson (1947) seem to have had little direct familiarity with contemporary philosophy. With few exceptions, of which Hutchison (1938) is the most striking, methodological works of the 1930s and 1940s made few explicit references to the work of the positivists or Popper.

9.1 Terence Hutchison and the initial challenge

The positivist challenge that caught the attention of the economics profession was Terence Hutchison's.[3] In *The Significance and Basic Postulates of Economic Theory*, Hutchison criticizes theoretical economics, which he regards as without empirical content, and he recommends that economists concentrate on the discovery of empirical laws that will permit "prognoses." Hutchison was influenced by the logical positivists and Popper, with whose work Hutchison was remarkably familiar.

Hutchison's principal criticism of theoretical economics, of, in his terminology, "propositions of pure theory," is that they do not have testable implications. Either one is served up disguised tautologies or the lawlike assertions are so hedged with *ceteris paribus* clauses that their unambiguous interpretation and testing is impossible.[4] It is hard to interpret this criticism, because it is unclear what is a "proposition of pure theory." Hutchison seems to regard the law of diminishing marginal utility as an empirical law (1938, p. 64), while the claim that firms are profit maximizers is supposed to be a proposition of pure theory.

Hutchison does not condemn all uses of *ceteris paribus* clauses. He claims:

We suggest that the *ceteris paribus* assumptions can only be safely and significantly used in conjunction with an empirical generalisation verified as true in a large percentage of cases but occasionally liable to exceptions of a clearly describable type. (1938, p. 46)

Hutchison is suggesting justification conditions on the legitimate use of *ceteris paribus* clauses that are similar to those developed in chapter 8 (and indeed my work was influenced by studying Hutchison's account). On the basis of these sketchy and, in my view, unreasonably stringent

---

[3] A little before Hutchison published his work, Leslie Fraser published his *Economic Thought and Language* (1937), which has positivist themes, but few explicit references to their work. Fraser's book is not often cited and seems not to have had much influence. Earlier in the 1930s, Felix Kaufmann, a philosopher conversant with the work of the positivists, published a small book in German on the philosophy of the social sciences with applications to economic methodology as well as some essays in English (1933, 1934, 1942). But Kaufmann's work also seems not to have been influential and (so typical of philosophers) he is already criticizing over-simplified positivist construals and making use of other traditions such as American pragmatism (1944). Hutchison mentioned to me that he believes that his book was particularly influential because of Frank Knight's lengthy and vehement denunciation of it (1940). See also Hutchison 1941 and Knight 1941.

[4] Klappholz and Agassi (1959, pp. 63–4; 1960) and Rosenberg (1976, p. 154) accuse Hutchison of regarding *ceteris paribus* claims as tautologies, for which there is some textual basis (1938, p. 42). This is, however, an ungenerous reading that Hutchison repudiates (1960, pp. 158–60). Vagueness and untestability are bad enough.

justification conditions, Hutchison turns immediately to criticism. For the economic generalizations to which *ceteris paribus* clauses are appended are not almost universally true. Exceptions are widespread. Economists are not just covering their ignorance of the causes of infrequent failures. Furthermore, economists have done little to classify the cases in which their generalizations fail. They cannot specify what interferences are ruled out by the *ceteris paribus* clauses. So the reliance on *ceteris paribus* clauses in economics is, in Hutchison's view, illegitimate.

Hutchison also criticizes what he calls the "hypothetical" or "isolating" method – the method of theorizing about simplified states of affairs with the hope of reaching an understanding of actual economies via "successive approximation" (1938, pp. 43, 119–20). He is thus forthrightly rejecting Mill's deductive method. Hutchison maintains that the "inexact" laws upon which economists rely are not laws at all. Without their qualifications, they are not true, and, with their qualifications, they are not testable or empirically significant.

Hutchison argues further that it is no defense to claim that economic laws are statements of "tendencies." In making this argument he focuses on the following quotation from Hayek,

There seems to be no possible doubt that the only justification for this [special concern with equilibrium analysis] is the existence of a tendency towards equilibrium. It is only with this assertion that economics ceases to be an exercise in pure logic and becomes an empirical science.[5]

Hutchison criticizes Hayek by distinguishing between two kinds of tendencies. In the first "the position *actually is* regularly arrived at..." while in the second there is no assumption that one even comes close to the position toward which there is a supposed tendency (1938, p. 106). Hutchison finds talk of tendencies in the second sense cheap. One might talk of human tendencies toward immortality that are, to our sorrow, always counterbalanced by other tendencies. Whether or not generalizations express tendencies, they are inadequate unless, at least for a specified set of conditions, they are nearly always true – in other words, unless Hutchison's stringent reliability condition is satisfied. Talk of tendencies does not resolve the problem of justifying purported laws that are apparently false.

Hutchison's basic criticism is that claims qualified with *ceteris paribus* clauses and theories relying on extreme simplifications are untestable and empirically empty. Hutchison extends this criticism in various ways:

---

[5] Hutchison 1938, p. 105. Hutchison does not give the source, but Bruce Caldwell identified it for me as from Hayek 1937.

by stressing how pervasive the inaccuracies of economic generalizations are and how economists have failed to specify sharply what classes of phenomena these generalizations are supposed to apply to, by pointing out that the method of isolating causal factors and successively approximating the complexities of reality never gets beyond its first step, and by arguing that claims about tendencies have little content unless the supposed tendency is not often counteracted. The basic criticism is that economics does not make testable empirical claims.

According to Hutchison, economic theorists need to free themselves from abstract, tautologous, contentless theorizing and concentrate on the inductive development of empirical laws that permit genuine prognoses (1938, p. 166). How this task is to be accomplished is not clear. Hutchison has no definite program for economics, apart from his call to face the facts of uncertainty, and his philosophical apparatus is unsophisticated. Yet he seems to be pointing out real problems in traditional economic theory. The simplifying assumption to which he most vehemently objects (1938, chapter 4), the attribution of perfect knowledge to economic agents, still bears a heavy burden in contemporary theory. Can economists justifiably claim to have evidence for purported laws that are not supposed to apply precisely to any real economy? Successive approximations that begin with models such as Samuelson's overlapping-generations model never get very "close" to economic reality. How can such work be of value? Might one not be better off eschewing such theorizing altogether?

Hutchison's attack was disquieting. Did microeconomic theory measure up to the standards for science defended by up-to-date philosophy of science? Those who first rose to answer Hutchison's challenge, such as Frank Knight (1940, 1941) may have aggravated rather than allayed this disquiet, for Knight explicitly repudiates the empiricist or positivist philosophy of science upon which Hutchison's challenge relied. Knight accuses the positivists of overlooking the complexity and uncertainty of testing in all sciences (1940, p. 153) and argues at length that positivist views of science are particularly inappropriate with respect to economics, which, like all sciences of human action, must concern itself with reasons, motives, values, and errors, not just causes and regularities. Less philosophically sophisticated economists than Knight might have wondered whether there was any way to respond to Hutchison without repudiating up-to-date philosophy of science. Indeed, in his review, Knight worries about the pernicious effect Hutchison's book may have on the young (1940, pp. 151, 152). Knight was right to worry, for, although few wound up fully accepting Hutchison's criticisms, even the defenders of economics wound up accepting Hutchison's central philosophical premises.

9.2   Paul Samuelson's "operationalism"

Given how sketchy and hard to implement Hutchison's constructive suggestions were, it might appear that Knight had little to worry about. But, at about the time Hutchison issued his challenge, Paul Samuelson sketched out an "operationalist" program for economic theory that apparently offered a new empirically respectable way of doing economics.

Samuelson's views on the assessment of economic theories are scattered through his economics. I shall focus on his most explicit discussions of methodology[6] and on the exemplification of his methodological commitments in his early work on revealed preference theory.

The relevant part of Samuelson's (1963) argument goes as follows: let B be a theory and C be the set of all its empirical consequences. Then (so Samuelson maintains) B if and only if C. If all of C is correct, then B is a good (perhaps a perfect) theory. If only some part of C, C-, is correct, then only that portion of B, B-, that implies and is implied by C-, is good theory. The remainder of B is false and ought to be discarded. The application of the HD method is thus rendered more difficult in some ways, since *all* the consequences of the theory need to be tested, but simplified in another, since there are no longer any inductive leaps. Since theories supposedly entail and are entailed by the complete set of their empirical consequences, inferences concerning the correctness of theories are deductive.

Samuelson illustrates what he means by referring to his own work on revealed-preference theory. In the late 1930s he showed (for the two-commodity case) that an individual maximizes a complete and transitive utility function that is an increasing function of quantities of the two commodities if and only if the individual's choices satisfy the weak axiom of revealed preference.[7] The weak axiom of revealed preference states that if an individual chooses the bundle b, which is more expensive than commodity-bundle b' at one set of prices, p, then the individual will not choose b' over b when b' is more expensive than b. If the chosen bundles were both the more expensive options at the respective prices, then the individual would violate the weak axiom of revealed preference. Samuelson believes that he has "shown that the regular theory of utility maximization implied, for the two-good case, no more and no less than that 'no

---

[6] These are found in his contribution to a famous symposium on Milton Friedman's "Methodology of Positive Economics," which was published in the *American Economic Review*: *Papers and Proceedings* (May, 1963) and in his responses to subsequent criticisms (Samuelson 1964, 1965).

[7] Samuelson 1938. In the general market case, choices must also satisfy the strong axiom of revealed preference to rule out choice cycles. See Houthakker 1950 and section 1.3 above.

two-observed [sic] points on the demand functions should ever reveal...[a] contradiction of the Weak Axiom'" (1964, p. 738).

Samuelson is proposing a radically "behaviorist" reformulation of economic theory, on the lines of revealed-preference theory. But few economists (and certainly not Samuelson himself) do such behaviorist theorizing. Nor could they without dramatic loss. For the general view Samuelson espouses, of replacing theories insofar as possible with representations of their correct empirical implications, is incoherent and unhelpful, and to attempt to implement it would mean abandoning the whole enterprise of economic theory.

The incoherence of Samuelson's proposal is a consequence of the fact that the "implications of economic theory" are not implications of economic theory alone, but of economic theory coupled with statements of initial conditions concerning beliefs, market structure, etc., and auxiliary theories concerning, for example, data generation, and *ceteris paribus* clauses. The notion of "the set of empirical consequences of a theory" has meaning only relative to these other stipulations. If an individual falsely believes that bundle b is not available in the circumstances in which b' is more expensive than b, then the choice of b', which violates the weak axiom of revealed preference, does not falsify "the regular theory of utility maximization."[8]

Not only is the set of empirical consequences of a theory relative to the other theories one accepts (which cannot thus themselves be equivalent to their "sets of empirical consequences"), but there is no empirical advantage in insisting on this equivalence. Although each individual empirical consequence is observable, the correctness of the whole infinite set (whatever it is) is no more observable than the correctness of the theory, and an inductive leap is equally necessary.

Third, even if one could formulate a clear notion of the set of all the empirical consequences of a theory and could somehow determine that all the empirical consequences in some infinite subset were correct, there would in general be no feasible way to replace the original theory with a pared-down version that implied only this correct subset. Unless one were extraordinarily lucky, all that would be left would be a long and useless list of conditional statements.

Finally, in attempting to eschew all theorizing that goes beyond observable consequences, one surrenders all explanatory ambitions. Standard

---

[8] The example incidentally also shows either that the equivalence claimed between "the regular theory of utility maximization" and the weak axiom is mistaken (or rests on a mistaken interpretation of the former) or that the revealed-preference approach does not avoid reference to subjective states. The weak axiom of revealed preference is not equivalent to utility theory interpreted as in chapter 1. See esp. section 1.3.

utility theory apparently *explains why* individuals choose the consumption bundles they do (in terms of their beliefs and preferences and the constraints on their choices). Revealed-preference theory permits no such explanations and no way of linking choice behavior in the market to other sorts of rational choice behavior.

One might respond that the notion of explanation is just excess metaphysical baggage and that the possibilities of theoretical unification do not justify a refusal to pare theories down to their empirical consequences. But such a response is hardly tenable for most economists, who, like Samuelson, make use of theoretical idealizations and simplifications that have many false empirical implications. Just recall Samuelson's "Exact Consumption-Loan Model..." in chapter 7. What bearing could his views on theory appraisal have on work such as this, apart from roundly condemning it? When Fritz Machlup pointed out this apparent conflict between Samuelson's preaching and practice (1964), Samuelson replied, "Scientists constantly utilize parables, paradigms, strong polar models to help understand more complicated reality. The degree to which these do more good than harm is always an open question, more like an art than a science." (1964, p. 739) But what can the word, "understand," mean here?

Juxtaposing the author of "An Exact Consumption-Loan Model..." with the methodologist whose views I have been discussing, one might reasonably suppose that these are two different people who happen to have the same name. This is a vivid example of the methodological schizophrenia of contemporary economics, and it is found in "the very model of a modern neoclassical."[9] What causes it? Why does Samuelson espouse a methodology that he so regularly violates? The reason, I conjecture, is that he believes that the equation of a theory with its empirical consequences is mandated by up-to-date philosophy of science. Since he is not about to reject this authority nor to keep his economic theorizing within behaviorist boundaries, he chooses instead to live with the contradiction.

9.3   Fritz Machlup and logical empiricism

During the 1940s empirical qualms concerning economic theory grew in response not only to Hutchison's critique and Samuelson's operationalist

[9] Mirowski 1989, p. 182. Mirowski goes on to maintain (correctly, I think) that, "However much the average economist cited Milton Friedman's 1953 essay on 'method,' it was Samuelson, and not Friedman, who both by word and deed was responsible for the twentieth century self-image of the neoclassical economist as 'scientist.'" As we shall soon see, Friedman's methodological schizophrenia is almost as severe as Samuelson's.

program but also to efforts of economists to test fundamental propositions of the theory of the firm. For example, Richard Lester tried to determine whether firms attempt to maximize expected returns, whether they face rising cost curves and whether they in fact adjust production until marginal revenue equals marginal cost.[10] Lester's tests, which consisted of surveys sent to various businesses, were not well designed. But they attracted considerable attention and provoked angry responses (esp. Machlup 1946, 1947; Stigler 1947), partly because everybody knew that Lester was right, that firms did not behave precisely as the theory of the firm maintains. As Fritz Machlup, one of Lester's harshest critics, wrote in response to Hutchison's critique (1956):

Surely some businessmen do so [maximize net returns] some of the time; probably most businessmen do so most of the time. But we would certainly not find that all of the businessmen do so all of the time. Hence, the assumption of consistently profit-maximizing conduct is contrary to fact. (1956, p. 488)

But how could Machlup confess that Lester was right without granting Lester's point? To criticize the details of Lester's surveys, while conceding the relevance of more sophisticated studies of the same kind, seems to surrender the traditional neoclassical ship to the rising tide of logical positivism.

Machlup defends economic theory from empirical criticisms such as Lester's and from philosophical criticisms such as Hutchison's by applying more philosophically sophisticated views of theory structure and theory appraisal defended in later work of the logical positivists or, as they preferred to be called, "logical empiricists."[11] Although Machlup's reasons are different than Samuelson's or Hutchison's, he rejects Mill's deductive method as completely as they do. In attempting to reply to what he calls "ultra-empiricist" criticisms of economic theory, Machlup argues that the truth or falsity of the basic postulates of economics is not open to direct observation or test. For example, he compares the notion of "money illusion" to that of the neutrino:

With the help of the new construct the consequences deduced from the enlarged system promised to correspond to what was thought to be the record of observation; but the construct is without direct reference to observables and no one could reasonably claim to have any direct experience of illusions suffered by other minds. The reference to observed phenomena is entirely indirect. (1960, p. 579)

---

[10] 1946, 1947; see also Hall and Hitch 1939. Mongin 1986b and 1990–1 contain valuable discussions of the importance of these inquiries to the development of methodology in the 1950s.

[11] See particularly Braithewaite 1953, Carnap 1956, and Nagel 1961.

Since there is no direct way to observe or test the assumptions or basic postulates of economics, one can only assess them indirectly by testing the observable consequences that one can derive with their help.[12] At times (1955, 1956) Machlup suggests an instrumentalist view, whereby it is inappropriate to assess the truth or falsity of theoretical claims at all. The only relevant question is whether such claims are good tools for making predictions concerning observable market phenomena. At other times (1960), Machlup suggests instead that such theoretical claims are "partially interpreted" through their links with observational consequences and may justifiably be judged true or false, according to whether their consequences are true or false. Either way, the denial that these propositions can or should be (directly) tested *themselves* is central to Machlup's position:[13]

Unfortunately, writers on verification have all too often overlooked the important difference between the (direct) verification of a single empirical proposition and the (indirect) verification of a theoretical system consisting of several propositions, some of which need not be directly verifiable and need not be composed of operational concepts. These are not directly verifiable propositions and these non-operational concepts may be perfectly meaningful. (1960, p. 559)

Machlup's response to Hutchison, to Lester, to Samuelson, and to all who question fundamental theory is to accuse them of the methodological error of attempting to assess directly the basic postulates of economic theory, instead of focusing on their observational consequences. Machlup contends that up-to-date philosophy of science supports the view that fundamental theory need do no more than demonstrate its fruitfulness

---

[12] Machlup mistakenly attributes this view to Mill, Senior and Cairnes, "This methodological position...at least denying the independent objective verifiability of the fundamental assumptions, had been stated in the last century by Senior and Cairnes, but in essential respects it goes back to John Stuart Mill." (1955, p. 6) One wonders how Machlup could know that "consistently profit-maximizing conduct is contrary to fact" (1956, p. 488), if firms and their conduct are unobservable.

[13] At times there are hints of a different defense. The following passage suggests that Machlup may find the "ultra-empiricist" critique of basic theory mistaken because basic theory should be regarded as just a model that does not make any claims about reality, not because basic theory is concerned with unobservables: "Such propositions [the heuristic postulates and idealized assumptions in abstract models] are neither 'true or false' nor empirically meaningful. They cannot be false because what they predicate is predicated about ideal constructs, not about things or events of reality....They cannot be 'falsified' by observed facts, or even be 'proved inapplicable,' because auxiliary assumptions can be brought in to establish correspondence with almost any kinds of facts..." (1956, p. 486)

I do not know how much to make of such passages. In any event, such a view provides no defense of the use of basic theories to make assertions about phenomena and to explain or to predict phenomena.

in deriving correct observational consequences. Just as sophisticated logical positivists recognize the legitimacy of theories in physics that concern unobservable phenomena, yet have correct observational implications, so should economists recognize the legitimacy of theories in economics that have correct observational implications. Thus Hutchison is mistaken about which criteria must be satisfied by the statements of "pure theory," Lester is mistaken about what to test, and, in identifying theories with their consequences, Samuelson is mistaken about the role of theory in systematizing data. With a more sophisticated understanding of philosophy of science, the empiricist criticisms dissolve.[14]

Although superficially plausible, the analogy between the unobservable claims of particle physics and the false claims of equilibrium theory is indefensible. The first problem is that, except in some irrelevant absolute sense, economic theories rarely make claims about unobservable things. Let us grant that in some "absolute" sense of "direct observation" or of "direct testing" one cannot directly test whether individuals suffer from money illusion. To test whether individuals suffer from money illusion would require "indirect" tests such as, for example, asking a sample of salaried employees who have had a 3% raise in a period of 4% inflation whether they are richer or poorer than they were a year ago. But such a test is no more "indirect" than are the econometric tests one might employ to assess the supposedly observable implications of economics concerning price changes.[15] No interesting claims in any of the sciences are appreciably more observable than is the claim that laborers suffer from money illusion. In any scientifically relevant sense of "direct testing" or "direct observing," many of the behavioral postulates of economics are directly testable. The problem with claims such as "People's preferences are transitive" or "Firms attempt to maximize profits" is not that they are untestable, but that they are apparently false.

Why does Machlup defend this thesis? In part he is motivated by a philosophical view of the privacy of subjective experience, but he is also driven to it by his attempt to exploit contemporary philosophical work

---

[14] Machlup's views have another dimension, with which I am not concerned here. He insists repeatedly that all constructs in the social sciences should pass the additional condition of "empathic understanding" or "imagined introspection" (1960, pp. 579–80). Indeed, he is as much a follower of Max Weber and Alfred Schutz as of the logical positivists. But this additional test of good social theory only complements rather than qualifies or negates Machlup's response to empiricist criticisms of the basic postulates of economics.

[15] Nor are they more indirect than, for example, tests of whether an object is falling with a constant acceleration. The mentalistic fact that my children prefer chocolate ice cream to onions is much more easily observed than are most facts about markets.

concerning theoretical physics. Given the failure of attempts to relate theoretical claims closely to observational claims via either explicit definition or reduction sentences, the logical empiricists retreated either to non-cognitive instrumentalist or "partial interpretation" views of theoretical claims.[16]

Machlup gives the instrumentalist and partial interpretation views a strange twist when he applies them to defend equilibrium theory. Unlike the logical empiricists, he is not trying to show how statements might be legitimate even if one cannot test them directly. He argues instead that one *should not test the basic assertions of equilibrium theory individually and that one should ignore their apparent falsity* (Mäki forthcoming b, pp. 21-2). But there is nothing in the work of the logical positivists that supports an injunction not to test or not to heed the results of tests. Apart from the spurious analogy with the instrumentalist or partial interpretation views of the logical empiricists, Machlup has no argument against testing such claims by, for example, psychological experimentation or surveys, no matter how unsettling the results may be (see chapters 12 and 13 below). And, since Machlup insists forcefully on the explanatory role of theories, he cannot consistently urge one to overlook the apparent falsity of the basic explanatory principles of economics. Machlup has no coherent answer to Hutchison's philosophical critique and no way to dismiss as irrelevant Lester's survey results. This conclusion is not surprising, for survey results can be relevant (see for example Blinder and Choi 1990). One of the most damaging methodological legacies that Machlup, and, as we shall see, Friedman left behind was a repudiation of all survey research.

9.4   Friedman's pragmatic instrumentalism

The most influential way of reconciling economics and up-to-date philosophy of science was not Machlup's, but Milton Friedman's. Friedman's essay, "The Methodology of Positive Economics" is by far the most influential methodological statement of this century. It is the only essay on methodology that a large number, perhaps a majority, of economists have ever read. Although Friedman does not explicitly refer to contemporary philosophy of science, he, too, attempts to show that economics satisfies positivist standards. In "The Methodology of Positive Economics" (1953c), Friedman offered the apparent way out of the

---

[16] See A.7. For various reasons, including especially doubts about the distinction between theory and observation, even these weaker conceptions of the relations between theory and observation have been largely abandoned (see esp. Suppe 1977).

empirical difficulties raised by Lester and others which has proven most popular with economists.[17] It is that apparent way out, not the possible intricacies of Friedman's views, with which I shall be concerned.

After distinguishing positive and normative economics, Friedman begins his response to critics of economics, such as Lester, by asserting that the goals of a positive science are exclusively predictive (1953c, p. 7). Economists seek significant and usable predictions, not understanding or explanation. The view that science, or at least economic science, aims only at prediction is a contentious one, for which Friedman offers no argument, and it might reasonably be challenged (see A.2). Since Friedman's methodological views are untenable, even if one grants his claim that the goals of economics are exclusively predictive, let us not contest it here.

In Friedman's usage, any implication of a theory whose truth is not yet known counts as a prediction of a theory, even if it is not concerned with the future. Since the goals of science are exclusively predictive, a theory which enables one to make reliable predictions is a good theory. In the case of a tie on the criterion of predictive success, simpler theories or theories of wider scope (that apply to a wider range of phenomena) are to be preferred, unless they are inconvenient to use (1953c, p. 10).

Friedman stresses that there is no other test of a theory, in terms of whether its "assumptions" are "unrealistic" (1953c, p. 14). When Friedman speaks of the "assumptions" of a theory, he includes both fundamental assertions (such as the claim that consumers are utility maximizers) and additional premises needed in particular applications (such as, for example, the claim that different brands of cigarettes are perfect substitutes for one another). It is not clear what Friedman or the critics he is responding to mean by the term, "unrealistic." Friedman equivocates. Sometimes he means simply "abstract" or "not descriptively complete." But usually, when he calls an assumption unrealistic, he means (as he must if he is to respond to Lester's challenge) that it is not true, perhaps not even approximately true, of the phenomena to which the theory is applied.

---

[17] Despite its influence, Friedman's essay has not been admired by other writers on economic methodology. With the exception of Boland 1979, 1987, Frazer and Boland 1983, and, in a very different vein, Hirsch and De Marchi 1986 and 1990, Friedman's methodology has been uniformly condemned. See Archibald 1959, 1961, 1967, Bear and Orr 1967, Blaug 1980a, Bray 1977, Bronfenbrenner 1966, Brunner 1969, Caldwell 1980a, 1982, Coddington 1972, 1979, Cyert and Grunberg 1963, Cyert and Pottinger 1979, De Allessi 1971, Helm 1984, Hollis and Nell 1975, Jones 1977, Koopmans 1957, Mason 1980–1, Melitz 1965, Musgrave 1981, Nagel 1963, Nooteboom 1986, Pope and Pope 1972, Rosenberg 1976, Rotwein 1959, 1962, Samuelson 1963, Simon 1963, Wible 1987, and Winter 1962.

Friedman can then argue that researchers such as Lester mistakenly attempt to assess the "assumptions" of economic theory instead of its predictions. In dismissing any assessment of assumptions, Friedman is also responding to writers in a critical tradition which extends back to the German Historical School via American Institutionalists, such as Veblen (1898, 1900, 1909). These authors question the worth of abstract theorizing and object to the unrealistic assumptions of economic theory. Friedman apparently enables one to reject all such criticism as fundamentally confused.[18]

But Lester's case cannot be dismissed so easily. For Lester apparently showed that economic theory makes false predictions concerning the results of his surveys. The distinction between assumptions and implications is a shallow one that rests on nothing but the particular formulation of a theory. Assumptions trivially imply themselves, and theories can be reformulated with different sets of assumptions that have the same implications. False assumptions concerning observable things will always result in false predictions.

For a standard instrumentalist (A.2) who regards all and only the observable consequences of a theory as significant, this difficulty is insuperable, but Friedman is *not* such a standard instrumentalist. When one looks hard, one can find ample evidence. Consider the following seven passages:

Viewed as a body of substantive hypotheses, theory is to be judged by its predictive power for the class of phenomena which it is intended to "explain." (1953c, pp. 8–9)

For this test [of predictions] to be relevant, the deduced facts must be about the class of phenomena the hypothesis is designed to explain... (1953c, pp. 12–13)

Misunderstanding about this apparently straightforward process centers on the phrase "The class of phenomena the hypothesis is designed to explain." The difficulty in the social sciences of getting new evidence for this class of phenomena and of judging its conformity with the implications of the hypothesis makes it tempting to suppose that other, more readily available, evidence is equally relevant... (1953c, p. 14)

the relevant question to ask about the "assumptions" of a theory is...whether they are sufficiently good approximations for the purpose in hand. And this question can be answered only by seeing whether the theory works....The two supposedly independent tests thus reduce to one test. (1953c, p. 15))

---

[18] Lee Hansen told me that he recalls economists in the 1950s reacting to Friedman's essay with a sense of *liberation*. They could now get on with the job of exploring and applying their models without bothering with objections to the realism of their assumptions.

Clearly, none of these contradictions of the hypothesis is vitally relevant; the phenomena involved are not within the "class of phenomena the hypothesis is designed to explain"... (1953c, p. 20)

The decisive test is whether the hypothesis works for the phenomena it purports to explain. (1953c, p. 30)

the question whether a theory is realistic "enough" can be settled only by seeing whether it yields predictions that are good enough for the purpose in hand... (1953c, p. 41)

Although some ambiguities are hidden by taking these quotations out of context, they show that Friedman *rejects* a standard instrumentalist view whereby *all* the predictions of a theory matter to its assessment. A good tool need not be an all-purpose tool. The goal of economics and of science in general is "narrow predictive success" – correct prediction for "the class of phenomena the hypothesis is designed to explain." Lester's surveys are irrelevant because answers to survey questions are not among the phenomena that the theory of the firm was designed to explain. Those who reject any inquiry into whether the claims of the theory of choice are true of individuals reason the same way.

Friedman's views are thus a distinctive form of instrumentalism. Even falsity of predictions is of no importance unless it detracts from a theory's performance in predicting the phenomena it was designed to "explain." A theory of the distribution of leaves on trees which states that it is *as if* leaves had the ability to move instantaneously from branch to branch is thus regarded by Friedman as perfectly "plausible" (1953c, p. 20), although of narrower scope than the accepted theory. On Friedman's view, if a theory predicts accurately what one wants to know, it is a good theory, otherwise not.

When Friedman says that it is *as if* leaves move or *as if* expert billiard players solve complicated equations (1953c, p. 21), what he means is that attributing movement to leaves or higher mathematics to billiard players leads to correct predictions concerning the phenomena in which one is interested. And a theory which accomplishes this is a good theory, for a "theory is to be judged by its predictive power for the class of phenomena which it is intended to 'explain'" (1953c, p. 8). It may thus seem obvious that the realism of a theory's assumptions or the truth of its uninteresting or irrelevant implications is unimportant except insofar as either restricts the theory's scope. Since economists are not interested in what business people say, it makes no difference what Lester's surveys show.

I suggest that Friedman uses his view of the narrow predictive goals of science as a premise in the following implicit argument:

1 A good hypothesis provides valid and meaningful predictions concerning the class of phenomena it is intended to explain (premise).
2 The only test of whether an hypothesis is a good hypothesis is whether it provides valid and meaningful predictions concerning the class of phenomena it is intended to explain[19] (invalidly from 1).
3 Any other facts about an hypothesis, including whether its assumptions are realistic, are irrelevant to its scientific assessment (trivially from 2).

If (1) the *criterion* of a good theory is narrow predictive success, then one is tempted to say that surely (2) the *test* of a good theory is narrow predictive success, and Friedman's claim that the realism of assumptions is irrelevant follows trivially. This is an enticing argument.

But it is fallacious. (2) is not true, and it does not follow from (1). To see why, consider the following analogous argument.

1' A good used car drives reliably (over-simplified premise).
2' The only test of whether a used car is a good used car is whether it drives reliably (invalidly from 1').
3' Anything one discovers by opening the hood and checking the separate components of a used car is irrelevant to its assessment (trivially from 2').

Presumably nobody believes 3'.[20] What is wrong with the argument? It assumes that a road test is a conclusive test of a car's future performance. If this assumption were true, if it were possible (and cheap) to do a total check of the performance of a used car for the whole of its future, then there would indeed be no point in looking under the hood. For we would know everything about its performance, which is all we care about. But a road test only provides a small sample of this performance. Thus a mechanic who examines the engine can provide relevant and useful

---

[19] This is overstated, and (to repeat) I am not concerned to provide the best interpretation of Friedman's whole methodology. In his essay Friedman concedes a role for assumptions in facilitating an "indirect" test of a theory: "Yet, in the absence of other evidence, the success of the hypothesis for one purpose – in explaining one class of phenomena – will give us greater confidence than we would otherwise have that it may succeed for another purpose – in explaining another class of phenomena. It is much harder to say how much greater confidence it justifies. For this depends on how closely related we judge the two classes of phenomena to be..." (1953c, p. 28) The last sentence still limits the relevance of the correctness of predictions concerning phenomena that are remote from those which the theory is designed to explain, and Friedman believes that the evidential force of indirect tests is much less than that of tests concerning the range of phenomena that the theory is intended to "explain."

[20] Those who do should get in touch. I will find some fine old cars for you at bargain prices.

information.[21] The mechanic's input is particularly important when one wants to use the car under new circumstances and when the car breaks down. One wants a sensible mechanic who not only notices that the components are used and not perfect, but who can also judge how well the components are likely to serve their separate purposes.

Similarly, given Friedman's view of the goal of science, there would be no point to examining the assumptions of a theory if it were possible to do a "total" assessment of its performance with respect to the phenomena it was designed to explain. But one cannot do such an assessment. Indeed the whole point of a theory is to guide us in circumstances where we do not already know whether the predictions are correct.[22] There is thus much to be learned by examining the components (assumptions) of a theory and its "irrelevant" predictions. Such consideration of the "realism" of a theory's assumptions is particularly important to provide guidance when extending the theory to new circumstances or when revising it in the face of predictive failure.[23] Again what is relevant in the messy world of economics is not whether the assumptions are perfectly true, but whether they are adequate approximations and whether their falsehood is likely to matter for particular purposes. Saying this is not conceding Friedman's case. Wide, not narrow predictive success, constitutes the grounds for judging whether a theory's assumptions are adequate approximations. The fact that a computer program works in a few instances does not render study of its algorithm and code superfluous or irrelevant.

As is implicit in the remarks above, there is some truth in Friedman's defense of theories containing unrealistic assumptions. For failures of

---

[21] This is true even when the user is able to make extremely sensitive performance assessments. My wife, who is a classical pianist, would never buy a used piano without having a technician find out what is responsible for the flaws she can feel or hear and look for problems with the piano that are imperceptible to her now, but which will come to affect the piano's touch or sound.

[22] Friedman partially recognizes this point when he writes, "The decisive test is whether the hypothesis works for the phenomena it purports to explain. But a judgment may be required before any satisfactory test of this kind has been made, and, perhaps, when it cannot be made in the near future, in which case, the judgment will have to be based on the inadequate evidence available." (1953c, p. 30)

[23] With what seems to me inconsistent good sense, Friedman again partly recognizes the point, "I do not mean to imply that questionnaire studies of businessmen's or other's motives or beliefs about the forces affecting their behavior are useless for all purposes in economics. They may be extremely valuable in suggesting leads to follow in accounting for divergences between predicted and observed results; that is, in constructing new hypotheses or revising old ones. Whatever their suggestive value in this respect, they seem to me almost entirely useless as a mean of *testing* the validity of economic hypotheses." (1953c, p. 31n)

assumptions may sometimes be irrelevant to the performance of the hypothesis with respect to the designated range of phenomena. Just as a malfunctioning air-conditioner is irrelevant to a car's performance in Alaska, so is the falsity of the assumption of infinite divisibility unimportant in hypotheses concerning markets for basic grains. Given Friedman's narrow view of the goals of science (which I am conceding for the purposes of argument, but would otherwise contest), the realism of assumptions may thus sometimes be irrelevant. But this practical wisdom does not support Friedman's strong conclusion that only narrow predictive success is relevant to the assessment of an hypothesis.

One should note three qualifications. First, we sometimes have a wealth of information concerning the track record of theories and automobiles. I may know that my friend's old Ford has been running without trouble for the past seven years. The more information we have about performance, the less important is separate examination of components. But it remains sensible to assess assumptions or components, particularly in circumstances of breakdown and before applying them in a new way. Second, intellectual tools, unlike mechanical tools, do not wear out. But, if one has not yet grasped the fundamental laws governing a subject matter and does not fully know the scope of the laws and the boundary conditions on their validity, then generalizations are as likely to break down as are physical implements. Third (as Erkki Koskela reminded me), it is easier to interpret a road test than an econometric study. The difficulties of testing in economics make it all the more mandatory to look under the hood.

When either theories or used cars work, it makes sense to use them – although caution is in order if their parts have not been examined or appear to be faulty. But known performance in some sample is not the only information relevant to the assessment of either. Economists must (and do) look under the hoods of their theoretical vehicles. When they find embarrassing things there, they must not avert their eyes and claim that what they have found cannot matter.

Thus, even if one fully grants Friedman's view of the goals of science, one should still be concerned about the realism of assumptions. For there is no good way to know what to try when a prediction fails or whether to employ a theory in a new application without judging its assumptions. Without assessments of realism (approximate truth) of assumptions, the process of theory modification would be hopelessly inefficient and the application of theories to new circumstances nothing but arbitrary guesswork. Even if *all* one wants of theories are valid predictions concerning particular phenomena, one needs to judge whether the needed assumptions are reasonable approximations, and one thus needs to be concerned about incorrect predictions, no matter how irrelevant.

I have dwelled on Friedman's views not only because of their influence but because they show the same methodological schizophrenia that we saw in Samuelson's work. Friedman's confidence in "the maximization-of-returns hypothesis" and in neoclassical theory in general purportedly rests entirely on "the repeated failure of its implications to be contradicted" (1953c, p. 22; but see pp. 26–30 on indirect testing). On this, Friedman is at one with Popperian methodologists such as Blaug (1980a,b). But the implications of economic theory have certainly been contradicted on many occasions. This would be so even if the theory lived up to its highest praises. All it takes is some disturbance, such as a change in tastes, a new invention, or a real or imagined invasion from Mars.[24] Does *any* economist really accept neoclassical theory on the basis of "the repeated failure of its implications to be contradicted"? Is this not rather a doctrine piously enunciated in the presence of philosophers or of their economist fellow travellers and conveniently forgotten when there is serious work to do (Mäki 1986, pp. 137–40)?

9.5   Conclusion: Koopmans' restatement of the difficulties

In concluding this survey of methodological revolution of the 1930s, 1940s and 1950s, it is instructive to look back to the perceptive book by Tjalling Koopmans, *Three Essays on the State of Economic Science* (1957).[25] Koopmans' *Essays* was written in the wake of Hutchison's and Friedman's works (to which Koopmans refers) and at about the same time as Machlup's views, but before the great wave of comment and criticism directed toward Friedman's "Methodology of Positive

[24] Objections that readers have voiced to these examples instructively support my point. One objected that economic theory obviously allows for "shocks." But, unless it does so by means of a not fully specified *ceteris paribus* clause, there will still be refutations of the kind cited. And, if not fully specified *ceteris paribus* clauses are permitted, the "repeated failure of its implications to be contradicted" is a cheap triumph. Another reader objected that better examples are those in which the assumptions involved in the particular application of the theory are satisfied. I agree, but this is certainly not a line that Friedman or others who rest everything on the success of predictions can follow. For we are not supposed to pay any attention to whether the assumptions are satisfied – that is, to whether the assumptions are "realistic" for the situation at hand. There are examples in which predictive failures are more puzzling and disturbing than in the cases cited in the text. Consider the fact that even in inflationary circumstances many firms evaluate their inventories on a first in, first out basis or the fact that shares in closed-end mutual funds sometimes sell for less than the value of the assets of the funds (Stiglitz 1982).

[25] For a more recent methodological statement see Koopmans 1979.

Economics" broke out. Koopmans cogently rejects Friedman's methodological position, but also expresses hesitation about the exaggerated
claims Robbins makes for the obviousness of the basic assumptions of
economics (see above p. 125). Koopmans incisively links his methodological comments to the details of particular problems in economics and
argues that some problems call for more mathematical investigation of
the implications of fairly obvious postulates, while others require more
empirical work. He relies upon philosophical distinctions much stressed
by the positivists, such as the distinction between syntax and semantics
(see above section 5.1), to defend the importance of purely logical and
mathematical explorations in economics, yet he also defends a non-
positivist notion of model building that is similar to the notion developed
in chapter 5 above. He states his overall conclusion concerning the
assessment of economic theory as follows:

Whether the postulates are placed beyond doubt [as in Robbins], or whether
doubts concerning their realism are suppressed by the assertion that verification
can and should be confined to the hard-to-unravel more distant effects [as in
Friedman] – in either case the argument surrounds and shields received economic
theory with an appearance of invulnerability which is neither fully justified nor
at all needed. The theories that have become dear to us can very well stand by
themselves as an impressive and highly valuable system of deductive thought,
erected on a few premises that seem to be well-chosen first approximations to a
complicated reality. They exhibit in a striking manner the power of deductive
reasoning in drawing conclusions which, to the extent one accepts their premises,
are highly relevant to questions of economic policy. In many cases the knowledge
these deductions yield is the best we have, either because better approximations
have not been secured at the level of the premises, or because comparable
reasoning from premises recognized as more realistic has not been completed or
has not yet been found possible. Is any stronger defense needed, or even desirable?
(1957, pp. 141–2)

Depending on one's aims, perhaps no stronger defense is needed. But
a clearer one is. Although Koopmans' general vision exudes good sense,
he has avoided rather than answered the criticisms of Mill's deductive
method. Is it scientifically acceptable to rely on premises "that seem to
be well-chosen first approximations"? How can such a methodology
make use of the results of observation or experiment? Can such a
methodology be legitimate? Given the inexactness of the premises, are
the conclusions "highly relevant to questions of economic policy"? Is
the test of whether this "knowledge" "is the best we have" (as Koopmans
implies) a comparison only with other deductively structured and derived
theoretical systems? As I shall argue in chapter 12, Koopmans' views
are partially defensible. But their defensible core was not understood,

and his remarks did nothing to head off another three decades of misconceived methodological debate largely divorced from methodological practice.

Since Koopmans' time, empiricist criticisms and calls for reconstructing economics have come to depend more on the philosophical views of Karl Popper and of his interpreter, disciple and then critic, Imre Lakatos. When writers on economic methodology in the 1970s and 1980s criticize or defend economic theory, they typically rely on Popper or Lakatos, rather than on the views of the logical empiricists. Popper's and Lakatos' views are, however, no more hospitable toward the deductive method than are those of the logical positivists and logical empiricists. Indeed, if Popper's or Lakatos' view of theory assessment is correct, then the traditional methodology that Koopmans reaffirms is completely untenable.

10   Karl Popper and falsificationism in economics

In chapter 9 we criticized contemporary alternatives to traditional views of theory appraisal in economics. But we need to look deeper to the philosophical underpinnings of this reaction. The philosopher who has had the greatest influence is Karl Popper (Mäki 1990b). He is often invoked by Mark Blaug, Terence Hutchison, and lesser writers on economic methodology. His philosophy even influenced a major introductory textbook, Richard Lipsey's *An Introduction to Positive Economics* (1966). If Popper is right about what scientific methodology requires, then the traditional Millian view of justification in economics developed above in chapter 8 is indefensible.

This chapter presents and answers the Popperian challenge to Mill's views by criticizing Popper's philosophy of science. These criticisms of Popper's views are widely accepted among philosophers.[1] Although I share Popper's concern that scientific theories be testable, Popper's philosophy prevents one from coming to terms with the problems of testing in economics. A reasoned concern with testability leads one, I shall argue, to reject Popper's philosophy of science and to reconsider the Robbins–Mill view of theory appraisal in economics.

10.1   The problems of demarcation

Throughout his work Popper has been concerned with what he calls "the problem of demarcation," the problem of distinguishing science from non-science (A.12). He is careful to stress that this is *not* the problem

---

[1] The critique of Popper's views on induction to a considerable extent follow criticisms made by Levison (1974), Lieberson (1982a, 1982b), Putnam (1974), Grünbaum (1976), and Salmon (1981), although only Lieberson was a major influence. Jonathan Lieberson's early death deprived me, and the intellectual community at large, of his invaluable criticisms and insights. Isaac Levi's work (1967, 1980) has also influenced this critique, and in my argument for the possibility of verifications, I was assisted by Nisbett and Thagard's discussion of induction in their (1982). Lakatos' criticisms of Popper and his plea for a "whiff of inductivism" is much weaker, since his own treatment of induction, discussed briefly below in section 11.3, differs so little from Popper's (see Lakatos 1974). For some defense, see Miller 1982.

of distinguishing what is true from what is not, for science may lead us astray, and non-sciences or even pseudo-sciences may happen on the truth. Popper has been a persistent critic of the popular misapprehension that science accumulates proven, uncontestable, indeed infallible truths. Scientific results are not conclusively proven, and even the most successful scientific theories, such as Newton's theory of motion, can be found in error.

But, if the demarcation of what is scientific from what is not scientific is not a demarcation of the true from the false, why should one care whether some enterprise or theory is scientific? Of course it matters when it comes to membership in the American Academy for the Advancement of Science or to the receipt of grants from the National Science Foundation. Our culture values science. Other cultures value sorcery. Does the question of whether something is scientific or not have any further significance?

The answer to which Popper subscribes is simple and intuitive, although it has had its share of recent philosophical critics (Feyerabend 1975; Laudan 1983; see also A.12). What is important about science and justifies a concern with the problem of demarcation is that science has a particularly excellent *method* of weeding out truth from falsity. In non-Popperian terminology, the conclusions of science have a special claim to be believed. Nancy Reagan's reliance on the advice of an astrologer was disturbing because there is no good reason to believe astrologers, not because astrologers are always wrong.[2] The distinction between the questions, "Is this claim true?" and "Are we justified in believing this claim?" is critical to clear thinking in the philosophy of science (see pp. 267 and 289).

Popper argues that what distinguishes scientific *theories*, such as Newton's or Einstein's, from unscientific theories, such as Freud's or those endorsed by astrologers, is that scientific theories are *falsifiable*. A theory is falsifiable if it is not guaranteed that it will pass all tests. There must be some possible tests or observations which, if the results are unfavorable, would be evidence that the theory is false. "All swans are white" is the sort of statement which is appropriate in science, because the observation of a non-white swan would establish its falsity (Popper's own example, 1968, p. 27).

---

[2] Popper and his followers would object to my language, since, as I explain below, they deny that scientific claims are ever justified, and their concern is knowledge, not belief. In my view, if the demarcation between science and non-science is important, it must be because science has some special claim on our beliefs. The critical virtues of science that Popper stresses are of interest only because of a thesis that Popper denies: that what survives harsh criticism has a better claim on our beliefs.

Popper refines this intuitive notion by distinguishing a class of "basic statements" upon whose truth agreement is easily obtained. Basic statements are true or false reports of observations that are of an "*unquestioned empirical character*" (1969a, p. 386; see also 1968, sections 28, 29).[3] Accepted basic statements are not certain, infallible, or incorrigible. One is not *forced* by the facts to accept them. But people do (albeit tentatively) *decide* to do so, and they rather easily reach agreement on which basic statements to accept. Basic statements have a special importance because of this agreement, because they are easy to test, and because, as empiricists, scientists take test reports to be central in assessing scientific theories.

Popper defines a theory to be falsifiable if and only if it is logically inconsistent with some finite set of basic statements (which need not be true). A falsifiable but true theory will not be inconsistent with any set of *true* basic statements, but it will be inconsistent with false observation reports. What is important is that it will not be consistent with whatever might be claimed to have been observed. A falsifiable theory will forbid some possible observations.

I cannot judge how important logical falsifiability is to Popper, since he apparently contradicts himself on the question.[4] In an introduction to the *Postscript to The Logic of Scientific Discovery* written in the early 1980s he writes:

It is of great importance to current discussion to notice that falsifiability in the sense of my demarcation criterion is a purely logical affair. It has to do only with the logical structure of statements and of classes of statements...

A statement or theory is, according to my criterion, falsifiable if and only if there exists at least one potential falsifier – at least one possible basic statement that conflicts with it logically. (1983, p. xx)

Here Popper seems to be claiming that the demarcation between science and non-science depends entirely on whether the statements of the discipline are logically falsifiable. Yet in *The Logic of Scientific Discovery* itself, Popper writes:

Indeed, it is impossible to decide, by analysing its logical form, whether a system of statements is a conventional system of irrefutable implicit definitions, or whether it is a system which is empirical in my sense; that is, a refutable

---

[3] By regarding basic statements as singular rather than existential, I am simplifying – as, indeed, Popper also does (1972, p. 7).

[4] Although Popper (1983, pp. xxii–xxiii) is correct to distinguish logical falsificationism from what Lakatos calls "dogmatic falsificationism" pp. 95–103, its vices are, I shall argue, just as serious.

system....*Only with reference to the methods applied* to a theoretical system is it at all possible to ask whether we are dealing with a conventionalist or an empirical theory. (1968, p. 82)

By a "conventionalist theory" Popper means a theory whose claims are taken, as a matter of convention or decision, to be true, or at least beyond questioning. Here the demarcation seems to depend not on the logical properties of the statements of a discipline, but on the methods of the practitioners.

According to the first quotation, logical falsifiability demarcates science from everything else. If so, then the problem of demarcation must be to distinguish scientific *theories* or *statements* from *theories* or *statements* that are not scientific. But throughout his career Popper has stressed the importance of methodological decisions and has also taken the problem of demarcation to be the problem of distinguishing scientific *practices* from *practices* that are not scientific. Popper argues, for example, that through the use of "conventionalist stratagems" people can cling unscientifically to theories such as Marx's, which were falsifiable, and were, in Popper's view, falsified. Let us first examine how Popper distinguishes scientific *theories* from theories that are not scientific.

10.2   Logical falsifiability and Popper's solution to the problem of induction

As a corollary of logical falsifiability, Popper emphasizes an "*asymmetry* between verifiability and falsifiability; an asymmetry which results from the logical form of universal statements" (1968, p. 41; see also 1983, pp. 181-9). A universal statement concerning an infinite or an unbounded domain may be falsifiable – that is, it may be inconsistent with some basic statements. But it will not be verifiable – it will not be deducible from any finite set of basic statements, and its negation will not be inconsistent with any finite set of basic statements. For example, "This swan is black" falsifies "All swans are white." But no set of observation reports entails "All swans are black." It is not possible to verify any truly universal statement, but one can falsify it or verify its negation. Although Popper makes too much of this asymmetry, he is right to insist that the results of science are not proven.

Popper argues that this asymmetry between falsifiability and verifiability leads to a solution to the problem of induction.[5] In more or less the formulation Popper prefers (1972, p. 7), Hume's problem of induction is the problem of finding a good argument with only basic statements as premises and a universal statement as a conclusion.[6] If by "good argument" one means "valid deductive argument," as Popper does, then there are no good arguments with universal statements as conclusions and with only basic statements as premises.

Thus far Popper agrees with Hume. But Popper argues that one need not accept Hume's skeptical conclusion that human inductive proclivities have no rational justification. Since one can provide valid deductive arguments *against* universal statements, one can (albeit fallibly, since basic statements are not themselves infallible) find out that theories are wrong.

By itself this observation would not solve the problem of induction, for only the fallacy of elimination enables one to find theory T meritorious merely because an alternative theory T' has been refuted. But Popper is also proposing to cut the linkage between knowledge and justification altogether. Conjectures about the world constitute knowledge if they are true. In attempting to falsify them, scientists sometimes find out that they are false and not knowledge at all. That which has not been falsified one takes to be knowledge. Justification has no role. Hume is correct that justification is not available, but Popper maintains that it is not needed either.

I cannot accept this dramatic problem shift. Popper only apparently escapes Hume's challenge by redubbing unsupported conjecture that has

---

[5] It is important to keep separate three different problems, each of which might be called a problem of induction: (1) How do people discover or formulate generalizations or claims about things not yet observed? When philosophers and scientists speak of induction, they are often concerned with questions concerning scientific discovery. Popper, for example, argues forcefully that scientific laws are never discovered by any inductive process (for example, 1969a, pp. 46–8). Although the distinction between questions of discovery and justification will not bear much weight (see A.9), one can distinguish a second question, this time concerning inductive justification: (2) How, *in fact*, do scientists go about defending or justifying scientific laws? Hume's problem of induction (3) is, at least as he conceived of it, separate from both of these. Regardless of how generalizations are discovered and regardless of what sorts of arguments scientists use to support various purported laws, Hume is issuing a skeptical challenge: show how to provide a rational defense for what people actually do. See A.11.

[6] I do not concur with Popper's sharp separation of what he calls the "logical" from the "pragmatic" problem of induction. There is basically only one problem here. Although literally correct, given Popper's definitions, the following claim is misleading: "For anybody who adopts an instrumentalist view, *the* [logical] *problem of induction disappears.*" (1983, p. 117) As Popper notes (1983, p. 120) the point is a trivial one, since the instrumentalist faces the analogous problem of deciding rationally which statements to rely on. Popper's formulation seems to have misled Lawrence Boland, who argues that instrumentalism is a response to the problem of induction (1979, p. 508).

not yet been falsified "knowledge." Although his conclusion is clothed in soothing words about how rational the procedure is (for example, 1972, pp. 22, 27, 58, 81, 95), it is as skeptical as Hume's, for Popper explicitly denies that there is any room for argument in support of any theory or law. He writes, for example, "that in spite of the 'rationality' of choosing the best-tested theory as a basis of action, this choice is *not* 'rational' in the sense that it is based upon *good reasons* for expecting that it will in practice be a successful choice; *there can be no good reasons in this sense, and this is precisely Hume's result*" [Popper's emphasis] (1972, p. 22). One has no better reason to expect that the predictions of well-tested theories will be correct than to expect that untested theories will predict correctly. This skeptical view is central to Popper's philosophy of science. For, if Popper were to admit that the results of testing can give one reason to believe in the reliability or approximate truth of claims about the world, then he would have to face the problem of induction and attempt to explain how they can do so. Popper's option is simpler, but it fails.

Although I reject Popper's solution to the problem of induction, I think that his proposed revision of the concept of knowledge is in the correct direction; it is merely too extreme. As argued in section 11.4 below and sketched in A.11, we should reject Hume's view that human knowledge is, as a whole, in need of justification. But rather than surrender justification altogether, we need to temper our justificatory demands.

Whether or not one accepts Popper's (and Lakatos') radically non-justificatory notion of knowledge, Popper's purported solution to the problem of induction presupposes that individual scientific statements or individual scientific *theories* are falsifiable. But scientific theories are not logically falsifiable. Statistical and probabilistic claims are obviously not logically falsifiable. Even a million heads in a row does not logically falsify the claim that a particular coin is unbiased. The claim that a coin is unbiased is not logically inconsistent with any finite set of basic statements. More seriously, all claims that cannot be tested *individually* are not themselves inconsistent with some finite set of basic statements and not logically falsifiable. And virtually no scientific claims of any interest and none of the conjunctions of such claims that constitute recognizable scientific theories are, *by themselves*, inconsistent with sets of basic statements. To falsify so simple a scientific claim as Galileo's law of falling bodies requires non-basic statements concerning whether non-gravitational forces are present. To falsify the law of demand requires a non-basic assertion of the absence of interferences. Predictions are not deduced from single statements or theories alone, nor from theories conjoined with statements of initial conditions. Only conglomerates of various theories, statements of initial conditions, and auxiliary assumptions concerning the absence of interferences will entail a prediction. Only such conglomerates are logically falsifiable (see A.10). If statements or theories can be regarded as scientific only if they are logically falsifiable, all non-trivial science is not science after all. The criterion of demarcation that demands that scientific theories must be individually falsifiable demands too much.

Although Popper typically talks of the falsifiability of scientific theories, he recognizes that they are not logically falsifiable; and he has discussed at length the role of background knowledge in testing and the "conventionalist stratagems" one might employ to shield theories from falsification. Sometimes he backs away from this recognition and mistakenly takes individual theories to be falsifiable, as, for example, when he argues against Lakatos that the observation of a dancing tea cup would, *by itself*, falsify Newton's theory of motion and gravitation.[7] But Popper has an answer to this difficulty. His answer is that *logical falsifiability is not a criterion that scientific statements or even whole scientific theories have to satisfy individually*. What distinguishes scientific theories from non-scientific theories is that whole systems of scientific theories, auxiliary assumptions, and statements of initial conditions created to derive predictions are falsifiable (1983, p. 187). One can deduce testable predictions from a set of statements including the theory under test only if the set is logically falsifiable. Let us call such sets or conglomerates "test systems." Galileo's law of falling bodies is not itself logically falsifiable, but conjoined with claims about resistance and friction and other forces, one has a falsifiable test system.

To insist that scientific theories be incorporated into logically falsifiable test systems, is weak, inadequate as a criterion of demarcation, and inconsistent with Popper's purported solution to the problem of induction. It is weak because logical falsifiability plays a small role in the actual process of theory rejection or revision.[8] Step 2 of the hypothetico-deductive method (A.10.1) is not much of the method. The fact that a

---

[7] 1974, p. 1005. Watkins criticizes this passage in his 1984, p. 326.

[8] Zahar's proposed phenomenological reconstrual of basic statements (1983, pp. 156-61) and of logical falsifiability only underscores how small a role logical falsification plays in the process of theory revision. Popper disputes this criticism, which was emphasized by Duhem (1906, p. 187), by arguing that $H2$ might entail P, while $H1$ entails P when $H1$ and $H2$ are conjoined to a common set of additional premises, S. But even in such a case $H2$ does not follow deductively from P. S is still needed, and we still need to decide (for whatever reasons) to regard the members of S as true. See Grünbaum 1976, pp. 248-50 and the critique of Popper's methodological rules below. See pp. 185f and footnote 17 below.

theory is part of a logically falsifiable test system only enables the further methodological rules that guide the scientist to get some grip.

Yet, in demanding only that test systems be logically falsifiable, one is demanding too little to distinguish science from pseudo-science. Virtually nothing fails to count as science. For example, Freud's psychological theories, which Popper regards as unfalsifiable, are not unfalsifiable in this sense. On the contrary, analysts and amateurs alike are constantly deriving predictions about how people will talk and act from Freudian theory and a wealth of other assumptions. The problem is not that these predictions (and thus the test systems from which they are derived) are never inconsistent with sets of basic statements. What bothers Popper about Freud's theories is rather that the logical falsifications are not taken by analysts as evidence against the theories.[9] The criterion of demarcation, that requires only that whole test systems be logically falsifiable demands too little.

Furthermore, Popper's concession that only whole test systems are logically falsifiable rules out his solution to the problem of induction. Since individual scientific theories need not be falsifiable, there is no logical asymmetry between the verifiability and falsifiability of particular scientific *theories*: *They* are neither logically verifiable nor logically falsifiable. Accepted basic statements and deductive logic can get one to the falsity of whole test systems and no further. One can deduce neither scientific theories nor their negations from basic statements only. Even if one grants Popper's reconceptualization of knowledge, Popper still has no solution to the problem of induction.[10]

Whether a condition on individual scientific claims or a condition that applies only to test systems, logical falsifiability and the logical asymmetry between falsification and verification are of little interest to economic methodologists. Few theoretical claims in economics are by themselves logically falsifiable, but this is no fault, for logical falsifiability of individual theories is too much to demand. There are no economic theories which cannot enter into logically falsifiable test systems (which would include specifications of statistical techniques and *ceteris paribus* clauses in addition to theories from economics and from other domains). But this is no great virtue, for it is not enough to demand logical falsifiability only of whole test systems. Popper's claims about the asym-

---

[9] "But what kind of clinical responses would refute to the satisfaction of the analyst not merely a particular analytic diagnosis but psycho-analysis itself?" (1969a, p. 38n).

[10] As we shall see later in section 10.4, Popper explicitly allows that one can also make use of what he calls "background knowledge" to achieve falsifications, but in this section I have been concerned exclusively with logical falsifiability.

metry of logical falsifiability and logical verifiability, as applied to whole test systems are uninformative and provide no solution to the problem of induction.

10.3   Falsificationism as a methodology – as norms to govern science

Popper has always stressed that methodology is concerned with rules, not simply with logic. Indeed, as documented above, he sometimes addresses the problem of what distinguishes scientific *practices* from practices that are not scientific, and he offers a set of norms for scientists to follow.

Popper's basic intuition is that what distinguishes scientists from non-scientists is that scientists have a *critical attitude*. They look for hard tests and they take their results seriously. Scientists do not treat their theories as articles of faith but as corrigible hypotheses that should be put to serious tests. Such a critical attitude does not separate scientists from classical scholars, historians, or literary critics, but it does highlight the dogmatism of "scientific creationists" or of many astrologers (for example, West and Toonder 1973).

Descending from this plausible and salutary general vision to a more detailed level, Popper's account runs into difficulties, because he demands too much and rejects all empirical justification. Popper's falsificationist methodology – his account of what a critical attitude is – consists in outline of three rules addressed to scientists: (1) propose and consider only contentful and thus testable theories; (2) seek only to falsify scientific theories; (3) accept theories that withstand attempts to falsify them as worthy of further critical discussion, never as certain, probable, or close to the truth.

In somewhat more detail these rules can be restated as follows:

1 Although untestable theories may be true and suggestive, consider as candidates for scientific knowledge only theories that have a great deal of content and can be subjected to hard tests. A hard test is a test that, given background knowledge or the alternatives, one should expect the theory to fail. Prefer theories with lots of content and many possibilities for falsification.

2 Scientists should, at least collectively, have a critical attitude; they should try to falsify existing theories, not to confirm them. This attitude requires that scientists look for harsh tests of existing scientific theories. To do so, they must accept not only basic statements but also some non-basic statements as true. Otherwise there would be no way to falsify

anything except whole test systems. In other inquiries, scientists can test their presuppositions, although these further tests will have their own further presuppositions. When a theory fails a test, and scientists cannot find a reasonable excuse, then they must reject the theory and look for an alternative. A reasonable excuse must at least be readily tested. A scientist might, for example, question whether a particular instrument was operating properly. There is no simple algorithm stating when it is unreasonable to make further excuses, but, provided that one is seeking to falsify rather than to hold on to theories, no algorithm is needed.[11]

3 If a theory has not yet been falsified, scientists should accept it tentatively as worthy of testing. Theories that survive harsh testing are not better supported or more worthy of belief than are untested theories. They are merely difficult to falsify and worth testing further. "The theoretician's choice" in Popper's view, "is the hypothesis most worthy of *further critical discussion* (rather than *acceptance*)" [Popper's emphasis] (1969a, p. 218n). Although Popper argues that there may sometimes be evidence that one theory has more true and fewer false consequences than another (1972, pp. 58, 81–2, 265), there is never, in his view, any good evidence that a law or a theory is correct or even close to correct.

What we do – or should do – is to *hold on, for the time being, to the most improbable of the surviving theories* or, more precisely, to the one that can be most severely tested. We tentatively "*accept*" this theory – but only in the sense that we select it as worthy to be subjected to further criticism, and to the severest tests we can design.[12] [Popper's emphasis] (1968, p. 419)

Are these good rules? The answer presumably depends on what the objectives of scientists should be. And therein lies a tangled story, which

---

[11] This requirement, like the last, is not so much a requirement of each individual scientist as it is of the institution of science (1969b, p. 112; but see 1972, p. 266). Provided that there is open and free communication, the institution as a whole may be critical, even though individual scientists attempt to protect their own theories from criticism.

[12] Popper chides Lakatos (1974, p. 1003) for in effect ignoring the sentence that follows: "On the positive side, we may be entitled to add that the surviving theory is the best theory – and the best tested theory – of which we know." But this last sentence does not change what Popper takes corroboration and "acceptance" of scientific theories to be. Popper also had a theory of "ontological" verisimilitude, which met with an unfortunate formal demise (Tichy 1974, Miller 1974). But regardless of formal vicissitudes, Popper has insisted that corroboration is no evidence of verisimilitude and that verisimilitude is not an epistemic notion. In very special and limited circumstances one can justifiably maintain that one theory has a greater verisimilitude than another, but there is never any justification for maintaining that a theory has a high verisimilitude (1972, pp. 47f).

we had better avoid tackling here. Let us temporarily simplify: since realists and instrumentalists (see A.2) agree that one fundamental goal of science is to provide correct predictions, let us consider how well scientists would accomplish this goal if they followed Popper's methodology. Popper might object that this "simplification" is biased, but as I shall argue below (p. 187), the criticisms can be reformulated and remain valid even if one maintains that the goals of science are not at all predictive. We can also ask whether Popper has provided any good arguments in defense of his methodological rules. For, given their implausibility, something needs to be said on their behalf.[13]

One can grant the first rule, that science should seek theories with lots of content that can be tested harshly and in many ways. But, apart from the important insistence on content, there is no news in the first rule. Inductivists have been saying these things since at least the seventeenth century (Grünbaum 1976, pp. 17f).

The second and third rules are disputable. It seems strange to claim that scientists should seek only to falsify theories, never to support them and that they should never regard theories as more than conjectures that may be worthy of criticism.[14] Why should anyone accept them? Would accepting them serve the goals of science? Popper offers four reasons in defense of these two rules. First, he maintains that confirming evidence is worthless since "It is easy to obtain confirmations, or verifications, for nearly every theory – if we look for confirmations." (1969a, p. 36). So it is a mistake to look for confirmations or to regard what one finds as supporting evidence. But only cheap and comparatively worthless confirmation is readily available. From a Bayesian perspective, for example, a good test requires not only a high likelihood $(\Pr(e/H))$, but also an unlikely prediction, a low $\Pr(e)$ (A.10.2). Good supporting evidence is hard to obtain and leads one to seek harsh tests (see Grünbaum 1976, pp. 215–29).

---

[13] One might object that it is unfair to demand supporting argument, for just as Popper maintains that science provides no good reason to believe its conclusions, so philosophers cannot be required to defend their methodological rules. But Popper has not drawn so radical a metaphilosophical conclusion. To avoid the absurdity of philosophy without supporting argument, this line of thought would require clear and convincing distinctions between the claims for which one could offer supporting arguments and those for which only critical arguments were possible.

[14] And indeed Popper is unable to consistently follow his own advice, for he writes, "What we believe (rightly or wrongly) is not that Newton's theory or Einstein's theory is true, but that they are *good approximations* to the truth, though capable of being superseded by better one.

But this belief, I assert, *is* rational." (1983, p. 57)

Second, Popper argues that to seek confirmation or to believe that one has found it shows a dogmatic attitude rather than the critical attitude shown by those who seek falsifications (1969a, pp. 49f). But someone who seeks confirmation for a theory need not be credulous, closed-minded, or dogmatic. A person seeking the solution to a problem, who is concerned *both* with confirming and with disconfirming evidence, does not automatically qualify as a dogmatist.

Third, Popper suggests that to seek supporting evidence or to regard scientific theories as sometimes well-established falsely supposes that scientific knowledge is infallible, and the overthrow of Newtonian physics renders such a view untenable. But knowledge claims may be both well supported and fallible.[15] To regard K as fallible does not require that one's subjective degree of belief in K be close to zero.

Popper's fourth argument for the injunction to seek to falsify theories and never to seek to support them rests on the thesis that it is impossible for evidence to support scientific theories. Scientific theories simply *cannot* be confirmed, so it is a mistake to attempt to do so. Popper says bluntly, "there *are* no such things as good positive reasons; nor do we need such things..." (1974, p. 1043). There is no such thing as supporting evidence.[16] This argument may appear to be inconsistent with the claim that supporting evidence is easy to obtain. But there is no real contradiction here. In Popper's view, evidence that *truly provides* positive reason for accepting a scientific claim cannot be had, while evidence that inductivists *mistakenly take to support* scientific theories is easy to obtain.

It would be foolish to seek confirming evidence, if such evidence were unattainable. But why believe that one *never* has good reason to accept any scientific claims or that one *never* has good reason to believe that some claims are more likely to pass future tests than others?

What convinces Popper that one can never have genuine confirming evidence is the problem of induction. There are no good arguments with only basic statements as premises and scientific theories as conclusions. So there is no supporting evidence, no sense in seeking it and no justification for believing that one has found it. In Popper's view, it

---

[15] And Isaac Levi has even argued that one can regard one's knowledge as *in*fallible, without regarding it as incorrigible. See his 1980.

[16] There are verbal difficulties here, since Popper offers an explicit analysis of what it is for evidence to support a theory (see esp. 1983, pp. 236f). This is not a contradiction, however, for in the unfamiliar Popperian sense in which evidence "supports" or "corroborates" theories, it gives one no reason to believe that the theory is true or close to the truth and no reason to believe that the theory will pass any future tests. Popper denies that evidence that "supports" or "corroborates" theories in his sense supports theories in any usual sense.

remains rational to seek to criticize scientific theories, because such theories are falsifiable: there may be good arguments against them.

But this argument restates Popper's solution to the problem of induction, which in turn depends on the mistaken view, which is explicitly denied by Popper, that individual laws and theories in science are falsifiable. So this argument derives its specious plausibility from Popper's lack of clarity about whether individual theories or only whole test systems are supposed to be falsifiable. If the problem of induction gave one good reason not to seek confirming evidence, it would also give one good reason not to seek falsifying evidence.

10.4   Decisions, evidence, and scientific method

Since scientific statements and theories are not individually falsifiable, how could one carry out Popper's methodological rules insisting that one formulate falsifiable theories and test them as harshly as possible? Popper's answer is that it is legitimate for the purpose of testing to make further *decisions* to take non-basic statements as unproblematic background knowledge. These further decisions make it possible to falsify specific scientific theories.[17]

Let us call falsifications whose premises include both basic statements and background knowledge "conventional falsifications" as opposed to logical falsifications whose premises include only basic statements. (These labels may be misleading. The tentative acceptance of basic statements as true is just as conventional as the decision to regard non-basic statements as background knowledge.) Perhaps Popper's solution to the problem of induction (and the methodological injunctions that depend on this purported solution) can be saved, if Popper is interpreted as defending a conventional asymmetry thesis: scientists can provide good falsifying arguments whose premises include both basic statements and background knowledge, but they cannot provide good supporting arguments. I shall argue that the conventional asymmetry thesis is false, and,

[17] It might be thought that such decisions are not always necessary. Suppose the conjunction (S and U) has been logically falsified. The problem is to determine which is the culprit. If S and various alternatives to U, (S and U'), (S and U''), (S and U'''), etc., are not falsified while at least one of (S' and U), (S'' and U), (S''' and U), etc. is logically falsified, one may, it is contended, conclude that U is the culprit not S (see Popper 1957, p. 132 and Zahar 1983, pp. 155f). As Glymour (1980, pp. 34–5) has pointed out, this suggestion faces serious formal difficulties. Moreover, this suggestion does not obviate the need to decide to regard some statements as part of background knowledge. The failure to falsify (S and U'), (S and U''), (S and U'''), etc. is being used to provide an unacknowledged inductive justification for S and hence for taking the logical falsification of (S and U) as a falsification of U. See footnote 8 above.

unless the decisions Popper would have us make are evidentially supportable, science could not pursue its goals efficiently.

Others have tried to show that there is no asymmetry of conventional falsification and verification by arguing that, if scientists cannot verify statements, then they cannot get beyond mere logical falsification of whole test system conglomerates (Lieberson 1982b). In answer to this criticism, Popperians maintain that *decisions* will do in place of verifications (Watkins 1984). Although formally correct, this answer creates some serious difficulties, to which I shall turn shortly.

Regardless of the basis for the decision to rely on some propositions to falsify others, such decisions are unavoidable. But, if it is permissible to include background knowledge among one's premises in order to make conventional *falsifications* possible, then one also makes conventional *verifications* possible. The conventional asymmetry thesis fails, and Popper has failed to defend his claim that scientists should seek falsifications only.

Consider, for example, a scientist attempting to determine the spectrum of a newly discovered metallic element (see Nisbett and Thagard 1982). The scientist already knows that the spectrum of an element is invariant in particular ways from pure sample to sample. Given (a) this background knowledge, (b) the report of a particular bunsen burner's flame turning orange, and (c) the claim that the particular sample was pure, the scientist can *deduce* that all pure samples of the element will turn a bunsen burner's flame orange. Given background knowledge in addition to basic statements, one can provide good arguments for as well as against universal statements. There is no claim to incorrigibility or infallibility in pointing to such possibilities of verification, and one need be no more dogmatic in offering such arguments, than one is when one relies on basic statements and background knowledge to falsify scientific claims.[18]

Not only does the reliance on decisions fail to set apart falsification and verification and to ground Popper's methodological rules, but not to insist on evidential *justification* for these decisions would be disastrous.

---

[18] The possibility of providing such arguments also appears to be independent of the question of whether there exists an inductive logic, in the sense of a rational procedure according to which the acceptance of basic statements might justify the acceptance of non-basic statements. But appearances may be deceptive here, since an inductive argument can always be formulated as a deductive argument that includes an inductive principle as a premise. In the argument above, the claim that the spectrum of an element is invariant in particular ways from pure sample to sample is an inductive principle. It is a highly restricted version of Mill's principle of uniformity. Mill's own account of induction is closely related to the possibilities of making arguments such as these. See Mill's *Logic*, 3.3, esp. 3.3.3 and 3.3.4.

If a central goal of science is to provide correct predictions, then the methodological rules that guide science should provide an efficient means toward this end. How do Popper's rules compare in this regard to the non-Popperian norms that govern scientific conduct? In actual practice in both science and everyday life, people make estimates of how well-established and plausible various claims are, and how likely they are to lead one astray. These estimates may be mistaken and may be revised, but they are *used* in pure science as well as in everyday action and engineering. Estimates of the extent to which particular claims have been established may, for example, be crucial to the interpretation of experimental failures. If, for example, someone reports that price increases were followed by demand increases, economists would conclude that there was some statistical error or that other causal factors were involved. This conclusion is based on the judgment that the law of demand is a good approximation to the truth. Weaker links are more likely to break (see 9.4 and 12.1). Popper alleges that such judgments are unsupportable, and a Popperian scientist would not make them. He is calling for a revolution in human conduct.

Consider how a scientific practice would work that relies on evidentially unsupported decisions to regard statements as a part of background knowledge. Could there even *be* a completely non-inductivist Popperian science (see Watkins 1984 and sections 11.1 and 11.2 below)? In deciding what to do in the light of the failure of a prediction of a whole theoretical system, one might, perhaps, be guided entirely by consideration of which revisions are maximally content increasing, least *ad hoc*, etc. Questions about how well supported the various constituents of the system are would play no role. Such an enterprise is radically unlike the science we are familiar with, and, indeed, Popper is hesitant in presenting it. Zahar (1983, p. 168) quotes the following passages from Popper's (1979) (written in 1930-1), which illustrate vividly Popper's early hesitance.

We unquestionably believe in the probability of hypotheses. And what is more significant: our belief that many a hypothesis is more probable than others is motivated by reasons which undeniably possess an objective character (*Grunde, denen ein objecktiver Zug nicht abgesprochen werden kann*) ([1979], p. 145).

The subjective belief in the probability [of hypotheses] can be based on their corroboration, but it goes beyond what corroboration can effectively do. This belief assumes that a corroborated hypothesis will be corroborated again. It is clear that without this belief we could not act and hence that we could not live either. There is in this belief nothing further which should intrigue us. Its objective motives are clarified by the notion of corroboration to such an extent that this belief should not give rise to the deployment of any further epistemological questions (*ibid.* p. 155)[19]

Popper seems to grapple with the problem ("without this belief we could not act..."), but then to back away from it with words that baffle me.

Popper also writes,

There is first the layered structure of our theories – the layers of depth, of universality, and of precision. This structure allows us to distinguish between more risky or exposed parts of our theory, and other parts which we may – *comparatively speaking* – take for granted in testing an exposed hypothesis. (1983, p. 188)

Perhaps this passage is consistent with Popper's philosophy, since he could maintain that evidence does not determine how "exposed" or "risky" a part of our theory is and that we do not need to judge how well supported the propositions are. But it seems that Popper has a hard time avoiding all reliance on evidential support.

A non-inductive Popperian science would be inefficient. For just as I argued with respect to Friedman's dismissal of questions concerning the realism of assumptions (in section 9.4 above), one good way to proceed in the case of failure and one basis for determining whether extensions of a theory to new domains are likely to work is to consider how well supported are the various components of one's theory. It should not take detailed philosophical argument to defend the truism that it matters for predictive purposes how well supported claims are. (But it may require a great deal of philosophical analysis and argument to clarify this truism and make it precise.) Moreover, the difficulties cannot be avoided by insisting on a purely theoretical view of science, for theoretical scientists, just as much as engineers, need to be able to rely on some statements in order to test others (see pp. 198–200 below).

So Popper has provided no good arguments for his implausible second and third methodological rules and no answer to the simple argument that degree of confirmation is important to accomplishing efficiently the goals of science. Popper has not shown that one should not seek evidence in support of scientific theories, and he has not shown that one should never regard scientific theories as well-established. And, indeed, these injunctions are mistaken. It is sometimes sensible to regard theories that have been well tested and that have passed these tests as close to the

---

[19] Compare these remarks to Lakatos' defense of a tentative metaphysical inductive principle below, pp. 194f.

truth and as admissible into the background knowledge that one relies upon in developing and testing new theories – just as it is sometimes sensible to regard such theories as a reliable basis for engineering purposes. In learning more we are stuck on Neurath's boat (appendix, p. 314), and as it becomes more sea worthy, we can repair it better.

10.5   Why are economic theories unfalsifiable?

Even if Popper's rules for scientific procedure were free of the difficulties discussed above, they would be of little value to economists.[20] For, within Popper's philosophy of science, there are no interesting questions to be asked concerning the falsifiability of economic theory! The only Popperian questions are: (1) Are economic theories logically falsifiable by themselves? – No, but neither are any interesting theories in science. (2) Can economic theories be incorporated into logically falsifiable test systems? – Yes, but the same goes for theories of practically all disciplines, no matter how patently unscientific they may appear. (3) Can one take the other statements in such test systems to be background knowledge and regard economic theories as conventionally falsifiable? – Yes, but there is little difficulty in taking any statement to be conventionally falsifiable. It all depends on whether one is willing to decide to take other statements to be background knowledge, and such decisions are, in Popper's view, not evidentially based.

So if one is concerned about whether economic theory is falsifiable, as many economists have been, what question is one asking? Economists have wanted to know whether one could come, as the result of experiment or observation, to have *good reason* to believe that economic theories are correct or mistaken. That it be possible to incorporate such theories into logically falsifiable test systems is only a necessary condition. What is needed in addition is that one have good reason to believe that the other statements in such test conglomerates are true or close to the truth or that their falsity does not matter for the particular inquiry. But, according to Popper, one never has such good reason. One can never justify the decision to regard a claim as part of background knowledge on the grounds of its confirmation or corroboration (Lieberson 1982b). Consequently there is no way within Popper's philosophy of science to capture the questions economists ask concerning the falsifiability of their

---

[20] For a comprehensive overview of Popper's philosophy of science and a more sympathetic view of its applicability in economics, see Caldwell 1991.

theories. To understand in what way economic theories have seemed unfalsifiable, one must reject Popper's third methodological rule prohibiting scientists from regarding theories as more than conjectures.

Although it might be reasonable to demand such a non-Popperian falsifiability of scientific theories, it is still not reasonable to follow Popper's second methodological rule requiring scientists to seek falsifications only, and unflinchingly to discard falsified theories. If science consisted only of falsifiable but unfalsified claims, economic theory would be either an empirical failure or an unfalsifiable metaphysical theory that might be of use in the development of empirical theories. In his discussion of "the logic of the situation," Popper seems inclined to regard economics as a metaphysical theory (Hands 1985a). Even though one might still find economics to be useful metaphysics, the costs of such an interpretation are considerable. For, in such a view, there are no empirical discriminations to be drawn between neoclassical economics and other approaches (unless, unlike neoclassical economics, some of the other approaches actually qualified as scientific) nor could one discriminate which propositions of economic theory were better supported by the evidence.

The most prominent economic methodologists who have defended parts of the Popperian vision (Blaug 1980a,b, 1985, Hutchison 1977, 1978, 1981, 1988, and Klant 1984) have been unwilling to draw such drastic conclusions. They have instead argued only for the importance of criticism and testing. Such advice might appear harmless, like defenses of motherhood or apple pie. But it may have distracted economists from the real difficulties that stand in the way of developing better tested theories.

For example, consider the allegations of Popperian methodologists such as Mark Blaug (1) that economists rarely formulate their theories in ways which facilitate testing, (2) that they carry out few tests, and (3) that they pay little attention to negative results. Popperians and non-Popperians agree that one prominent feature of good science is a serious concern with testing and with the results of testing, even when they are unfavorable. Presumably economists know at least this much methodology.

Why then is testing so unimportant in economics? Is there a lapse in scientific conduct, which can only be explained by sociological or institutional facts, or are there some good reasons as well? Is there something about economic theories or data or about the phenomena economists study that explains the scarcity of testing? One Popperian answer would be that economic theories are *themselves* untestable. But, as already argued, this answer, if understood in one of the ways that Popper would have us understand it, is unsatisfactory. If the accusation is that economic theories are not by themselves logically falsifiable, then the accusation is true but trivial, for no interesting theories are falsifiable in this sense. If, on the other hand, the accusation is that economic theories cannot be combined with other statements to derive testable predictions, then it is false. Furthermore, even if it were true that economic theories are in some significant sense unfalsifiable, this would only push the explanatory question back one step. In asking why testability has so little grip in economics, one surely wants also to know why economic theories are untestable, if indeed they are.

So it seems that the only explanation for the apparent methodological failings of economics that the Popperian methodologist can give is Mark Blaug's: that there has been too little methodological nerve. Toward the end of *The Methodology of Economics* Blaug argues:

Mainstream neoclassical economists do not have the same excuse. They preach the importance of submitting theories to empirical tests, but they rarely live up to their declared methodological canons. Analytical elegance, economy of theoretical means, and the widest possible scope obtained by ever more heroic simplification have been too often prized above predictability and significance for policy questions. The working philosophy of science of modern economics may indeed by characterized as "innocuous falsificationism." (1980a, p. 259)

It seems to me, on the contrary that economists are so little involved with testing because, first, many are involved with non-empirical conceptual work (see sections 5.3 and 6.3 above). Second, even those who are interested in empirical theory are also relatively uninvolved with testing (in comparison with biologists or chemists) because, given the subject matter they deal with, they do not know enough to formulate good tests or to interpret the results of tests. To test a theory requires not merely that one derive a testable prediction from the theory and a set of further statements. One must also have good reason to regard these further statements as unproblematic in the context. One cannot arbitrarily will them or declare them to be unproblematic. Testing requires knowledge and simple phenomena, so that few auxiliary theories are needed to derive predictions. Facing a complex subject matter and lacking such knowledge, economists cannot effectively test their theories (see section 12.5 below). If there is a cure, it can only come as a result of acquiring better experimental techniques and more detailed knowledge. This requires methodological reform – particularly of the commitment to economics as a separate science (sections 6.4–6.6, 12.7, and chapter 15) – but not better standards of theory assessment. Moral entreaty to be good scientists will not help, and it can even hurt; for it disguises the real problems. Popper's philosophy of science does not permit one to pose the central problems of theory appraisal in economics and does not help to resolve them.

11 Imre Lakatos and economic methodology

Imre Lakatos was a follower of Popper's, but their views came into conflict shortly before Lakatos died. Lakatos' writings on the philosophy of science date from the late 1960s and early 1970s and had no role in the development of the alternative views discussed in chapter 9. Over the last two decades Lakatos has had a tremendous influence, exceeded only by Popper's.

Although Lakatos' views are a brilliant modification of Popper's, they fall prey to the same fundamental difficulties,[1] and this chapter will conclude with some general words of appraisal concerning both Popper's and Lakatos' views. Despite his indebtedness to Popper, Lakatos defends a strikingly original vision of science that has fascinated the leading contemporary writers on economic methodology.

11.1 Sophisticated methodological falsificationism

Lakatos grants many of the criticisms I made of Popper in chapter 10, but he thinks them unfair, for Lakatos argues that Popper was moving toward a more sophisticated position to which the criticisms do not apply. Lakatos calls this new position, "sophisticated methodological falsificationism."[2] One can best grasp what sophisticated methodological falsificationism requires by contrasting its basic three rules of scientific conduct with the three rules of Popper's methodology (pp. 180–1 above).

1 Where Popper required that theories worthy of scientific attention possess a great deal of *content* (and thus be testable), the sophisticated

---

[1] Indeed, despite Popper's and Lakatos' focus on theoretical science and their unambiguous repudiation of instrumentalism, the most important difficulties they face turn out to be similar to those that confront Milton Friedman's views discussed above in section 9.4. For a useful critical overview see Hacking 1979.

[2] In Lakatos' view, Popper is not a consistent sophisticated methodological falsificationist (1974, p. 143), and, except in section 5 of "Truth, Rationality and the Growth of Scientific Knowledge" (1969c), I do not see much of sophisticated methodological falsificationism in Popper. But my concern here is with Lakatos' position, not with the accuracy of his interpretation of Popper.

methodological falsificationist requires that scientific theories possess *excess content* when compared to the "touchstone" theories that were previously entertained. To be more precise, the sophisticated methodological falsificationist requires of every new theory T' that

(i) T' must explain all the corroborated content of the previous theory T.
(ii) T' must have implications in addition to those of T and of any "interpretative" theories T^* falsifying T, and
(iii) Some of the "excess content" of T' must be "novel predictions."

The phrase, "novel predictions," has three different meanings in Lakatos' work:[3] (a) predictions of phenomena not yet known, (b) implications that were not considered when the theory was generated, and (c) new interpretations of known phenomena. Predictions that are novel in sense (a) will be novel in senses (b) and (c), but not necessarily vice versa. A theory T' which explains all the corroborated content of a previous theory T and also makes novel predictions shows "theoretical progress." Popper is concerned with the content of the new theory, while Lakatos is concerned with the content of the *change*.

2 Popper's second rule required that scientists attempt to falsify theories. Doing so requires looking for harsh tests, accepting certain statements as unproblematic background knowledge for the purpose of testing, and rejecting theories when they fail such tests. The second rule of the sophisticated methodological falsificationist, in contrast, calls upon scientists:

(i) To modify existing theories by proposing alternatives that make novel predictions.
(ii) To test the novel predictions of the proposed alternatives. If some of these are corroborated, the alternative shows "empirical progress."
(iii) To reject existing theories when some of the novel predictions of a proposed alternative are corroborated or, in some circumstances, when the alternative shows merely theoretical progress.

The object of appraisal shifts from individual theories to sequences of theories. Criticism is more difficult and more constructive than in Popper's view. The methodological directives of sophisticated methodological falsificationism are also, Lakatos argues, less risky and more in accord

---

[3] Hands (forthcoming b) counts five senses of "novel prediction," while Murphy (1989) counts six.

with the history of science. One no longer needs to regard some claims
as unproblematic background knowledge in order to test others, which
Lakatos objects to on historical grounds and on the grounds of risk (*not*
on the grounds that such decisions must not be arbitrary). When faced
with an empirical "anomaly" – the falsification of a "test system" (see
p. 178 above),

> we do not have to decide which of the ingredients of the theory we regard as
> problematic and which ones we regard as unproblematic: we regard all ingredients
> as problematic in the light of the conflicting basic statement and try to replace
> all of them. If we succeed in replacing some ingredient in a "progressive" way
> (that is, the replacement has more corroborated empirical content than the
> original), we call it "falsified" (1970, pp. 40–1)

The sense in which sophisticated methodological falsificationism is "falsificationist" is peculiar, for "the few crucial *excess-verifying instances*
are decisive" (1970, p. 36). "the only relevant evidence is the evidence
anticipated by a theory..." (1970, p. 38).

3 Finally, for Popper, if a theory survives harsh testing, then it becomes
particularly testworthy, nothing more. Although such a view is consistent
with the first two rules of sophisticated methodological falsificationism,
Lakatos argues that increasing corroboration must be taken as evidence
of increasing "verisimilitude," or else science becomes a mere game.
Science must not be disconnected from theoretical concern to learn the
truth or from practical concern with the technological application.

> We have to *recognize* progress. This can be done easily by an inductive principle
> which connects realist metaphysics with methodological appraisals, verisimilitude
> with corroboration, which reinterprets the rules of the "scientific game" as a –
> conjectural – theory about the *signs* of the *growth of knowledge*, that is, about
> the signs of *growing verisimilitude of our scientific theories.* (1974, p. 156)

There are thus two crucial shifts in Lakatos' sophisticated methodological
falsificationism. First there is the shift of focus from individual theories
to series of theories. What distinguishes science from non-science is not
how scientists test and criticize individual theories but how scientists
modify their theories. Second, Lakatos retreats from Popper's repudiation
of all inductive principles and insists that successfully following the rules
of sophisticated methodological falsificationism permits the tentative
conclusion that science is moving towards its epistemic goals rather
than away from them. Before considering and assessing Lakatos'
modifications, there is one further piece of the puzzle that must be put
into its place.

11.2   The appraisal of scientific research programs

Although Lakatos attributes sophisticated methodological falsification-ism to Popper, there is one further Lakatosian step to take. Sophisticated methodological falsificationism leaves unexplained the *continuity* that persists across theory modifications. As far as the rules of the sophisticated methodological falsificationist are concerned, the shift from T to T' would be theoretically progressive if T' merely tacked on to T some unrelated bold conjecture. But to offer a sensible appraisal of a series of theories, T, T', T'' requires an account of what links these theories and *generates* the theory modifications.

Research programs thus play an important part not only in Lakatos' account of the global theory structure of science (see above section 6.2), but also in his account of appraisal within science. For Lakatos stresses,

The idea of growth and the concept of empirical character are soldered into one. (1970, p. 35)

The weight of evidence is not merely a function of a falsifiable hypothesis and the evidence; it is also [a] function of temporal and heuristic factors. (Lakatos and Zahar 1976, p. 180)

We accept theories if they indicate *growth* in truth-content ("progressive problem-shift"); we reject them if they do not ("degenerate problemshift"). This provides us with rules for acceptance and rejection even if we assume that all the theories we shall ever put forward will be false. (1968, p. 178)

the essence of science is growth: fast potential growth...and fast actual growth. (vol. 2, p. 180; see also vol. 2, pp. 183–4)

The real unit of appraisal is the research program. The heuristics of a research program are responsible for its progress, although luck, genius, and nature have a small role to play, too. Within research programs there are also appraisals of particular theory modifications, but the standards for these appraisals are largely determined by the heuristics of the research program. Appraisals of research programs are fundamental to the under-standing of science and to the demarcation between science and non-science.

Lakatos reinterprets the problem of demarcation as the problem of distinguishing between "scientific and pseudo-scientific *adjustments*, between rational and irrational changes of theory" (1970, p. 33). The "new, nonjustificationist criteria for appraising scientific theories" are "based on anti-ad hocness." The failures of theory modifications all involve *ad hoc*ness of one variety or other.

I distinguish three types of *ad hoc* auxiliary hypotheses: those which have no excess empirical content over their predecessor (*ad hoc*$_1$), those which have such excess content but none of it is corroborated (*ad hoc*$_2$) and finally those which are not *ad hoc* in these two senses but do not form an integral part of the positive heuristic (*ad hoc₃*) (1971, p. 112n)

The essential feature of science is *growth*, and what distinguishes sciences is the *autonomous* and *rapid* manner in which they grow. Lakatos' views, like Popper's, cut science off from ordinary inquiry, but Lakatos retains one thin thread linking science to human interests: the fallible metaphysical hypothesis that increasing corroboration is a sign of increasing verisimilitude.

One can appreciate why Lakatos' views have been so appealing to economists. For they are well suited to the defense of contemporary microeconomics and general equilibrium theory. Lakatos makes the heuristic power of a research program, in which microeconomics is rich, central to its assessment, greatly downplays the importance of refutations of particular theories, and dismisses criticisms of the central propositions as methodologically misguided. Thus one finds Lakatosian defenses of microeconomics in Latsis 1976 and Weintraub 1985a,b, 1987, 1988.[4]

11.3   Why the methodology of scientific research programs cannot work

Lakatos' work is a brilliant caricature that calls attention to features of science that others have overlooked. But his account of appraisal is unworkable and misconstrues scientific progress. Even if it could be used, it exaggerates the importance of growth. Moreover, Lakatos' concessions to inductivism do not go far enough to meet the objections to Popper's views argued above in section 10.4. Both in practical applications and in theoretical science, decisions to rely on particular claims depend on judgments of how well supported they are. The knowledge that T' has not been falsified or that T' represents progress over T is not enough.

Lakatos argues that the shift from theory T to theory T' is not progressive unless T' includes all the corroborated content of T, and T' makes novel predictions. Since these conditions are seldom met, Lakatos' account is unworkable and misdescribes progress. Theory shifts typically involve some loss, as well as gain of content. For example, some of the corroborated content of the law of diminishing marginal utility was lost

---

[4] One also finds methodological and historical writings on economics influenced by Lakatos that are critical of microeconomics. Blaug's somewhat critical (1980a) was influenced by both Popper and Lakatos. See also Hands 1985b. Other discussions of Lakatos and economics are Ahnonen 1989, Blaug 1987, Blaug and de Marchi 1991, Cross 1982, Dagum 1986, Fisher 1986, Fulton 1984, Hamminga forthcoming, Hands 1979, 1988, forthcoming a,b, Jalladeau 1978, Rizzo 1982, Robbins 1979, and Rosenberg 1986, 1987.

in the shift to ordinal utility theory, which is nevertheless regarded by economists as an important step *forward.*[5] Phlogiston theory explained things that Lavoisier's oxygen theory could not explain. To insist that corroborated content must not be lost in theory modifications would block most theory modifications. The insistence on novel predictions is also inconsistent with the history of science, as Lakatos' shift (p. 193 above) to progressively weaker senses of "novel predictions" reveals. Lakatos is right to point out that scientists are greatly impressed by successful novel predictions, but there is little support for the view that this is the only evidence they are concerned with (appendix, p. 310).

Like Popper, Lakatos believes that theoretical science can dispense with the notion of supporting evidence for theories or for theory changes. Moreover, in his view, it is a mistake to inquire, "Yes, I can see that T' is indeed much better than T, but how good is T'?" Lakatos recognizes that such questions may be unavoidable in practical life,[6] but they have, for Lakatos, *no* role in theoretical science. In this, Lakatos is still a follower of Popper's and his view of science inherits the central flaws of Popper's view.

Unlike Popper, Lakatos tackles the objection that practical applications depend upon judgments of reliability. In his view, the knowledge needed for engineering emerges from theoretical science as follows:

But which are the most "verisimilar" theories? I think that these can (tentatively) be constructed in the following way: we take the extant "body of science" and replace each refuted theory in it by a weaker unrefuted version. Thus we increase the putative verisimilitude of each theory, and turn the inconsistent body of scientific theories (accepted$_1$ and accepted$_2$) into a consistent body of accepted$_3$ theories, which we may call, since they can be recommended for use in technology, the "body of technological theories."[2]

[2] If we have two rival, inconsistent theories in the body of science such that neither of them has superseded the other, then their "trimmed," "technological" versions may still be inconsistent. In such cases we may either cautiously choose the maximal consistent subset of the propositions of the two theories, or daringly choose the theory with the more empirical content. [Lakatos' footnote]

Technological choice follows scientific choice: acceptable$_3$ theories are modified versions of acceptable$_1$ and acceptable$_2$ theories: the way to the acceptable$_3$ theories leads through acceptable$_1$ and acceptable$_2$ theories. *For the appraisal of trustworthiness the methodological appraisals are indispensable.* [Lakatos' italics] (1968, p. 183; see also 1978a, pp. 218–19)

[5] For similar criticisms see Hands (1985b), and his response to criticisms (1990) by Ahnonen (1989) and Blaug (1987). See also the conclusion to Hamminga (forthcoming).
[6] If a doctor asks my permission to use a drug on my sick child, I want to know what evidence there is concerning its safety and effectiveness. I will not be satisfied to learn that a theory which implies its safety and effectiveness has shown empirical progress over its predecessor.

This account has three central features, all of which are questionable. First, theoretical science is autonomous. It has nothing to learn from engineering. Lakatos' comments imply that if there were no technological knowledge, scientific theory would not miss a step. Second, engineering knowledge derives from theoretical knowledge through weakening the bold claims of theory. Engineering possesses no autonomy. Its concern is entirely application. There seems to be no such thing as engineering research. Third, there is a radical discontinuity in the methods of theoretical and applied science. In theoretical science, growth and heuristic power are everything, while in engineering, the concern is with reliability.

When stated so baldly, it is easy to see the flaws in this account. First, theoretical science needs technological knowledge not only to build its experimental devices but to judge which claims are unlikely to be responsible for apparent refutations. Second, much of what we call "science" is devoted to determining nitty gritty "facts," such as the density and tensile strength of various materials, the price elasticity of demand for various commodities, or the toxicity of various chemicals. It is unhelpful to have to classify this work as engineering or as theoretical science, but from Lakatos' perspective one must do so. If one classifies such work as engineering, then engineering is not just applying theoretical science. If one classifies it as theoretical science, then theoretical science sometimes seeks facts, not just progress. Either way, there is no radical discontinuity between the methodology evinced by work designed to provide technologically useful results and work in theoretical science.

Lakatos links scientific theory to human concerns only via the speculative connection between corroboration and verisimilitude. His account thus places heavy reliance on the concept of verisimilitude, which was undermined by work published at the time of Lakatos' death.[7] Lakatos distinguishes the formal notion of verisimilitude from an intuitive notion of closeness to the truth:

"*Verisimilitude*" has two distinct meanings which must not be conflated. First it may be used to mean intuitive truthlikeness of the theory; in this sense, in my view, all scientific theories created by the human mind are equally unverisimilar and "occult". Secondly, it may be used to mean a quasi-measure-theoretical difference between the true and false consequences of a theory which we can never know but certainly may guess. (1970, p. 101)

---

[7] See Tichy 1974 and Miller 1974. For an important discussion of the importance of the concept of verisimilitude in the development of Lakatos' philosophy of science, see Hands forthcoming a.

But with the demise of the measure of this measure-theoretical difference, all that is left is the intuitive notion with respect to which in Lakatos' view there is *no* increase in verisimilitude with the growth of science. Moreover, even if the formal notion were sustainable, it would not do the work that assessments of reliability need to do. For example, Lakatos argues that, "*Thus we cannot grade our best available theories for reliability even tentatively, for they are our ultimate standards of the moment.*" Thus there are no grounds for the common belief that physical theories are more trustworthy than economic theories or that it is a better bet that properly maintained bridges will last for another five years than the rate of unemployment in one year will be as predicted. But this is to deny a *datum* that Lakatos ought to be explaining. Philosophy might convince us that we are wrong in matters this fundamental to ordinary life – but it will take an awful lot of convincing.[8]

Lakatos recognizes that actions are based on beliefs, that not all beliefs are equally reliable, and that science has something to tell us about the reliability of beliefs. But he does not want to permit any questions of justification into theoretical science. The unsatisfactory result is the above account of "acceptability$_3$."

But both science and technology need non-comparative assessment of the extent to which various claims are supported by evidence. Without any such "justificationism," Lakatos' science will be as inefficient as Popper's or Friedman's. For, to repeat an argument already made twice before (pp. 167–8 and 187–8) and to be repeated yet again (section 12.1), one needs to judge how well supported claims are in order to modify theories efficiently in the face of apparent disconfirmations. Lakatos would advise scientists to attempt to modify everything[9] and to see which modifications are progressive (1970, pp. 40–1 and p. 45; see also p. 194 above). This is just like the mechanic who repairs a car by replacing its components one by one until it runs again (see pp. 167–8 above). Such a brute force method may sometimes work best, but it is typically a waste of time.

[8] Popper draws a sharp distinction, endorsed by Lakatos, between the psychological "world" of beliefs and the "world" of objective knowledge, and both insist that they are concerned with the growth of *knowledge* not at all with belief, rational or otherwise (see esp. Popper 1972). Even if this sharp divide were defensible, knowledge does bear on belief, desire, and action, and any acceptable account of knowledge should show how this is possible.

[9] Except the hard core, if they wished to remain within the research program. But proliferation of research programs is a good thing, and scientists should be attempting to modify the hard core propositions, too, and to launch new competing research programs.

11.4   Further comments on induction, falsification, and verification

Let me return to the problem of induction sketched in A.11. For it is essential to the wrong turn that Popper and Lakatos take and to the differences between Popper and Lakatos that led to their intellectual parting. Moreover, the issues are central not only in Popper's and Lakatos' philosophy but in most accounts of the nature of science.

Hume's problem of induction follows from the combination of (1) his *empiricism*, which limits empirical evidence to reports of sensory experiences and which treats these reports as self-justified, and of (2) his *foundationalism*, which stipulates that a statement is justified only if it is self-justified or follows from self-justified statements by means of a good argument. Although I shall argue against foundationalism, it is a plausible view of justification. If everything needed justifying, then the process of justification could never get started, but according to most epistemologies, including empiricism, there is a base or foundation that is not itself in need of any further justification. Real justification relies on nothing that is not part of this foundation.

Empiricism and foundationalism jointly create an insoluble problem of induction. There are no valid deductive arguments with general laws as conclusions and nothing but basic statements as premises. But the correct reaction is neither to conclude, with Hume and Popper, that all generalizations are equally unsupported, nor to conclude, with Popper, that support is never needed, nor to conclude, with Lakatos, that induction is a metaphysical leap in the dark to give some point to the game of science. The proper reaction is to take seriously the piecemeal, non-foundational justification of generalizations relative to what one regards as unproblematic background knowledge. This piecemeal "internal" justification is what matters in both science and practice. As Isaac Levi has rightly stressed, justification plays its part in responding to specific challenges and in changing our knowledge (1980; compare Williams 1977 and Popper 1969a, p. 228). We need to justify a particular claim when it is challenged or when we run into conflicts within our set of beliefs.

Popper aims in the right direction, but overshoots the target, and Lakatos' correction is too slight. Popper and Lakatos stress that human knowledge does not rest on any epistemically privileged foundations. Even basic statements are not certain. One decides to accept them, even though such decisions may lead one astray. And one's decisions do not stop there. In Popper's view one advances beyond the uninformative logical falsification of a whole test system by *deciding* to take a large portion of the system as "background knowledge" and to attribute the error to the remaining part. In doing so one may blunder, but Popper believes that without doing so one cannot learn. In Lakatos' view decisions are also unavoidable, although they are less haphazard, for they are determined by the heuristics of a research program.

Scientists need more than mere logical falsification, and, if they want science to grow efficiently, they cannot live with Lakatos' sophisticated methodological falsificationism either. They need a rational basis for deciding which statements to take to be true in order to test others. Popper denies that the extent to which a hypothesis is "corroborated" by the data ever provides such a basis. In his view, one may decide to take claims to be part of background knowledge, but one never has good reason to believe that they are true, probable, or good approximations to the truth. Lakatos will allow a metaphysical presumption of verisimilitude, but he permits this metaphysical conjecture no methodological role within theoretical science and winds up like Popper proscribing the efficient use of knowledge in the acquisition of knowledge.

This question of whether scientists can rely on what they think they have established in learning more about the world goes to the heart of traditional discussions of economic methodology. As argued at length above in chapter 8, the mainstream view of justification in economics, as enunciated by Nassau Senior, John Stuart Mill, John Neville Keynes, or Lionel Robbins, maintains that economics explores the deductive consequences of well-established principles such as "Agents prefer more commodities to fewer." These deductions constitute reasons to accept their conclusions.

So, for example, the strongest argument for the hypothesis of rational expectations is not that it survives hard tests, but that it seems to follow from equilibrium theory, once one accepts the claim that knowledge is, from an economic perspective, a commodity like any other. Consider the famous argument that John Muth offered:

I should like to suggest that expectations, since they are informed predictions of future events, are essentially the same as the predictions of the relevant economic theory....

If the prediction of the theory were substantially better than the expectations of the firms, then there would be opportunities for the "insider" to profit from the knowledge – by inventory speculation if possible, by operating a firm, or by selling a price forecasting service to the firms. The profit opportunities would no longer exist if the aggregate expectation of the firms is the same as the prediction of the theory..." (Muth 1961, pp. 316, 318)

This argument can be reformulated as deductively valid – that is as an argument whose conclusion must be true if all its premises are (see Hausman 1989a, pp. 5–9 and section 14.1 below). The conclusion is that, *ceteris paribus*, the expectations of firms "are essentially the same as the predictions of the relevant economic theory." Some of the premises, such as that few firms run by economists make extraordinary profits or that the expectations of some firms coincide with the predictions of economic theory, are roughly reports of observations. But also involved are premises concerning the advantages of accurate predictions and the accuracy of the predictions of economic theory. These are not observation reports. Some of these premises are questionable, but the argument is still valid, and the premises are largely contained within the background knowledge of a neoclassical economist. If one permits scientists to make use of background knowledge – as one must if there is to be any science – then there are valid arguments with accepted premises for the truth of general scientific conclusions.[10]

If one surrenders foundationalism and countenances conventional falsifications and verifications, one can offer a partial solution to the problem of induction: conclusions that transcend observation can be defended by good arguments if one permits large parts of our purported knowledge to supply the premises. This "solution" turns crucially on reformulating the problem and changing what one expects of justification. Hume would certainly cry "Foul." As a foundationalist, he would insist that the premises themselves have a foundational justification. He would not permit economists to help themselves to the premises in the above argument that are not reports of perceptions. But, if one rejects a foundationalist epistemology, there is no reason to insist that the only admissible premises are observation reports. Popper and especially Lakatos correctly note that epistemology should be concerned with *changes* in our body of knowledge. But, in the repudiation of all justification, which is central in Popper's and Lakatos' philosophy of science, Popper slides backwards toward the foundationalism that he rejects, while Lakatos steps away from assessing theories at all.

11.5   Concluding remarks on Popperian and Lakatosian methodology

Even if the advice to be a better falsificationist is more helpful than I have suggested, it is still unwise to rely on a mistaken philosophical doctrine. Some of Popper's and Lakatos' slogans can be retained, for

---

[10] McCloskey's (1985a, chapter 6) discussion of the sense in which it is metaphorical to claim that knowledge is a commodity is not needed in order to understand why many economists accept the hypothesis of rational expectations without waiting for experimental confirmation, although his points may provide an additional explanation. See section 14.3.

they are consistent with the reasoned consensus within the philosophy of science. Empirical criticism is crucial to science, and scientific theories must, however indirectly, be open to empirical criticism. The most important evidence in support of scientific theories comes from hard tests and analogous explanatory achievements, not from adding up favorable instances. Scientific knowledge is corrigible, and scientists may be forced to surrender even the best established theories. All of these Popperian theses may be used to criticize irresponsible proponents of unsupported theories.[11]

Similarly Lakatos is correct to emphasize the role of heuristics in the development of science, and he may be right to argue that heuristic power is important in theory assessment. One must take seriously the competition between different theories and research programs, and one should not lightly surrender a powerful scientific theory until one can find a better alternative.

But once economists tie themselves to a philosophical system such as Popper's or Lakatos', they will be trapped with its unattractive consequences. A greater measure of philosophical agnosticism among economic methodologists would, I think, be sensible.

Popper's and Lakatos' methodology have dramatic flaws both from the perspective of knowledge acquisition and from the perspective of error avoidance. Popper's decisions about what to regard as unproblematic background knowledge and Lakatos' decisions about how to modify theories must depend on the evidence. Just as engineers want theories to be well supported when they rely on them to build bridges or to manage inflation, so scientists want the theories they use to test other theories to be well supported. We need confirmations to decide which theories to use in practice and to decide which theories to rely on when testing others. And, as I have shown, if we can have falsifications, we can have confirmations, too.

One might object that this critique of Popper and Lakatos is just semantics. Popper writes, for example, "...the decision to ascribe the refutation of a theory to any particular part of it amounts, indeed, to the adoption of a hypothesis; and the risk involved is precisely the same" (1983, p. 189). Perhaps Popper is only denying that scientists can have foundational justifications for their claims. Similarly Lakatos insists that corroboration can be taken as evidence of verisimilitude and emphasizes the importance of corroboration and of the acceptance of theories in the falsification of others.

---

[11] Although, as I argue in the appendix, p. 316, the most effective criticism will be detailed and substantive, not abstract and methodological.

But to regard Popper and Lakatos as granting the importance of supporting evidence in determining which claims theoretical scientists should rely on would eviscerate their philosophies. If Popper conceded that there are non-foundational justifications, he would have to surrender his central theses and his methodological rules. He would even have to reject falsificationism as an apt label for his views, for science would be devoted to seeking verifications as well as falsifications. Essential to Popper's life's work has been not the platitude that scientists should be critical and take disconfirming evidence seriously, but the striking thesis that there is nothing to scientific rationality except conjecture, evidentially unsupported methodological decision, and refutation. The rejection of "justificationism" in theoretical science is just as essential to Lakatos' vision. Lakatos insists that heuristic power and empirically progressive theory changes are all that scientists should be concerned with. I doubt that an enterprise that functioned according to either Popper's or Lakatos' methodology could exist. It would be a poor tool for acquiring knowledge and inefficient in practice.

The last three chapters canvassed the main alternatives to the method *a priori*. None shows how economists can rationally commit themselves to a highly inexact science such as economics. Each of the alternatives runs into internal philosophical difficulties, and (except Koopmans') each implies drastic changes in methodological practice.

Perhaps methodological practice in economics is due for a major overhaul. But first let us look again at that practice to see whether it is as mistaken as has been alleged. Since that practice appears largely to conform to the inexact method *a priori* (summarized on pp. 147-8 above),[1] its appraisal seems to turn on the appraisal of the inexact method *a priori*.

The inexact deductive method has been subject to logical, methodological, and practical criticisms:

1 The logical criticism maintains that inexact (*ceteris paribus*) laws are scientifically illegitimate, because they are meaningless or unfalsifiable. But the arguments of sections 8.2 and 8.3 show that qualified claims are not meaningless or untestable and, as argued above in section 10.2, no interesting scientific claims are logically falsifiable.

2 The methodological criticism of the inexact deductive method is that it is too dogmatic, since it rules out the possibility of disconfirming the basic "laws." Adhering to the deductive method thus, it is alleged, impedes the progress of economics and leads to the sort of *ad hoc* response to apparent disconfirmation characteristic of a degenerating research program. I shall accept this criticism of the *method*, but not of economists, who, despite appearances, do not adhere to it.[2]

---

[1] I have no systematic argument in support of this assertion, and in any case not all branches of economics display the same methodology. In a decade of presenting this view to economists, few have denied that microeconomics appears to conform to Mill's deductive method.

[2] This claim is not true of all economists, for one can surely find maniacal dogmatists among them. Economists are people and as various as people are. I know of no stylistically graceful way to avoid the appearance of overgeneralization.

3 Furthermore, methodological vice is alleged to lead to practical impotence. Even if the inexact laws and the other statements needed to deduce a prediction are true, the unspecified *ceteris paribus* clauses mean that the prediction follows only if there are no interferences. But, since these *ceteris paribus* qualifications are vague, it is hard to know when they are satisfied. And, if economists do not know when they are satisfied, then economic theory is of little use in practice. Even if Milton Friedman's views are mistaken, at least he is concerned about when theories actually work. Does not the reliance on the deductive method render economics useless?

Can these objections be answered? Can the existing methodological practice be defended? Can the apparent dogmatism be justified? Do economists in fact disregard apparent disconfirmations? Can they learn from experience? Can the method of discovery and appraisal employed by economists make it rational to rely on economic theories for policy purposes?

Although the methodological rules of the method *a priori* as presented in chapter 8 cannot be defended, I shall nevertheless defend the existing practices of theory assessment among economists. These practices appear to follow the inexact method *a priori*, but they are, I shall contend, also consistent with the recommendations of standard methods of theory appraisal in the special circumstances with which economists have to cope. Although apparent Millians in practice, economists can be good Bayesians or hypothetico-deductivists in principle.[3] After demonstrating this possibility in the next two sections, I shall sketch the method of theory appraisal economists actually employ, and discuss the large and legitimate role of pragmatic factors in economic theory choice. Only then will I discuss the practical objection. This chapter will conclude by pointing to the real source of dogmatism in economics.

12.1   Apparent dogmatism and the weak-link principle

One of the rules of the method *a priori*, that one should *never* attribute apparent disconfirmations to shortcomings in one's laws, is unacceptable. To this extent, the critics of the deductive method are correct. To follow

---

[3] As noted (p. 146n above), Mill might agree with the critique of what I have formulated as the inexact method *a priori*. It is, in my view, more consistent with the texts to attribute to Mill the view that the invulnerability of the laws is due to the difficulties of disentangling the effects of different causes, not to methodological rule.

such a rule would truly prevent one from discovering inadequacies in one's laws. It would hinder theoretical and empirical progress. Such a rule is objectionably dogmatic.

Yet one should not leap to the conclusion that economists are following this rule. It looks as if they are, but appearances may be misleading. Given the tasks and difficulties economists face, "standard" theories of confirmation, such as the Bayesian and hypothetico-deductivist views, recommend confirmational practice that is almost indistinguishable from what Mill's inexact method *a priori* recommends. The methods of theory appraisal economists employ may be defensible, even though the method *a priori* is indefensible, and economists appear to conform to it.

It is not unacceptably dogmatic to refuse to find disconfirmation of economic "laws" in typical failures of their market predictions. When the anomalies are those cast up by largely uncontrolled observation of complicated market phenomena, it may be more rational to pin the blame on some of the many disturbing causes, which are always present. Since the confidence of economists in the simplifications and *ceteris paribus* assumptions necessary to apply economic theory to actual market phenomena will generally be *much* lower than their confidence in the basic laws, the more likely explanation for the apparent disconfirmation will usually be a failure of the simplifications and *ceteris paribus* assumptions. In consequence, little can be learned about the purported laws from such observations, but the failure will lie in the difficulties of the task, not in any methodological mistake. The possibility of discovering errors in the "laws" of equilibrium theory may be foreclosed by the inadequacies in the data and limitations in economic knowledge, not by unjustifiable methodological fiat.

In responding this way to apparent disconfirmation, economists are implicitly relying on what one might call "the weak-link principle."[4]

(The weak-link principle) When a false conclusion depends on a number of uncertain premises, attribute the mistake to the most uncertain of the premises.

This is but one of many principles that one might use and is neither inviolable nor always appropriate. For example, details concerning the failure of the conclusion might point to a different premise as the culprit. But scientists and non-scientists alike use the weak-link principle (which is why Popperian methodology is revolutionary, since it permits no appraisals of degrees of uncertainty), and it is rationally justifiable to do so. If either G or B is false and the subjective probability of B is less

---

[4] Greg Mougin helped me to clarify my thinking on this point.

than that of G, then (other things being equal) it is more likely that B is false than that G is.

Since the simplifications and *ceteris paribus* clauses needed to derive predictions concerning uncontrolled market phenomena from equilibrium theory are the weak links, mistaken predictions never wind up disconfirming the theory. Hence one can see why Mill's views seemed so plausible, were so easily refuted, yet methodological practice continues apparently to conform to them.

Given their subject matter, economists are bound to look like followers of Mill's deductive method. Powerful tests require either experimentation, with its possibilities of intervention and control, a great deal of knowledge, or fabulous good fortune, and without such tests (or superior alternatives) it would be irrational to react to apparent disconfirmations by surrendering credible hypotheses with great pragmatic attractions. If economists could do experiments, then they could control for disturbances and avoid the complexity of the phenomena with which they are presented non-experimentally. If they knew enough, they could exert much the same control even if experiments were not possible. If, on the other hand, they were blessed with a comparatively simple set of phenomena such as those of celestial motion, then neither the inability to experiment nor the paucity of their knowledge would be crippling. But the combination of these handicaps makes knowledge of economic phenomena hard to garner.

Limitations in the ability to test could make the basic "laws" of economics *de facto* unfalsifiable, even if economists were explicitly employing a Bayesian account of confirmation (A.10.2). Let H be either a "law" of equilibrium theory or a conjunction of such laws and A be the conjunction of all the other statements needed to derive a prediction, e from H. The prior probability of H, $\Pr(H)$ is much larger than the prior probability of A, $\Pr(A)$. In the case of uncontrolled market predictions, $\Pr(A)$ will be tiny. For each of the simplifications and *ceteris paribus* qualifications is improbable, and the probability of the conjunction will be much smaller than that of the separate conjuncts. To keep things simple, although at the cost of a little unreality, let us suppose that H and A are probabilistically independent of each other, so that $\Pr(H.A) = \Pr(H).\Pr(A)$. Personalist Bayesians typically suppose that the relevant probabilities are known, and I shall temporarily join them, although the assumption is fantastic.[5] From Bayes' theorem, the independence of H

[5] But I do not follow Dorling (1979) or Howson and Urbach (1989), pp. 96–102, whose crisper argument for the same conclusion assumes that the likelihoods of H and A, $(\Pr(e/H), \Pr(e/A)$, etc.) are known. See p. 309.

and A, the fact that $Pr(e/H.A)$ is one, and some simple algebra, one can derive the following two equations:

$$Pr(H/e)/Pr(H) = [Pr(A)/Pr(e)] + Pr(\sim A).Pr(e/H.\sim A)/Pr(e) \quad (1)$$

$$Pr(H/\sim e)/Pr(H) = Pr(\sim A).[Pr(\sim e/H.\sim A)/Pr(\sim e)] \quad (2)$$

Since $Pr(A)$ is close to zero and $Pr(\sim A)$ is close to one, the two ratios on the left-hand sides, which one may take as indices of the extent to which H is confirmed or disconfirmed by the observation respectively of e or not e, depend on $Pr(e/H.\sim A)/Pr(e)$ and $Pr(\sim e/H.\sim A)/Pr(\sim e)$. If one believes that, given H, e is much more probable and $\sim e$ is much less probable than given not-H, even if A is not true (that is, if one believes that $Pr(e/H)$ is higher than $Pr(e)$ and $Pr(\sim e/H)$ is lower than $Pr(\sim e)$), then the first ratio will be greater than one, and e will confirm H, while the second ratio will be less than one and $\sim e$ will disconfirm H. But typically economists have little idea what $Pr(e/H.\sim A)$ and $Pr(\sim e/H.\sim A)$ are and no reason to believe the former to be larger than $Pr(e)$ or the latter to be smaller than $Pr(\sim e)$. And if $Pr(e/H.\sim A)$ does not differ from $Pr(e)$ and $Pr(\sim e/H.\sim A)$ does not differ from $Pr(\sim e)$, then H is neither confirmed by e nor disconfirmed by $\sim e$. Given how weakly evidence bears on H, the credible "laws" with which economists begin will be *de facto* non-falsifiable.

12.2   Why believe equilibrium theory?

The deficiencies of market data coupled with the weak-link principle will mimic the inexact method *a priori* only if economists judge the "laws" of equilibrium theory to be much more probable than the simplifications and *ceteris paribus* claims that are needed to test them. But, given the empirical problems with those "laws," can such a judgment be defended? And, if it cannot be defended, then are not economists as unjustifiably dogmatic as critics of the method *a priori* have alleged?

Economists do not regard the "laws" of equilibrium theory as proven or obvious truths. Only some fancy philosophical footwork permits one to regard these "laws" as true (see section 8.2), and it is questionable whether they can be regarded as well-established (see section 8.3). Why then do economists show such apparent confidence in these behavioral postulates? Why do they cling to them in the face of apparent disconfirmation? Is it introspection, as Mill maintains, or everyday experience, as in Robbins' view, or are these assumptions implicit in the very concept of action, as has been maintained by Austrian theorists such as von Mises (1978, p. 8)?

A full answer would take us back to the discussion of the theoretical strategy of economics in chapter 6 or forward to the conclusion of this chapter. But everyday experience and introspection are sufficient to establish that some of these laws, such as diminishing marginal rates of substitution and diminishing returns, are reasonable approximations. Without qualifications and a margin of error, they are false, but, with these, they seem true; and economists have good reason to be committed to them.

Furthermore, each of the laws of equilibrium theory possesses *pragmatic virtues,* for each plays an important role in making the theory mathematically tractable, consistent, and determinate. Indeed, this is about the only virtue of the postulate of constant returns to scale, to which economists are not nearly as committed. Constant returns to scale figures in many economic theories for essentially mathematical reasons, and because it is hoped that its falsity does not do much harm.

Claims such as consumerism and profit maximization are not such good approximations to the truth as are diminishing returns or diminishing marginal rates of substitution, but neither are they as far from the truth as constant returns to scale. There is a great deal of truth to them, and their virtues in permitting determinate mathematical formulations are considerable. Firms pursue all sorts of objectives besides profits, and a usable theory that heeds these facts should be more accurate. But the accuracy would be purchased at the cost of simplicity, and such complications could destroy the normative force equilibrium theory has, when it is coupled with minimal benevolence. In such circumstances pragmatic factors may justifiably be more than empirical tie-breakers. If the empirical benefits of a theory change are small – that is, if (a) a slightly more accurate theory does not serve the purposes of economists appreciably better and (b) economic theorists do not believe that an appreciably more exact economic theory is feasible – then the pragmatic virtues of current theory may be decisive. It may be more sensible to treat other objectives of managers and other behavioral generalizations concerning individuals as disturbing causes that may usually be ignored, even if they are important in particular contexts.[6]

So one finds a combined empirical and pragmatic basis for refusing to regard the basic propositions of equilibrium theory as disconfirmed. Although not necessarily unjustifiably dogmatic, there is a serious risk that economists become so entranced by their models that they overlook

---

[6] Although reminiscent of Friedman's views (section 9.4), this practical thought must be distinguished from Friedman's position. For there is no presumption here that it is a mistake to consider the "realism" of one's assumptions. For a more extensive discussion of the pragmatic factors in theory appraisal, see section 12.4.2 below.

anomalies and are unwilling to consider alternatives. As Mill so presciently remarked (though only when criticizing his father, not his own work!):

We either ought not to pretend to scientific forms, or we ought to study all the determining agencies equally, and endeavour, so far as it can be done, to include all of them within the pale of the science; else we shall infallibly bestow a disproportionate attention upon those which our theory takes into account, while we misestimate the rest, and probably underrate their importance. (1843, 6.8.3)

In my view, the dogmatism of economists, such as it is, lies in an exaggerated commitment to equilibrium theory and to the theoretical strategy underlying it, not in a mistaken view of theory appraisal.

12.3 Do economists follow the inexact deductive method?

Economists have reasonable grounds for judging their basic laws to be less open to revision than are the simplifications and *ceteris paribus* claims that are also needed to derive predictions about market phenomena. It is possible for them to behave in the way that the inexact deductive method recommends, without being committed to a dogmatic view of theory appraisal. The apparent dogmatism may be just the result of the good fortune of beginning with a set of plausible generalizations coupled with the bad luck of being unable to perform good tests.

How can one tell whether economists are committed to the inexact method *a priori* or whether they are good Bayesians or hypothetico-deductivists doing the best they can in the face of poor data? If the only data economists could gather were the results of uncontrolled observations of markets, then we might not be able to find out. But experimentation in economics is not impossible, and in some experiments the "auxiliary assumptions" – the additional premises needed to derive predictions from equilibrium theory – have been sufficiently strong links that the experimental results could actually disconfirm the theory. By examining how economists have responded in such cases, one can determine whether they are proponents of a dogmatic theory of confirmation or whether their apparent dogmatism in non-experimental circumstances is a rational response to weak evidence.

In the next chapter I will consider how economists seem to have responded to a particular set of experimental results. That case study provides evidence that the dogmatism of economists does not stem from a mistaken view of theory appraisal. But first we need to clarify how one can disconfirm the sort of inexact laws upon which economics depends, what role pragmatic factors can play, and how alternative theories might figure in the process of theory appraisal.

12.4   Expected utility theory and its anomalies

To address these questions, I shall go slightly out of the way and consider some of the controversies concerning expected utility theory (section 1.4 above). Expected utility theory has many of the same axioms as equilibrium theory (including completeness, the axiom I shall focus on). It is, like parts of equilibrium theory, a theory of rationality, and it is accepted on the same sort of grounds as equilibrium theory. But unlike equilibrium theory it is readily testable. Consequently it is easier to consider how apparent disconfirmations bear on expected utility theory.

The case for expected utility theory, as for equilibrium theory, *seems* to rest upon an application of the inexact method *a priori.* Consider the following remarks of Daniel Ellsberg:

> However, this proposition [that individuals have cardinal expected utility functions], which we will call the Hypothesis on Moral Expectations, has little inherent plausibility. The major feat of von Neumann and Morgenstern is to show that the Hypothesis on Moral Expectations is *logically equivalent* to the hypothesis that the behavior of given individuals satisfies certain axiomatic restrictions. Since the axioms appear, at first glance, highly "reasonable," the second hypothesis seems far more intuitively appealing than the equivalent Hypothesis on Moral Expectations. It is thus more likely to be accepted on the basis of casual observation and introspection, although the two hypotheses would both be contradicted by exactly the same observations. (Ellsberg 1954, p. 277)

Ellsberg is pointing out that economists sometimes accept theories, such as expected utility theory, because the axioms appear "reasonable." The credibility of the axioms is largely prior to any testing of the theory as a whole.

One cannot regard the axioms of expected utility theory as proven scientific truths, though one may say on their behalf (1) that they are, as Ellsberg notes, "reasonable," (2) that there is some experimental evidence that confirms them, and (3) that, if people do not conform to the axioms of expected utility theory, then, contrary to observation, they will make fools of themselves.[7] These grounds provide the axioms with some credibility, and (via the weak-link principle) they provide the theory

---

[7] I refer to the Dutch-book and money-pump arguments (pp. 16 and 25 above). Those whose beliefs do not conform to the calculus of probabilities can find themselves committed to accepting a series of bets that they must inevitably lose, while those whose preferences are not transitive can find themselves paying for a sequence of exchanges that necessarily leaves them worse off.

with an ability to withstand casual falsifications. But, unlike equilibrium theory, expected utility theory is readily testable, and the assumptions necessary to derive predictions from the theory need not always be weak links.

Psychologists and decision theorists have shown that human behavior sometimes does not conform to the "laws" of expected utility theory. Some of these "anomalies" can be explained as the consequence of non-rational disturbing causes – as, for example, the result of minor peculiarities in how people process information or of people's failure to take small differences in probabilities seriously.[8] Others are more troubling. Let us see how one ought to deal with some of these.

12.4.1 The Allais problem

In the early 1950s Maurice Allais formulated the problem shown in the following table.[9] A ball is drawn from an urn containing one red ball, eighty-nine white balls and ten blue balls. So the probabilities are known. Depending on the color and the choice of A or B in problem I or of C or D in problem II, one receives one of the prizes in the table:

| | | | Payoffs | |
Problems	Choices	Red (1)	White (89)	Blue (10)
I	A	$1mil	$1mil	$1mil
	B	$0	$1mil	$5mil
II	C	$1mil	$0	$1mil
	D	$0	$0	$5mil

Many people are inclined to prefer option A to option B in problem I and to prefer option D to option C in problem II. Even the Bayesian

[8] As in the case of the so-called "common ratio effect." Suppose an agent is offered a choice between two pairs of gambles. In the first the agent chooses between (I) $1 m. with probability 0.75 and $0 otherwise or (II) $5 m. with probability 0.60 and $0 otherwise. In the second the agent chooses between (III) $1 m. with probability 0.05 and $0 otherwise and (IV) $5 m. with probability 0.04 and $0 otherwise. Many prefer I to II and IV to III, which is irrational not only according to expected utility theory, but also according to many of the alternatives to it. See Allais 1952, pp. 90–2, Hagen 1979, pp. 283–97, MacCrimmon and Larsson 1979, pp. 350–9, and Kahneman and Tversky 1979, p. 267. The particular example is quoted from Levi 1986, p. 46. My discussion is heavily influenced by Levi's essay.
[9] See Allais and Hagen 1979, Savage 1972, pp. 101–2, or Levi 1986, p. 39. The formulation here follows Levi and Savage.

statistician, Leonard Savage, was at first so inclined (Savage 1972, p. 103). If these choices reflect preferences, then they violate the independence principle, for the only difference between the choice pairs is in the magnitude of the payoff if a white ball is drawn, which should be irrelevant to the choices because it does not depend on whether A or B in problem I or C or D in problem II is selected. Thus, A should be preferred to B if and only if C is preferred to D.[10] Yet many individuals are unpersuaded. In one view,

In Situation X [Problem I], I have a choice between $1,000,000 for certain and a gamble where I might end up with nothing. Why gamble? The small probability of missing the chance of a lifetime to become rich seems very unattractive to me.

In Situation Y, there is a good chance that I will end up with nothing no matter what I do. The change [sic] of getting $5,000,000 is almost as good as getting $1,000,000 so I might as well go for the $5,000,000 and choose Gamble 4 [D] over Gamble 3 [C]. (Slovic and Tversky 1974, p. 370)

If expected utility theory is a correct normative theory of rationality, then this reasoning must be fallacious or irrational.[11]

Allais devised the example as a criticism of the normative adequacy of expected utility theory not as an empirical refutation. So, even if people do stubbornly choose A in problem I and D in problem II, one can still ask whether these choices are evidence against subjective expected utility theory or evidence of human irrationality. The latter view would be supported, if one could find some obvious sign of irrationality, but there is none. If many people are inclined to choose A over B and D over C, and a variety of thoughtful decision theorists are prepared to defend the rationality of choosing A and D, such as Allais himself, Levi (1986), or Sugden (1986), then there are significant grounds for questioning the independence condition as a normative condition of rationality.

If one is concerned with independence as a generalization about how people actually choose, then it might seem that it does not matter *why*

---

[10]   Alternatively, let V be the utility of $5 m., U be the utility of $1 m., and 0 be the utility of $0. Then $EU(A) = U$, $EU(B) = 0.89 U + 0.1 V$, $EU(C) = 0.11 U$ and $EU(D) = 0.1 V$. If A is preferred to B, then $EU(A) > EU(B)$. So $U > 0.89 U + 0.1 V$, or $0.11 U > 0.1 V$. So if A is preferred to B, then C must be preferred to D. These choices violate the independence condition only if one takes choice to reflect preference and regards the monetary outcomes as standing in some monotone relation to preferences (utilities). If, for example, the outcome of choice B when a red ball is drawn is not just $0 but intense regret, then these choices are consistent with expected utility theory. See for example Eells 1982, p. 39. But "saving" expected utility theory by redefining the outcomes greatly decreases the content of the theory.

[11]   As initially posed, Allais' problem was not a controlled experiment; and, even when repeated as a controlled experiment, it has flaws since it examines what people say they would choose rather than how people actually choose. But for the purposes of this discussion these flaws are unimportant.

people make these choices. The fact that they do is sufficient to show that they do not act in accordance with expected utility theory. But predictions do not follow from expected utility theory all by itself, and the diagnosis of the reasoning responsible for the anomalous decisions may still be important. Since we believe that people's choices are influenced by their reasoning and that fallacious reasoning is unstable, such a diagnosis remains of the utmost importance. For paradoxes such as Allais' call for fundamental modification of expected utility theory as an inexact positive theory of choice behavior only if the choices cannot reasonably be attributed to disturbing causes of secondary importance. Indeed, there is another regard in which examples such as these may have *less* force in an empirical critique of expected utility theory than in a challenge to its normative adequacy, for it might be objected that choice problems such as these are unusual and unimportant.

Are people's choices in the Allais problem evidence against subjective expected utility theory or do they show that there is some disturbing cause? There is little evidence of irrationality, but perhaps the interference might be some further rational factor. One might want to *supplement* subjective expected utility theory with some further *rational* tendency counteracting the independence principle. Expected utility theory is falsified only if such a hypothesis is inferior to one which denies rather than merely qualifies one or more of its "laws." What makes this issue more tractable than those raised by the myriad of apparent "falsifications" of equilibrium theory revealed by market data is the possibility of experimentation. Instead of an impenetrable mess in which one can do no better than to hold on to what is independently plausible, one has a partially penetrable mess from which one may learn how to correct or improve what one begins with.

12.4.2   Qualification versus disconfirmation

One important effect of mitigating the empirical difficulties that stand in the way of testing inexact claims is to make the conceptual difficulties clearer. To explain away an apparent disconfirmation by changing an auxiliary hypothesis or citing a disturbing cause (whether rational or non-rational) is to change one's applied theory in response to apparent disconfirmation. The new applied theory has different empirical consequences than the old. Hence it is wrong to say that those who always cite some interference to explain away unfavorable evidence ignore disconfirmations. Perhaps they do not react correctly, but they do react.

Disturbing causes, like all causes, have their (inexact) laws, and to explain away a disconfirmation by citing an interference may not be purely *ad hoc* (at least in Lakatos's first two senses (1970, p. 112n; see p. 196 above.) The disturbing cause cited is to be expected in similar circumstances, and the modification has some non-vacuous empirical content – although the complexity of the phenomena may make testing impossible. The more general the disturbing cause, the more contentful and less *ad hoc* is the hypothesis that cites it.

Once one has largely ruled out failures of rationality, the question, "Does the Allais paradox reveal mistakes in expected utility theory, or does it merely reveal a mistake in some simplification or the influence of some disturbing cause?" turns out to be less straightforward than it might appear. The right question in a well-controlled experimental context is not "Is the theory disconfirmed or is there an interference?", but "What should one do about this disconfirmation? Should one add a qualification to the theory (which might in many contexts harmlessly be ignored), or should one revise the theory in some other more fundamental way?" One cannot draw any sharp line between qualifications and modifications, but one does not need to do so either. In both cases empirical evidence exerts some control over theory change. *The difference is pragmatic: qualifications can often be dropped, while modifications leave a permanent mark.* The significant question is whether theorists can, for particular purposes, ignore the necessary changes and employ the original theory.

Another way of grasping the issue would be to ask how one is supposed to know, in Mill's terminology, that equilibrium theory has captured the "*greater*" causes of economic phenomena.[12] Introspection provides evidence that consumerism is a significant causal factor affecting economic phenomena, but it does not give one solid reason to believe that consumerism is a more important cause of economic behavior than, for example, the attitudes toward risk that seem to influence choices in the Allais paradox.

How can one decide whether a disturbing cause is "major" or "minor" and whether one may justifiably regard expected utility theory as capturing the "greater causes" of choice behavior? The quantitative statistical question, "How much of the variation in some dependent variable is due (in the actual complicated circumstances) to a particular independent variable?" is subject to fairly direct, though fallible statistical investigation. But Mill's concern in distinguishing major and minor causes is not simply quantitative. "Major" causes are fundamental and have universal scope, while minor causes are more superficial and have narrower scope. So the decision whether to deal with an empirical anomaly by changing one's theory or by citing a disturbing cause is tantamount to the decision

---

[12]   I am indebted for this way of thinking about this question to Joseph Stiglitz.

whether to treat the factors mentioned by one's current theory and only those factors as the "major" causes. If expected utility theory leaves out a major cause that is responsible for the Allais paradox, then a serious theory change is called for. If it encompasses all the major causes, then anomalies such as the Allais paradox only call for qualifications, which for many purposes can be ignored. The decision depends on both pragmatic and empirical factors.

In its pragmatic aspect this question demands that one be clear about both practical and theoretical *employments* and *aspirations* for the theory. What does one want the theory for and what sort of theoretical grasp of the subject matter does one think possible?[13] Although this way of thinking is most congenial to instrumentalists, it carries no instrumentalist commitments. For realists can also think about the cognitive jobs they want particular theories to do and how well they think such jobs can be done. Some of the pragmatic virtues of the axioms of expected utility theory of the "laws" of equilibrium theory have already been mentioned: they lead to a mathematically tractable and determinate theory. But there are other pragmatic virtues, to which I will return shortly, which are related to the fact that these are also theories of rationality.

The decision whether to qualify or to modify also hinges on the empirical scope, frequency, and distribution of the apparent disconfirmations experimenters have uncovered. If, for example, the disconfirmations are not very important in the domain that is of the greatest theoretical and practical importance, and one does not believe that a much better theory is likely to be found (which, obviously will depend on what alternatives have been suggested), then it would be reasonable to account for the disconfirmations in terms of "interferences." If, on the other hand, the qualifications need to be invoked often and one believes that considerably more exactness is possible, then it would be more reasonable to seek to modify the theory decisively.

The presence and promise of alternatives also influences one's theory choices. Indeed, it is fair to say (following to some extent Lakatos' views, p. 203 above) that what converts anomalies or difficulties such as Allais' paradox into disconfirming evidence demanding fundamental theory modification is the formulation of alternatives, which accommodate such

---

[13] "the critics of the simplified psychology used by economic theorists have made little headway in bringing forth substitute principles. I do not believe they ever will. Their strictures are valid as *limitations* on the familiar reasoning, not as negations. The principles of the established economics are partial statements, but sound as far as they go, and they go about as far as general principles can be carried." (Knight 1921, p. 145) This response seems to suppose that the limitations are unsystematic errors. See 15.3 below. The weight of these factors varies depending on the extent to which one is a pure theorist or also an economic actor. Advertisers pay much more attention to human foibles than economic theorists do.

anomalies within a theory that can do the job done by expected utility theory.

At this point a distinctive element enters the picture about which I will have more to say below in section 15.3. For one job that expected utility theory, like ordinal utility theory, does is provide a theory of rationality. Should the fact that utility theory is a theory of rationality affect its empirical appraisal?

The mere suggestion seems ludicrous. To argue that utility theory is a good theory of how people actually behave because it is also a theory of how they ought to behave seems like the argument that people do not cheat on their taxes because they morally ought not to do so. The argument seems to presuppose what is in question, which is whether people behave as (according to this theory) they ought rationally to behave.

But this response does not settle the matter. Irrationality can be costly, and the costs of irrational behavior may make it unstable. Although people's behavior diverges from that predicted by expected utility theory, it may be that there can be no better general theory precisely because of the instability of these divergences. Furthermore, people's behavior is influenced by its theoretical description. There is evidence that students who learn economics also learn to conform to utility theory (Marwell and Ames 1981). So the defense of utility theory as a first approximation may be self-supporting, while espousing non-rational theories of choice may be self-defeating. The fact that utility theory is a theory of rationality seems to provide some grounds to believe that it is a correct theory of how people actually choose.

Furthermore the fact that utility theory is a theory of rationality may provide pragmatic reasons not to give it up and to accommodate anomalies via qualifications or interferences. There are two quite different pragmatic considerations here. First, the fact that utility theory is a theory of rationality permits explanations in economics to be reason-giving explanations in addition to causal explanations (see 15.3 and A.14.2). Explanations in economics justify as well as explain, and they con-sequently depend on the same factors that economic agents focus on and find of interest. A quite different sort of explanation might be more successful empirically, but the costs of severing the links between economics and "folk psychology" (A.14.2) and the concerns of economic agents are not trivial and give one reason to favor current theory or some alternative that is simultaneously an empirical theory of choice and a theory of rationality.

But there is an even more striking pragmatic argument in favor of preserving a theory of rationality as one's basic theory of actual choices. For one might reasonably hold that, when people behave irrationally, the theorist's response should not be to revise utility theory, but to encourage agents to change their behavior. Those who are unclear on what rationality requires or who are lazy or ineffective in their efforts to conform need reeducation. This educative function of expected utility theory provides a good pragmatic reason for accepting it, unless there is a competitor that is much better supported by the evidence or is better able to guide choice. I am not proposing that theorists pretend that people behave according to expected utility theory even when they do not do so. But the educative function of a theory of choice gives one reason to describe the divergences as lapses or interferences and to retain expected utility theory (or some alternative with the same normative aspect) rather than opting for a non-normative alternative. This reason may not be decisive, for the empirical advantages of a non-normative alternative might be overwhelming. But such pragmatic grounds are neither trivial nor irrational.[14]

The reasoning involved in such theory assessment, with its complex mixture of empirical and pragmatic elements differs decisively from the inexact method *a priori*. What drives economists to regard interferences as minor disturbing causes is not the manifest truth of the basic axioms nor any methodological rule prohibiting revisions of them, but the nature of the disconfirmations coupled with the pragmatic attractions of accepted theory.

12.4.3 *Incomplete preferences: Levi's alternative*

It is useful to consider an argument for an alternative to expected utility theory to illustrate how this complicated process of theory assessment might work. There are several alternatives to expected utility theory which purport to inherit its normative and predictive virtues and to accommodate anomalous examples, of which Allais' problem is but one instance: regret theory, theories which surrender the independence principle, such as Edward McClennen's (1983) and Mark Machina's (1987), theories which surrender completeness, such as Isaac Levi's (1980), and theories which surrender independence and completeness such as Edward McClennen's (1990). I shall discuss only one of these, Levi's proposal, not because it is clearly superior to the others, but because it brings out the methodological points clearly. Levi's views, unlike Machina's, for example, have little following within economics, but the issue here is the structure of rational criticism and theory change, not the extent to which

---

[14] In addition there are less defensible links between the commitment of economists to utility theory and the fact that utility theory is a theory of rationality. When even pigeons and rats conform to utility theory, the unstated argument is that people cannot be such fools as not to conform. See Battalio, Green, and Kagel 1981, Battalio, Kagel, and Green 1979, Kagel and Battalio 1975, and Rachlin *et al.* 1981. To admit to our irrationality may be embarrassing.

economists have actually endorsed this criticism and change. For a case study concerning how orthodox economists *behave* in the face of apparently disconfirming evidence see chapter 13.

As stressed above in section 1.1.2, one apparently weak link in both utility theory and expected utility theory is completeness or comparability – that among any two options x and y a rational agent will either prefer x to y or y to x or will be indifferent. If asked whether one prefers x to y, people are sometimes inclined to say, "I don't know." The related claim that agents can and should form precise subjective probability judgments, which is required by completeness of preferences over gambles, is similarly dubious.

The standard defense of completeness assumes that choice demonstrates preference. What one chooses is what one prefers. But, as discussed before (section 1.3), the standard defense gives rise to spurious intransitivities and will not do. The only remaining grounds upon which to accept completeness are that it is a reasonable approximation or a harmless idealization that permits development of a simple and systematic theory of rationality. Levi argues that paradoxes such as Allais' – as well as a pragmatic perspective on inquiry – suggest that this idealization is not harmless.

In Levi's view, people are often unable to rank options with respect to expected utility, owing to indeterminacies in their utility functions or in their probability judgments. Given this inability, they *ought to* suspend judgment, as indeed people often do, rather than making arbitrary presumptions. After screening out those options that are unambiguously inferior with respect to expected utility for *any* admissible utility function or probability judgment, one should choose on the basis of secondary criteria such as security. Consider the Allais problem again (p. 213 above). Option A, $1 million for sure, obviously beats option B on this criterion of security. It is, however, less obvious that D is more secure than C, although Levi argues that it is.[15]

---

[15] The worst outcome in both C and D is $0, but the second worst outcomes are, respectively, $1 m. and $5 m. Thus, Levi argues, D has the higher security level. But if one *improves* option D by offering ten dollars if a red ball is drawn, then, in Levi's view, individuals would prefer C to the improvement of D. Although there is no preference inconsistency here, for C is not ranked with respect to D or the improvement of D, and the improvement of D would be preferred to D (unless the agent overlooks small differences (see Levi 1989, 1991)), this result is nevertheless hard to believe. Further criticisms are presented in Maher 1989 and Maher and Kashima 1991. It is, however, possible to calculate security levels in other ways, and it is also consistent with Levi's general pragmatic approach to countenance the existence of other secondary or tertiary principles of choice apart from security, which might lead to the choice of D over C. One might, for example, regard C and D as essentially tied with respect to expected utility and security and employ a tertiary criterion recommending choosing the alternative with the largest possible gain.

Levi argues that his account of rational choice, which surrenders ordering and sharply distinguishes preference and choice, accounts for a wide range of choice behavior that conflicts with expected utility theory and in which (as in the Allais paradox) many subjects refuse to see the error of their ways. Furthermore, permitting indeterminacies in probability judgments and utilities is not *ad hoc*, but is required by a pragmatic theory of inquiry that takes ignorance seriously, and the theory that results is neither normatively nor empirically empty (Seidenfeld, Schervisch, and Kadane 1987). If these claims are defensible – which I leave to others to judge – then Levi has presented a strong case *disconfirming* expected utility theory.

Levi's alternative cannot be classified unambiguously as a fundamental theory change, although this is clearly how Levi would classify it (compare Kaplan 1989). Since expected utility theory is preserved as a special case within Levi's theory, when one has precise preferences and precise probability judgments, one might plausibly argue that Levi is offering a theory that includes *more* causal factors and thus *supplements* rather than replaces expected utility theory. Yet Levi believes that circumstances in which agents can be treated as if they had precise preferences and precise probability judgments are exceptional rather than paradigm cases and that failures of completeness should not be treated as unusual complications.[16]

There was never any question of an empirical *proof* of completeness, let alone of its importance to the explanation of choice behavior. At best it appeared a reasonable approximation. Levi argues that these appearances are misleading. The example shows that theories that are regarded as inexact and that are defended by means of what looks like Mill's deductive method are not fully immunized against refutation.

12.5 The economists' deductive method

We are now in a position to formulate a schema sketching a "deductive" method of theory appraisal that is both justifiable and consistent with existing theoretical practice in economics, insofar as that practice aims to appraise theories empirically. For, as I stressed above (sections 5.4, 6.3, and 6.4), a great deal of theoretical work in economics is concerned with conceptual exploration, not with empirical theorizing.

---

[16] The example may make it seem as if the choice between modification and qualification is just a choice of terminology. But even in a case such as this one, the choice affects what one takes the "ordinary" case to be. In other circumstances, one may face a choice between distinct theory modifications, some of which are more naturally described as qualifications than others.

To facilitate the comparison of what I am calling the economists' deductive method with Mill's inexact method *a priori*, I have juxtaposed sketches of the two methods below.

1. *Borrow* proven (*ceteris paribus*) laws concerning the operation of relevant causal factors.

2. *Deduce* from these laws and statements of initial conditions, simplifications, etc., predictions concerning relevant phenomena.

3. *Test* the predictions.

4. If the predictions are correct, then regard the whole amalgam as confirmed. If the predictions are not correct, then *judge* (a) whether there is any mistake in the deduction, (b) what sort of interferences occurred, (c) how central the borrowed laws are (how major the causal factors they identify are and whether the set of borrowed laws should be expanded or contracted.

1. *Formulate* credible (*ceteris paribus*) and pragmatically convenient generalizations concerning the operation of relevant causal factors.

2. *Deduce* from these generalizations, and statements of initial conditions, simplifications, etc., predictions concerning relevant phenomena.

3. *Test* the predictions.

4. If the predictions are correct, then regard the whole amalgam as confirmed. If the predictions are not correct, then *compare* alternative accounts of the failure on the basis of explanatory success, empirical progress, and pragmatic usefulness.

Note that the economist's deductive method is as much a repudiation of the inexact method *a priori* as it is a revision of it, for it is consistent with standard views of confirmation. What justifies continuing to call it a deductive method, despite its concessions that the inexact laws with which one begins are not proven and that they can be refuted by economic evidence? First (in sharp contrast to the methodological views discussed in the last three chapters), independent confirmation of the basic inexact laws plays a crucial role. Second, refutation is largely proscribed, albeit by the circumstances, not by methodological rule. Since economists are typically dealing with complex phenomena in which many simplifications are required and in which interferences are to be expected, the evidential weight of predictive failure will be very small. It will rarely be rational to surrender a well-supported hypothesis because of a predictive failure in circumstances such as these. The Allais problem atypically exaggerates the weight of evidence because of its quasi-experimental basis.

The simplified account of the economist's deductive method sketched above follows the hypothetico-deductive method precisely in steps 2 and 3 and is consistent with it in steps 1 and 4, where it is merely more specific (see section A.10.1). The HD method is mute on where hypotheses to be tested come from and permits one to begin with a theory with known empirical and pragmatic virtues.

The fourth step of the economist's deductive method abbreviates section 12.4.2 above. It is consistent with the HD method, which merely requires that the correctness or incorrectness of the predictions contribute to the appraisal of the hypothesis tested. The empirical grounds for discriminating between theories in the economist's deductive method remind one of Lakatos' formulations, and they direct one to consider what theory modifications or qualifications best explain the data and best increase the confirmed empirical content of the theory. Given the acute *practical* Quine-Duhem problem in economics (pp. 177–8 and 306–7), which is a consequence of how dubious are the various auxiliary hypotheses necessary in order to perform most tests, it will be extremely difficult to judge theory modifications on empirical grounds. Pragmatic grounds may consequently play a large role. For if one cannot tell which theory modification is empirically better, it is sensible to choose the one that has greater pragmatic virtues – that is, the one that it is easier to use, gives sharper advice, lends itself to cleaner mathematical expression, and so forth.[17]

Yet, when experiments are possible and when alternatives are available that inherit the initial credibility of the accepted theory and offer similar pragmatic advantages, then the economist's deductive method favors theory change. If one studies how economists respond to experimental anomalies, one can see that they are not committed to a dogmatic view of confirmation, such as the inexact method *a priori*. So I will argue in the case study in the next chapter. The dogmatism one does find in these responses results more from a commitment to an image of economics as a separate science than from any theory of confirmation. Many modifications are proposed, discussed, and tested. Although Levi's particular alternative to expected utility theory has not found favor, there are extensive discussions in leading economics journals of other alternatives.

12.6   The deductive method and the demands of policy

The one remaining criticism of the deductive method is practical: in following a deductive method, economists allegedly condemn their work

---

[17] Although there is one Lakatosian element in this method, it is very different from Lakatos' sophisticated methodological falsificationism or his methodology of scientific research programs. For there is no hard core and no rejection of justification. Hypotheses can be tested rather than merely compared. Novel predictions are not the only relevant evidence. Pragmatic concerns have a powerful role to play.

to practical futility. But this criticism is specious. The economist's deductive method does not rule out theory changes when doing so will increase the empirical content of the theory – on the contrary it mandates them. Nor does it – or any other variety of the deductive method – condemn empirical generalization. Mill is explicit in endorsing common sense on this point: if something works, use it (though with due caution). Moreover, the development of empirical generalizations, for which no deductive derivation is currently possible, is of great *theoretical* importance, too, for such generalizations constitute the most important *data* for which theories need to account. There are, as we saw in section 6.5, methodological rules against employing *ad hoc* generalizations – that is generalizations that do not permit rational choice explanations, that do not give pride of place to consumerism, that have narrow scope, or that rule out the possibility of equilibrium. But these result from the vision of economics as a separate science, not from any distinctive views of theory appraisal.

The deductive method does not recommend repudiating useful empirical generalizations or abandoning accurate predictive devices. Instead it condemns naive reliance on unreliable empirical generalizations and offers an *additional* means of getting a predictive grasp on the phenomena. Whether the best way to aim an artillery piece is by firing it in various circumstances and fitting a curve to the data points or by calculating from fundamental laws is an empirical question. Rather than forbidding the first procedure, the deductive method offers a way of improving, correcting, and extending the results one gets by it.

If the standard theory of the firm has all the empirical virtues claimed for it by Milton Friedman and others, then one should make use of it for relevant practical purposes. The economist's deductive method does not recommend the sort of theoretical purism that spurns useful tools that are not in perfect condition or perfectly understood. But by considering the realism of a theory's assumptions – the constituent causal processes and their laws – one may be able to get some guidance concerning when the predictions of the theory are likely to break down and concerning how to modify the theory in the face of apparent disconfirmation.

12.7   Conclusion – economics as a separate science

What may stand in the way of developing generalizations that are of practical utility is not the deductive method, *per se*, but Mill's vision of economics as a *separate* science, as a discipline that is concerned with a domain in which a small number of causal factors predominate. This vision of economics as a separate science, although not often expressed in this terminology, remains, or so I argued in chapter 6, central to contemporary microeconomics. The whole project of microeconomics and general equilibrium theory presupposes that a single set of causal factors underlies economic phenomena and determines their broad features. Other relevant causal factors are regarded as disturbing causes. Their effects are allegedly significant with respect to a narrow range of cases; while, without its many specific qualifications, the basic theory is still purportedly a good general guide. As noted briefly above (pp. 145–6), Mill makes such a pragmatic case:

the ascertainment of the effect due to the one class of circumstances alone is a sufficiently intricate and difficult business to make it expedient to perform it once for all, and then allow for the effect of the modifying circumstances; especially as certain fixed combinations of the former are apt to recur often, in conjunction with every-varying circumstances of the latter class. (1843, 6.9.3)

To surrender the vision of economics as a separate science would be to part with the grand vision that a single theory could provide one with a basic grasp of the subject matter. The temper and character of modern economics still embodies the Millian vision of the discipline as a separate science.

Can one better understand economies by applying equilibrium theory, or would economists do better to develop a variety of different theories with smaller domains and a larger repertory of causes? The latter alternative would lower the barriers between economics and other social sciences, since the causal factors with which sociologists and psychologists have been concerned may be important in particular economic subdomains. Although the question is an empirical one, the answer also depends on the objectives and uses of economic theories. For a "separate science" such as general equilibrium theory has enormous aesthetic appeal, heuristic power, and normative force, none of which economists will willingly sacrifice unless the more fragmented and less purely "economic" alternatives have similar virtues and fit the data much better. So long as the data consist of noisy economic statistics, I doubt that the sacrifice could ever appear worth while.

But, with the development of experimental economics and with increasingly sophisticated field research, this situation *may* change; and a generation from now central "economic" theories may have more structural similarities to the sorts of theories favored by institutionalist economists[18] than to contemporary microeconomics and general equilibrium theory. But I have no crystal ball, and it may be impossible to generate significant theories that provide any appreciably better grip on the data than does equilibrium theory. In that case, economics will go on as it has; and critics may continue to complain that economists are not behaving as responsible scientists should. But before criticizing prematurely, they should recognize that the apparent dogmatism can arise from the circumstances in which economists find themselves – blessed with behavioural postulates that are plausible, powerful, and convenient, and cursed with the inability to learn much from experience.

Economists are committed to equilibrium theory because they regard its basic laws as credible and as possessing heuristic and pragmatic virtues. Their response to anomalous market data, which mimics the inexact method *a priori*, is not illegitimately dogmatic. It is, on the contrary, fully consistent with standard views of theory assessment, once one takes account of how bad these data are. The problem is not a moral failing among economists – their inability to live up to their Popperian convictions – but a reflection of how hard it is to learn about complex phenomena if one does not know a great deal already and cannot do controlled experiments.

[18] The institutionalists are a school of American economists, who have been influenced by the German historical school, by developments in the natural sciences, and by the philosophical work of the American pragmatists. Their theorizing has been much shallower and focused on particular institutional structures. See Gruchy 1947 and, for methodological distinctions, Wilber and Harrison 1978, and Dugger 1979. The *Journal of Economic Issues* is largely devoted to work by institutionalists. Herbert Simon remarks, "It is not clear that all of the writings, European and American, usually lumped under this rubric have much in common, or that their authors would agree with each other's views. At best, they share a conviction that economic theory must be reformulated to take account of the social and legal structures amidst which market transactions are carried out." (1979, p. 499) There are also many intriguing contemporary alternatives, although none has a wide following. Some striking and programmatic texts include Cyert and March 1963, Etzioni 1986, 1988, Granovetter 1981, 1985, Leibenstein 1976, Nelson and Winter 1974, 1982, North 1990, Smith 1990, and Williamson 1985. See also section 14.2.3 below.

13   On dogmatism in economics: the case of preference reversals

What happens when economists come across disconfirming experimental evidence? In this chapter, I will discuss one fascinating case. I chose it because of its tractability and because the anomalous results have been discussed repeatedly in prominent economic journals. It is more an illustration than an argument for the interpretation of economic methodology defended above. Although it provides some evidence that economists are not committed to the inexact method *a priori*, one case obviously proves nothing.

13.1   The discovery of preference reversals

No economist is under any illusion that the axioms of utility theory are exceptionless universal laws, but utility theory may still be a reasonable first approximation that is useful in predicting and explaining behavior. What should be worrisome to economists would be evidence that people's choices differ *systematically* from those predicted by utility theory.

One way in which people's choice behavior does apparently deviate systematically from that predicted by utility theory involves so-called "preference reversals." Paul Slovic and Sarah Lichtenstein describe the discovery of this phenomenon as follows:

The impetus for this study was our observation in our earlier 1968 article that choices among pairs of gambles appeared to be influenced primarily by probabilities of winning and losing, whereas buying and selling prices were primarily determined by the dollar amounts that could be won or lost....Subjects setting a price on an attractive gamble appeared to start with the amount to win and adjust it downward to take into account the probability of winning and losing, and the amount that could be lost. The adjustment process was relatively imprecise, leaving the price response greatly influenced by the starting point payoff. Choices, on the other hand, appeared to be governed by different rules.

In our 1971 article, we argued that, if the information in a gamble is processed differently when making choices and setting prices, it should be possible to construct pairs of gambles such that people would choose one member of the pair but set a higher price on the other. We proceeded to construct a small set of pairs that clearly demonstrated this predicted effect. (1983, p. 597)

Lichtenstein and Slovic called the bets with a high probability of winning "*P*-bets," while bets with large prizes are "$-bets." Given their earlier conjectures, Lichtenstein and Slovic predicted that among pairs of bets with positive expected value individuals who choose the *P*-bets should often be willing to pay more for $-bets. For example, consider the *P*-bet (*P**) consisting of a gamble in which one wins $4.00 if a roulette wheel comes up with any number except 1 (that is, with a probability of 35/36) or loses $1.00 if the roulette wheel comes up 1 (that is with a probability of 1/36). Lichtenstein and Slovic paired it with the $-bet ($*) in which one has an 11/36 chance to win $16.00 and a 25/36 chance to lose $1.50. The expected monetary value of the two gambles (that is the sum of the prices times the probabilities) are respectively $3.86 and $3.85. Lichtenstein and Slovic made the conditional prediction that if individuals preferred the *P*-bets in pairs such as (*P**,$*), they would be likely to pay *more* for the $-bets. I shall call such reversals "predicted." A reversal in which an individual prefers a $-bet and prices a *P*-bet higher is "unpredicted."

13.1.1   The first experiments

In their essay, "Reversals of Preference Between Bids and Choices in Gambling Decisions," (1971) Lichtenstein and Slovic report the results of three experiments in which subjects were first asked to choose among bets with approximately the same expected value such as *P** and $* above. Then the subjects were distracted with other tasks before they were asked to put a price on bets presented to them one at a time. In the first two experiments, subjects were paid for participating, and there was no actual gambling. In the third experiment, the bets were played, and the subjects were paid their winnings. In the pricing part of Experiment I, subjects were asked to suppose that they owned tickets to play the lotteries and to state the minimum price they would accept to sell their tickets. In Experiment II, subjects were asked to state the highest price they would pay to purchase each lottery. In Experiment III, choices were all repeated three times (with prompting concerning prior choices) and a special device (to be described shortly) was used to give subjects strong incentives to state accurately the minimum selling prices for lotteries. In the first experiment nearly three-quarters of the subjects reversed their preference *every time* they chose the *P*-bet in the pairwise comparison. There were few unpredicted reversals. In Experiment II the results were not as striking, but more than two-thirds of the subjects had a higher rate of conditional predicted reversals than of conditional unpredicted reversals. In Experiment III, which used only fourteen subjects, six always made conditional predicted reversals, five sometimes made them, and unpredicted reversals were infrequent. As Lichtenstein's and Slovic's hypotheses concerning choices and valuations of gambles implied, reversals were most frequent when the loss in the $-bet was larger than in the P-bet, which led subjects to prefer the P-bet more often, and when the win in the $-bet was large relative to the win in the P-bet, which led individuals to bid more for the $-bet.

To encourage subjects to reveal their true minimum selling price Lichtenstein and Slovic arranged in the third experiment to purchase the bet from a subject whenever a chance mechanism generated a purchase price exceeding the subject's selling price. If a subject announced a selling price higher than the probabilistically generated purchase price, then the subject would play the lottery instead. Given this arrangement, there is nothing to be gained by understating one's minimum selling price and there may be real costs, for doing so may result in selling the lottery for less than it is worth to one. To overstate the minimum selling price again brings no additional revenue, and doing so may lead one to play the lottery when one would prefer to sell it at the price offered. This method is due to Becker, deGroot, and Marschak 1964.

In the case of bets with negative expected values and improbable but large losses, Lichtenstein and Slovic predicted the opposite reversals among those preferring the $-bets to the P-bets. This implication was not tested in the experiments reported in the 1971 paper. But when the above results were replicated in a later paper (Lichtenstein and Slovic 1973) this additional implication was also confirmed. In this later paper, the experiment was carried out on the balcony of the Four Queens Casino in Las Vegas, and the experimental subjects, who included professional gamblers, played with their own money (Lichtenstein and Slovic 1973)! Once again Lichtenstein and Slovic found frequent conditionally predicted reversals and infrequent unpredicted reversals (see also Lindman 1971).

13.1.2 Apparent significance

Assuming that individuals prefer more money to less, preference reversal apparently involves gross choice inconsistency.[1] As the economists

---

[1] But see below, p. 237.

David Grether and Charles Plott point out,

Taken at face value the data are simply inconsistent with preference theory and have broad implications about research priorities within economics....It suggests that no optimization principles of any sort lie behind even the simplest of human choices and that the uniformities in human choice behavior which lie behind market behavior may result from principles which are of a completely different sort from those generally accepted....

Notice this behavior is not simply a violation of some type of expected utility hypothesis. The preference measured one way is the *reverse* of preference measured another and seemingly theoretically compatible way. If indeed preferences exist and if the principle of optimization is applicable, then an individual should place a higher reservation price on the object he prefers. (1979, p. 623)

Suppose I prefer bet a to bet b and place a price of $\$x$ on a and a price of $\$y$ on b. If we assume that I place a price of $\$x$ on a if and only if I am indifferent between a and $\$x$ and similarly for b and $\$y$, then I must prefer $\$x$ to $\$y$. This equivalence between pricing and indifference is called "procedure invariance" by Tversky *et al.* (1990, p. 205). If I am indifferent between $\$x$ and a, which I prefer to b, and I am indifferent between b and $\$y$, then, by, transitivity, I must prefer $\$x$ to $\$y$. If, in addition, I prefer more money to less, $\$x$ must be larger than $\$y$. Yet, in the case of preference reversals, individuals who prefer P-bets price $\$$-bets higher. So preferring a P-bet and pricing a $\$$-bet higher violates either transitivity or procedure invariance.

13.2   Grether and Plott's experiments

Not surprisingly, these results were greeted with skepticism by economists. But those who have reacted to them in print have not argued that such results cannot shake their confidence in the fundamental propositions of economic theory. They have shown neither the dogmatism implied by the inexact deductive method nor that which follows from Milton Friedman's argument against considering the realism of assumptions. Economists have, of course, considered the possibility that the results are due to disturbing causes or that they arose only because of peculiarities of the experimental set up. But these possibilities suggest experiments rather than providing automatic excuses. Thus Grether and Plott comment,

There is little doubt that psychologists have uncovered a systematic and interesting aspect of human choice behavior. The key question is, of course, whether this behavior should be of interest to economists. Specifically it seems necessary to answer the following: 1) Does the phenomenon exist in situations where economic theory is generally applied? 2) Can the phenomenon be explained by applying standard economic theory or some immediate variant thereof? (1979, p. 624)

Grether and Plott did not dismiss the results as due to experimental error or economically insignificant disturbing causes. Instead they attempted to see whether in properly designed experiments the preference reversal phenomenon would disappear. Grether and Plott are explicit about how they *want* the experiments to come out, for they say bluntly that the purpose of their experiments was "to discredit the psychologists' works as applied to economics" (1979, p. 623). But whether the fundamental theory can be saved depends on the experimental results, not on methodological fiat.

Accordingly, Grether and Plott constructed a list of possible explanations for the preference reversal phenomenon. On the list are psychological explanations, including two in terms of human information processing procedures. The first of these is Lichtenstein's and Slovic's, in terms of the different methods devoted to different cognitive tasks, while the second, which is not their view, although it might complement their view, explains the preference reversals in terms of information processing strategies designed to lessen the costs of decision-making. The other possible psychological hypotheses on Grether's and Plott's list cannot explain the data.

In addition the list includes various explanations in terms of faults in the experiment – misunderstanding among unsophisticated subjects, expectations produced by the knowledge that these were psychological experiments, etc. Grether and Plott do not believe that Lichtenstein and Slovic have botched their experiments, but, just to be sure, they try to control for these unlikely sources of the odd results.

13.2.1 How preference reversals might be explained away

Grether and Plott are particularly interested in the following four ways in which economists might attempt to explain away the preference reversal phenomenon. If supported by the evidence, these explanations would show that the preference reversal phenomenon poses no serious challenge to economics. The four possible "economic" explanations are:

1 **Poor incentives**: the incentives in the experiment were insufficient to get people to behave as they would in real life when significant decisions have to be made.
2 **Income effects**: as people acquire more wealth they may rationally come to be willing to gamble more. This change in aversion to risk as a result of increases in wealth could contaminate the results in some of Lichtenstein's and Slovic's experiments, in which many gambles were played and wealth changed between separate choices.

3 **Indifference**: in Slovic and Lichtenstein's experiment, subjects were not allowed to say that they were indifferent between the two bets. If subjects were nevertheless indifferent between the P- and $-bets, when they said they preferred the P-bet, then there would be less irrationality in pricing the $-bet higher.[2]

4 **Strategic pricing**: finally, subjects might not be telling the truth when asked to state the minimum price they would accept to sell a lottery. It is often advantageous to ask more than one would truly be willing to accept, and since it is hard to exaggerate the value of the P-bet, this general strategy may account for the reversals.

Grether and Plott endeavored to control for these factors to see whether the conditionally predicted preference reversals would then go away (see also Grether and Plott 1982). Before discussing their experiments, it is worth noting that these alternatives to accepting Lichtenstein's and Slovic's hypothesis are implausible and generally insufficient.

1 **Poor incentives**: since the same results obtained in Slovic's and Lichtenstein's experiments whether the gambles were played, whether it was the subject's own money, and whether individuals were driven to attend carefully, it is hard to believe that the preference reversals result merely from the weakness of the incentives. And, while it would be reassuring to economists if preference reversals went away when the incentives were substantial, it seems to me that economists should still be curious why weak incentives would lead only to the predicted, not the unpredicted reversals.

2 **Income effects**: it is hard to believe that these could be important, since the results obtained whether the gambles were played or not; and, as is noticed in the first excuse, the stakes were low. Furthermore, the opposite reversals in the case of bets with large possible losses, which were predicted and observed in the Las Vegas replication, are inconsistent with a purported explanation in terms of income effects.

3 **Indifference**: even if individuals were indifferent between P- and $-bets when they announced a preference for the P-bet, it would still be inconsistent with rational choice theory to price the $-bet higher. Indifference would also not explain the asymmetry between the frequency of conditionally predicted reversals and unpredicted reversals. Furthermore, although Lichtenstein and Slovic did not permit

---

[2] Levi argues that preference reversals might be due to incompleteness rather than indifference. The "preferences" expressed for the P-bets might reflect their greater security (1986, p. 48).

individuals to register indifference, they did ask them to indicate strength of preference on a four-point scale: "slight," "moderate," "strong," and "very strong," and the mean strength of preference indicated was "strong."

4 **Strategic pricing**: strategic misrepresentation would not explain reversals, when individuals were only asked to price gambles rather than to state buying or selling prices and would predict that, when asked to state buying price, individuals would understate the prices of $-bets.

13.2.2   Grether and Plott's results

So it not surprising that Grether and Plott failed to make the preference reversal phenomenon go away by controlling for these factors. Here is what happened.

1 **Poor incentives**: to determine the importance of incentives, Grether and Plott varied them. But the phenomenon was unaffected, so the explanation in terms of weak incentives was largely refuted. The fact that incentives had little effect was taken by Grether and Plott as evidence against the explanation in terms of information processing costs, since individuals should devote more care to adjusting for probabilities as the stakes increase.

2 **Income effects**: to control for these, subjects played only one of the gambles (which was chosen randomly) and the order of choosing versus bidding varied. But the phenomenon persisted.

3 **Indifference**: Grether and Plott permitted subjects to register indifference as well as preference, but scarcely any subject ever did, so the phenomenon did not arise from indifference.

4 **Strategic pricing**: Grether and Plott used the same Becker–deGroot–Marschak mechanism as Lichtenstein and Slovic in order to elicit a truthful statement of minimum selling price, and they also compared the result with simply asking people to state what they believed a lottery was worth. The amounts stated when pricing and evaluating were not appreciably different, so the explanation in terms of strategic responses was ruled out.

Thus Grether and Plott conclude

Needless to say, the results we obtained were not those expected when we initiated this study. Our design controlled for all the economic-theoretic explanations of the phenomenon which we could find. The preference reversal phenomenon which is inconsistent with the traditional statement of preference theory remains...
(1979, p. 634)

What is surprising to me is not the result of Grether's and Plott's experiment, but why the result should have surprised them. Given how implausible are the alternatives to Lichtenstein's and Slovic's hypothesis, which incidentally managed to predict this phenomenon before it was ever observed, it seems, at least with hindsight, that Grether and Plott should not have expected any different results.

13.2.3   Apparent dogmatism: Grether and Plott's conclusions

What then do Grether and Plott conclude? Here is what they say.

The fact that preference theory and related theories of optimization are subject to exception does not mean that they should be discarded. No alternative theory currently available appears to be capable of covering the same extremely broad range of phenomena. In a sense the exception is an important discovery, as it stands as an answer to those who would charge that preference theory is circular and/or without empirical content. It also stands as a challenge to theorists who may attempt to modify the theory to account for this exception without simultaneously making the theory vacuous. (1979, p. 634)

After the preceding openminded discussion and the striking concession that the preference reversal phenomenon really does appear to be a refutation of a central behavioral postulate of contemporary economics, these words (which constitute the last paragraph in Grether's and Plott's conclusion) are a letdown. It is almost as if they conclude, "Since these awful data cannot be discredited, economists should ignore them, although not without first congratulating themselves for possessing such a splendidly non-vacuous theory." Is this caricature completely unfair? Is their response justifiable?

13.3   Dogmatism and the commitment to economics as a separate science

Dogmatism is sometimes justifiable. As philosophers such as Lakatos have pointed out, theories are too valuable and too hard to generate to be easily dismissed, even when they face serious problems, unless better alternatives are available.

Moreover, Grether and Plott use their experiments to test the explanations of preference reversal proposed by some psychologists, and they argue that some of these hypotheses are unsuccessful, too (1979, p. 634).

So they suggest that they are confronting a mysterious phenomenon rather than rejecting a well-confirmed alternative hypothesis. But, as Grether and Plott concede, Lichtenstein's and Slovic's own hypothesis anticipated the experimental results and is well confirmed by these new experiments. At least at first glance, Grether and Plott's reaction seems indefensibly dogmatic.

What explains this dogmatism? The usual accusation made against economists is that they employ something like the deductive method and are unwilling to take evidence seriously. But Grether and Plott are not committed to the inexact deductive method. They do not refuse to take the disconfirming evidence provided by Lichtenstein and Slovic seriously, and they are not content to say merely that the problem must be caused by some interference. On the contrary, here is an instance where respected economists, who are committed to standard economic theory, are prepared to conclude that the evidence has disconfirmed one of the most central claims of economics. But having done so, little is changed.

Why? How else might one explain this dogmatism? The reason Grether and Plott give for refusing to move from refutation to theory change or modification is that, "No alternative theory currently available appears to be capable of covering the same extremely broad range of phenomena." This way of defending economic theory is familiar. Recall the comments quoted from Koopmans above, p. 170. At first glance the defense seems completely reasonable. The theory is only a first approximation, so disconfirmations are not decisive. And, in any case, theory assessment is comparative. As problematic as economic theory may be, there are no alternatives which provide "better approximations...at the level of the premises" (Koopmans 1957, pp. 141–2) and enable one to draw from such alternative premises conclusions comparable to those which can be drawn from accepted theory. Milton Friedman offers a similar defense when he remarks that "criticism of this type is largely beside the point unless supplemented by evidence that a hypothesis...yields better predictions for as wide a range of phenomena" (1953c, p. 31).[3] But Friedman's and Koopmans' defenses of economics, like Grether's and Plott's, have a tacit premise: that any good economic theory must, like the accepted theory, have both comprehensive scope and a compact or parsimonious theoretical core. The stipulated standard that an alternative theory must

---

[3] Earlier Friedman argued that one can use considerations of scope to choose among "alternative hypotheses equally consistent with the available evidence" (1953c, p. 10). This is perfectly reasonable. But in the later passage quoted in the text, Friedman, like Koopmans and Grether and Plott is ruling out theories with narrow scope, even if they are *more* consistent with the evidence.

meet is that it "be capable of covering the same extremely broad range of phenomena."

Grether and Plott, like Koopmans and Friedman, are committed to a vision of economics as a "separate science," as a science of economics that explains and predicts all central and significant economic phenomena by means of a single systematic and parsimonious theory. Such a theoretical strategy precludes accepting hypotheses concerning gambling choices and bidding such as Lichtenstein's and Slovic's, for that theory has a narrow scope. Its causal factors are significant for only a small set of phenomena; they are not significant factors in all economic phenomena.

Grether and Plott, Koopmans, and Friedman are not just saying that it is reasonable to hang on to accepted theory, since there are no alternatives that are better confirmed. Instead, they implicitly demand that any alternative to accepted theory must preserve a peculiarly "economic" realm to be spanned by a single unified theory. They are not merely defending simplicity, unity, and broad scope as methodological desiderata or as criteria to be employed when there are ties or near-ties on empirical grounds. Instead one finds a constraint in operation here against considering a narrow-scope hypothesis, regardless of its empirical vindication.

As I have argued before, this requirement seems unjustified. In defense of it in this context, one might argue that since utility theory is a theory of rationality, as well as a set of generalizations about how people in fact behave, it should not have a piecemeal structure. But this is to legislate that the theory of choice must also be a theory of rational choice. As argued in the previous chapter, there are pragmatic grounds for preferring theories of choice that are also theories of rational choice, but those grounds must take second place to solid empirical evidence. It would be nice if a better alternative possessed such unity and scope, united positive economics and the theory of rationality, and preserved the peculiar moral authority of economists, but one cannot inflate these methodological desiderata into methodological constraints against considering alternatives, no matter how much better they fit the data.

13.4   Further responses by economists

It might seem unfair to focus exclusively on Grether and Plott. How have other economists reacted? Among the relatively small number who have discussed preference reversals, none seems to have paid any careful attention to Lichtenstein's and Slovic's hypothesis (that people employ different cognitive processes when pricing than when choosing), and there has been no attempt to incorporate it into economics. There is little theoretical collaboration between economists and psychologists in this area,[4] and the continuing work by psychologists on aspects of preference reversals is not cited by economists.

In the decade since Grether and Plott published their results, there have been further discussions by economists of the preference reversal phenomenon, and most of them have been published in the *American Economic Review*, which is one of the most prestigious economic journals. In the immediate aftermath, Pommerehne *et al.* (1982) and Reilly (1982) tried even harder to make the preference reversal phenomenon go away and were able to reduce the frequency of preference reversals (although in doing so, they also blunted Grether and Plott's criticism of the information-processing-costs explanation). But the phenomena cannot be made to go away. Pommerehne *et al.* found that, although experimental subjects can learn from repetitions to accept more profitable gambles, they do not learn to avoid preference reversals (1982, p. 573). In a more dramatic demonstration of just how robust the phenomenon is, Berg *et al.* (1985) ran a series of experiments in which they exploited the choice inconsistencies to lead the subjects through a "money-pump" cycle of exchanges in which they paid money to wind up back where they started. The effect was to decrease the dollar amount of the preference reversals, but not to eliminate them (Roth 1988, p. 1015).[5] All of this confirms Lichtenstein's and Slovic's initial hypothesis.

But economists did not start studying contemporary psychology. Instead, some still tried to explain away the phenomena. Thus Holt (1986) and Karni and Safra (1987) pointed out that the experimental results may be explained by a failure of the independence axiom, rather than by a failure of transitivity. Since independence is not a part of ordinal utility theory and is not as central to the theory of rationality, this was an encouraging result. With odd preferences for money and a strange function relating degrees of belief to objective probabilities, one can explain the experimental results as what Karni and Safra call "announced price reversals" that show no intransitivities. In a similar vein, Segal (1988) pointed out that the preference reversals in some of Grether and Plott's experiments could be due to a failure of the reduction postulate,[6] which is an even less important part of the theory of rational choice. Since equilibrium theory incorporates only ordinal utility theory

---

[4] Richard Thaler is a striking exception.

[5] But, as discussed in the next chapter, p. 249, Chu and Chu (1990) report experiments in which repeated and transparent money-pumping did eliminate preference reversals.

[6] The Becker, de Groot, and Marschak method of getting subjects to state their true selling prices involves in effect a compound lottery. So, if individuals do not relate the values of compound and simple lotteries in the way specified by the reduction postulate, they might show preference reversals without violating transitivity or independence.

and does not rely on either the independence principle or the reduction postulate, these alternatives would save equilibrium theory from apparent disconfirmation.

But these ways of "saving" transitivity are implausible and do not account for the details of the data. The purported explanation of preference reversals in terms of a failure of the independence condition requires attributing to people, in an *ad hoc* way, bizarre preferences and subjective probability judgments, for which there is no independent evidence.[7] Furthermore, no single set of such beliefs and preferences can account for the whole series of choices subjects make in the experiments. The purported explanation in terms of a failure of the reduction postulate is just as *ad hoc* and, as noted by Tversky *et al.* (1990, p. 209), it cannot explain the asymmetry in preference reversals.[8] Tversky *et al.* also establish that a random mixture of P-bets and $-bets is not preferred to the P-bets and $-bets for sure, as it should be if there is a failure of independence (1990, p. 209). Furthermore, the explanation in terms of a failure of the reduction postulate is refuted by the result that the selling prices elicited by the Becker, deGroot, and Marschak mechanism do not differ significantly from the other valuations subjects make.

Although these alternative explanations for the preference reversal phenomenon are of interest mainly as evidence of how unwilling economists are to accept the disconfirmation or to take seriously psychological hypotheses, they have nevertheless been tested. In a recent (1989) essay (also published in the *American Economic Review*), Cox and Epstein report the results of tests of the explanations of preference reversals in terms of failures of independence or of the reduction postulates. The paper begins with a misstatement of the preference reversal phenomenon: it is described simply as any inconsistency between the pricing and choice of $- and P-bets rather than pricing $-bets higher than chosen P-bets. The authors do note the point in a footnote (p. 409), in which they mention that a referee pointed it out, but attention to the details of the phenomenon and to the psychological hypothesis that predicts just these reversals seems an afterthought.

To determine whether reversals might be due to failures of independence or of the reduction postulate, Cox and Epstein jettison the Becker-deGroot-Marschak elicitation mechanism. Instead, subjects were asked

---

[7] In Karni and Safra's example, the utility of money function $u(x)$ is $30x + 30$, for $x \le \$ - 1$, $10x + 10$ for $\$ - 1 \le x \le \$12$ and $6.75x + 49$ for $x \ge \$12$. The function relating degrees of belief to objective probabilities is $1.1564p$ for $0 \le p \le 0.1833$, $0.9p + 0.047$ for $0.1833 \le p \le 0.7$, $0.5p + 0.327$ for $0.7 \le p \le 0.98$, and p for $0.98 \le p \le 1$ (1987, p. 678). Although the general point that concerns Holt and especially Karni and Safra is of real interest, it would be an *ad hoc* maneuver to "save" transitivity by such belief and utility attributions.

[8] But see the argument of Safra *et al.* 1990, p. 927.

to price both of the gambles in a pair at the same time and were told that they would get to play the gamble with the higher price and would be paid a fixed amount for the gamble with the lower price (1989, p. 412). This experimental procedure is faulty, for it makes pricing just a way of stating a choice. Indeed, Cox and Epstein themselves conjecture, "that most of our subjects realized that the particular numbers they stated for prices were irrelevant except for their relative magnitudes. This was evidenced by their comments and by their propensity to state prices such as 1,000 francs for lottery A and 999 francs for lottery B in any given (A, B) pair." (p. 422)

The procedure removes the central difference between the *tasks* of pricing and choosing that led Lichtenstein and Slovic to predict the reversals in the first place, and there is no reason to expect the phenomena to present itself in these circumstances. Indeed, were Cox and Epstein's procedure to show the same preference reversals, one would have grounds to doubt Lichtenstein's and Slovic's account of the source of the phenomenon.

Cox and Epstein do not find the standard (asymmetrical) preference reversal phenomena. But they conclude that these results disconfirm Lichtenstein's and Slovic's work. Cox and Epstein write, "However, if the anchoring and adjustment theory is to be immunized to the apparent falsifying evidence of our experiments, it will have to be extended to incorporate more than a message space explanation of choice reversals." (p. 422) They take their study's result that the frequency of reversals in the predicted direction is not higher than in the unpredicted direction as falsifying Lichtenstein and Slovic's hypothesis. What they mean by the "message space explanation of choice reversals" is an explanation in terms of whether bids rather than choices are elicited. But their conclusions are unpersuasive. What matters in Lichtenstein's and Slovic's view is the *task* subjects are asked to carry out, not the way the task is worded. Cox and Epstein find reversals in either direction about one-third of the time, but in the absence of any inquiry concerning how consistently the subjects otherwise choose, it is impossible to diagnose the causes of these reversals.

Although one sees in this history little evidence of a distinctively dogmatic view of theory appraisal, one does see insularity and dogmatism of a different sort. In particular, economists have shown little interest in or even patience with the hypotheses psychologists have formulated to explain this aberrant choice behavior. The reason is, I believe, that the possibilities that valuation might be variegated and that the connections between choice and valuation might be complex and indirect threaten the structure of theoretical economics.

The unwillingness to take seriously the theoretical work by psychologists is a little ironic, for, although Lichtenstein's and Slovic's hypothesis concerning information processing is not compatible with standard models of economic choice, it can be modeled with similar mathematical tools and combined with much that is standard in economic theory. It owes a great deal to the work of less orthodox economists such as Richard Cyert, James March, or Herbert Simon (Cyert and March 1963; Simon 1959). But to incorporate Lichtenstein's and Slovic's hypothesis within an economic theory would be to move toward a theory of economic behavior with many behavioral postulates rather than few and with behavioral postulates that apply only to a comparatively narrow range of phenomena. And economists are generally unwilling to surrender their vision of a single unifying economic theory.

Despite attempts such as Holt's, Karni and Safra's, and Segal's to "save" the standard theory, attention among decision theorists and theoretical economists has shifted in the past few years to proposing alternatives to utility theory to account for the phenomenon. Loomes and Sugden (1983) argue that their revision of expected utility theory, "regret theory" (1982) can explain the preference reversal phenomenon (see also Loomes et al. 1989). Levi (1986) has suggested that the preference reversals may be due to incompleteness in preferences, which ought anyway to be modeled in an adequate theory of rational and actual choice. Machina (1987) suggests that formal choice models involving intransitive preferences can be formulated. Notice that respected economists such as Machina are willing to consider discarding even such a central postulate of equilibrium theory as transitivity. What economists refuse to give up is not their theory, but their theoretical strategy. All of these proposals for modifying utility theory cling to the vision of a separate science of economics.

13.5   Preference reversals and "procedure invariance"

The most recent contributions of psychologists concerning preference reversal undermine these theories, for they suggest that preference reversals are not due to a failure of transitivity after all![9] Recall that pricing the $-bet higher than the P-bet violates transitivity only if one assumes that, in pricing a bet, an individual is indifferent between the stated price and the bet. Failures of this assumption of procedure invari-

---

[9] There is an irony here in the fact that psychologists are defending transitivity against economists. But, as we shall see, the diagnosis of preference reversals offered by Tversky et al. 1990 is even less palatable to economists than is surrendering transitivity.

ance rather than failures of transitivity might be responsible for preference reversal. In a recent paper, Tversky, Slovic, and Kahneman point out this fact and report on experiments designed to discriminate intransitivities from procedural variances.

Suppose an individual A is offered a choice between not only P- and $-bets, but also between these bets and some payoff for certain, X. Let (P) and $($) represent the prices the individual would put on the P- and $-bets, and assume in each case the following preference orderings hold:

$($)	P-bet
$X	
(P)	$-bet

We know the orderings within the two columns, but we do not necessarily know where items in one column fit in the ordering in the other. Depending on how these are combined, preference reversals in the predicted direction can arise in four different ways (Tversky *et al.* 1990, p. 206).

1 **Intransitivity**: Given procedure invariance, the P-bet goes in the same row as (P) and the $-bet goes in the same row as $($) and one has the intransitive ranking:

$($), $-bet
$X
(P), P-bet
$-bet

2 **Overpricing the $-bet**: Subjects are indifferent between (P) and the P-bet and $X is preferred to both the bets. The consistent preference ordering is:

$($)
$X
(P), P-bet
$-bet

3 **Underpricing the P-bet**: Subjects are indifferent between $($) and the $-bet and consequently both bets are preferred to $X. The consistent preference ordering is:

P-bet
$($),$-bet,
$X
(P)

4 **Overpricing the $-bet and underpricing the P-bet**: One consistent prefer-
ence ordering is[10]

$$\$(\$), \ P\text{-bet}$$
$$\$X$$
$$\$(P), \ \$\text{-bet}$$

Procedure invariance requires one to place the bet and its price in the
same row and leads to intransitivity. If it is not assumed, then the bets
can be placed in various places in the monetary ranking, and purely
transitive preference orderings are possible.

As summarized in the table below, the four cases above provide testable
criteria for intransitivity, overpricing, underpricing, or both over and
underpricing as explanations of preference reversals. In a sizeable study,
Tversky et al. tested for the frequency of these four patterns. It seems
that procedure variance, in particular overpricing of the $-bet, is a much
more important factor in preference reversals than is intransitivity. The
results are written at the bottom of each column.

$-bet	$X	P-bet	P-bet
$X	P-bet	$-bet	$X
P-bet	$-bet	$X	$-bet
intransitivity	overpricing $-bet	underpricing P-bet	over and underpricing
10%	65%	6%	18%

These data are compatible with Lichtenstein's and Slovic's original explanation for preference reversals. In pricing, agents pay more attention to
pay-offs than in stating a preference. But this explanation is superficial,
and Tversky et al. offer a conjecture with a wider scope. They argue that
human thinking is influenced by what they call "scale compatibility." If
asked to answer a question about quantities in a particular unit, people
give a larger role to data expressed in the same units. Dollar amounts
have a greater influence in the pricing task, because dollars are the units
in which one prices. So preferences and pricing of bets that involve
non-monetary prices should be much more consistent, as has indeed
been shown by a study done by Slovic et al. (1990). And, if one examines

[10] There are others, for the ranking of $($) and the P-bet and of $(P) and the $-bet has
not been specified.

rankings and pricing of monetary options in which there is no explicit element of risk, similar reversals should be found. This implication is supported by the results of a second experiment by Tversky *et al.* 1990, pp. 212–14 in which subjects were asked to rank and to price options involving different time patterns of incomes. Many who prefer smaller short-run gains place a higher price on larger longer-run gains.

The implications for economics are disturbing. Tversky and Thaler conclude a recent summary piece as follows:

The discussion of the meaning of preference and the status of value may be illuminated by the well-known exchange among three baseball umpires. "I call them as I see them," said the first. "I call them as they are," claimed the second. The third disagreed, "They ain't nothing till I call them." Analogously, we can describe three different views regarding the nature of values. First, values exist – like body temperature – and people perceive and report them as best they can, possibly with bias (I call them as I see them). Second, people know their values and preferences directly – as they know the multiplication table (I call them as they are). Third, values or preferences are commonly constructed in the process of elicitation (they ain't nothing till I call them). The research reviewed in this article is most compatible with the third view of preference as a constructive, context-dependent process. (Tversky and Thaler 1990, p. 210).

This context-dependence has serious implications, for, as Tversky *et al.* conclude

These developments highlight the discrepancy between the normative and the descriptive approaches to decision-making, which many choice theorists (see Mark Machina 1987) have tried to reconcile. Because invariance – unlike independence or even transitivity – is normatively unassailable and descriptively incorrect, it does not seem possible to construct a theory of choice that is both normatively acceptable and descriptively adequate (1990, p. 215).

What seems to be required is the sort of theorizing that has traditionally been most repugnant to economic theorists. The pragmatic preference for a theory of choice that is also a theory of rational choice will have to be abandoned. The hope of a unitary account of all economic choice behavior vanishes. There also seems to be a case here for the sort of subjectivist perspective that contemporary Austrian economists defend. For, in eliciting preferences, we must attend to how agents *interpret* our actions and questions (Schick 1987). The independence between belief and preference that is fundamental to standard decision theory is cast into doubt.

Contrast these disturbing implications to Machina's recent (1987) discussion of preference reversal. Although Machina takes the phenomenon seriously, holds no hope for making it disappear, and indeed seems to urge economists to consider what sort of influence such anomalies may have in real market behavior,[11] his theoretical prescription is to seek an alternative general formal theory of utility maximization that permits intransitivities. Piecemeal theorizing that relies on substantive generalizations with limited applicability is apparently not worth considering. But such theorizing seems to be needed.

The general complaisance with which most economists continue to regard the claims of economic theory and their unwillingness to take seriously relevant psychological hypotheses is hard to defend. The attractions of a separate science run deep, but there is no justification for insisting on such a structure, and doing so creates unreasonable barriers to theoretical and empirical progress.

[11] 1987, p. 140. Some business-school economists have done so. Mowen and Gentry (1980) have replicated the phenomena among marketing students asked both to choose among investment opportunities and to price them. They also found more frequent reversals among *groups* facing such problems than among individuals (1980, esp. p. 721). In a fascinating recent study confirming the compatibility hypothesis, Schkade and Johnson (1989) actually test for subjects' cognitive processes by studying how they manipulate a computer "mouse" to retrieve information and register reactions.

Part III

Conclusion

Part I explored the structure and strategy of neoclassical economics, that is – or so I argued – of equilibrium theory and its applications, while part II addressed the problems of theory assessment in economics and showed how these can be clarified by the conclusions of part I. What is philosophically distinctive about economics is not the view of theory assessment accepted by economists but the structure and strategy of economic theorizing. The problems that have been addressed are central to the practice of economists, to epistemological problems of interest to philosophers of social science, and to the attitudes of philosophers, economists, politicians, and others toward the discipline of economics and the conclusions it defends.

Although I have emphasized the vision of economics as a separate science as the key to its methodological peculiarities, this book has defended many detailed theses, and I shall summarize the most important of these in chapter 15. Much of what I have written can be regarded as a defense of puzzling features of neoclassical economics. For I have maintained that the 'obvious falsehoods' upon which economic theory depends can be regarded as qualified truths and can be justifiably accepted and employed in some contexts. Along the way I have criticized both general philosophical views that would condemn such theorizing, and specific accounts of economic methodology such as those defended by Hutchison, Samuelson, Machlup, and Friedman.

My remarks concerning the structure and strategy of economic theorizing have been more critical, though I found good reasons even for what I have taken to be mistakes. Given the distinction between models and theories in chapter 5, one can appreciate the conceptual explorations that are so prominent in theoretical economics, free of misplaced concerns with empirical testing. The account of the global theory structure of microeconomics in chapter 6, as a 'separate science' in Mill's sense, helps explain why equilibrium theory dominates the thinking of economists and partially justifies that dominance. But I argued that the commitment of many economists to equilibrium theory is exaggerated and seems,

245

especially in the case of normative economics, to prevent economists from coming to terms with important problems. The insistence that a single unified theory span a separate economic realm can be justified only if it leads to theoretical success.

Before pulling together the threads of the argument in chapter 15, I need to address remaining defenses of equilibrium theory as well as a challenge to my whole project. Chapter 14 is accordingly devoted to these tasks and to an examination of specific methodological implications of my position.

I have argued that the insistence that economic phenomena be treated by a single unified theory – equilibrium theory in particular – has no general justification. Whether equilibrium theory is the best way to proceed is an empirical question; and there is little reason to reject other approaches because they cannot be integrated into a unified theory of an economic realm. But in reaching this, my principal critical conclusion, I have not yet addressed two powerful arguments that apparently establish the permanent hegemony of equilibrium theory. And, even if these arguments can be answered, I have said little about the upshot of my philosophizing for the practice of economics. Finally, even if I can defend the claim that equilibrium theory has no methodologically privileged position and show what the implications are for the practice of economics, one might reasonably question whether an outsider could challenge the methodological practice of an established discipline such as economics. Is not such a challenge futile and arrogant? What possible authority could I have to preach to economists?

14.1   The hegemony of equilibrium theory

Suppose a theorist were to offer a maverick explanation of some economic phenomenon P, which employed "*ad hoc*" behavioral generalizations that violate the strictures of section 6.5. In assessing this explanation relative to equilibrium theory, there are three possible cases: (1) there is a competing explanation of the phenomenon P in terms of equilibrium theory and permissible additions; (2) equilibrium theory does not appear to have any relevance to P at all; and (3) P is anomalous from the perspective of equilibrium theory, which apparently implies that the phenomenon ought not to occur.

If (1) the phenomenon were also explicable in terms of equilibrium theory and permissible additions, then one might argue that the standard microeconomic explanation is necessarily preferable to the deviant explanation. For the standard explanation employs a systematic theory and links P to an immense range of other phenomenon. Since unification is one goal of scientific explanation (Michael Friedman 1974), the microeconomic explanation is, *ceteris paribus*, the better explanation. Furthermore, as Max Weber (1949), Fritz Machlup (1969), and many of the Austrian economists emphasize, one constraint, or, at the very least, *desideratum* on the explanations of social phenomena is that they show such phenomena to be consequences of intelligible or understandable human action (A.14.2). Microeconomic explanations do this in a particularly powerful way, since they are extensions of the standard folk-psychological account of human action in terms of beliefs and desires (see A.14.1, esp. pp. 322–3). It is hard to see how a genuine alternative to equilibrium theory could possess these explanatory virtues to nearly the same degree as equilibrium theory does. The alternative might be better confirmed – in better accordance with the facts – so economists might be driven from their allegiance to equilibrium theory. But, given the difficulties involved in testing and confirmation in economics, this is an unlikely prospect.

In case 2, in which equilibrium theory was not relevant at all, one might question whether the phenomenon P truly belonged to the domain of economics. Since economics is defined by its causal factors, it could not be irrelevant to any genuinely "economic" phenomenon, and it is hard to see how equilibrium theory could fail to be relevant to any phenomenon in its standard domain. Again this thought is strengthened by the tradition of Weber and the Austrians who emphasize that the social phenomena of interest to us are those upon which human action and deliberation bear (A.14.2).

The most interesting case is the last. Suppose one has an explanation of some economic phenomenon P, which employs a theory such as Tversky, Slovic, and Kahneman's "compatibility hypothesis" (section 13.5 above), where P would apparently be ruled out by equilibrium theory and standardly accepted auxiliary assumptions. Such phenomena constitute an argument for revising equilibrium theory or limiting its scope. One can always defend equilibrium theory by *ad hoc* attributions of particular tastes, information failures, and the like, but significant success by some alternative theory in explaining behavior that is largely inexplicable in terms of equilibrium theory presents a major challenge (like that posed – in the opinion of some economists – by Keynes' theory). Yet most economists neither seek alternative theories nor believe that they can be found.

Russell and Thaler list three reasons why economists have been critical of anomalous experimental findings, and consequently unwilling to consider alternative theories that explain those findings:[1] (1) "In the real world, people will learn," (2) "Economists are interested in aggregate behavior and these individual errors will wash out when we aggregate," and (3) "Markets will eliminate the errors" (1985, p. 1074). The second response is a non-starter, when, as in the case of preference reversal, the errors are systematic, and I shall have no more to say about it. The first and third responses, on the other hand, call for careful discussion.

14.1.1 People will learn

As mentioned above (p. 237), there is evidence, at least with respect to preference reversals, that people do not learn easily. But it is hard to believe that people will not learn at all, and, in the latest experimental results concerning preference reversals, Chu and Chu (1990) show how to make people stop showing preference reversals. The experimental subjects were asked to state their preferences with respect to a single pair of a P-bet and a $-bet (such as [$4,$-1,35/36] and [$16,$-1.50,11/36]) and to state prices for the two bets. Those who showed preference reversals were then "educated" by the following sequence of exchanges. They had to purchase the $-bet from the experimenter for the price stated, make the exchange of the $-bet for the P-bet, which they claimed to prefer, and then to sell the P-bet back to the experimenter for the price they had stated. After the round was complete, they were, of course, poorer by $($-bet) - $($P$-bet). Individuals could then revise their preferences or their pricing and the game was repeated. Few continued to be reversers after two rounds, and after having been educated to stop reversing their preferences with respect to one pair, individuals also avoided reversing their preferences with respect to other pairs.[2] So people do indeed learn. In some environments, irrational behavior is inherently unstable.

Chu and Chu are careful not to leap to conclusions concerning how efficacious is the education provided by actual markets, and the weakness in the general claim that learning makes irrational behavior unimportant is precisely at this point. For markets do not always underline our mistakes so clearly. (If they did, then individuals should have learned not to show preference reversals before the experiments began.) Chu and Chu's results and the general argument that people will learn provide some hope that phenomena such as preference reversals will not be important factors in

---

[1] Apart from *specific* concerns about the incentives in experiments or the applicability of the experimental results to non-laboratory circumstances.

[2] This description oversimplifies the experiments slightly.

economic life. But such hope does not justify dismissing experimental findings of irrationality as obviously insignificant.[3]

14.1.2 Arbitrage arguments

The third ground Russell and Thaler (1985) mention, "Markets will eliminate the errors," might sound like a restatement of the first, since markets can eliminate errors by facilitating learning. Russell and Thaler are however referring to another function of markets and a different form of argument. This form of argument is prevalent in economics and of the utmost importance. Arguments of this form[4] purport to show that disequilibria are *impossible*, except temporarily or as unimportant curiosities. They also apparently provide good reason to dismiss most evidence gathered from surveys, experiments, or field observation as *irrelevant*.

Phenomena that are anomalous from the perspective of equilibrium theory are disequilibria. Suppose that some significant disequilibrium phenomenon P apparently obtained. For example, suppose P were the fact that women workers with the same abilities as male workers are paid a lower wage.[5] This disequilibrium apparently implies a failure of maximization, for demand for the cheaper but not less able female labor should increase and demand for more expensive male labor decrease until equal wages are paid to equally qualified workers. Field studies suggest a variety of explanations for wage discrimination in terms of entrenched expectations, prejudices, and customs.

The "arbitrage argument" rules out the phenomenon altogether. Regardless of what the data might appear to show, disequilibrium cannot persist.[6] Either there are constraints on knowledge, action, or preference

---

[3] For example, Kahneman, Knetsch, and Thaler (1990) argue that the "endowment effect" (valuing something more highly when it becomes part of one's endowment) and the asymmetrical attitude people adopt toward losses as opposed to forgone gains persist even in market environments which provide opportunities to learn. Ausubel (1991) explains the striking failure of competition in credit-card markets in terms of the irrational unwillingness of credit-card users to believe that they will borrow on their cards.

[4] They are pejoratively described by Russell and Thaler (1985, p. 1071) as "the knee-jerk reaction of some economists that competition will render irrationality irrelevant..."

[5] See the Symposium in *The Journal of Economic Perspectives* 3,1 (Winter, 1989), especially Bergmann 1989 and Fuchs 1989.

[6] Consider McCloskey's, "sad little Five-Hundred-Dollar-Bill Theorem:

If the Axiom of Modest Greed applies, then today there exists no sidewalk in the neighborhood of your house on which a $500 bill remains.

Proof: By contradiction, if there had been a $500 bill lying there at time $T - N$, then according to the axiom someone would have picked it up before T, before today." (1990, p. 112) McCloskey seems here to suggest the more radical conclusion that disequilibria can never exist. All disequilibria are $500 bills on sidewalks, though they are not all quite so easy to spot or exploit. See also Alchian 1950.

that perpetuate the apparent disequilibrium and make it an equilibrium after all, or the data are misleading. Except in the case of a nearly universal "taste for discrimination," or legally mandated wage differences, etc., the minority of firms that hire without regard to sex will seize profit opportunities presented by less expensive but equally able women workers. Those firms will earn higher profits. The other firms that continue to hire more expensive male workers will find themselves financially pressed, and ultimately the discriminating firms will either change their hiring practices, or they will be driven out of business. The market insures that equal wages are paid to equally qualified workers. All it takes is competition and a few firms who are only concerned with the bottom line.

So equilibrium theorists can cheerfully concede that people are driven by all sorts of motives and that people may be irrational in countless ways. But the market mechanism, coupled with the rationality of some, implies that phenomena drastically inconsistent with equilibrium theory are either transitory or require nearly universal divergence between actual behavior and that postulated by equilibrium theory. Surveys, experiments, and field reports may provide material for interesting anecdotes, but, for the true believer, things must be as equilibrium theory predicts. Although most economists are not such true believers, few would dismiss such arguments altogether.[7] Most would say that, while competitive markets may not guarantee that discrimination will be eliminated, they do move society in the right direction.

This form of argument, which I have elsewhere dubbed an "arbitrage argument" (1989a), is used in other fields, too. In an essay mainly focusing on biology, Elliott Sober calls such arguments "equilibrium explanations" (1983). They seem to be enormously powerful, for they apparently require so little knowledge. To make an arbitrage argument, one need not pay attention to the actual causal mechanisms that supposedly eliminate any disequilibrium outcomes. All that is required is that a minority act on the perceived advantage and that the environment be competitive enough to permit them to thrive at the expense of others.

But, if one does not attend to the motivation, the institutional facts, and the actual mechanisms that supposedly insure outcomes explicable by equilibrium theory, then one can easily go astray. For it may not be

---

[7] In the Fall of 1983, George Akerlof delivered a version of an essay criticizing the application of this form of argument to racial discrimination in hiring (an early version of Akerlof 1985) to an audience of social scientists at the Institute for Advanced Study in Princeton. The economists and the other social scientists in the audience had similar reactions to Akerlof's conclusions, but strikingly different reactions to the object of his criticisms. Even those economists who rejected the conclusion that market forces will eliminate racial discrimination took the arbitrage argument seriously, while the non-economists found the argument unpersuasive, even silly.

the case in real circumstances that hiring equally able but less expensive women workers will lower costs, and even if hiring women does lower costs it may not be the case that firms that hire women will thrive.[8] Only attention to the messy facts from which arbitrage arguments abstract will enable one to know whether these assumptions are true and whether the relevant equilibrium must obtain. One cannot concede that the world is a messy place with many factors influencing choices and their outcomes without recognizing that actions that appear to lower costs from the armchair may not actually do so. Similarly, one cannot concede that there are many relevant causal factors and still cling to the *a priori* conviction that the existence of competitive markets guarantees that the factors encompassed in equilibrium theory always dominate all others. The evidence supporting the claim that equally able women are paid less than men is impressive (Bergmann 1989), and, if one removes the spectacles (or blinders) provided by equilibrium theory, many of the explanatory factors are not difficult to see.[9]

The arbitrage argument does not defend equilibrium theory from all empirical doubts, but it does pose interesting questions. Since there is a great deal to be said for equilibrium theory, and, since the weaker presumptions that drive arbitrage arguments are plausible, phenomena that appear to be incompatible with equilibrium theory are puzzling and demand explanation. Sometimes apparent conflicts can be explained away, but sometimes one uncovers factors that significantly influence economic phenomena, from which equilibrium theory abstracts. These can always be treated as mere disturbances, but they may be susceptible to systematic theorizing. There should be no methodological rule against studying these other factors.

Although there might possibly be an *a priori* case for the irreplaceability of a folk-psychological, belief–desire account of human action in terms

---

[8] See Akerlof 1985. To combine the services of workers (as opposed to units of raw materials) requires more than merely technical knowledge. Workers must work together within the firm and must interact successfully with individuals outside of the firm. Hiring an "equally able" woman might be extremely costly, if, for example, she was resented and her efforts sabotaged by only a few male workers. (One might then question whether such a woman was "equally able," but to take effect on total costs as the criterion of ability would embed the effects of discrimination into the notion of ability and render tautologous the claim that hiring equally able women at lower wages would lower costs.) It might be thought that the claim that firms with lower labor costs do better on the market was not subject to similar questions, but this claim is true only *ceteris paribus*, and there are many possible disturbing causes. One cannot know whether they are present without looking. Furthermore, even if the argument's conclusion is correct, the rate of adjustment may be extremely slow.

[9] Moreover, in addition to the objections I have alluded to above and discussed at length in my 1989a, the argument does not go through formally when there are "too many" non-rational agents (Russell and Thaler 1985) and when, as is common, the costs to the discriminator are tiny (Akerlof and Yellen 1985).

of the aims and interests we have in inquiring about social phenomena (A.14.2), neither arbitrage nor learning constitute a blanket *a priori* defense of utility theory, the particular version of folk psychology embedded in equilibrium theory; and there is no *a priori* case to be made for the other constituents of equilibrium theory.[10] To what extent economics ought to be a unified separate science as opposed to a collection of specific theories of narrower scope cannot be decided by methodology. It is an empirical question. Given the limited predictive power of equilibrium theory, there should be no presumption that alternative theories can be dismissed on general methodological grounds.

14.2   How to do economics

Suppose that the conclusions of the previous chapters concerning confirmation and theory appraisal in economics are correct: economists employ an uncontroversial method of theory assessment. Unfortunately, owing to poor data (relative to the state of economic knowledge), little can be learned about which theories are better confirmed. Given the initial credibility of the basic behavioral postulates of economics, it is rational to remain committed to them in the face of apparent disconfirmations. The consequence of such a defense is to leave economists unable to learn very much from typical economic data.

If my account is right, economists desperately need better data in order to advance their theoretical knowledge, and serious redirection of effort among economists is called for. Such data gathering must not be divorced from specific objectives and problems, both practical and, especially, theoretical. One must be prepared to consider alternative kinds of theorizing, or else there is little point to such data gathering. Ways of getting better data include:

1 A major commitment of resources to take advantage of experimental opportunities. Experimental economics has grown rapidly over the last two decades. This is a positive development and should be encouraged.[11]

---

[10] Alternatives to utility theory, such as Herbert Simon's notion of "satisficing," are also consistent with folk psychology, which demands neither perfect consistency of preferences nor maximizing. See Simon 1979 for a historical overview, and A.14.2, p. 322.

[11] Roth describes one scenario as follows, "Directions in which to develop theory become clearer as experimental evidence builds up about systematic bargaining phenomena, and developments in theory suggest questions to investigate experimentally." (1987, p. 39) See Roth, ed. 1987, 1988, Smith 1978, 1982, and Thaler 1980, 1987. But as Jon Elster points out, one cannot expect too much from experimentation. "Laboratory experiments have the great value of isolating and controlling factors so that we can see the mechanisms in their pure form, but they are limited help in explaining the tug of war between mechanisms that is the rule in social life." (1989a, p 216).

2 A general willingness to make use of observational data of all kinds. Much can be done to refine the techniques of field reports and "social experimentation."[12] Economists need to overcome the animus they feel toward the laborious process of gathering such data and the precarious process of interpreting them.

3 More active engagement by economists in the process of data gathering in order to appreciate better the limitations of particular data sets. Although econometricians have recognized and emphasized this point, the structure of rewards within the economics profession makes involvement with data gathering costly to individuals.

4 Further work on improved statistical techniques for the analysis of data.

Of course, even improved data will not help theoretical knowledge in economics grow, if economists are unwilling to entertain alternatives because of methodological commitments to a single style of theorizing. If unfamiliar explanations can command empirical support, they should be pursued.

So I would defend three changes in theoretical economics:

1 More work should be devoted to exploring alternatives to elements of standard microeconomics that have already been proposed, such as Levi's proposal to surrender completeness, Machina's proposal to surrender transitivity and the independence principle, Loomes' and Sugden's regret theory, McClennen's notion of "resolute choice," Kahneman and Tversky's "prospect theory," or Simon's theory of procedural, bounded rationality.

2 More serious attention should be paid to the work of other social scientists. Whether economists have anything to learn from any particular instance of psychological or sociological research is an empirical question. The only legitimate reason to dismiss all work of other social scientists as of little interest would be if the separate science of economics were a smashing success.

3 Quite different styles of theorizing, such as that exemplified by the institutionalists should be encouraged, and empirical work studying problems faced by particular firms or groups of employees (which is often carried out by business school economists rather than by members of economics departments) should be taken seriously by economic theorists.

[12] Herbert Simon cautions, however, "Among the reasons for the relative neglect of such [field] studies, as contrasted, say, with laboratory experiments in social psychology, is that they are extremely costly and time consuming, with a high grist-to-grain ratio, the methodology for carrying them out is primitive, and satisfactory access to decision-making behavior is hard to secure." (1979, p. 501) For a fascinating critique of social experimentation that is still less sanguine about the prospects for progress here, see Neuberg 1988.

What do these generalities mean in detail? (It is here that I am most painfully aware of the limitations of my own knowledge of economics and of the fact that I am not a practicing economist.) The best I can do is to consider specific examples, some of which exemplify the above methodological recommendations and some of which do not, and to call attention to their methodological virtues and vices.

But, before doing so, two central qualifications are required:

> *Economics is a diverse enterprise, and there is no reason why it should become less diverse.*

Economists face many different tasks and questions. My focus is only on theoretical economics. Second:

> *There is absolutely no reason why all economists should employ the same styles and strategies of theorizing.*

If my methodological recommendations were to find general favor among economists, work devoted to the further elaboration of a separate science of economics – that is, to the articulation and application of equilibrium theory – should still be done. There is no alternative that is so obviously superior that it would justify everyone abandoning the current orthodoxy. What is wrong with economic theorizing is not what economists are doing, but what they are not doing and what they refuse to do.

14.2.1 Samuelson's overlapping generations model revisited

Recall Samuelson's essay "An Exact Consumption-Loan Model..." Samuelson's stated purpose was to determine what effects the desire to save for retirement has on the rate of interest. He was also interested in the mathematical and conceptual problems raised by the infinity of time periods, but these interests were supposedly subordinated to answering his empirical question.

But, as we saw, Samuelson abandons his main question and focuses on conceptual and implicitly normative issues. There is nothing wrong with conceptual and normative inquiry, and this particular essay is a fertile and intriguing contribution, which raises fascinating questions about the influence of expectations of the future on the present, about the notion of optimality in a dynamic context, and about the possible interplay between market and "social-contract" in solving dynamic inter-generational problems. What bothers me is the view of what such models can accomplish that is implicit in Samuelson's essay and, more dramatically, in Wallace's account of fiat money. These models do not answer empirical questions and it is hard to see how they could do so. Samuelson's and Wallace's over-optimism and Wallace's theoretical purism can be explained by attributing to them a vision of equilibrium theory as the core of a separate science of economics. Only a very strong commitment to equilibrium theory could lead one to share Wallace's belief that an explanation for the value and existence of fiat money requires an infinity of generations (see Hahn 1982, pp. 6f).

In the discipline as a whole, it is probably a good thing that there are theorists with the strong commitments Wallace shows. No one without them would be willing to explore such complicated models. There is a methodological failing here only when such theorizing gains a hegemony over the profession and attracts all the prestige and all the most talented students.

14.2.2 Preference reversals

The phenomenon of preference reversals suggests that there is something to be learned from experimentation and that economists do not subscribe to a dogmatic deductive method that prevents them from investigating anomalous data. Such dogmatism as there is results from economists' commitment to economics as a separate science.

Even when economists came to recognize the reality of preference reversals, which were successfully anticipated by a plausible psychological hypothesis, their reaction was to attempt to generalize or weaken parts of equilibrium theory rather than to utilize the theoretical contributions of psychologists. While economists were pondering implausible explanations in terms of violations of independence or the reduction postulate, psychologists were doing the theoretical and empirical work that seems to have revealed the source of the phenomenon in "procedure variance" (pp. 230, 240f) and the "scale compatibility" hypothesis (p. 242). Let me stress that I see no methodological mistake in Machina's (1987) programmatic call for a revised abstract separate science. The problem is rather that for most economists this appears to be the only possible response.

There are several methodological lessons here. First, experiments can have a dramatic impact. What else plausibly could have led leading theorists to concede that individual choice could be so drastically inconsistent with utility theory?[13] Second, experimental results are (obviously)

---

[13] Although the significance of experimental results for non-laboratory circumstances remains in each case to be demonstrated, experimental findings can be relevant to market phenomena and can make us aware of pervasive, but unnoticed facts. The importance of "framing" demonstrated in the laboratory (Tversky and Kahneman 1981) is, for example, vividly manifested in market phenomena. Gas stations offer discounts for using cash rather than surcharges for using credit cards, for the latter anger customers. Similarly, restaurants offer "early-bird" dinner specials rather than charging surcharges for prime-time dining. Such phenomena matter. See Kahneman, Knetsch, and Thaler (1986) and (1990).

subject to interpretation. By themselves even a long series of experiments only poses a problem. Third, economists, unlike astrologers, do not dismiss anomalous data.[14] They do not like such data, and they try to discredit them by analysis and experimentation, but they do not hide them either. Not only do some economists take the results seriously, but the major journals in the field now readily publish reports of experimental results and discussions of these results. Indeed one even finds reports of survey results![15] The accusation that economics is not an empirical discipline (Rosenberg 1983) cannot be sustained. But commitment to equilibrium theory and especially to the theoretical strategy and structure that it exemplifies runs deep. This commitment "closes" economics to the consideration of relevant theories proposed by other disciplines and generates an unjustifiable dogmatism.

14.2.3   Stretching microeconomics

Although economists of some schools, such as the institutionalists, have been willing to make use of theories and empirical findings from other disciplines, "orthodox" economists have clung to their separate science. This claim might be regarded as merely definitional: to have behaved otherwise would automatically classify one as non-orthodox. But it is possible to develop abstract mathematical models that incorporate both postulates of equilibrium theory and theoretical generalizations proposed by social theorists. For example, Russell and Thaler (1985) define a notion of "quasi-rationality" in formulating a model in which maximizing agents make mistakes about the mapping between goods and their characteristics, which are the true arguments of individuals' utility functions. Modifications of equilibrium theory such as these lie at the limits of

---

[14] As discussed in chapter 9, Machlup and Friedman justify dismissing survey results on the grounds that fundamental theory is not directly testable (Machlup) or on the grounds that survey results do not concern "the phenomena the theory was designed to explain" (Friedman). Their arguments would also justify dismissing most experimental findings. Although the arguments of Machlup and Friedman continue to discourage survey research, few economists accept the full implications of Friedman's and Machlup's positions.

[15] Blinder and Choi's recent essay reports the findings of a small survey designed to investigate why wages are sticky. "We actually *asked* a small sample of wage-setters about the nature and sources of wage rigidity in their own companies." (p. 1003) Among other things, they found that more than a quarter of the firms they interviewed had lowered some money wages during a period of relative prosperity and low unemployment, and they note that economists do not know even so elementary a fact as how prevalent wage cuts are (p. 1005). Their most significant finding was that perceptions of fairness apparently have a major role in wage setting.

economics as a separate science. They include many of the standard behavioral postulates of equilibrium theory, and, in particular, they portray individuals as maximizing a well-defined utility function. In mathematical style and in willingness to abstract and to simplify, they are completely standard. But, in attempting to model the findings of psychologists, they open a chink in the wall that keeps economics separate.

In a series of striking papers, George Akerlof has demonstrated that it is possible to combine orthodox tools and modeling style with theories from other social disciplines. I shall discuss two examples among the many that Akerlof's work provides. In "Labor Contracts as Partial Gift Exchange" (1982), Akerlof begins with the results of an empirical study by the sociologist, George Homans (1953), which showed that "cash posters" (clerks who recorded payments) at a utility company processed, on average, 17% more bills per hour than the company required. If the marginal utility of effort for the cash posters is negative, then minimum satisfaction of the work rules would be maximizing. If, on the other hand, the marginal utility of effort is positive (and decreasing), then the company and the workers could both be better off if higher pay were offered for more output. Either way, the data suggest a failure of maximizing on the part of the workers or the company.

The explanation Akerlof defends draws on the work of anthropologists, sociologists, and philosophers (Mauss 1954; Titmuss 1971) and is intuitively plausible. In working for a firm, employees develop sentimental attachments to one another and to the firm itself. These attachments lead employees to make a *gift* to the firm of extra work. Such gifts will, however, only be provided if the employees feel that the firm is fairly reciprocating with gifts of its own in the form of lenient work rules that reduce the pressure on less able workers and better pay or benefits than some salient reference. Such gift exchanges can lead to wages above the market-clearing rate and involuntary unemployment.

Thus far the explanation smacks of sociology and anthropology, which is, in the view of most economists, a damning indictment indeed. Moreover, the data Akerlof cites in support of his claims are drawn from sociological studies including (gasp!) surveys (Stouffer, Suchman *et al.* 1949 and Stouffer, Lumsdaine *et al.* 1949). But Akerlof goes on to sketch a mathematical model in which firms attempt to maximize net revenue and employees attempt to maximize utility, but in which gift exchanges take place. The abstract model has three main components.

1 Quantitative effort norms are mathematical functions of wages, work rules requiring minimum effort, worker's utilities, wages paid by other

firms, the unemployment rate, and unemployment benefits. Firms know that effort norms depend on these factors.

2 The utility of employees depends on the effort norms, the employee's individual effort, the wage, and individual tastes. Workers choose whether to be employed, which job to take, and what level of effort to exert on the job in order to maximize their utility, subject to the constraint that they satisfy a firm's work rules.

3 The output of a firm depends on the number of employees and their level of effort. Given limited knowledge of workers' individual tastes, firms decide on wages, work rules, and size of labor force in order to maximize net revenue.

The specific behavior of the cash posters is modeled in a more particularized model with a fixed wage, specified parameter values, and the further assumption that greater differences in work rules for different kinds of workers has a negative effect on output norms. Given the existence of norms that depend on the factors mentioned and the dependence of individual effort on such norms, gift exchange can result from the maximizing efforts of employees and firms.

Let us turn to the other example. In "The Economic Consequences of Cognitive Dissonance," Akerlof and Dickens (1982) suppose that beliefs are, to some extent, *chosen* both directly and through manipulating sources of information and that, once chosen, beliefs tend to persist. These suppositions enable them to take account of the apparent fact (explained by the theory of cognitive dissonance) that people adjust their beliefs in order to maintain a favorable view of themselves (see Aronson 1979). For example, bettors at a race track think it is more probable that their horse will win after placing their bets than they did before. Workers in risky jobs tend to underestimate the risks.

The crucial step in the model Akerlof and Dickens present is to include as a non-pecuniary cost of employment in a hazardous industry a psychological cost that depends on the worker's assessment of the risks. The riskier one judges one's employment to be, the less well off one is. So workers can become better off by changing their assessment of the risks involved in their work. In all other ways the workers are completely rational. They even have rational expectations and correctly anticipate how their beliefs will change. By making such a psychological factor an argument in an individual's utility function and using standard techniques of constrained maximization, it is possible to integrate cognitive dissonance theory into microeconomics (see Schlicht 1984). Such a revised version of microeconomics has applications, Akerlof and Dickens argue, to problems of innovation, advertising, social security, and the theory of crime. Cognitive dissonance exerts its influence on these phenomena via the maximizing choices of individuals.[16]

It might appear from this discussion that all is well with the vision of economics as a separate science. What further demonstration could one ask of the flexibility of equilibrium theory than the fact that these empirical generalizations from psychology and anthropology can be so smoothly incorporated into it? But to someone committed to a separate science of economics, Akerlof's formulations are deeply *ad hoc*₃ (p. 196 above). Although Akerlof's models are rational choice models (section 6.6), the sociological and psychological generalizations concerning gifts and cognitive dissonance do not satisfy the constraints listed in section 6.5. The additional generalizations concerning preferences and beliefs that Akerlof relies on have a comparatively narrow scope, undermine the dominance of consumerism and have no explanation in terms of equilibrium theory itself. Just as economists have objected to adaptive expectations on the grounds that it was not derived from equilibrium theory and makes exploitable fools of individuals, so might the defender of the separate science of economics object to the generalizations Akerlof borrows from other social sciences. Akerlof makes the same point with an elegant analogy:

economic theorists, like French chefs in regard to food, have developed stylized models whose ingredients are limited by some unwritten rules. Just as traditional French cooking does not use seaweed or raw fish, so neoclassical models do not make assumptions derived from psychology, anthropology, or sociology. (1984, p. 2)

I would add that, if French chefs resembled neoclassical economists, French cuisine would be more monotonous, for the chefs would use very few ingredients. They would also strenuously insist that food containing any other ingredients was not French. In stretching and opening microeconomics, Akerlof is transcending the vision of it as a separate science.

In Akerlof's combinations of microeconomics and other theories, microeconomics has two roles that should be distinguished. In its mathematical treatment of utility theory, economics provides a means to render determinant the implications of the empirical "force" captured in the generalizations borrowed from other social scientists. But, second, it also supplies one "force" of its own, greed. Fusing cognitive dissonance theory or the theory of gifts with a mathematical treatment of utility

---

[16] As Elster points out (1989b, p. 22n), there are some serious difficulties with this model, for, even though people do come to hold beliefs that reduce cognitive dissonance, beliefs cannot be deliberately chosen.

theory, consumerism, and profit maximization, consequently has implications that the psychological or anthropological theories by themselves did not have. Akerlof shows how hypotheses formulated by other social theorists can sometimes be neatly presented within a formalism familiar to economists, but a single set of behavioral generalizations is no longer doing the work for all economic problems and the vision of economics as a separate science has been abandoned.

It is possible to regard the behavioral generalizations offered by psychologists as simply further facts to be incorporated into microeconomics in the same way that technological knowledge or institutional constraints are incorporated. But to do so would be to countenance a radical change in strategy, because the models economists employ would then depend on substantive social and psychological theories, and economics would be a separate science in style only. If the explaining is being done by "*ad hoc*" psychological laws, and the economic framework is imposing a merely stylistic unity, then one has largely given up the aspiration of being able to separate off an economic realm, subject only to its own laws. Akerlof's marvelous ability to incorporate the insights of psychologists and sociologists into abstract mathematical models is deeply subversive of the style of theorizing to which it apparently conforms.

Although models such as Akerlof's and Dickens' or Russell's and Thaler's are concerned with empirical questions of positive economic theory, they are normatively loaded; and resistance to modifying microeconomics may have political and ideological as well as methodological sources. For, if workers in risky industries systematically underestimate the risks involved in their employment, the bargains they make with their employers may not protect their interests. If individuals irrationally refuse to think about their retirement, then there is a stronger case for mandatory social security. If economic behavior is significantly influenced by distinctive psychological and sociological traits in addition to rational acquisitiveness, or if there is any systematic irrationality, then the identification of well-being as the satisfaction of preferences is cast into doubt and the argument for competitive markets from minimal benevolence (section 4.6) no longer goes through. The case for government intervention in economic life is consequently strengthened.[17] However separable positive

---

[17] If gift exchange is a pervasive feature of labor contracts, then there can be involuntary unemployment; and there are stronger moral grounds for unemployment benefits. Akerlof's "A Theory of Social Custom, of Which Unemployment May be one Consequence," (1980) and his "Discriminatory, Status-Based Wages among Traditional-Oriented, Stochastically Trading Coconut Producers" (1985) might be used to justify government intervention to alleviate discrimination. His memorable model of adverse selection in "The Market for 'Lemons': Quality Uncertainty and the Market Mechanism" (1970) provides an additional argument for medicare.

and normative questions – questions of is and ought – may be in principle, they are here, as in Samuelson's overlapping generations model and in economics generally, constantly intertwined in fact.

14.2.4   What is to be done

If my general story is correct, what can be done to improve economics? One thing to do is to write books such as this one and attempt to convince economists of the need for change.[18] But, given the structure of academic economics, rational persuasion will take a long time, and those who are persuaded will face criticism and other sanctions within the discipline. Those persuaded by my arguments will need to undertake institutional changes as well.

One should not suppose that the incentives within the discipline will automatically favor the optimal mix of methodological commitments. The "meta-level" arbitrage argument that economists who employ a better methodology will convert or bankrupt those who employ a worse methodology is even weaker than the arbitrage argument concerning the behavior of economic agents. For the competitive structure of scientific disciplines (see Hull 1988) is quite different than the structure of markets. The obstacles in the path of empirical success in economics are so profound and the costs of empirical research so high that standards of excellence in economics, such as mathematical prowess, can persist indefinitely regardless of whether they contribute to or hinder progress in the discipline.[19]

I am not competent to map out the specific reforms that economists ought to undertake. The most important step is to comprehend the source of the problems. Once the problems are understood, then many detailed changes need to be made in the education of economists,[20] in the incentives in the profession, and in the tenuous relationships between theorists

---

[18] I am not, of course, alone in doing so. For other examples, see Bell and Kristol 1981, Eichner 1983, Klamer 1984, Mirowski 1990, Nelson 1986, Samuels 1980, Weintraub 1990.

[19] See Debreu's unconvincing praise for the accomplishments of mathematical economics (1991). I frankly do not know whether economists would be better economists if they were better mathematicians. But it is easy to see how mathematical competence could become probably the most important mark of excellence as an economist. For (1) most great physicists are strong mathematicians, (2) mathematical ability is sufficiently rare and mathematical competence sufficiently difficult to acquire that such competence discriminates among economists, (3) mathematical competence is easily judged, and (4) the implicit program for progress in economics shared by most theorists sets forth mainly mathematical problems.

[20] According to Colander's and Klamer's survey, more than half of the students at major universities believed that excellence at mathematics is very important to success in graduate school, while only 3 per cent believed that "having a thorough knowledge of the economy" was (1987, p. 100; see also Klamer and Colander 1990).

in business schools and in economics departments or between economists and other social theorists. I think that the discipline is in need of a major overhaul.

14.3   Epistemology, methodology, and the practice of economics

Having climbed briefly and precariously on my soap box, I am pleased to get down and to address the philosophical question of whether I had any right to up be there at all. First, one might question the possibility or point of "external" criticisms: could any outsider have a good enough understanding of the constraints governing the different tasks economists undertake to be able to offer sensible advice? And second, regardless of how well supported such advice were, could it possibly have any effect?[21] Even religious moralists with the authority of divine writ have had a hard time changing people's behavior. How then could a philosopher, with nothing but complicated arguments, change practices that are intelligently devised and diligently carried out by smart, dedicated, and highly educated economists? Indeed one's reaction at this point might shift from cynicism to anger. What impertinence! How dare Hausman pretend to legislate for economists?

But these questions suggest only healthy skepticism. For they can be asked about all normative enterprises. Consider the analogy (see A.13, p. 318) between philosophers of science studying science and economists studying business. Can economists know enough about business to offer advice? Can their advice possibly have any effect? Is it not arrogant to suppose that economists could know more about how to run a business than individuals who have devoted their lives to business and whose livelihood depends on their success? Such questions counsel caution, but they do not demand a repudiation of all economic advice.[22] The analogous doubts about normative methodology do not automatically discredit the recommendations offered by a philosopher.

With regard to the complaint that methodology is futile, remember that the influence of this book depends on you as well as me. There is no doubt that normative theorizing, like all theorizing, generally has little immediate influence on human practice. But this realization provides no better reason to dismiss all methodological advice than to dismiss all moral precept. Economists are, no doubt, and *should be* reluctant to change their practices, and the force of argument is limited. But arguments

---

[21] See Caldwell's forceful exposition of the objections to economic methodology (1990).
[22] George Stigler doubts whether economists can give much useful advice to either business or government (1976) and McCloskey 1990, chapters 8 and 9 doubts whether they can give any. So my rhetorical questions will not persuade McCloskey. But, as argued in footnote 26 below, McCloskey's skepticism is unjustified.

can persuade, and good arguments can persuade rationally. If a case is clear, cogent, and accessible, let us be optimistic enough to suppose that it can have some effect, too.

More interesting than these general complaints against all methodological criticisms are arguments directed particularly against accepting the advice of philosophers (hiss!). For (1) the philosophical theories that supported previous methodological advice have, one after another, collapsed with their own internal problems. Moreover (2) philosophical claims to special authority in methodological matters have been progressively undermined by the development of philosophical thought itself. Finally (3) the most influential philosophical advice of the twentieth century, that supplied by the logical positivists (at least in popularized versions such as Ayer's *Language Truth and Logic* (1936; see A.1.1) and that offered by Popper and Lakatos, is in my view largely bad advice. Why should this book be any better?

These objections to philosophy of economics call for some comments on the nature of my enterprise. In doing so I shall also react to recent work by Donald McCloskey, who has pressed such objections with particular force. In his book, *The Rhetoric of Economics* (1985a), McCloskey repudiates the whole enterprise of METHODOLOGY.[23]

McCloskey and I agree that the distinguishing feature of economic methodology is its concern with the relationship between the practices and products of economics and general cognitive ends such as truth and predictive reliability. Methodology is concerned with whether the claims of economics are reliable and true and how one can judge whether they are reliable or true; and it is concerned with whether the practices of economists lead to conclusions that one ought to rely on or to believe. This is not to say that methodology is exclusively concerned with questions of theory assessment, which has obviously not been the only issue in this book. But much of methodology is normative, and the standards employed are in part "external" general standards, such as those stating when one is justified in relying on claims for practical purposes and when one is justified in regarding claims as close to the truth.

When McCloskey argues for an end to methodology, he is arguing against any connection between specific evaluative standards and the concerns of epistemology. Why deny this connection? Obviously there are evaluative standards; norms are unavoidable features of every human

---

[23] McCloskey's general position was first presented in his 1983. More recent statements such as his 1988a, 1988b, and 1989 show a more moderate epistemology. His 1990 is less epistemologically ambitious and makes more explicit the links between McCloskey's commitment to rhetoric and his libertarianism. For interesting criticisms see Bicchieri 1988 and Fish 1988.

enterprise. But one might question whether any norms are better than any others in leading scientists to acquire predictively valuable or true conclusions. Paul Feyerabend comes close to defending this extravagant conclusion (1975), but this extreme view is not McCloskey's.

A slightly more moderate view is that no norms can be *shown* to be better than others in achieving predictively valuable or true conclusions. One might argue for this claim by maintaining that "good" arguments in economics are simply those that accord with whatever standards happen (for no good reason) to be prevalent among economists. Many have read McCloskey as defending this radically skeptical conclusion. I do not think this interpretation is correct, because rhetoric, his replacement for methodology, is supposed to be concerned with good arguments, that is arguments that not only happen to persuade but which ought to persuade (1985a, p. 29). Furthermore, McCloskey criticizes the conflation between economic and merely statistical significance, which is common in leading economics journals and thus presumably persuasive to many economists (1985a, chapter 9).

If McCloskey then agrees that there are grounds to believe that some norms are better than others, why does he deny that there are specifically *epistemological* grounds for distinguishing which are better and which are worse? Although some of McCloskey's reasons apply to all methodological inquiry, many are directed only against a particular kind of methodology, which one might call "*a priori*" or "conceptualist." "Positivists" or, more generally (in McCloskey's terminology) "modernists" are often taken to believe that methodological standards are determined by the analysis of concepts.

Whether or not McCloskey correctly interprets traditional conceptualist methodology or justly criticizes it, his critique of specifically "modernist" methodology is not an argument against all methodology. In my view, philosophical theses about how knowledge ought to be acquired and structured, such as those defended in this book, are justified just as other theses are. One asks, "How well do they enable my body of knowledge, including my perceptual beliefs, to hold together?" Epistemology is, in Quine's terminology, "naturalized" (1969). Like physics or phrenology it aims to help improve our beliefs. Only the narrowness of its questions, which is dictated by its normative role, distinguishes epistemology from other empirical studies of the acquisition and revision of human beliefs.

The sort of empirical methodological inquiry exemplified here embodies this vision of philosophy. People acquire knowledge, and, to find out how, one must study what they do. There is no presumption that there is only one good way to learn. To find out how people have learned and to find out which methods have been successful in which circumstances, one must study what has been done and how well it has worked. In so far as McCloskey is only insisting that those interested in economic methodology must study how economists argue, I fully agree.

But McCloskey wants to draw more radical conclusions.[24] He wants to repudiate all methodology, not merely *a priori* methodology. Apart from his critique of *a priori* methodology, he seems to have three main reasons for denying that economists can be held to "external" cognitive standards justified by epistemological considerations.

First, McCloskey asserts, "Nothing is gained from clinging to the Scientific Method, or to any methodology except honesty, clarity, and tolerance" (1983, p. 482). His point seems to be that all external standards are vacuous. Truly informative and substantive standards are context-dependent. They will be determined by features internal to economics, not by general epistemological considerations. The failed efforts of philosophers to provide contentful context-free accounts of notions such as confirmation or scientific explanation do indeed suggest that substantive norms will be context-specific (Miller 1987). But the conclusion that no significant transdisciplinary claims can be made and that there can be no role for epistemology depends on the false assumption that such claims can make no reference to context. Just how methodological rules should depend on features of the context of inquiry remains a vital epistemological question.

Second, McCloskey argues that "It would be arrogant to suppose that one knew better than thousands of intelligent and honest economic scholars what the proper form of argument was" (1985a, p. 139). But epistemology seems arrogant only if one falsely assumes that these scholars agree on an internally consistent methodology that coheres reasonably with the rest of their beliefs and that the methodologist drops from a philosophical cloud. As we have seen, there is plenty of methodological controversy among economists, and philosophers can learn some economics before issuing edicts. Since there need be no arrogance when economic scholars themselves invoke epistemological concerns, it is not automatically arrogant of outsiders to do so.

Finally, McCloskey argues that the methodological standards defended by the epistemologist depend on a chimerical notion of Truth (with a capital T) (1985a, pp. 46–7; 1985b, pp. 136–7; 1988a, pp. 255–6). Truth cannot be a standard or an objective. McCloskey argues that the standard of good argument is whatever persuades the majority of competent

---

[24] He here follows literary theorists such as Booth (1974, 1979), Burke (1950, 1961), and Fish (1980), and philosophers such as Rorty (1979).

economists. There is no other success to be obtained and no other objective to aim for.

This argument rests on a failure to distinguish among different issues. First, it is not true that all invocations of epistemology are bound up with the notion of truth, for not all epistemologies are realist (A.2).[25] The instrumentalist wants only predictively useful hypotheses. Second, although both instrumentalist and realist economists aim to persuade other economists, they seek to persuade not as an ultimate goal or as an end in itself, but because they take success in persuasion to be a fallible *result* and a fallible *indication* of having made a good argument. Working among a set of corrupt and depraved colleagues, one might indeed be disconcerted by persuasive success.

Third, the fact that truth and future reliability are not now *grounds* for accepting conclusions is entirely consistent with the aspiration of making true or reliable claims (see p. 173 above and appendix, p. 289). The truth of *P* is not an *argument* in favor of believing *P*. One might persuade someone by pronouncing with an air of great certainty: "The best reason to believe that tariffs decrease economic welfare is that it is true that tariffs decrease economic welfare," or by shouting: "It's true! It's true!" But these are not arguments. One might as well simply recite: "Tariffs decrease economic welfare. Tariffs decrease economic welfare. Tariffs decrease economic welfare." Truth is what one *seeks*, not one's *evidence*. Similarly, the greater future predictive success of *P* as compared to *Q* is no evidence or argument now in favor of *P*. Future predictive success, like truth, is a goal, not a kind of evidence. This platitude gives one no reason to be suspicious of the notions of truth or predictive reliability and no reason to attempt to analyze the truth or predictive reliability of *P* and *Q* in terms of beliefs concerning *P* and *Q*.[26]

[25] Mäki 1988a criticizes the implicit instrumentalism in McCloskey's defense of rhetoric, and McCloskey replies in his 1988c. See also Mäki's rejoinder, 1988b.

[26] McCloskey also argues, "A scholar in possession of a scholarly formula more specific than Work and Pray would be a scientific millionaire. Scientific millionaires are not common. Methodology claims prescience in scientific affairs. The difficulty with pre-science is that it is exactly 'pre-science' – that is, knowing things before they are known, contradicting itself. Methodology entails this contradiction. It pretends to know how to achieve knowledge before the knowledge to be achieved is in place. Life is not so easy." (p. 53) By parity of reasoning, economics can make no useful predictions (an implication which McCloskey apparently accepts (1985a, pp. 15–16, 89; 1990, chapters 8, 9)). Useful advice is impossible, because useful advice would make one a millionaire. But the scarcity of scientific millionaires is consistent with any level of success and progress in methodology, just as the scarcity of economist millionaires is consistent with any level of success and progress in economics. If it were easy to make useful improvements in methodology or economics, there would be lots of people busy doing so. When they succeeded, they would be unable to monopolize their success, and they would not earn windfall profits.

In addition, although this is not one of McCloskey's arguments, one might argue that empirical philosophy of science is hopelessly circular. The proposal to find out how to do science by studying scientifically how people do science seems multiply paradoxical. If one does not already know what science is, one will not know which practices to study, and if one does not already know how to do science, one will not know how to study those practices. Either one cannot start at all, or one must begin by assuming that one already knows the answers one is looking for. But, if one must beg all the significant questions, what point can the exercise have? (see Hausman 1980 or 1981a, postscript).

The trick is to beg the questions in the right way. There is nothing wrong with beginning with the presumption that one knows how to find out what norms govern institutions such as theoretical economics, provided that one's initial presuppositions are subject to correction in the course of inquiry (Michael Friedman 1979). I began this methodological study of economics with many unavoidable presuppositions, which I have tried to scrutinize, piecemeal. Philosophy of economics, as I have attempted to practice it, thus resembles history, sociology, literary criticism, and economics itself as much as it resembles conceptual analysis.

I see no grounds to conclude that this sort of empirical methodological inquiry is misconceived. There is no good general philosophical case against the possibility of investigating empirically how people learn, what sorts of methods work best for which sorts of problems, or how one can best insure against the sort of mistakes people are prone to make. Such questions are not purely psychological, although psychological evidence may bear on them. Investigations into the history and current state of science are also relevant to their answers. In any event, they are real questions. They do not appear to be unanswerable, and their answers may be of normative importance. Thus I attempted in the previous section to draw out the practical implications of my account of the structure, strategies, and difficulties of economic theorizing.

Moreover, appraisals of economics that draw on epistemological theses are inevitable. For the very terms in which one describes the practices of economists – theorizing, testing, deducing, modeling, sampling, and so forth – carry philosophical baggage. McCloskey unavoidably begins with such notions, and his object – the discourse of economists – is already penetrated through and through with philosophical influences. Could these philosophical influences on the methodological inquirer or on the object of inquiry ever be transcended? I doubt it, and, even if they could, they will be with us for a long while yet.[27]

---

[27] McCloskey pointed out to me in correspondence that one can make the same argument for the inevitability of rhetoric. Notice that I have been defending methodology, rather than attacking rhetoric.

Furthermore, at least one kind of normative epistemological theory, the Bayesian view of confirmation (A.10.2), is itself an application of central claims of economic theory. For economists to refuse to pay attention to the norms proposed by Bayesian epistemologists would be to refuse to heed implications of more or less their own models. Epistemology is unavoidable.

Finally, as Alexander Rosenberg has argued so pointedly (1988a), if economics ever succeeded in repudiating all epistemology and answered only to its own standards, it would lose its influence on non-economists and its rational hold on economists themselves. If the standards of acceptance among economists had no connection to epistemologically significant goals, such as reliability or truth, then the fact that a particular conclusion was accepted by most economists would be of as little interest to policy-makers as is the fact that a particular conclusion is accepted by most astrologers. Indeed, pursued to its logical conclusions, the notion that a distinctive kind of investigation should answer only to its own standards would dissolve economics not into a single cult, but into many.

None of these comments constitute a defense of the specific conclusions or recommendations of this book. They stand or fall on their merits. I have only argued that there is nothing misconceived about the project of appraising the discipline of neoclassical economics as a purported contribution to human knowledge.

15   Conclusions

This book has focused on the epistemological peculiarities of a very special human cognitive enterprise – neoclassical microeconomics. It has not broached the central problems of epistemology or of philosophy of science in their full generality. Its conclusions concern economics and not all are relevant to other disciplines, even other social disciplines. But some of its conclusions are of general significance. For example, although Richard Miller in his recent *Fact and Method* eloquently insists upon the importance of the particular problems and standards that characterize different disciplines, he endorses the philosophical platitude that scientific theories postulate the existence of unobservable things to explain generalizations at the level of observations (1987, p. 135). To make sense of economic theory, one must reject this view. Similarly the extent to which the view of models and theories defended in section 5.3 helps to illuminate economics provides an argument for the cogency of that general view. The discussion of Milton Friedman's methodology helps one to disentangle different positions that might be called instrumentalist (A.2) and shows what concern for truth instrumentalists need to have. The discussion in chapters 12 and 13 of how evidence bears on utility theory illuminates the tenuous general relations between theory and data.

It would be tedious to compile a long list of examples such as these, and, in any event, my main concern is economics, not general philosophy of science. Instead, in closing, I shall attempt to bring together the main theses of this book and to show how they clarify and explain the most prominent methodological peculiarities of economics. The fact that economics is a social science, a science of human beings (A.14), turns out to be crucial to its distinctive methodological problems.

15.1   The structure and strategy of neoclassical theoretical economics

In part I I tried to give a general account of the structure and strategy of theoretical economics, which is summarized in figure 15.1. I argued that equilibrium theory lies at the heart of neoclassical theoretical

270

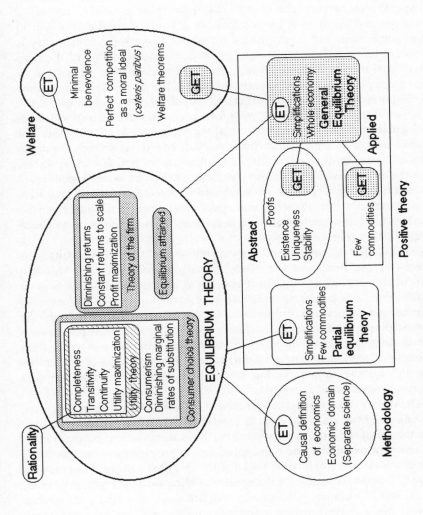

Figure 15.1. Theoretical neoclassical economics

economics. Neoclassical economics *is* the articulation, elaboration, and the application of equilibrium theory.

It is unhelpful to maintain that equilibrium theory is the hard core of a Lakatosian scientific research program, because this claim is both unspecific and untrue. For neoclassical economists are free in particular inquiries to drop some of the constituents of equilibrium theory and even to replace them with contraries. Commitment to equilibrium theory is only commitment to some subset of its components. Some of the laws that constitute equilibrium theory are more central than others, but, if one attempts to say what theoretical economics is by identifying some common core of propositions that are shared by every model or theory, one will not be able to give an informative characterization. So what Lakatosians might be inclined to call the "negative heuristic" does not forbid tampering with equilibrium theory. It effectively forbids removing rational greed and the possibility of equilibrium from their central places, but the characterization of this "pseudo-hard-core" is left open: non-satiation can be replaced with satiation, but claims about cognitive dissonance are not allowed. Incompleteness or intransitivities can be explored, but psychological generalizations about procedure variance are probably forbidden.

Equilibrium theory consists of the theory of consumer choice, the theory of the firm, and the thesis that equilibrium obtains. This last constituent fits awkwardly, for it appears as a theorem rather than as an axiom, but it is a central constituent nevertheless. All of the parts of equilibrium theory are problematic. Of the theory of the firm, only the law of diminishing returns is relatively solid. Constant returns to scale seems false and shows up more to insure mathematical coherence than because of any conviction of its correctness. Maximization of net returns not only appears to be false, but it is in conflict with utility maximization in most institutional settings.

The theory of consumer choice consists of utility theory, consumerism, and diminishing marginal rates of substitution. It is less problematic than the theory of the firm, for consumerism and diminishing marginal rates of substitution seem to be reasonable first approximations, at least with respect to market behavior, and (ordinal) utility theory is perhaps a plausible approximation. In the context of choices among a finite number of options, continuity is harmless, and, although transitivity may break down, there is obviously a good deal to be said for its correctness. Completeness is most problematic, though perhaps not in the context of complete certainty (but that context is itself problematic).

As I construed theories, they consist of sets of lawlike statements that are systematically interconnected; and I thus identified equilibrium theory with the laws of the theory of the firm and of consumer choice, plus the assertion that equilibrium obtains. But these laws do no work by themselves, and, in theoretical and empirical work in economics, they are always combined with simplifications and specifications of relevant circumstances. Some of these simplifications, such as infinite commodity divisibility, perfect information, or perfect competition are pervasive and help determine the character of theoretical economics. But these simplifications are not assertions or discoveries of economics. Theories in economics can be classified into partial or general equilibrium accounts. Partial equilibrium analyses attempt to treat markets in relative isolation, while general equilibrium theories attempt to deal with the general interdependencies among markets, although this is less true of highly aggregative general equilibrium models with few commodities. Mathematical investigations of abstract general equilibrium models have been methodologically puzzling, since the models are not true of existing economies. I argued that they are best interpreted as conceptual investigations, investigations of possibilities, or as attempts to develop heuristically useful tools. Equilibrium theory, *not* general equilibrium theory, is the fundamental theory of neoclassical economics. General equilibrium theories augment equilibrium theory with simplifications or specifications concerning the circumstances to be studied. They serve as a proving ground for new tools and are used to explore whether equilibrium theory will be able to serve as the core of a separate economic science.

To make sense of this theoretical enterprise also requires distinguishing between models and theories. Models are definitions of kinds of systems. The assumptions of models are clauses in definitions and not true or false assertions about the world. The investigation of models is a fully defensible part of science, for one crucial component of science is the articulation of new concepts in terms of which to theorize. When one offers a general theoretical hypothesis asserting that a model is true of some realm of reality, then one is offering a theory; and in offering the theoretical hypothesis one is committed to treating what were the assumptions of the model as assertions about the world. Despite what they sometimes say, economists do not treat equilibrium theory as merely a fundamental model, to which no empirical commitments pertain. For economists believe that they can predict and explain economic phenomena in terms of equilibrium theory.

Central to mainstream economics has been the thought that economists are concerned with a set of causal factors or "laws," which turn out to be predominant in a particular domain of social life. These laws are generally well-known and make up accepted economic theory, which provides a unified and complete, but inexact account of the entire economic realm (though not all of economics is concerned with the economic realm). This vision expresses a methodological commitment to what Mill called "a separate science" of economics. Other generalizations about preferences, beliefs, and constraints may be added to economic models and theories, provided that they do not conflict with the central place within the economic realm of rational greed or make equilibrium impossible. To employ any other generalizations is *ad hoc*. No changes in fundamental theory itself are permissible unless they preserve its universal scope. The further features of human behavior that psychologists and sociologists discover are typically *ad hoc* and have only narrow scope. They are usually not suitable for inclusion in particular economic models and are virtually always disqualified from inclusion within fundamental theory. The methodological commitment to a separate science leads to the view that equilibrium theory is (at a suitable level of abstraction and approximation) the whole theoretical truth about economics.

This methodological commitment to the structure and strategy of a separate economic science explains why economists theorize as they do. I argued that it is unjustifiably dogmatic. The methodological commitment to a separate science of economics preserves the scientific appearance of economics and spares economists the maddeningly difficult and disorderly task of floundering among disparate data, attempting to identify significant causal factors. It preserves the aesthetic attractions of economics and keeps it a tractable subject for mathematical exploration. The commitment to a separate science maintains the identification between the empirical theory of how people choose and the theory of how they rationally ought to choose, which in turn provides a strong pragmatic argument for treating apparent disconfirmation as error. And this commitment is essential to the normative argument for perfect competitive equilibrium, which underlies both conservative defenses of *laissez-faire* and liberal analyses of market failures.

But, however appealing this vision of economics is and however easy it is to understand why economists are so deeply committed to it, it stands in the way of empirical progress.

15.2   Appraising microeconomics and general equilibrium theory

Part II of this book was concerned with theory appraisal, and it was as much critical as constructive. Many hundreds of unhelpful pages have been written concerning how to assess economic theories, in large part because questions of theory appraisal in economics have rarely been joined to a detailed treatment of its structure and strategy. So, when economists fail to take apparent disconfirmations as refutations, they are seen as adhering to an unreasonably dogmatic theory of confirmation or as failing to live up to their scientific standards, when their actions are instead consistent with an uncontroversial view of theory assessment, given the best knowledge economists have and their commitment to economics as a separate science. If economists are sometimes unreasonably dogmatic, it is because of this last commitment, not because of their views of theory appraisal.

Further complicating the story are Milton Friedman's influential views, which direct economists to be guided entirely by the success of the relevant predictions of their theories. With respect to microeconomics at least, this advice is entirely impractical, quite apart from the internal problems with Friedman's methodology. Friedman's advice has rarely been followed, and to implement it would require that microeconomics be radically transformed. Yet, since Friedman presents his views in defense of theoretical "business-as-usual" against critics of standard economics, one finds economists espousing Friedman's methodology, who would never dream of seriously acting on it.

Add in the influences of Popper and Lakatos and the confusions deepen. Popper is a natural authority to look to, for he is a leading philosopher of science and a marvelous writer, and his political views and his views concerning the methodology of the social sciences appeal to many economists. Moreover, his message appears at first glance consonant with Friedman's (Blaug 1976). But, if Popper were right about how to do science, then economics would show a massive failure of methodological nerve. If one takes seriously what Popper says about falsifiability and the critical attitude, then the methodological practice of economics is not only mistaken, it is stupid and intellectually reprehensible. Although this book has been critical of features of the methodology of economics, it has shown how researchers of intelligence and scholarly integrity could be mistakenly committed to it.

One can better defend the honor of economists by using Lakatos's methodology of scientific research programs, since it is flexible enough that few practices can be unequivocally condemned. Yet some developments in economics that are widely regarded as central theoretical advances (such as the switch from cardinal to ordinal utility theory), must be seen from Lakatos' perspective as evidence that the "neoclassical research program" is degenerating. Furthermore, Lakatos' categories do not fit the practices and products of economics easily and his rejection of "justificationism" is an invitation to epistemological disaster.

Friedman, Popper, and Lakatos, each in his own way, would prevent us from relying on supporting evidence. But, in interpreting experimental failures and in gambling on theories in new circumstances, we need to make careful use of the evidence in support of the propositions involved. Indeed it is only because of the importance of such evidence that there is a special difficulty about testing in economics. There is no special logical problem deriving predictions from economic theory and other statements. The difficulty is that the other statements are so unlikely to be true that the test results tell us nothing about economic theory. It is difficult even to envision an activity that paid no attention to supporting evidence. It would be nothing like the sciences we know.

To appraise economic theory sensibly, one must also come to terms with its inexactness. While inexactness is not a virtue, it must be distinguished from other sorts of empirical shortcomings; and one must explain how inexact sciences can be understood and defended. The inexactness of equilibrium theory should be understood mainly in terms of counterfactuals or vague *ceteris paribus* qualifications. Until one understands how counterfactual or qualified claims can be true or false, valuable or valueless, and confirmed or disconfirmed, one is in no position to recognize the extent to which equilibrium theory is true, valuable or confirmed.

The theory of confirmation is very difficult and puzzling, and I do not know exactly how theories should be appraised. Neither do scientists, including economists. If progress in science depended on having scientific method exactly right, there would be no progress in science. There is a good deal of truth to the simple story that says that one derives predictions from an hypothesis and other premises and draws conclusions concerning how likely it is that the hypothesis is correct "on the basis of"[1] the success or failure of those predictions. Economists do exactly this, but they are blessed with the knowledge that there is a great deal of truth to equilibrium theory, and they are cursed with such difficulties in testing that they are rarely in any position to change their initial assessment. The weakness of the empirical control exerted by economic data provides for a legitimately large role for pragmatic factors. Choices about whether to deal with disconfirmations by means of fundamental theory modification or by the introduction of disturbances or interferences (which in many contexts do not need to be mentioned) will turn not only or mainly on the data, but on the sort of exactness one thinks obtainable, on the sorts of jobs the theory is supposed to do, and on the sort of aesthetic, systematic, and normative virtues the alternatives may have.

This looks like Mill's method *a priori*, his deductive method, but it is not a special theory of confirmation at all; and its apparent dogmatism

---

[1] This phrase is intentionally vague. There are enormous problems with this simple story, too. See A.10 and especially the discussion of Richard Miller's views of confirmation on pp. 303–4.

arises from the bad data coupled with the good reasons economists have to find some truth in equilibrium theory.

15.3 Reasons and causes: rationality and economic behavior

If one says that Elizabeth's preferences are complete, transitive, and continuous, one is offering empirical generalizations about her. These generalizations assert matters of fact. They are testable. And, unless Elizabeth is unlike the rest of the species, they are not all true, although there is a good deal of truth to them. Similarly, to connect Elizabeth's actions to her preferences by asserting that Elizabeth never prefers an option she believes to be feasible to the one she chooses, is, on the ordinary understanding of the notion of preference, an empirical claim (although the theory of revealed preference takes it as defining preference). As many have pointed out, this generalization is not easy to test (Boland 1981, Caldwell 1983; see also appendix, p. 323). To employ these generalizations – that is, utility theory – to explain why Elizabeth chose some option is to say only that she chose it because she most preferred it. Hamlet killed Claudius because he preferred to. Such explanations are vacuous, completely lacking in "depth" (appendix, p. 291). They can be regarded as causal, although they also allude, vacuously, to the agent's reasons. Utility theory can be used to explain Elizabeth's choices on the basis of Elizabeth's preferences and beliefs, but the preferences and beliefs, not utility theory, are doing the explanatory work.

If one explains why Elizabeth chose some bundle of commodities by means of consumer choice theory – that is, not only utility theory, but also consumerism and diminishing marginal rates of substitution, one gives Elizabeth's reasons more clearly, and one also seems to provide a more definite causal explanation. Consumerism and diminishing marginal rates of substitution are substantive "laws" of preferences. They have no obvious connection to rationality, *per se*, and they are easier to test. Consumerism is the motive force ("greed"), and diminishing marginal rates of substitution is a psychological constraint governing economic preferences. Utility theory guarantees the consistency of the chooser and derives a choice from the force, the psychological constraint, and further facts. Both the causal story and the reason for the choice are clearer than in an explanation employing only utility theory.

Since an explanation employing consumer choice theory can be construed as a causal explanation, one might be tempted (as, until recently, I was) to regard the reason-giving aspect and the fact that utility theory is a theory of rationality as merely extra detail, some "local color" that is irrelevant to the explanatory logic of theoretical economics. But it seems to me that many of the distinctive methodological characteristics of economics can be understood better if the reason-giving feature of explanations in economics is taken seriously. In particular, I suggested that the fact that utility theory is a theory of rationality helps to explain:

1 Why the notions of Pareto optimality and Pareto superiority are so pervasive and appealing in welfare economics and why ethical concerns are so often intermingled in positive economic theorizing (section 4.6 and chapter 7).
2 Why economists have such a strong empirical commitment to utility theory as the best account of how agents in fact choose (chapters 12 and 14).
3 Why economists follow their distinctive theoretical strategy (chapter 6).

Much of the methodological distinctiveness of economics stems from the remarkable fact that a theory of rationality lies at its theoretical core.

1 In section 4.6 above I sketched an argument for the moral approval (*ceteris paribus*) of perfectly competitive equilibrium on the basis of equilibrium theory and "minimal benevolence" (that, *ceteris paribus* it is a morally good thing to make people better off). Equilibrium theory identifies an individual's good with the satisfaction of his or her preferences, and it provides the premises for the welfare theorems which show that perfectly competitive equilibria are Pareto efficient and that all Pareto optima can be achieved as competitive equilibria. Rationality, in the form of utility theory is specifically presupposed by the notion of Pareto efficiency and is central to the welfare theorems and to the identification of well-being with the satisfaction of preferences. It is because preferences are *reasons* that the satisfaction of preferences has a claim to be a matter of prudence and thus a claim on the beneficence of others.

Consequently, any challenges to the empirical adequacy of equilibrium theory, or to the argument for the Pareto optimality of the consequences of individually rational behavior in competitive markets bear immediately and forcefully on the argument on the basis of minimal benevolence for perfect competition. Hence a positive conceptual investigation such as Samuelson's has immediate moral reverberations that are evident in Meckling's and Lerner's responses. Challenges or qualifications to individual rationality or to its consequences undermine the moral claims of competitive markets.

2 As I argued above (section 12.4.2), the fact that utility theory is a theory of rationality can give one additional reason to believe that it is to be preferred as an empirical theory of human preference and choice.

The instability of irrational behavior and the educative effects of theories of rationality provide reason to believe that a theory that portrays individuals as behaving rationally is more likely to be true than a theory that depicts them as behaving irrationally. Furthermore, a theory which depicts actual behavior as rational permits explanations to be reason-giving as well as causal. These explanations can be accepted by economic agents as well as economic theorists and permit actions to be appraised.[2] Such a theory may also have better *effects* on how people will behave than a theory that describes people as irrational. Although these last pragmatic factors must take second place to empirical adequacy, they can have a large influence on theory choice in a discipline such as economics in which empirical adequacy is so hard to judge.

3 There are many reasons why it is hard to get knowledge in economics. In particular I have stressed the inadequacies of the data with which economists have to work. Some of the limitations in this data have been economists' own fault, since they have avoided gathering or using certain kinds of evidence; but both the multiplicity of causal factors and the practical and moral problems of experimentation are unavoidable difficulties.

One impediment to progress in economics, about which economists can do something, is the hegemony of the vision of economics as a separate science. This hegemony is due in large part to the fact that equilibrium theory contains a theory of rationality. Utility theory links equilibrium theory to the plausible explanatory strategy embedded in everyday "folk" psychology. Generalizations concerning social phenomena that are not in terms of the beliefs and preferences of agents or the constraints on their actions are *ad hoc* and in need of explanation in these terms. Generalizations that *cannot* be explained in these terms are inherently unstable, because "people will learn" or at least enough of them will that the competitive pressure of the market will bring them into line.

Theoretical constraints are necessary to focus research and to motivate the investigation of esoteric questions. But the justification for a particular paradigm or research program, like the justification for the commitment to economics as a separate science, is success and progress, including especially empirical success and progress. Since economics has not been

---

[2] As Donald Davidson (1980) and Jon Elster (1983, 1989a, 1989b) have argued, irrationality must be exceptional, or folk psychology and the attribution of beliefs and desires to people must be abandoned. But, as Davidson and Elster recognize, this argument does not show that the best theory of human behavior cannot contain appreciable elements of irrationality.

very successful and has not made much empirical progress, economists should be exploring alternatives. When theorists and experimenters in other disciplines have generated potentially relevant generalizations and data, economists should be eager to reach out and incorporate this material into their theorizing.

When one recognizes the centrality of rationality, one can understand better why so many economists are deeply committed to equilibrium theory and to the image of economics as a separate science. Linked to the notion of a separate science is not only the heuristic power of microeconomics but also the rational prescriptive force of utility theory and the moral argument for perfectly competitive equilibrium. Any step away from microeconomics weakens these links between purported facts, rational oughts, and moral oughts and surrenders the grand vision of a unified theory of all economic phenomena. It is hard to give up so much.

But, unless equilibrium theory has captured the major causes of economic phenomena, the separate science of economics can never be successful. If, as seems likely to me, there are systematic and important failings of human rationality, and economic behavior is significantly influenced by many motive forces, apart from consumerism and diminishing marginal rates of substitution, then equilibrium theory is not a very good theory, whether or not there is anything better. If it leaves out important causes, then no mathematical expertise or elegance in modeling will make equilibrium theory into a good theory.

The edifice of contemporary microeconomics is elegant, even gorgeous, and it can sometimes solve specific predictive problems. But its empirical difficulties are legion, and, if the speculative thoughts of these pages are correct, it will never conquer them. Furthermore, concerns about rationality are unavoidable, and normative policy implications will always be close at hand to generate bias. So the case of economics might seem hopeless. But there are better ways forward. Although some theorists should keep pushing the current strategy as hard as they can, I would urge economists to be more eclectic, more opportunistic, more willing to gather data, more willing to work with generalizations with narrow scope, and more willing to collaborate with other social scientists.

Appendix

An introduction to philosophy of science

Science is a human cognitive enterprise, and philosophy of science is a part of epistemology (the theory of knowledge), although philosophers of science also face logical, metaphysical, ethical, and aesthetic questions. Questions concerning the nature of science go back to the beginnings of philosophy, but philosophy of science only became a separate subspecialty about a century ago. Important figures in the early development of modern philosophy of science are David Hume (1738, 1748), Immanuel Kant (1787), John Stuart Mill (1843), William Whewell (1840), and major scientists themselves such as Galileo, Descartes, Newton, and Herschel. Only at the end of the nineteenth century was the field launched with striking monographs by scientists or historians of science such as Ernst Mach (1942), Piere Duhem (1906), and Henri Poincaré (1905).

In the first half of the twentieth century the so-called "logical positivists" dominated thinking about the philosophy of science, although Karl Popper's views also exerted a growing influence. In the 1960s philosophy of science took a historical and empirical turn that has become dominant over the last generation, although many contemporary philosophers of science do abstract formal work that resembles in style the work of the logical positivists. Recent developments in cognitive science have begun to have a strong influence on philosophy of science, but it is too early to judge how significant this influence will be (see Giere 1988, Goldman 1986, Holland *et al.* 1986, Langley *et al.* 1987, and Thagard 1988). Contemporary philosophy of science is a lively field in which disagreement predominates. Although I shall attempt to sketch a "consensus" view on the issues, I cannot avoid making controversial claims.

In the overview that follows, I shall try to say something about most important issues under discussion in contemporary philosophy of science, but I shall pass quickly over those of comparatively little importance to economics. These issues can be divided into thirteen groups:

1 What are the goals of science? Does science aim exclusively to provide correct predictions, which may be of practical use, or should science seek explanations and truth?

2 What is a scientific explanation?
3 What are scientific laws? How important are laws to explanation?
4 What is causation? What role should causal judgments play in science?
5 What is a scientific theory and what are scientific models? How are theories related to models and to laws? Why are theories important and how are they used?
6 How are claims about unobservable things related to the results of observations? Can observation lead to knowledge of imperceptible entities such as electrons?
7 Paradigms and research programs: How are particular theories related to one another? What sort of "global" theory structure is characteristic of science?
8 How are scientific theories and laws discovered or constructed?
9 The problems of confirmation and appraisal: How do scientists test and appraise scientific theories and how do scientists compare competing theories?
10 The problem of induction: How is it possible to establish generalizations and claims about the future on the basis of observation?
11 The problem of demarcation: How can one distinguish the claims and practices of scientists from those of non-scientists?
12 What attitudes, practices, and rules characterize scientists? What are the rules of scientific "method"?
13 The unity of science: Can human actions and institutions be studied in the same way that one studies nature?
   (a) Is a science of society possible?
   (b) Do explanations in the social sciences have the same logic and structure as explanations in the natural sciences?
   (c) Do the social sciences employ the same "extensional" logic that the natural sciences do? Are the social sciences reducible to the natural sciences, and do they develop in the same way?
   (d) How are the intimate links between social theories and values to be understood? Do these links make the social sciences any less objective than the natural sciences?

Question number 9 – the general problem of appraising and comparing scientific theories – has been of most interest to writers on economic methodology; and it is central to this book, as well. But it is important to remember how many other important philosophical questions there are.

This way of grouping the questions is arbitrary, and I make no claims for it apart from expository convenience.

A.1   Historical and philosophical background

In discussing the thirteen sets of issues listed above, I shall need to say something about the positivist and Popperian ancestors of contemporary views, for current philosophy of science is best understood as a reaction against the views of its predecessors, and logical positivist and particularly Popperian views are still influential among economists. So I shall begin with some of this background. Otherwise I shall say little about the history of the philosophy of science.

A.1.1   Logical positivism

Logical positivism was a philosophical movement beginning in the 1920s in Berlin and Vienna and continuing (thanks to Hitler) mainly in the United States into the 1950s (see Ayer 1959 and Hanfling 1981a,b). It was an exceptionally influential intellectual movement. Although most of its distinctive theses were untenable, the logical positivists (or, as they preferred to be called by the 1950s, "logical empiricists") generated the refutations themselves and faced them with an unrivaled honesty (see Nagel 1961).

Although there were many influences on the logical positivists, who had diverse intellectual backgrounds, there were four main inspirations: (1) twentieth-century physics, especially Einstein, (2) late nineteenth- and early twentieth-century formal logic, (3) empiricism, especially as espoused by Hume and Mach, and (4) Kant's "critical" philosophy.

Although Kant had held that scientific knowledge requires sensory data, he regarded the products of sensation as cognitively empty apart from the conceptual "synthesizing" imposed by the "understanding." Mathematics and mathematical physics were the best exemplars of how systematic relations imposed on sensory data constituted objective knowledge. Like Kant, the logical positivists regarded objective knowledge as possible only insofar as sensory experiences are systematically related to one another. Like Kant, the logical positivists regarded mathematics and mathematical physics as paradigmatic of objective knowledge. But they rejected Kant's notion that space and time were "pure intuitions" and his consequent claims for the necessary applicability to experience of mathematical systems such as Euclidean geometry (see Michael Friedman unpublished).

Although the Kantian background of logical positivism was inconsistent with a crude empiricism that takes knowledge to be just an accumulation of sensory experiences, empiricism remained central to logical positivism, and it presented one tempting way to show how scientific knowledge could be objective. Empiricism consists of two related theses: (1) all evidence bearing on "synthetic" statements (statements concerning matters of fact) derives from sense perception; and (2) predicates are meaningful or "cognitively significant" only if it is possible to tell however indirectly by means of sense perception whether something belongs to their extension.[1] Science must be purged of sentences that contain terms that are not cognitively significant. Scientific theories should be formulated so that the bearing of empirical evidence is precise and transparent.

In the positivist's view, formal logic could be marshalled in the empiricist cause, for logicians such as Frege and Russell appeared to offer the possibility of a new language for science that avoids the vagueness and ambiguity of ordinary language and sets new standards for rigorous analysis (Russell's 1905 was one paradigm). The distinction logicians came to draw between syntactic notions such as well-formedness, proof, or consistency and semantic notions such as truth, reference, and meaning became especially important to the positivists. They saw formal logic as liberating empiricism from the psychological and metaphysical garb in which it was presented by Hume and Mach and as permitting one to distinguish analytic or inconsistent statements, which are true or false by virtue of logic and meanings, from the statements which must pass the test of observation (Ayer 1936, chapter 4).

Finally both formal logic and empiricism could help explain the breakthroughs of contemporary physics and contribute to further scientific progress. For the logical positivists saw Einstein's contribution as in part the conceptual discovery that the Newtonian notion of simultaneity of spatially separated events was not cognitively significant: there is no way to tell whether pairs of spatially separated events belong to the extension of the Newtonian predicate "is simultaneous."[2] This revolution in physics showed the importance of formulating theories precisely enough that the cognitive significance of their predicates could be assessed by intellects less lofty than Einstein's. Despite the deep empiricist commitments of the positivists, their work was always constrained by a respect for the achievements of the natural sciences. If a philosophical model wound up condemning the major achievements of contemporary physics, then it, not the physics, was regarded as suspect.

---

[1] Examples of predicates are phrases such as "is red" or "is shorter than." The extension of a predicate is the set of all those things of which the predicate is true, the set of all red things in the first case, the set of all ordered pairs of which the second is taller than the first in the second example. The empiricist view of meaning, "conceptual empiricism" is not meant to apply to purely logical predicates such as "is identical to."

[2] Theorists such as P.W. Bridgman (1927, 1938), the main proponent of "operationalism," also saw Einstein's contribution this way. See Hempel 1965, pp. 123–34.

The work of the logical positivists consisted of trying (1) to formulate precisely central philosophical notions such as a criterion of cognitive significance or the distinction between analytical claims that are true by definition and synthetic claims that must be testable (Carnap 1936, 1937, Hempel 1965, pp. 101-22); (2) to develop precise construals of central scientific notions such as theory, explanation, confirmation, etc. (Hempel 1965, pp. 3-46, 173-228, 245-90, 331-496); and (3) to show that significant scientific work was consistent with positivist conceptual analyses or to reveal the need for changes in these conceptual analyses (Hempel 1965, pp. 231-44, 297-330). As I discuss major features of science in the succeeding sections, I shall repeatedly take the positivists' construals as the point of departure.

A.1.2   Karl Popper's philosophy of science

Since Karl Popper had a more direct and powerful influence on economics than have the logical positivists, his views are discussed at length in chapter 10. So the remarks here will be brief. Popper differed from the logical positivists in placing less emphasis on formal reformulations of science, in refusing to equate science with cognitive significance (or to regard metaphysics and non-sciences as "meaningless"), and, most centrally, as stressing that scientific theories boldly transcend the data and are subject only to empirical *falsification*, never to empirical *verification*. What distinguishes sciences from non-sciences in Popper's view is that scientific theories are falsifi*able* (not false or falsified) – that is, that scientific theories take risks and might possibly be falsified by reports of observations or experiments. The mark of sciences, as opposed to pseudo-sciences, is that scientists are critical and subject their theories to the harshest tests that they can design.

Despite important differences between Popper and the logical positivists, there is also a great deal of common ground. Popper has the same view of scientific explanation, the same admiration for the exact sciences, similar empiricist inclinations, and a strong Kantian inheritance. Like the positivists, he has specific views on detailed questions concerning science, and I shall touch on these in succeeding sections. As argued in chapter 10, Popper's views are as inadequate as are those of the logical positivists, although for different reasons.

A.2   The goals of science: realism versus instrumentalism

One of the longest-standing disagreements among scientists concerns the goals of theorizing and the attitudes one should have toward the unobservable things so often mentioned in scientific theories.[3] There have been two main schools of thought. So called "scientific realists" have held that science should not only enable us to make accurate predictions, but it should *also* enable us to discover new truths about the world and to explain the phenomena. When a theory is very well supported, the realist holds that one can regard its claims, even those which talk about unobservable things, as true, although realists concede that the findings of science are *corrigible* – that is, subject to correction. Copernicus, for example, was a realist.[4] He sought an alternative to Ptolemy's earth-centered astronomy not mainly because of its inadequacies in predicting the positions of heavenly bodies, but because its account of the heavens made no physical sense and therefore could not be true (Dreyer 1953, p. 320; Toulmin and Goodfield 1961, 178-9).

Members of the other school, so-called "instrumentalists," *agree* that scientific theories are important, but instrumentalists have been more reserved about whether one can regard the claims that theories make about unobservables as true. For instrumentalists insist that the goal of science is the development of tools which enable one to make reliable and useful predictions. Thus Osiander, in his preface to Copernicus' *De Revolutionibus* (1543) argued that the merits of Corpernicus' astronomy lay in the accuracy of its predictions and that one ought not to take seriously its account of the earth whirling through space around the sun (Dreyer 1953, p. 319). Had Galileo been an instrumentalist, he would not have run afoul of the inquisition. (Realists might also argue that he would not have revolutionized science, either, by searching for a physics compatible with Copernicus' astronomy.)

Notice that realists and instrumentalists *agree* that scientists should develop theories which apparently talk about unobservables. Instrumentalism and realism should thus be distinguished from extreme anti-theoretic views like those defended by B. F. Skinner in psychology and Paul Samuelson in economics (section 9.2). Unlike realists and instrumentalists, Skinner and Samuelson want to eschew all theory that goes beyond identifying regularities among observable phenomena (Skinner 1953, 1974).

Some instrumentalists have laid great stress on the *practical* importance of scientific predictions, while others have simply been suspicious of the possibility of finding the truth about unobservables (Laudan 1981).

---

[3] For important contributions and overviews see Boyd 1984, Hempel 1965, pp. 173-228, Miller 1987, part III, Nagel 1961, chapter 6, and Toulmin 1953.

[4] This seems to me to be the consensus in contemporary scholarship. For an opposing view (which concedes that Copernicus did not always resist realist temptations), see Duhem 1908, chapter 5. Kuhn (1957) provides a fascinating account.

Realists and instrumentalists disagree about two things: the goals of science and the interpretation of claims about unobservable things (Morgenbesser 1969). Since these two issues are distinct, one finds instrumentalists about the goals of science who are realists about theoretical entities (Dewey 1939a, pp. 534–45; 574–5) as well as virtual realists about goals who are instrumentalists about theoretical entities.[5] Bas van Fraassen, for example, sees explanation as a goal of science, but holds an instrumentalist view of claims about unobservables. In his view, explanation does not require truth, and scientists do not aim at finding out the truth about unobservables. Science aims instead at "empirical adequacy" (1980; see also Churchland and Hooker 1985). (A theory is empirically adequate if and only if all of its observable implications are true.)

Problems about unobservables seldom arise in economic methodology, because economic theories rarely postulate unobservable things (but see the discussion of Machlup's views in section 9.3). Economists have however been attracted to instrumentalism concerning the goals of science. In "The Methodology of Positive Economics" (1953c) Milton Friedman espouses a distinctive and extremely influential instrumentalist view of science (see section 9.4). I do not know whether most economists are instrumentalists or whether most are realists, but certainly both positions are widely held (Mäki 1988a,b, 1990a,c, forthcoming a).

Who is right? Should scientists confine themselves to forging tools which enable people to make reliable predictions and thus to control inflation, or should they aim "higher" at the truth about nature and society? There is no settled opinion among philosophers, and the fortunes of realism and instrumentalism have oscillated over the past few decades. Scientists are just as divided. Realism has a firm foothold in most areas, but the peculiarities of quantum mechanics have led many physicists to instrumentalism.

It should not be thought that a realist who hopes that scientific theories can lead us to new truths about the world must find theories *valueless* unless they are true. Ptolemy's astronomy, which places the earth in the center of the solar system, may be useful for navigation even though it is full of false claims. There is no reason why the realist cannot use Ptolemy's theory to navigate, too. Realists want more from science than useful theories, but they are not about to throw away vanilla ice cream

---

[5] Many more complicated variations are also possible. Nancy Cartwright (1983), for example, denies that the evidence for theoretical laws ever justifies belief in their truth or in the existence of their theoretical entities. But when *causal claims* are well confirmed, then we are justified in believing them to be true and in accepting the existence of the postulated unobservable entities. See also Hacking 1983.

when chocolate cannot be had. The realist can also recognize that engineers and policy-makers may be more interested in reliable predictions than in theoretical truths.

A.3   Scientific explanation

An explanation answers a "Why?" question. It removes puzzlement and provides understanding and has an important pragmatic aspect (emphasized by Bromberger 1966, van Fraassen 1980, and Achinstein 1983). One naive view is that explanations make unfamiliar phenomena familiar. But explanations often talk of things that are *less* intuitively comprehensible than what is being explained. What could be more familiar than that water is a liquid at room temperature? Certainly not the explanation physicists give for its liquidity.

In his recent *Scientific Explanation and the Causal Structure of the World* (1985), Wesley Salmon distinguishes three intuitive views of explanation: (1) Explanations show that the phenomenon to be explained was *to have been expected.* (2) Explanations show that the phenomenon to be explained was *necessary.* (3) Explanations reveal the *causes* of the phenomenon to be explained.[6]

The dominant view has been the first: a scientific explanation shows some happening or some regularity to be an instance of a broader or "deeper" regularity. Where there was contingency and multiplicity, science reveals the unity of an underlying regularity. A scientific explanation shows that the thing being explained did not just "happen." It was the sort of thing that could have been expected to happen in the circumstances. Notice that, in explaining something as an instance of a more fundamental law, one need not have any explanation for that law itself. Explanations come to an end at the current frontiers of science.

This expectability or subsumption view of explanation goes back to the Greeks, but it receives systematic development in essays by Carl Hempel (1965, see also Michael Friedman 1974 and Railton 1980). Although Hempel was a logical positivist when he began his work on explanation, his basic notion antedates the positivists and has survived logical positivism's collapse. Hempel develops two main models of scientific explanation, the deductive-nomological and the inductive-statistical models. The inductive-statistical model as its name suggests is concerned with statistical explanations and raises additional serious difficulties. My emphasis will be on Hempel's deductive-nomological or DN model.

---

[6] For a recent overview of the whole subject, see also Salmon 1990 and Kitcher and Salmon 1989.

In a deductive-nomological explanation, a statement of what is to be explained is **deduced** from a set of **true** statements which includes **essentially** at least one **law**. Schematically, one has:

> True statements of initial conditions
> Laws
>
> _____
>
> Statement of what is to be explained

The solid line represents a deductive inference. One shows the phenomenon to be explained to be an instance of broader regularities, by deducing a statement of what is to be explained from laws and other true statements. The presence of at least one *law* in a deductive-*nomological* explanation is essential. To deduce that this apple is red from the true generalization that all apples in the bowl are red and the true statement that this apple is in the bowl does not explain *why* the apple is red. "Accidental generalizations," unlike laws, are not explanatory.

Furthermore, to have truly explained some phenomena, one must be able to deduce it from a set of *true* statements. If one *believes* that the statements in a purported explanation are true (and that the other conditions are satisfied), one will *believe* that one has given a good explanation, but one has not actually done so if the statements one makes are not true. Some philosophers, such as van Fraassen, relax this requirement and demand only empirical adequacy – truth of their observable implications – rather than truth (1980). Empirical adequacy, like truth, is a semantic property and an ontological aspiration, not a standard of belief or justification. Good *evidence* rather than *truth* provides the *grounds* for belief, while belief in some proposition is belief in its truth, not belief in its justification. Hempel's concept of DN explanation is thus not *epistemic*. Whether some set of statements explains another is not a matter of our beliefs but a matter of fact.

That explanations require laws and truth is important in thinking about economics. For economists are often hesitant to regard their basic generalizations as laws, yet economists nevertheless claim to be able to explain economic phenomena. These questions are discussed in chapter 8.

Recall that the DN model is only an account of deterministic, or non-statistical explanations. If one has only a statistical regularity, then one will not be able to *deduce* what is to be explained, but one may be able to show that it is highly probable, which is what Hempel's inductive-statistical model requires.

The deductive-nomological model of scientific explanation partly captures the intuitive notions that explanations show the necessity of the phenomenon to be explained and that explanations reveal the causes. The intuition that explanations reduce contingency is explicated as the claim that explanations show that descriptions of the phenomenon to be explained are *entailed* by statements of the relevant laws and initial conditions. Causal intuitions are accommodated by noting that the initial conditions from which, in accordance with laws, the phenomenon to be explained follows will typically be its causes (see also p. 295 below).

But the DN model is problematic. Not only is it limited to non-statistical explanations, but an argument may satisfy all its conditions without being an explanation. Consider the following example:

Nobody who takes birth control pills as directed gets pregnant. George takes birth control pills as directed.

George does not get pregnant (Salmon 1971, p. 34).

If George is a man, nobody would regard this argument as explaining why George does not get pregnant. If one assumes for the sake of this discussion that the first premise is a law and that George does faithfully take his birth control pills, then the conditions of the DN model are met, but one has not explained why George does not get pregnant.

Why not? The intuitive answer is that it does not matter whether George took birth control pills. His taking the pills was not causally relevant. The factors explanations cite must be causally relevant.

Explanation apparently requires not only causal relevance, but explanations should also be in terms of causal influences, rather than causal consequences. For example, one can *deduce* that water is H_2O from the following four premises: (i) the law of the conservation of matter, (ii) the law that equal volumes of gases contain equal numbers of molecules, (iii) the fact that two volumes of hydrogen combine with one volume of oxygen to make two volumes of water vapor, and (iv) the fact that hydrogen and oxygen molecules are, respectively, H_2 and O_2. But such a deduction does not *explain* the chemical composition of water. On the contrary, that water is H_2O explains why two volumes of hydrogen combine with one volume of oxygen. The composition of water is a causal condition of the combining proportions, not vice versa. Similarly, from the fact that Fido is pregnant, one can deduce that she is female, but her pregnancy does not explain her sex. Effects do not explain their causes, and effects of a common cause do not explain one another.

Given the pervasiveness of facts such as these, Salmon and, from a different perspective, Richard Miller (1987), have argued that one should abandon the DN model and develop the intuition that explanations cite causes of the phenomena to be explained. The details of these accounts would take us far afield, but, since the core idea that explanations cite causes is so intuitively appealing, I shall sketch Miller's view.

In Miller's view, explanation is adequate causal description. A list of causes is adequate if it (a) cites causes that were actually present, (b) cites causes that were sufficient in the circumstances for the explanandum, (c) conforms to an appropriate "standard causal pattern," and (d) possesses sufficient causal "depth." (a) requires little explanation except to note that Miller regards the concept of causation as an unanalyzable primitive. It develops through extensions of paradigm cases such as pushing something (1987, pp. 73–85). Since Miller thinks that few explanations can be deterministic, (b) needs heavy qualification.

(c) is a context-dependent feature. For various reasons, about which Miller has a great deal to say (1987, pp. 88f), disciplines establish different standard explanatory patterns. In medicine, for example, citing an infectious agent is generally taken to be sufficient to explain an illness, even though the presence of the agent is rarely a sufficient condition. The standard causal pattern for consumer choice theory involves citing preferences, prices, and incomes. Miller's claim that practical considerations influence the choice of standard causal patterns is of particular interest, for it suggests one way in which ideological considerations might influence economic theory (see Miller 1987, pp. 96–7, p. 110 and section A.14.4 below).

(d), the requirement of causal depth, rules out explanations that cite causes that are not necessary or are merely links between deeper causes and the phenomena to be explained. If the phenomena would in the normal course of events have occurred anyway, even if the cited causes had been absent, then the causal account lacks the first sort of depth. The explanation of why Hamlet killed Claudius in terms of Hamlet's preference that he kill Claudius lacks the second sort of depth. Miller argues that the requirement of depth also has a practical justification, for shallow causes are not good "levers" for manipulating the world (Hausman 1986a).

I have qualms about Miller's account, because of how greatly it lowers one's expectations of what a philosophical account of scientific explanation should do. Instead of a precise model of explanatory arguments such as Hempel's, one has a discussion of detailed, practical, context-dependent requirements on lists of "causes." Does an account such as Miller's provide an alternative philosophical account of explanation, or does it represent an alternative to providing a philosophical account of explanation?

If one does not want to scrap the DN model altogether, one can cling to it as providing necessary conditions for non-statistical explanations.

But even this weaker thesis requires qualifications, for explanations in science rarely fit the deductive-nomological model explicitly. Defenders of the DN model respond by arguing that actual scientific explanations are often elliptical or mere explanation sketches. Even if one accepts these excuses, the DN model seems to abstract from much of what is most significant about scientific explanations.

It seems to me that the DN model is an important starting point for approaching the problems of scientific explanation, and that there is something right and important about it. But here, as elsewhere, there is more to be learned by examining the matter in more detail. Attention should be paid to the specific demands on scientific explanations that scientists committed to particular research approaches have made. Furthermore, explanation of human behavior introduces other difficulties discussed in sections A.14.2 and 15.3. Most of the interesting features of explanations in economics are at a much lower level of generality.

A.4   Laws

When one thinks naively about science, one thinks of its many laws: Newton's laws of motion and gravitation, Coulomb's law of electrostatic repulsion, Mendel's laws of inheritance, and so forth.[7] Economics has at least one well-known law, too: the law of demand, although economists are in general hesitant to describe their generalizations as laws, for reasons explored in part I. How important are laws in science? What are laws?

Scientific laws are not prescriptive laws dictating how things *ought* to be, but true expressions of regularities. It is not as if the Moon would like to leave its orbit around the earth, but is prevented by a gravitational regulation. In my usage, to call something a law is to imply that it is true. Sometimes people use the word "law" without this implication of truth. To keep our language unambiguous, let us say that a "lawlike statement" is a statement which is just like a law although it might not be true (Goodman 1973, p. 22). It should be noted that laws rarely express regularities that are evident to observation. Much of the genius of science has involved abstracting from the *ir*regularities at the level of everyday experience.

What makes laws difficult to understand is that they are not just regularities, for there are also true generalizations that appear to be "accidental." Since explanations require laws, some distinction must be drawn between lawlike and accidental generalizations. It is easy to

---

[7] Though at least two of the most prominent contemporary philosophers of science, Nancy Cartwright (1989) and Bas van Fraassen (1989) argue that it is a mistake to regard laws as fundamental to science.

distinguish a generalization such as "All the candies in the jar are orange" from a law, because this generalization, unlike a basic law, is restricted to a particular place and time. But consider the generalization, "All buildings are less than 10,000 stories tall." This generalization is well supported, and it might well be true of the whole universe throughout the whole of time. Yet few would regard it as a law. Why?

The answers that first come to mind are not very enlightening. Many people would be inclined to say that laws state what *must be*. Since it is *possible* that a building more than 10,000 stories tall be built, the claim that none are so tall cannot be a law. This view is linked to the intuition mentioned before that explanation involves necessity. But, if laws express necessities, and all evidence comes from observations, how can scientists distinguish universal generalizations that happen to be true from universal generalizations that *must* be true.

A second way to distinguish laws from accidental generalizations runs into similar problems. Laws appear to support counterfactual conditionals, while accidental generalizations do not. A law, such as "Copper conducts electricity" supports conditional claims such as, "If this pencil were made of copper, it would conduct electricity." But an accidental generalization such as "All the candies in the jar are orange" does not support the counterfactual, "If this chocolate were in the jar, it would be orange" (Goodman 1973). Unfortunately, the empirical assessment of counterfactual claims is problematic. How is one to interpret and assess a generalization such as "If this chocolate were in the jar, it would be orange"? What people apparently do is imaginatively "hold fixed" as much as possible apart from the location of the chocolate and then consider what color the chocolate is. Another way of describing the procedure is to say that people consider whether in the "closest" possible "world" in which the chocolate is in the jar, it is also orange (Stalnaker 1968, Lewis 1973b). But these imaginative procedures are disturbingly vague, and it is unclear how evidence justifies judgments about possible worlds. Some philosophers have argued that controlled experiments provide evidence for the truth of counterfactuals, for the controls warrant the counterfactuals that it would have been with the experimental group as it in fact was with the control group and *vice versa* (Giere 1980). But this last view is controversial.

One less mysterious difference between laws and accidental generalizations is that laws are supported by, incorporated in, or derivable from accepted scientific theories (Berofsky 1971). If accepted theories of matter were inconsistent with the existence of a building of more than 10,000 stories, then one would cease to regard the generalization that all buildings are less than 10,000 stories tall as merely accidental (see Hempel

1966, p. 54–8). One would instead regard it as an uninteresting derivative law. So an attempt to understand what laws are leads one to attempt to understand what scientific theories are.

A.5 Causality, laws, and explanation

A traditional view of science was that it is an inquiry into the *causes* of phenomena, that laws describe the operations of causes, and that explanation involves the identification of causes (Aristotle 1958, book II, chapter 3). Perhaps a deeper understanding of causality might help one to understand laws.

But the notion of causality has been hard to understand and explicitly causal language fell out of philosophical favor, particularly when the influence of logical positivism was strongest. Indeed Bertrand Russell went so far as to claim that,

> the reason why physics has ceased to look for causes is that, in fact, there are no such things. The law of causality, I believe, like much that passes muster among philosophers, is a relic of a bygone age, surviving, like the monarchy, only because it is erroneously supposed to do no harm. (1912, p. 132)

This repudiation of causal notions was tied up with empiricism, which was as central to Russell's later views as it was to those of the logical positivists or to David Hume's arguments two centuries before. Hume wanted to know what observations could provide evidence for or against causal claims, and he argued that all one ever observes are that the cause and effect are "constantly conjoined" and that the cause precedes the effect.[8] The "necessary connection" supposed to obtain between cause and effect is empirically ineffable, and Hume offers a psychological explanation for how the illusion of some further connection arises from repetition (1748, section 7). All that causality "really" is "in the objects" is empirical regularity with temporal priority of the cause to the effect.

Although Hume generally speaks of "*the* cause" of an effect, and much effort in everyday discussion (Collingwood 1940, pp. 304f; Gorovitz 1969) and in the law (Hart and Honoré 1985) is devoted to singling out *the* (salient) cause from among the various causal influences and conditions, Hume's analysis can easily be adapted to the notion of "*a* cause or causal condition." It is this notion, not the notion of *the* cause, which is of interest to science. The best way of adapting it in the deterministic case

---

[8] At times Hume also argued that cause and effect are spatio-temporally contiguous, but this requirement runs into difficulty if one wants to allow causal relations among mental events, which seem not to have definite spatial locations.

is J. L. Mackie's. Although one would regard the striking of a match as a cause (indeed "the" cause) of its lighting, strikings of matches are not always followed by matches lighting, and matches that are not struck may be lighted in other ways. Mackie argues that the regularity that is implicit in the claim that striking a match caused it to light is that matches light if and only if either they are struck and a variety of other conditions (they are dry, oxygen is present, etc.) obtain, or some other set of factors obtains. Such claims are vague, but testable, and they highlight the facts that events can have different causes and that the joint presence of a number of separate causal factors is typically necessary in order to bring about a given effect. Causes are Insufficient but Necessary components in sets of factors that are Unnecessary but Sufficient for the effect to occur, or, for short, INUS conditions (Mackie 1974, chapter 3). To guarantee the asymmetry of cause and effect, some other condition, such as the temporal priority of the cause, must be added.

If causality is conceived of in these minimalist ways, then there can be no objection to scientific use of the notion, but there would be little reason to use it, either, except when one is unable yet to formulate explicitly the laws that are presupposed by the causal claims. Russell's view that causal notions have no role to play in mature science would be vindicated. Accepting Hume's notion of causality also dashes hopes that understanding causality will help distinguish laws from accidental generalities. For, apart from the temporal precedence of causes, causal relations are just regularities.

Hume's account of causality leads naturally to Hempel's view of explanation, for citing causes involves only identifying relevant regularities. But, given this notion of causality, some of the features of explanations discussed above become utterly perplexing. How can one deny that George's taking birth-control pills explains why he does not get pregnant (see p. 290)? Isn't one forced to assert that the fact that two volumes of hydrogen combine with one volume of oxygen explains why the chemical composition of water is H_2O (see p. 290)? Furthermore, whether a cause and its effect are ever simultaneous, which seems an empirical matter, is ruled out as logically impossible.

For reasons such as these, many philosophers are dissatisfied with Hume's account of causality (but see Beauchamp and Rosenberg 1981 and Horwich 1987, chapter 8 for spirited defenses). Moreover, there is now good evidence that (*pace* Russell), causal notions play a large role even in physics. However uncomfortable economists are with explicit talk of causation (partly because they mistakenly assume that causal talk commits one to *single* causes), causal notions are nevertheless ubiquitous in economics and central to economic theory. Most often such notions are formulated using terms such as "determine," which are ambiguous between "mathematically determine" and "causally (as well as mathematically) determine." But terms such as "influence," "depend on," or "determine," are almost always used by economists in their causal sense. Causal notions have also had a special importance in econometrics.[9]

Thus one finds among philosophers a growing recognition of the importance of causal notions and deep dissatisfaction with Hume's analysis. Yet promising alternatives have been difficult to generate. The only alternative to Hume's account with any appreciable following is the counterfactual analysis of causality.[10] In David Lewis' version (1973a), an event c is a cause of a distinct event e, if and only if there is a chain of events leading from c to e such that the successor to any event in the chain is counterfactually dependent on its predecessor. An event y is counterfactually dependent on an event x if and only if two counterfactuals or subjunctive conditionals are true: if x were to occur then y would occur and if x were not to occur then y would not occur. The counterfactuals are analyzed in terms of possible worlds and similarities among them. y is counterfactually dependent on x if and only if no possible world in which x occurs and in which y does not is more similar to the real world than a possible world in which x and y both occur, and no possible world in which x does not occur and y occurs is more similar to ours than a possible world in which both do not occur. If x and y both occur, then the first of the two counterfactuals will be trivially true (since the real world is maximally similar to itself), and attention will focus on the second.

Problems abound. What are possible worlds and what is this relationship of "comparative overall similarity" (Lewis 1979, 1986; Bennett 1984)? Do these similarity judgments presuppose the causal judgments one is attempting to analyze? Can such an account make sense of the *asymmetry* between cause and effect? What *evidence* bears on the truth of these counterfactual claims? If causality is analyzed in this vague and highly metaphysical way, can it have any use in science? Can one, alternatively, develop a contentful account of explanation, confirmation,

---

[9] On causality mainly as relevant to questions of identifiability, see Koopmans 1949, Simon 1953, Wold 1954, 1960, Strotz 1960, and Strotz and Wold 1960. On questions concerning the inference of causal relations from statistical data and, to a lesser extent on questions of identifiability, see Basmann 1963, Engle, Hendry, and Richard 1983, Geweke 1982, 1984, Granger 1969, 1980, 1985, Koopmans 1949, Leamer 1984, Orcutt 1952, and Sims 1972, 1977, 1981. For a good recent discussion of the issues, see Hoover 1990.

[10] I have my own theory, which is defended in "Causal Priority" (1984a) and "Causation and Experimentation" (1986).

and science in general that takes causation, as Richard Miller does (see above p. 291), as unanalyzable?

I must leave this subject in this unsettled state. The topic of causality is unfortunately not only a mess, but also unavoidable for those interested in economic methodology. In chapters 2 and 3, especially section 3.5, I show how to avoid the worst parts of this philosophical swamp.

A.6   Scientific theories and models

The attempt to understand scientific laws leads one to scientific theories, but theories are no easier to understand than laws. Theories appear to be collections of lawlike statements that are systematically related to one another. (Recall that a law is a true lawlike statement.) But, if in order to understand what theories are, one needs to know what laws are, then one cannot rely on the connection between laws and theories to analyze laws. All that one can say is that laws are systematically related to one another in ways that accidental generalizations are not.

The logical positivists made the notion of a "systematic relationship" precise, by arguing that theories form deductive systems. Theories are primarily "syntactic" objects, whose terms and claims are supposedly interpreted by means of "correspondence" rules (see Suppe 1977, pp. 3–118). Correspondence rules were originally conceived of as explicit definitions of a theory's terms, but the positivists soon realized that the relationship between theory and observation is more subtle and complicated (Carnap 1936, 1937). For a more detailed discussion of the positivist view of scientific theories see section 5.1.

The positivists were unable to formalize much of science, to do justice to how theories are constructed and used, or to offer a satisfactory account of how theories are related to observation. Consequently, many philosophers now settle for the looser informal construal of theories as collections of lawlike *statements* (not uninterpreted, purely syntactic sentences) systematically related to one another. But there are some contemporary alternatives (discussed at more length in chapter 5), one of which is of particular help in understanding theoretical *models* in economics.

A number of philosophers have argued that theories may be regarded as of the same logical type as are predicates such as "has two legs" or concepts like two-leggedness, or definitions of such predicates or concepts. According to this view, a theory such as Newton's does not make assertions about the world at all! It is instead a predicate such as "is a Newtonian gravitational system" or a definition of such a predicate. Scientists obviously make claims about the world, but, according to this view of theories, they do so by *employing* theories, by asserting that the predicates which theories constitute or define are true or false of systems of things in the world. One can regard economists as defining a "rational agent" as an agent with complete and transitive preferences and who chooses what she most prefers, and then as asserting that real people are rational agents so defined.

This roundabout procedure of first defining a rational agent and then saying that people are rational agents helps one to recognize the *two* kinds of achievements involved in constructing a scientific theory. Of course a theory must identify regularities in the world, and that is what ultimately counts in an empirical science. But science does not proceed by spotting correlations among well-known observable properties of things. The construction of new concepts, of new ways of classifying and describing phenomena is an equally crucial part of science. Such conceptual work has been prominent in economics.

A.7   Theory and observation

The logical positivists were empiricists about both assessment and meaning. Sensory experience constitutes the ultimate evidence, and non-logical terms have meaning only if one can tell by experience whether they apply. Because they were empiricists in both senses, the logical positivists found "theoretical claims" – that is sentences that purported to talk about unobservable things or properties – doubly problematic. How could such theoretical sentences be tested (Carnap 1936, 1937; Hempel 1965, pp. 101–22)? How could theoretical sentences have meaning (Hempel 1965, pp. 173–228)?

By the 1930s the logical positivists recognized that it was too much to demand either explicit definitions of theoretical terms or correspondence rules of the form, "T if and only if O," where "T" is a sentence containing theoretical terms and "O" is a sentence containing only observational terms. Consider even so simple a claim as T^*: "This bit of table salt is water soluble." It will not do to say T^* if and only if O^*, where O^* is: "if this bit of table salt is placed in water then it dissolves." For, according to the formal logic accepted by the positivists, O^* is true if the table salt is not placed in water – regardless of whether it is soluble or not. The most that one can say is R: "If this table salt is placed in water, then it is water soluble if and only if it dissolves." Carnap called sentences such as R "bilateral reduction sentences" (1936, 1937). R links the theoretical predicate, "soluble," to the observational predicate, "dissolves," and permits claims about solubility to be tested, but it does not *define* solubility or permit one to dispense with theoretical claims. The positivists

rejected extremely restrictive views such as operationalism, which demanded that all terms in science must be defined in terms of some measuring
operation.

The positivists made a variety of efforts to show how sentences which
apparently referred to unobservable things could be meaningful. Some
of the positivists looked to instrumentalism: theories could be regarded
as tools to help one make correct inferences about observable things,
and not as making true or false statements at all. But this sort of
instrumentalism seems only superficially to avoid commitment to truth
or falsity of theoretical claims. It provokes questions such as: How do
supposedly meaningless theoretical claims manage to be reliable "rules
of inference?" What are scientists doing when they ask about the size
or mass of electrons or the way in which electrons interact with other
unobservable "things?"

By the 1950s, most "logical empiricists" (as the logical positivists now
preferred to be called) had retreated to the weaker view that theoretical
claims are "partially interpreted" by the whole set of correspondence
rules (Carnap 1956, Campbell 1957). Theoretical terms and claims have
meaning and scientific legitimacy if their presence makes a difference to
a theory's testable implications. This view largely abandons the strict
empiricist ambitions of the early logical positivists, but the positivists
were more prepared to tinker with their epistemology than to repudiate
contemporary physics.

Few philosophers remain committed to even this weak partial interpretation view. For the very distinction between theory and observation is
widely questioned. As Popper had stressed back in the 1930s, and as
many others have argued over the past generation, observations are
heavily influenced by beliefs: observation reports are not the unvarnished
expression of sensory experience (see Maxwell 1962, Feyerabend 1965).
The positivists' distinction between "analytic" statements, which are true
by virtue of the meanings of their terms, and "synthetic" assertions about
the world has also been questioned (Hempel 1965, pp. 131f, Quine 1953),
as has the utility of regarding theories as formal systems. As a consequence
philosophers of science have largely *abandoned* the positivist's worries
about the meanings of claims about unobservable things, without really
resolving them.

In any case, these questions should not be greatly worrying to those
interested in economics, since economic theories rarely refer to anything
unobservable (in some loose intuitive sense of "observation"). In 9.3, I
criticize Fritz Machlup's effort to apply the views of the logical empiricists
to economics. The methodological problems of economics are serious
enough that there is no need to annex those of physics as well. The

problems raised by unobservables are of secondary importance in economics.

A.8   Paradigms and research programs

In coming to worry less about the relations between theory and observation, philosophers have come over the past generation to worry more about the relations among different theories. Even a cursory knowledge of science reveals that sciences are not amalgams of unrelated individual theories. Scientific endeavor is continuous and coherent. This fact is evident in contemporary economics, where the separate theories proposed within a particular tradition are intimately linked to one another. This feature of economics is documented in part I, and I argue for a particular interpretation of the global theory structure of neoclassical economics against the background of recent philosophical accounts of intertheoretic connections in chapter 6.

Philosophical attention to the global theory structure of scientific disciplines dates from Thomas Kuhn's influential book, *The Structure of Scientific Revolutions* (1970) (but see Morgenbesser 1956). Kuhn argues that "normal" scientific work is dominated by "paradigms." He means that normal science models itself after exemplary past scientific accomplishments and that normal science is governed by a set of implicit rules concerning what questions to ask, what procedures to employ in answering them, what sorts of answers are acceptable, in what order to proceed, what sorts of instruments to use, what quantities to measure, what terms to use in describing phenomena, and so forth. Paradigms structure problems and, when successful, make solvable puzzles of them.

Kuhn's historical and sociological insights have influenced other philosophical accounts of science that differ with Kuhn concerning the nature of scientific progress. Thus Imre Lakatos (1970) describes a "research program" as a collection of theories bound together by what Lakatos calls "heuristics." The "negative heuristic" instructs the scientist not to question fundamental claims, which constitute the "hard core." The claim that individuals are rational is the sort of thing that would belong to the hard core of neoclassical economics. The positive heuristic guides scientists in modifying the "protective belt" of testable theories, which incorporate the hard core of the research program. There are other significant accounts of the broader structure of scientific theories, such as Larry Laudan's (1977), and Dudley Shapere's (1974, 1984, 1985), which I am unable to discuss here. Kuhn's and Lakatos's views on paradigms and research programs are discussed at greater length in sections 6.1 and 6.2.

In addition to the sociological interest of these features of scientific inquiry, important philosophical questions arise. For one wonders whether the influence of paradigms or research programs weakens the scientist's claims to have discovered the truth. Kuhn maintains that those who accept different paradigms live in different worlds (Kuhn 1970, p. 121), and that there can be progress only within normal science. Lakatos and others have been rightly concerned to dispute these exaggerated claims. Even if paradigms determine what questions are of interest, one's theoretical vocabulary, and how to test and confirm, they do not necessarily determine what the correct answers will be. Historians of science have documented major, revolutionary changes that were readily made in response to conclusive experimental findings (Franklin 1986, chapters 1, 3).

A.9   Scientific discovery

Paradigms and research programs are of particular importance from the perspective of understanding how scientists make discoveries. In this century, most philosophers held that there was little of philosophical interest to be said about invention in science. Although Karl Popper titled his major work *Die Logik der Forschung* or, in its misleading English translation, *The Logic of Scientific Discovery*, he held that discovery was not subject to rational rules and that the normative interests of philosophers should be confined to the assessment of scientific theories (1968, p. 31). In Hans Reichenbach's well-known terminology, one can distinguish the context of discovery from the context of justification, and philosophy of science is concerned exclusively with the context of justification (Reichenbach 1938, pp. 6–7; Hoyningen-Huene 1987). Earlier epistemologists and philosophers of science, such as J. S. Mill, have been criticized for failing to distinguish these contexts clearly enough.

Writers on economic methodology have reiterated this repudiation of any logic of discovery.

The construction of hypotheses is a creative act of inspiration, intuition, invention; its essence is a vision of something new in familiar material. The process must be discussed in psychological, not logical, categories; studied in autobiographies and biographies, not treatises on scientific method; and promoted by maxim and example, not syllogism or theorem. (Milton Friedman 1953c, p. 43)

But this bit of methodological orthodoxy fits economics badly. The grounds for accepting economic theories are rarely distinct from the grounds upon which they were generated in the first place; and much of traditional economic methodology has been concerned as much with the context of discovery as with the context of justification. J. S. Mill's so-called "deductive" or *a priori* method, which dominated methodologi-cal thinking concerning the appraisal of economic theories for at least a century (and which I attempt to resuscitate in chapters 8 and 12) is primarily an account of how to *generate* plausible and credible economic theories.

And Mill's view is not the worse for being an account of theory generation, for here, as elsewhere, philosophical dogma has come into question (Nickles 1980 and Nickles, ed. 1980). Once one recognizes that one can study the abstract relations between various evidential features and the theories that may be generated in response rather than the causal processes involved in actual theory generation, there is little basis for denying that there can be a logic of discovery. Indeed some of the formal procedures for theory assessment proposed by the logical positivists are themselves procedures for theory generation (Kelly 1987). The existence of computer programs that actually generate theories from evidence vividly demonstrates that there can be rational procedures for scientific discovery (Langley *et al.* 1987; Glymour *et al.* 1987).

A.10   Testing and assessing scientific theories

Most philosophers, economists, and indeed "the man or woman in the street" are empiricists about theory assessment. They believe that the evidence that ultimately leads one to accept or to reject claims about the world is observational evidence. Economists believe that individuals generally prefer more commodities to fewer because this claim is borne out by experience.

Not all claims seem to be supported or refuted this way. Consider assertions such as "All tables are tables." "Triangles have three angles," or "This square is circular." These do not require testing, and confidence in their truth or falsity does not depend on test results. The logical positivists dealt with such cases by distinguishing *synthetic* claims – claims about the world – from *analytic* or contradictory claims whose truth or falsity depend solely on logic and on the meanings of the terms. But, largely owing to the critiques of W.V.O. Quine (1953, pp. 20–46) and Morton White (1956), few would now defend the epistemic import-ance of this distinction.[11] Consider, for example, the following claim: "*Ceteris paribus*, people will purchase more of y when the price of x increases and less of y when the price of x decreases if and only if x and y are substitutes" (see p. 29). Is this a synthetic empirical generaliz-

---

[11] Those who still defend the distinction, such as Katz (1988) defend it only as a legitimate element in linguistic theory.

ation or an analytic definition of a substitute (Rosenberg 1976, pp. 18–22)? On Quine's view, the question is an empty one (see also Putnam 1962). On Quine's view, acceptance or denial of such claims rests on their role in larger sets of propositions that have testable implications (see p. 307 below).

Although subject to difficulties, empiricism remains dominant. But it is not unchallenged. Kant argued in his *Critique of Pure Reason* that there are "synthetic" truths about the world that can be known "*a priori*" – that is, without empirical confirmation. Some propositions, such as the axioms of Euclidean geometry, are, Kant asserted, implied by the possibility of having conscious experience of the world. No perceptual evidence could lead one to reject such propositions.

Modern physics has refuted Kant's view that the axioms of Euclidean geometry are *a priori* truths. Yet Kant's general position still has supporters. Modern "Austrian" economists, especially Ludwig von Mises and his followers, believe that the fundamental postulates of economics are synthetic *a priori* truths (von Mises 1949, 1978, 1981; see also Rothbard 1957, 1976, pp. 24–5). Martin Hollis and Edward Nell (1975), argue on different grounds for the necessity of the basic propositions of their classical-Marxian economics. I shall not discuss either Hollis and Nell's or the Austrians' epistemological views, but shall focus on the dominant, generally empiricist views of theory assessment.

If one supposes the grounds for assessing claims about the world are the results of observations and experiments, one then faces the question of how such results provide evidence for or against scientific theories. Two different questions should be distinguished:

1 The problem of evidence: How does observational evidence provide any confirmation or disconfirmation (no matter how weak) of scientific hypotheses?
2 The problem of acceptance or choice: When are hypotheses strongly confirmed or disconfirmed on the basis of the results of observation and experiment?

My discussion will focus on the first question.

Richard Miller's recent *Fact and Method* defends the view that confirmation is fair causal comparison (1987, chapter 4). One examines competing causal accounts of the evidence and prefers that account that offers the better explanation (understood in Miller's way, see p. 291 above) of that evidence. Although there is more to be said, particularly about what sorts of "frameworks" are to be taken for granted in such causal comparisons, there is little more to be said in such abstract terms. All the substance lies in discipline-specific knowledge and standards that govern such causal comparisons. Perhaps Miller is right, and there is nothing more in general to be said, but let us first examine the more structured alternatives defended by most philosophers of science. Although none of these may ultimately be tenable, they are still important tools of analysis and criticism.

A.10.1   *The hypothetico-deductive method*

Given a commitment to empiricism and a rejection of any logic of discovery, the dominant view of how one tests scientific theories became the so-called "hypothetico-deductive (HD) method." (Notice that the name may mislead: this is an *inductive* method.) Reduced to its bare bones, this method consists of the following four steps:

1 *Formulate* some hypothesis or theory *H*.
2 *Deduce* some "prediction" or observable claim, *P*, from *H* conjoined with a variety of other statements. These other statements will include descriptions of initial conditions, other theories, and *ceteris paribus* ("other things being equal") clauses.
3 *Test P*. (One tests *H* only indirectly by means of the HD method.) Testing may involve complicated experimentation or simple observation.
4 *Judge* whether *H* is confirmed or disconfirmed depending on the nature of *P* and whether *P* turned out to be true or false. *"Confirmed" does not mean "proven" or "true," nor does "disconfirmed" mean "disproven" or "false," for false hypotheses may have true implications, and the falsity of* P *may be due to some premise from which* P *is derived other than* H.

These steps can be amplified or modified in a variety of ways. For example, in the case of statistical theories, it may not be possible to deduce *P* or, if it is, the testing of *P* may be problematic. If one seeks *good* evidence, as opposed to just some evidence, one will look for predictions that background knowledge or alternative theories render unlikely (see Giere 1983). But the four steps listed above capture the essential features of hypothetico-deductivism. Note that a "prediction" is any testable implication. It need not be about the future and its truth may already be known.[12]

The HD method preceded the logical positivists, but became a central part of their program. For, given their rejection of a logic of discovery and the fact that most theoretical claims are not reducible to claims about

---

[12] See Giere 1983 for a different view of what hypothetico-deductivism involves.

observables, they saw no other way that theoretical claims could be tested. Popper denies that successful prediction ever gives one reason to believe that a hypothesis is true, but he is otherwise committed to the HD method. Although the hypothetico-deductive account of testing and of evidential relevance faces serious philosophical difficulties, it is still an important starting point. Indeed, in the words of its most important critic, "the hypothetico-deductive account remains today one of the most popular. The reason, I think, is that it is so obviously the correct account of a great deal of the history of science." (Glymour 1980, pp. 47–8) Notice that the HD method is an account of how evidence supports or disconfirms some hypothesis – however strong or weak that support may be. It is not an account of what it is for a hypothesis to be *well-supported*.

The above sketch of the HD method also enables one to formulate the special problems of theory assessment in economics. Suppose one wants to test an economic hypothesis such as the law of demand. The law of demand states that a change in the price of some commodity or service causes (*ceteris paribus*) a change in quantity demanded in the opposite direction. When the price of gasoline goes up, people will demand less of it. From (a) the law of demand, (b) a statement describing a price change, (c) a *ceteris paribus* assumption, and (d) various assumptions about the reliability of the statistical data one is using, one can deduce a prediction about statistical demand data. And one can then observe whether the prediction is true. So, although there are practical problems in carrying out the first three steps of the HD method, there seems to be no fundamental philosophical difficulty.

The point of the HD method lies, however, in step 4, in deciding whether the evidence supports the hypothesis, and, ideally, to what extent. It is at this step that the problems of assessing economic theories arise. Suppose one finds that price and demand both decrease. Such apparently disconfirming data are readily available. Ought one to regard the law of demand as disconfirmed? Hardly. For demand also depends on other factors (section 2.1). That is why the law of demand states only that a change in price will, *ceteris paribus*, cause a change in quantity demanded. Given the multitude of "disturbing causes" in economics and the difficulty of performing controlled experiments to weed these out, it seems that little can be learned from experience. And, if this is so, one must question whether economics can be a science. How these difficulties should be dealt with is the major task of this monograph (see particularly chapter 12).

The general philosophical difficulties facing the HD method mainly involve the notion of evidential relevance. The hypothesis to be tested must play an essential role in the second, deductive step, or else, trivially, any hypothesis can be confirmed by conjoining it to some confirmable theory. But it is not easy to spell out adequately the notion of an "essential role." One might say that *h* is confirmed by *e* only if *h* and some theory *T* imply *e*, but *T* does not imply *e* by itself (Schlesinger 1976; Horwich 1978). But this condition can be satisfied trivially. Just take any hypothesis *h* and any true observation report, *e*, and let *T* be the true "theory": "if *h* then *e*." Then *h* is essential to the deduction of *e* from *T*, but not confirmed by *e*. In their search for criteria of "cognitive significance" the logical positivists devoted considerable effort to such problems, only to conclude eventually that they had no formal solution.

One appealing way to improve upon the HD method is summarized by the slogan that confirmation involves "inference to the best explanation."[13] On this view the second step of the HD method is the source of the problem. Rather than merely *deducing* any old proposition *P*, one looks for some proposition *P* that the hypothesis *explains* better than any alternative does. The truth of *P* then confirms the hypothesis. But this account of confirmation relies heavily on the theory of explanation, which, as we have already seen, is a troubled area. If explanation is conceived of as deductive-nomological, then confirmation as inference to the best explanation collapses into the general HD method. But no other account of explanation is generally accepted.

Although the problems of evidential relevance are serious, they seem to be "merely philosophical." Real economists do not cook up arbitrary theories such as "If *h* then *e*" in order to defend hypotheses with irrelevant evidence. But the problem cannot be dismissed, for a philosophical account of the relationship between theory and evidence ought to explain *how* scientists avoid these pitfalls of the HD method. In addition, the HD method provides no good way of explicating how evidence may be regarded as relevant only to particular *parts* of scientific theories. When predictions are faulty, where does the blame lie, and, when predictions are successful, which particular hypotheses should take the credit? The HD method tempts one to an unhelpful and untenable holism that assigns praise and blame only to whole amalgams of theories and auxiliary assumptions.

Both the specific difficulties about employing the HD method in economics and the general philosophical difficulties of evidential relevance are linked to the "Quine–Duhem Problem."[14] Piere Duhem, particularly in *The Aim and Structure of Physical Theory* (1906) pointed out that one never tests significant scientific propositions by themselves.

[13] Hanson 1961, Harman 1973. Miller (1987, chapter 4) talks instead of "fair causal comparison," but his account is similar.
[14] For an application to economics, see Cross 1982.

Testing an hypothesis involves deriving a prediction from a conjunction of many propositions, of which the hypothesis is only one. Even if one could capture formally the requirement that the hypothesis be essential to the deduction, there would still be the problem that a predictive failure could be due to the falsity of one of these other propositions. Consequently, one can always "save" any given hypothesis by casting the blame on some other claim. Moreover, if one takes the further step, which Quine endorses, of rejecting the distinction between analytic and synthetic statements and the notion of necessary truth, then the predictive failure could be due to a "mistaken definition" or perhaps even to the use of the "wrong" logic.

If the Quine–Duhem problem is posed as a purely logical difficulty, then it may not be in practice very serious. But, as argued in chapter 12, if one is unable to place much confidence in the other premises needed to derive a prediction P from an hypothesis H, then there is a serious practical problem. Indeed it becomes almost impossible to learn from experience. This is the situation in economics.

A.10.2 Bayesian philosophy of science

Actual testing and appraisal in science makes heavy use of substantive scientific commitments. Scientists generally know what phenomena an hypothesis ought to account for and what data are relevant. Arbitrary "theories" such as "if h then e," where h is any hypothesis and e is any true observation report are never formulated and would not be taken seriously if they were. By paying attention to heuristic rules that are central to "paradigms" or "research programs," one can perhaps compensate for the formal weaknesses of the HD method. Furthermore, Lakatos insists that all tests involve comparisons of competing theories. Although this view goes too far, as I argue in section 11.3 (and see Franklin 1986, chapter 1), it is an instructive exaggeration. Many problems of confirmational relevance are simplified when one is seeking evidence that will discriminate between competing hypotheses.

Although there is a good deal of truth to these last observations, they do not lend themselves easily to systematic development. Too much depends on the details of particular paradigms or research programs. Even if discipline-specific knowledge is of great importance, it is hard to believe that there is *nothing* more that can be said in general concerning the relation of theory to evidence.

One way to say more, which is commanding growing attention among philosophers of science and which should be attractive to economists, is espoused by so-called Bayesian philosophers of science (Dorling 1972, Eells 1982, Hesse 1974, Horwich 1982, Jeffrey 1983a,b, Rosenkranz 1977, 1983, Winkler 1972). Crucial to Bayesian philosophy of science is the view that individuals assign subjective probabilities to propositions – including propositions stating hypotheses and propositions stating evidence – and that they update these probability judgments in response to new observations or experimental results in accordance with Bayes' Theorem. Bayes' theorem states that $\Pr(A/B) = \Pr(A).\Pr(B/A)/\Pr(B)$, where $\Pr(A/B)$ is the conditional probability of A given B.[15] Let h be some hypothesis and e be an evidence proposition. Then Bayes' theorem can be restated as $\Pr(h/e) = \Pr(h).\Pr(e/h)/\Pr(e)$. $\Pr(h)$ is the "prior probability" of h, the probability an agent assigns to h prior to possessing evidence e. $\Pr(h/e)$ is called the posterior probability. Many Bayesians argue that it is the probability an agent should assign to h after possessing evidence e. $\Pr(e/h)$, the conditional probability of the evidence given the hypothesis is called the "likelihood" of the hypothesis given the evidence. When the hypothesis implies e, the likelihood is one. These probabilities are degrees of belief. There are disagreements about how these should relate to knowledge of objective frequencies. The dominant view, "subjectivist" or "personalist" Bayesianism, is very permissive about subjective probabilities. For a less subjectivist contemporary variant see Rosenkranz (1977, 1983).

The virtues of this bit of formal fiddling are first that it gives substantive discipline-specific knowledge a definite role in confirmation via the prior probabilities. In a cooked-up theory such as "If h then e," where h is any arbitrary hypothesis and e any true statement of evidence, h will have a low prior probability, and, since e is already known to be true, the denominator will be unity and the posterior probability will be the same as the prior probability.

Second, unlike the general hypothetico-deductive scheme, which is mute on how *much* some bit of evidence confirms a hypothesis, the Bayesian account apparently permits a simple and intuitive metric of degree of confirmation: $\Pr(h/e) - \Pr(h)$.[16] It also neatly explains why "hard tests" of hypotheses – tests in which $\Pr(e)$ is low – strongly confirm

---

[15] The proof is easy: by the definition of conditional probability, (i) $\Pr(A/B) = \Pr(A.B)/\Pr(B)$ and (ii) $\Pr(B/A) = \Pr(A.B)/\Pr(A)$. Solve (ii) for $\Pr(A.B)$, substitute in (i), and the theorem follows immediately.

[16] To say that e confirms h if and only if $\Pr(h/e) > \Pr(h)$ leads to paradoxical conclusions. As Salmon points out, e and e' may both confirm h, yet the conjunction of e and e' disconfirm h (1975, p. 104) and e may confirm h and confirm k yet disconfirm (h or k) (1975, p. 117)! Salmon's view (p. 121–2) is that the qualitative notion of evidence confirming or disconfirming a theory ought to be superseded by a quantitative notion of degree of confirmation. See also Carnap 1950, sections 69 and 71.

them, while mere addition of instances of the same kind contribute little confirmation. Various other intuitive confirmation principles follow. For example, logical truths or contradictions cannot be confirmed. If $\Pr(h)$ <1, then if e entails h, e confirms h. If $\Pr(h)$ and $\Pr(e)$ are not zero or one, then if h entails e, e confirms h. Moreover, the Bayesian account motivates these conditions on confirmation in a natural way.[17] Scientists want to avoid errors, and an increased probability means that error is less likely.[18]

In the simplest Bayesian vision the prior probabilities and the likelihoods are known. Plausible hypotheses have non-negligible priors, and good tests have high likelihoods and low prior probabilities of the evidence. When a test is carried out, the probability of h is up-dated as $\Pr(h/e)$ or $\Pr(h/\sim e)$, depending on whether e or $\sim e$ is observed. Since the likelihood, $\Pr(e/h)$ is known, so is the evidential relevance of e to h, and there is no Quine–Duhem problem.

All this seems too good to be true, and it is. If the priors and the likelihoods were known, and one had reason not to change them in response to test results, then it would be easy to know exactly what was the significance of an observation or experimental result. But this is just to say that, if all the problems of confirmation and theory assessment were solved, then they would be solved. For the Quine–Duhem problem and the problem of evidential relevance imply that we do not know the likelihoods of specific hypotheses. Although Bayesian views of theory appraisal are sometimes presented in this oversimplified form, I think it is less deceptive to make explicit what is hidden in the assumptions that the priors and likelihoods are known (see Sober's discussion of "nuisance parameters" (1988), pp. 102–10).

Let us then sketch a slightly more sophisticated Bayesian approach:

1 *Formulate* a hypothesis h that has a substantial prior probability.
2 *Calculate* $\Pr(h/PT)$ and $\Pr(h/T.\text{not-}P)$ such that:
  (a) $\Pr(T)$ is close to 1,
  (b) $\Pr(P/h\&T)$ is high, and
  (c) $\Pr(P/\sim h\&T)$ is low.
3 *Test P.*
4 *Update* the probability one assigns to h as approximately equal to $\Pr(h/PT)$ or $\Pr(h/T.\text{not-}P)$ depending on whether P is true or not.

[17] For a brief and extremely lucid discussion of these virtues of the Bayesian account, see particularly Eells 1982, chapter 2.
[18] Crucial to this claim are demonstrations that if the data are true and the true hypothesis has non-zero prior probability then, regardless of the prior probability of the hypothesis, Bayesian conditionalization will eventually converge on the truth (Savage 1972, section 3.6).

This sketch is subject to many additions and refinements. In formulating it, I have emphasized the parallelism between Bayesian and hypothetico-deductivist views. The sketch says nothing about whether hypotheses should ever be "accepted." All it talks about is their probability. The schema is also idiosyncratic, for Bayesians often suppress the mention of some background theory T and suppose that the likelihood of h $(\Pr(P/h))$ is known. But, as I already argued, this habit begs too many important questions. Notice that nothing is said about what is admissible as a part of "T" here, nor whether the probability of T might itself be revised as a result of this testing. But simple pictures still have their uses.

Since the Bayesian approach conceives of confirmation as a kind of rational decision-making, it may consequently be extended in a variety of intriguing ways, when one notices that science has other competing aims, such as acquiring information.[19] Such an aim may serve as an constraint, along with prior probability assessments, on which hypotheses are considered in the first place. One can conceive of theory appraisal as a problem of rational decision-making in circumstances of uncertainty and competing aims.

The possibility of integrating the theory of confirmation into a general account of rational scientific decision-making should make this approach attractive to economists, for Bayesian decision theory is an extension of the standard economic view of rational choice (see chapter 1). The Bayesian vision thus holds out the prospect that economic methodology can turn out to be an application of economic theory!

A.10.3 Bootstrapping

Despite the many virtues of the Bayesian approach, it faces serious problems, too (see especially Glymour 1980, chapter 3). Simplest to describe is the problem of old evidence. If the truth of e is known, then $\Pr(e) = 1$ and e cannot confirm h. But even if new evidence is better than old evidence, old evidence is not worthless.[20] Second, the Bayesian account gives precise directions about how to update probability judgments only if judgments of likelihoods $(\Pr(e/h))$ are known and may not be revised (as stressed by Miller 1987, pp. 314f). But, as the Quine–Duhem problem suggests (p. 306 above), it may be as reasonable to revise judgments of likelihood as to change one's degree of belief in the

---

[19] But it should be noted that there are also non-Bayesian accounts of scientific inference as rational decision-making. For a simple example, see Giere 1983. Closer to the Bayesian view, but still distinct alternatives are Kyburg 1974 and Levi 1967, 1980.

[20] For more on the problem see Eells 1985, Garber 1983, Howson and Urbach 1989, and Niiniluoto 1983.

hypothesis. As I discuss in chapter 12, this is a serious practical problem in economics. Furthermore, like the general HD schema, the Bayesian account has little to say about how the relevance of evidence to different parts of a theory is determined. Can one not say more about the structural and objective aspects of evidential relevance?

Clark Glymour attempts to supply such an account in his recent *Theory and Evidence* (1980, 1983; see also van Fraassen 1983a,b). Glymour endorses an alternative confirmational strategy, which he finds implicit in the work of Carnap (1936, 1937), Reichenbach (1959), and Weyl (1949). Although the formal presentation of the account is complicated,[21] the basic idea is that confirmation is always relative to some "theory," which one uses to *deduce from the evidence* an instance of the hypothesis one confirms. Glymour calls this view "bootstrapping," because one uses theories, including even the theory one is testing, in order to test theories. Provided that the procedure does not guarantee a positive instance, regardless of what the evidence is, there is nothing objectionable in this circularity. Here is Glymour's sketch of the basic idea:

The central idea is that the hypotheses are confirmed with respect to a theory by a piece of evidence provided that, using the theory, we can deduce from the evidence an instance of the hypothesis, and the deduction is such that it does not guarantee that we would have gotten an instance of the hypothesis regardless of what the evidence might have been. (Glymour 1980, p. 127)

Since different bits of evidence figure in the deduction of instances of different hypotheses within a theory, one can see how evidence can be relevant to parts of theories; and one can see how two theories which both account for the same data may not be equally confirmed by it. Bootstrapping is primarily an account of how evidence bears on theories, not of when to accept theories or how to choose among them, although Glymour offers some remarks on these problems, too (1980, pp. 152f).

Just as for the HD method and the Bayesian account, one can provide a simplified sketch of how the bootstrapping method is supposed to work:

1 *Formulate* an hypothesis *h*.
2 *Determine* some class of data *D* such that for some *P* in *D* and some theory *T*, *T&P* imply an instance of *h*, while for some *P'* in *D*, *T&P'* do not imply an instance of *h*.
3 *Gather* data from class *D*.
4 *Judge h* depending on whether *T* and the data gathered imply an instance of *h* or not.

---

[21] Reminiscent of "the fine print in an auto-rental contract" (Glymour 1983, p. 5).

Table A.1. Three views of confirmation

Hypothetico-deductive	Bayesian	Bootstrapping
1. *Formulate h.*	1. *Formulate h* with some prior probability.	1. *Formulate h.*
2. *Deduce P* from *h&T.*	2. *Find P*, s.t. $\Pr(T)$ is close to 1, $\Pr(P/h\&T)$ is high, and $\Pr(P/\sim h\&T)$ is low.	2. *Find* data class *D* s.t. for some *P* in *D*, *T&P* imply an instance of *h*, and for some *P'* in *D*, *T&P'* do not.
3. *Test P.*	3. *Test P.*	3. *Gather* data *d* from *D.*
4. *Judge h* depending if *P* is true.	4. *Update* $\Pr(H)$.	4. *Judge h* depending if *d&T* imply *h.*

This is a barebones account that can be filled out in various ways. Section 2.6 provides an example of how bootstrapping might be applied to the testing of consumer choice theory.

In its full generality Glymour's account runs into difficulties that are reminiscent of those that befall the hypothetico-deductive method,[22] and discipline-specific knowledge seems essential to prevent one from making nonsense of bootstrapping.

To tie together this long discussion of confirmation, let us juxtapose the three schemata in a single figure. As table A.1 makes clear, the Bayesian account of confirmation can be regarded as an elaboration of the hypothetico-deductive view, but the bootstrapping account is quite different.

A.11   The problem of induction

Although most people think it obvious that the only evidence for theories is, ultimately, perceptual, empiricist views of theory assessment face deep problems, some of which become evident when one tries to be more precise about confirmation. There is also a serious philosophical puzzle about the very possibility of confirmation. As David Hume argued in

[22] See Christensen 1983, 1990, Earman 1983, Earman and Glymour 1988, Edidin 1981, 1983, 1988, Grimes 1987, and Zytkow 1986.

the eighteenth century, observation or experimentation only leads one directly to accept singular statements about properties of things at particular times and places. Upon what, then, is one's confidence in generalizations or in singular statements about instances not yet observed based? As Hume himself put it:

If a body of like color and consistency with that bread which we have formerly eaten be presented to us, we make no scruple of repeating the experiment and foresee with certainty like nourishment and support. Now this is a process of mind or thought of which I would willingly know the foundation (1748, p. 47).

Hume is issuing a challenge: "Show me a good argument whose conclusion is some generalization or some claim about something not observed and whose premises include only reports of sensory experiences." Such an argument cannot be a deductive argument, because the conclusions of such arguments may be mistaken even when all the premises are true: Europeans had ample inductive evidence for the false generalization that all swans are white. Nor will an "inductive" argument do, since one has only inductive and thus question-begging grounds to believe that inductive arguments are good ones. The validity of inductive arguments is precisely what is being questioned.

This is Hume's *problem of induction*. It is primarily a problem concerning how singular claims about unobserved things or generalizations are to be *supported* or *justified*. It is not mainly a problem about the discovery of generalizations. Nor is it a problem about the actual arguments scientists make in defense of particular hypotheses, whose premises are never limited to observation reports. I believe that Hume's problem of induction is insoluble.

If the problem of induction cannot be solved, then either one can embrace Hume's skepticism and deny that there are good reasons to believe anything beyond logical truths and the immediate pronouncements of observation or one can reject Hume's problem. The first option is difficult to take seriously; indeed Hume himself found it impossible to do so when he left his study (1738, book I, part IV, section VII). The latter course is the only serious possibility.

What is wrong with Hume's problem of induction is Hume's "foundationalist" view of justification (Williams 1977). Hume wants an argument for each claim about the world from premises consisting only of reports of sensory experiences. If one rejects foundationalism and permits the premises in justificatory arguments to include parts of one's purported knowledge, then one faces the more tractable (although still very difficult) problem discussed in the last section. On the Bayesian view, for example, one cannot proceed without some prior probabilities. But, given such priors, evidence can make hypotheses more probable. Observations and experiments have a crucial role in the expansion and correction of empirical knowledge, but one cannot and need not trace knowledge claims back to any experiential foundation (Quine 1969; Levi 1980). To use a superb metaphor that Quine cites repeatedly: in learning about the world it is as if one is rebuilding a ship while staying afloat in it. In learning more, people rely on what they think they know.[23]

The ship metaphor is Otto Neurath's. Although Neurath was a member of the Vienna Circle, the logical positivists generally resisted such a view of scientific knowledge. Instead Carnap (1950) and others attempted to develop an inductive logic, a canon of thought whereby conclusions could be established with a certain subjective probability from premises, which included only logic, mathematics, analytical meaning postulates, and reports of observations and experiments. These efforts were not successful, but Carnap's work helped lead to the less foundational approaches to confirmation discussed in the last section.

A.12   The problem of demarcation

Part of what makes skepticism about human knowledge difficult to espouse has been the success of the natural sciences. Although some philosophers have questioned whether the natural sciences have increased human knowledge, their efforts make one wonder at their cleverness; they do not lead to doubts about science. Furthermore, the success of science has not come entirely from genius and good luck, but has something to do with the institutional structure of sciences and the rules which guide scientific practice. It seems worth asking what rules guide science, which is what this book does, and what distinguishes sciences from non-sciences or pseudo-sciences.

In autobiographical comments, Karl Popper writes that what led him into the philosophy of science was this problem, which he calls "the problem of demarcation." Popper often formulates the problem as: What is the difference between a scientific theory and a theory which is not scientific? Popper answers by maintaining that scientific theories are "falsifi*able*" – logically inconsistent with some finite set of true or false

[23] One may have qualms, for without foundationalism there is no guarantee that the results of inquiry are not castles in the air. Is the world knowable at all? Is there any reasonable chance that inquiry could arrive at the truth and nothing but the truth? These are serious questions that are susceptible to abstract inquiry (Kelly and Glymour 1989).

observation reports (see 10.2 for more detail). When the question is put in this way, one can say that the problem of demarcation was a crucial question for the logical positivists, too. For they wanted to be able to distinguish scientific theories from "meaningless" metaphysics. If one takes this formulation of the problem of demarcation literally, it consists of the problem of distinguishing those entities called "scientific theories" from other entities. This problem of demarcation cannot be completely separated from the problem of theory assessment, and I think it is best replaced with the problem of distinguishing good theories from bad.

Popper is also concerned to distinguish those attitudes, rules, and practices that characterize a scientific community from other human practices. What distinguishes sciences may not be their theories so much as what scientists think of their theories and what they do with them. Newton's theory of motion might become the dogma of a strange religious sect, while astrology might be subjected to careful scientific scrutiny. In my view the more important issue for those concerned with demarcation is to distinguish between science and non-science.

Popper maintains that what distinguishes scientists from non-scientists is that scientists have a "critical attitude." They propose bold conjectures and then seek out harsh tests. When the conjectures fail the tests, no excuses are permitted. The theories are refuted and new conjectures must be proposed and scrutinized. If Popper's proposal were carried out, it would be destructive. Theories always face unresolved difficulties. They are too important to be surrendered until alternatives are available, and alternatives are not easily generated. For details see chapter 10.

Imre Lakatos offers a criterion of demarcation that addresses these objections. Within the guidelines laid down by the heuristics of a scientific research program (see A.8 and 6.2), scientists attempt to improve theories. In "progressive" research programs, the positive heuristic enables practitioners to formulate theories that have additional empirical implications, some of which turn out to be correct. There is no sharp demarcation between sciences and non-sciences, but progressive research programs are characteristic of science, while extremely degenerating research programs are pseudo-scientific. Lakatos' account of demarcation is plausible, but, as argued in section 11.3, its details are flawed.

The problem of demarcation has both a political and a philosophical point. The political point arises from the fact that **SCIENCE** possesses great authority and prestige in our society. Deciding whether some discipline is a science determines its status. The political point is crucial in current debates concerning "scientific creationism." The creationists use Popper's views on demarcation, as well as specific remarks Popper made about the theory of evolution to argue that evolutionary biology is unscientific and should command no more attention or authority in the classroom than does the view that the universe and all the species came suddenly into existence less than 10,000 years ago.[24] The creationists have persuaded two states to pass laws embodying their views, and they have even found sympathy among justices on the United States Supreme Court (*Edwards v. Aguillard* 1986). The creationists have had a strong influence on local school boards, textbooks, and science education.

But the philosophical point of the problem of demarcation must not be forgotten amid this political dispute. There are *reasons* why science has authority and prestige. Although its status is a sociological fact, there is something distinctive and important about science that does not depend on the social attitudes toward science. The problem of demarcation could still be important if the status of scientists were no greater than that of welders.

What is special about science is not that its claims are uniquely *true*. It would be absurd to maintain that science is the only source of truth or that whatever scientists regard as well-established is true. If science has any special claim on our regard, it is as an engine of *discovery* and as providing particularly *good reason* to believe its assertions. Popper and Lakatos would not approve of this formulation, for they deny that there are ever good reasons to believe the claims of science and because Popper denied that there was any method to discovery. But the basic sentiment, that science has an especially effective way of contributing to the growth of knowledge, was one that they fully shared; and it motivated their work on the problem of demarcation.

Despite these good reasons to confront the question of what distinguishes science from non-science and pseudo-science, I agree with Laudan (1983) that it is not the right question to ask. For, in addressing the differences between sciences and non-sciences as a single problem, one is forced to draw a single distinction where many distinctions should be drawn, and one is driven toward the view, which should be independently considered, that all sciences share the same methods of discovery and confirmation. One may, of course, offer a summary comparison and contrast between a science such as physics and activities such as philology, history, "scientific" creationism, or, for that matter, golf – just as one may offer a summary comparison and contrast between a science such as physics and quite different sciences such as archeology, computer science, or economics. But both the philosophical and political demands that give rise to the problem of demarcation are better addressed by

---

[24] Morris undated, p. i. Popper's critique of evolutionary biology is found on p. 168 of his *The Unended Quest* (1976), and he has since retracted it (1978, pp. 345–8).

focusing on more specific questions. Accidents of US constitutional law may force one to phrase the political question as "Is scientific creationism scientific?" but, when possible, it is sounder instead to ask questions such as, "How well confirmed by the data is the hypothesis that all fossils result from a single world-wide flood?" "What new discoveries does scientific creationism lead to?", or "What contributions does scientific creationism make to other disciplines such as astronomy, nuclear physics, thermodynamics, and so forth?" (Kitcher 1982) Everything that is significant about the problem of demarcation is to be found in the specific problems of which it is constituted.

A.13   Scientific "method"

Even if one sets aside the problem of demarcation as the wrong problem to pursue, one would still like to know more about the special features of sciences: what rules, attitudes, and traditions govern scientific disciplines? How can one study markets or economies scientifically? The abstract discussions of the previous sections are motivated by such questions. For to understand theories and models, laws and explanations, confirmation and discovery, and the goals and observational basis of science is largely to understand what sort of human activities sciences are.

But nobody is going to learn how to do science from this appendix, for useful rules and hints lie at a lower level of generality and require more detail. One reason for writing a monograph such as this one is precisely the need to focus on the methodological details of a single discipline.

In thinking seriously not about the philosophical problems cast up by the sciences, but about *methodology* in a narrow sense,[25] about how to do the work of some discipline, it is important to be aware of the distinctively methodological perspective. Unlike the philosopher, who sees philosophy of science as a branch of epistemology and as casting up particular metaphysical, logical, conceptual, ethical, or aesthetic problems, the methodologist is primarily interested in understanding how a particular discipline works and how to make it work better. This distinction resembles the division of labor between theoretical and applied economics. Just as the methodologist wants to understand what makes

---

[25] The "term" methodology is used in different ways. Many, such as Fritz Machlup (1963) explicitly identify methodology with the philosophical problem of theory appraisal. This is much too narrow. I regard *any* feature of economics as a legitimate object of methodological study. What distinguishes methodology from the history or sociology of economics is not its object but its partly normative aim. Methodology can be used in a wider sense to include philosophy of science. See the introduction.

some scientific practice tick and how to improve it, so the applied economist wants to understand how particular markets work and how to make them work better (Railton 1980, pp. 686f).

Put this way, it is an open question whether a methodologist is well advised to employ the tools of a philosopher of science. Perhaps those of a sociologist or of a literary critic might serve methodologists better (see section 14.3). But some affinity between methodology and philosophy of economics is unavoidable, for in the attempt to improve economics the methodologist necessarily shares some of the normative concerns of the philosopher of science. Methodology cannot avoid its normative calling.

There is no reason why philosophy of economics cannot be in large part an empirical discipline, a sort of social science that studies the institutions and practices of economics in much the same way that economics studies the institutions and practices of economies. Questions about knowledge acquisition in economics can only be answered well if philosophers have learned what makes for good economic science. And, in my view, to learn about science, one needs to study science. This book is both methodology and philosophy of economics. In its concern with the particular problems that confront economists, it is intended as a contribution to economic methodology (particularly in chapter 14), but it focuses on epistemological questions cast up by economics.

If one goes to contemporary philosophy of science in search of hard and fast rules for scientific practice, one will be disappointed. Philosophers of science know a great deal about science, but that knowledge falls short of providing usable algorithms. Non-philosophers often express disgust with so much "useless philosophizing" and then proceed to do more of it, only less carefully and less knowledgeably. Many are tempted by a skeptical relativism that denies that there are any rules of scientific practice. As this monograph shows, such negative, relativist, and skeptical conclusions are unjustified, which is fortunate, for skepticism and relativism are cold comfort when one needs to decide what to do about unemployment (see 14.2).

In one's disappointment at finding no simple rules for doing science, one should not overlook what philosophers have learned. Even through the failures of oversimplified accounts of science, important lessons have been learned. There are some simple generalizations that apply to all empirical sciences – the "facts," the results of experiments and observations, are still what ultimately count – but such generalizations are not very useful. Sciences are not only very complicated institutions, but their norms depend on the content of current scientific knowledge. Valid and helpful accounts of the nature of sciences cannot be simple.

A.14   Social theory and the unity of science

One theme which has surfaced frequently is that sciences are not all alike, and that philosophers and methodologists must be sensitive to the details of the disciplines they study. Even within the physical sciences the differences are large. Consider, for example, the allied fields of chemistry and physics. In the molecular realm the two largely overlap, and parts of chemistry have been reduced to physics. But even here the differences must not be overlooked. Much of chemistry is, unlike physics, concerned with properties of particular substances and with the molecular structure that explains these properties. Even if the laws the chemist relies on to study benzene, for example, are physical laws, the attention of the chemist is on the properties and molecular structure of substances, not on the laws. Economists have drawn analogies between economics and physics without asking whether these are the right analogies to stress. Are the resemblances to physics more instructive than the resemblances to chemistry, biology, or paleontology? I am inclined to agree with Sidney Morgenbesser, who suggested to me that economics is more like chemistry than physics.[26]

It makes sense to look for similarities between sciences, but one should not forget to notice the differences. Philosophers have paid too little attention to the peculiarities of particular disciplines. For example, there are very few studies of electrical or chemical engineering by philosophers of science. One reason may be that the differences between engineering and theoretical physics are so large that philosophers had trouble seeing engineering as science at all. Yet electrical and chemical engineering are systematic empirical studies. They have theories and engage in extensive experimentation. Their results are used by "pure" scientists, and no sharp boundary can be drawn between them and physics and chemistry "proper." The neglect of engineering may be one reason why philosophers and methodologists have found economics so puzzling. For, as suggested to me by Hal Varian, economics may be more like engineering than it is like physics. Consider the repeated efforts of economists to show that economic conclusions follow even if one *denies* the basic behavioral generalizations of economics (discussed in 2.2 and 6.3). These efforts are deeply puzzling if one conceives of economics as a sort of social physics. Except to undermine support for particular physical laws, physicists are not trying hard to show that the phenomena would still obtain, even if

[26] Jon Elster defends the same analogy, "Ultimately, parsimony must take second place to realism. In physics, truth may be simple. In chemistry, it is likely to be messy. Social science, to repeat what I said in the Introduction, is closer to chemistry than to physics." (1989a, p. 250)

the laws of physics were different. But the practice makes perfectly good sense if economics is conceived of as a sort of engineering. For in engineering one wants "robust" conclusions that can be established in various ways.

In thinking about economics, one needs to recognize not only that there are important differences between physics, chemistry, and electrical engineering, but one must also pay attention to the fact that economics is a social science. As such, one might question whether it should be modeled after *any* of the natural sciences. Human beings and their social interactions are quite different objects of study than are planets, proteins, or integrated circuits. Should one's goals or methods in investigating societies be the same as those of natural scientists? Many writers on the social sciences have insisted that there are fundamental differences between the natural and the social sciences (see Morgenbesser 1970).

Those who have been concerned with this question of "social-scientific naturalism" - those who have asked whether the social sciences can be "real" sciences - have been concerned with several distinct questions. They have wondered about the possibility of social *laws*. Is there something about human behavior that makes the formulation of laws impossible? Second, they have been concerned about explanation in the social sciences and about the goals of social theory. Third, many have questioned whether the logic of social theories is the same as in the natural sciences, and whether social scientific theories develop in the same ways as do those in the natural sciences. Finally, the policy implications of disciplines such as economics raise questions about the limits of objectivity in social theory and about the relations between fact and value in the social sciences. I argue in the text that the fact that economics is a social science explains some of its most important methodological peculiarities.

A.14.1 Is social science possible?

Why would one question whether there can be social laws? One simple answer is that none have been found. Indeed, Alexander Rosenberg maintains that there has been no progress in developing laws of human behavior for the last twenty-five hundred years (Rosenberg 1980, pp. 2-3; 1983). New psychological facts about people in particular cultures have been noticed, as have correlations among aggregates (such as the negative correlation Durkheim notes between Catholicism and the suicide rate) (1951, pp. 152f). But Rosenberg contends that there has been no progress in developing genuine laws of individual or social behavior. This fact suggests to Rosenberg that such laws are unobtainable.

Second, many have been inclined to deny that social laws are possible, because they believe that free will makes human behavior unpredictable. But human behavior is not unpredictable. Not only can we predict the behavior of people we know well, but we often know what strangers will do. When we ask for directions in an unfamiliar city, we rely on people to give truthful answers. When we cross the street, we rely on strangers not to run us over. Whether or not human freedom sets limits to social theory, there are still uniformities in human behavior that social theorists may study (Hume 1738, book II, part II, sections 1 and 2 and Mill 1843, book VI, chapter 2).

Third, and of considerable importance in current economics, claims in the social sciences often involve a measure of reflexivity. Since expectations and beliefs influence behavior, awareness of or belief in social theories may change people's behavior. Prophesies and theories can be self-fulfilling or self-refuting. One school of contemporary economists explicitly models agents as acting on the correct economic theory, which is identified with the very theory being proposed (see Begg 1982; Hoover 1988). Analogues of the self-fulfilling prophesy have been found: in some models any of an infinite set of conflicting expectations may be such that, if the expectation is universal, then it is true (see p. 118 and Hahn 1986, p. 276). Although there are interesting puzzles here, such possibilities do not reflect fundamental difficulties (see Buck 1963 and Simon 1954), because social theorists can "factor in" the reactions of those who become aware of the theories. My hunch is that skeptics are implicitly relying on free will to foil the social theorist.

There are two other common arguments against the possibility of laws and of reliable predictions of human behavior, which are linked to issues to be discussed in the next two subsections. The first of these is offered by Rosenberg as a diagnosis for the nomological failings of the social sciences. Theories of human behavior typically incorporate "folk psychology" and conceive of action as determined by belief and desire. But belief and desire are irreducibly "intentional" notions, and there can be no intentional laws. This claim is discussed in A.14.3.

The last argument against the possibility of laws of human behavior that I shall mention maintains that regularities in human action are responses to meaningful norms, not causal uniformities. The self-deceived social scientist misidentifies the regular consequences of people adhering to meaningful rules as the blind and meaningless regularities of natural phenomena. Defenders of this position need not be committed to any metaphysical doctrine of free will (although here again I see its influence), for they can concede that there might be physical causes for every motion that a human being makes. But, in the terms that are appropriate for social theory, one is examining the relationship between rules, reasons, and actions, not the relationship between causes and their behavioral effects.

Since this view is also an account of the nature of explanation in the social sciences, let us consider what makes explanations in the social sciences so distinctive before saying more about it.

A.14.2 Explanations in the social sciences

Explanations in the social sciences introduce special difficulties. First are the questions usually discussed under the rubric of "methodological individualism."[27] In the social sciences one can find not only generalizations about individual behavior ("Individuals prefer more income to less"), but also generalizations about aggregates ("The rate of inflation depends on the rate of increase of the money supply"). Many philosophers and social theorists have argued that "rock-bottom" or fully satisfactory explanations in the social sciences must be "individualistic" – that is, they must employ only laws concerning individual behavior or, more stringently, they must not refer to any aggregates. Non-individualist claims and purported explanations may be significant, but one must not rest content with them, because the only actors in the social drama are individual human beings. Unless holistic explanations can be "reduced to" individualist terms, they are not scientifically acceptable. The stricter formulation of methodological individualism calling for the elimination of all non-individualistic terms is untenable (Levy 1985), but weaker versions are plausible. Methodological individualism is accepted by many economists and is sometimes used as a basis to criticize macroeconomic theories. For an excellent recent discussion, see Sensat 1988.

Most explanations of human action take one simple ("folk-psychological") form. One explains why an agent wrote a letter or sold a bond or stayed home from work by citing the agent's beliefs and desires. Although often elliptically formulated, such explanations are common in everyday life and in economics, too. When economists explain behavior in terms of utility functions, their explanations are of just this kind. But one can reject utility theory without rejecting folk psychology. For example, Herbert Simon's theory of individual choice in terms of "satisficing" rather than maximizing (1976, 1978, 1982) still explains choices in terms of beliefs and desires.

---

[27] See Brodbeck 1958, Hayek 1952, Hodgson 1986, Kincaid 1986, Levine *et al.* 1987, Lukes 1973, Macdonald 1986, Miller 1978, Popper 1957, 1966, vol. 2, Sensat 1988, Watkins 1953, 1968 and the collection by O'Neill 1973. See also section 6.6.

This familiar kind of explanation is philosophically problematic. For the "laws" it relies on are platitudes such as "People do what they most prefer." Some philosophers and economists have argued that these platitudes follow from the meanings of terms such as "action" and "preference" and are not empirical generalizations at all (von Wright 1971). But is it strictly *contradictory* to say that G wanted Y most of all, G believed that X led infallibly to Y and that nothing else led to Y, and that G did not do X?

A slightly different argument seems more forceful. Consider how one might go about testing the generalizations that individuals do what they most prefer. One would need to gather data about individual G's beliefs and desires in order to consider the relations between them and G's actions. But the investigator's only access to G's beliefs and desires depends on their connection to what G says and does. When, for example, we take G's words, "I did not know the road was slippery," as information about G's belief, we suppose that G knows what the words mean, wants to tell us the truth, and believes that saying these words is a means to this end. In inferring what an individual believes or wants from her actions or her words, one thus takes for granted the very generalization that one is supposed to be testing (Rosenberg 1988b, chapter 2)![28]

For reasons such as these, many philosophers have concluded that explanations of human behavior differ from explanations in the natural sciences. In explaining why Othello did what he did, one does not subsume his action under some general regularity. What then is one doing?

At the end of the last subsection, I sketched one answer: The social sciences aim at "understanding," rather than explanation. The aim is not to subsume some human action under a causal law, but to discover the *rules* (or *goals* or *meanings*) which guide the action and render it meaningful. And to understand rules, according to Peter Winch and others, requires *interpretation* (Winch 1958, 1964). Winch's views seem to rule out the possibility of scientific study of human behavior and institutions. They have accordingly been vigorously contested (Gellner 1973, MacIntyre 1967). At the very least one should notice that citing a rule only helps one to explain a human action, if one supposes that the rule led to the action. But how do rules "lead" people to act? One plausible answer is that recognizing or knowing the rule is one of the *causes* of the action. And, if this is so, then rules have a role *within* causal explanation rather than as a part of an alternative kind of explanation.

---

[28] Although disquieting, this circularity does not seem vicious, for it is not guaranteed that the results of our testing will come out favorably. This could be seen as an instance of the bootstrap methodology discussed above in A.10.3.

A second possible alternative to causal explanation, which has been influential in economics, goes back to Max Weber (1949, 1975), although it has been espoused by twentieth-century economists such as Frank Knight (1940; 1961) and Fritz Machlup (1969). It also resembles the perspective of the contemporary Austrian school (Dolan 1976). Weber argued that the social sciences should provide an understanding "from the inside," that one should be able to empathize with the reactions of the agents and to find what happens "understandable." Causal regularities of social phenomena cast in terms that are not *meaningful* to the participants or to us may be correct, but do not provide the sort of knowledge we seek.

This meaning- or value-relevance of social phenomena introduces an element of subjectivity into the social sciences that is avoidable in the natural sciences. Weber resists drawing the extreme conclusion that the social sciences cannot provide objective knowledge. He argues that people classify social phenomena in terms of culturally significant categories, and that explanations must be in these terms or they will not tell investigators what they want to know. But, in contrast to authors such as Frank Knight (1935a), Weber has no objection to causal (indeed deductive-nomological) explanation (Weber 1904, p. 79; Runciman 1972). Weber also maintains that when studying social phenomena we are interested in the concrete details rather than in general regularities (1904, pp. 72f). But I see this as a distinctive emphasis, which is shared by some natural sciences, such as paleontology, and not as demanding a different kind of explanation.

A more common view of explanations in the social sciences is that they give the agent's *reasons* rather than citing causes of action. Explanation in the social sciences is thus tied to *justification,* for reasons, unlike causes, may be good or bad; and an explanation in terms of reasons will thus vindicate or condemn (Knight 1935a).

It is true that a folk-psychological explanation gives the agent's reasons and makes possible evaluation as well as understanding. Beliefs and desires function as reasons for action. But cannot reasons also be causes? Indeed Donald Davidson (1963) has argued that they must be. Merely citing a reason the agent had does not explain the agent's action. One must cite *effective* reasons, reasons that actually led to action. Davidson argues that what makes reasons effective and hence explanatory is precisely their causal relation to actions.

Given the evaluative force of reasons, explanations in the social sciences will generally have an *additional* feature that explanations in the natural sciences lack, but why cannot explanations in terms of reasons still be roughly deductive-nomological in form? The "laws" involved are little more than platitudes, and their testing involves some circularity. But it is not clear what these complaints add up to. The case against seeing reason-giving explanations as also causal explanations is inconclusive and hotly contested.

Like most writers on economics, I regard explanations in economics as similar to explanations in the natural sciences, and I see no compelling philosophical objections in the above discussion (but see section 15.3). But not everyone agrees, and there are grounds for uneasiness.

A.14.3 Intentionality

The contention that the explanation of human action in terms of the reasons for action must be distinguished from causal explanation receives additional support from the fact that folk psychology is *intentional*. As economists have come increasingly to recognize, human beliefs and expectations, not just the realities about which people have beliefs and expectations, are crucial to understanding human behavior (Begg 1982). For people can, as Frank Knight stresses, make mistakes or fail to recognize things (1935a). As a first approximation, economists abstract from such difficulties by assuming that people have perfect information. In that way theorists can avoid worrying about what people believe. But this is only a temporary expedient.

Once one relaxes the assumption that agents know everything, difficulties arise which have no parallel in the natural sciences. For claims about beliefs and preferences possess a different logic: they are, in philosophical jargon, "intentional" (Anscombe 1969, 1981, Chisholm 1957, chapter 11, Quine 1960, chapters 4, 6). From a true *non-intentional* statement such as "Some people in Chicago took capsules from packages of Extra-Strength Tylenol" and the horrifying truth that somebody placed cyanide in those capsules, one can infer "Some people ingested cyanide-filled capsules." But from the true *intentional* statement that "Some people in Chicago *believed* that they were taking capsules from packages of Extra-Strength Tylenol" and the same horrifying truth, one cannot infer "Some people in Chicago believed that they were ingesting cyanide-filled capsules." Nor can one infer from the true claim that the individuals wanted to take capsules from the Tylenol packages that they wanted to take poison-filled capsules.

The logic of belief, preference and other such "intentional" terms is thus in some ways "subjective." Although one may change agent W's intentional state in a non-intentional way by, for example, hitting W over the head with a club or slipping a drug into W's food, many facts affect a person's intentional state only insofar as they are recognized.

Until the cyanide is recognized, its presence does not affect beliefs and desires. Such logical peculiarities and the subsequent need for a "subjective" treatment of expectations distinguish economics from the natural sciences. But the significance of this peculiarity is unclear. Members of the Austrian school argue in effect that these differences are of great importance, and, in chapter 15, I partly agreed.

Alexander Rosenberg lays great emphasis on the role of intentionality in the social sciences, for in his view this role explains the nomological failures of the social sciences and supports the view that the social sciences (in anything like their current form) can *never* succeed in formulating real laws of human behavior (1980, 1983, forthcoming). Nomological progress in the natural sciences often results from the discovery of more fundamental laws that explain and correct superficial regularities. Such nomological progress is impossible in the social sciences, Rosenberg contends, because the intentional concepts of folk psychology are not "natural kinds." Just as there are no laws of motion which involve concepts such as "blurriness in our visual field" or "closeness to home" so there are no laws of human behavior involving concepts such as belief and desire. Part of Rosenberg's argument for this claim is that such concepts make essential implicit reference to some spatio-temporal particular, and that laws, unlike accidental generalizations, must be universal (1980, pp. 131f). Moreover, the folk psychology that we have is supposedly an irreparable dead end: since intentional notions are irreducible to non-intentional notions, there is no way that its generalizations can be derived from and corrected by more fundamental laws. The disciplines that we currently call "social sciences" may accumulate gossip or spot correlations, but Rosenberg believes they will never succeed in formulating laws and theories with the force and fruitfulness of those in the natural sciences. Real sciences of human social life can emerge only out of neurophysiology from as it were "below" or from sociobiology from "above." Behaviorism appears to avoid intentional notions, but Rosenberg argues that this appearance is deceptive (1988b, chapter 3 and forthcoming).

Although Rosenberg's arguments have appeared faulty to many (see, for example, Sober 1985), his claims cannot be easily dismissed. The importance of intentional notions and their irreducibility to non-intentional notions does seem permanently to divide the social sciences from the natural sciences.

A.14.4 Policy relevance

The social sciences are also intimately connected to values and policies.

Not only do economists offer advice on economic policy, but much of their work is devoted to questions of economic policy (Diesing 1982). Of course the natural sciences guide our activities, too. The findings of physicists and chemists help us to build bridges or bombs. But the technological role of scientific knowledge seems unproblematic. Agent A has some given goals, and the scientist provides purely "factual" or "descriptive" knowledge, which determines what means best achieve the specified goals. The policy recommendation follows from the purely scientific knowledge and A's given aims.

Most writers on the methodology of economics construe the role of economics in determining policies in this way (Klappholz 1964, Solow 1971). The body politic or its representative may want to lower unemployment and inflation. The politician turns to the economist for information about how to accomplish these goals and about what other effects the possible means will have. The information the economist provides is supposed to be purely descriptive or "value-free." It would be equally useful to a malicious politician who wanted to wreck the economy. On this view economics and the other social sciences have no more connection to values or prescriptions than do the natural sciences. They have more influence on policy only because they provide information that is particularly relevant for policy making.

But social theorists do not only provide technical knowledge to decision-makers who already have definitely formulated goals. Economists help determine the goals, too. John Dewey (1939b) argued that the whole distinction between means and ends, as plausible and useful as it may sometimes be, can also mislead and confuse us, for our aims may change as we contemplate what means they require. The major economists of the past two centuries have also been social philosophers who have found inspiration in economic theory for their social ideals. Moreover, as illustrated in chapter 7, normative issues are constantly mixed with positive.

The simple picture of the economist who provides value-free technical information to the decision-maker is at best a useful caricature. It fits the activity of an economist who calculates the revenue losses that will result from a tax reduction, but it does not fit the activity of an economist who is asked for advice. For the political process never formulates explicitly what all the relevant goals and constraints are and how to weight them. If Jimmy Carter had asked Milton Friedman, "What is the 'best' way to reduce inflation?" Friedman would not have had a well-defined technical problem until he figured out what other objectives Carter had and what their relative weight was. At some point he would almost certainly have had to rely on some of his own values, too.

Economists who refuse to "dirty their hands" with ethical matters will not know what technical problems to investigate.

Furthermore, in explaining human behavior, social theorists offer generalizations about the reasons which move people. In doing so they touch on questions of prudence and morality. In a simplified economic model in which individuals are taken as acting for selfish reasons only, the absence of moral criticism *itself* conveys the implicit moral message that such reasons justify the choices made. Thus Donald McCloskey remarks that academic economists can be openly selfish in a way that would be unthinkable for English professors or historians (1990, p. 140). It is very difficult to talk about any feature of social life without at least implicitly evaluating it.[29]

There are social facts ("a five-pound bag of sugar is \$2.39 or (£1.50) at the supermarket"), and they constitute important evidence for social theories. But in my view it is almost impossible to do social theory without having the influence of one's values show and without at least implicitly offering or bolstering normative conclusion. Why this is particularly so for neoclassical economics is argued in sections 4.6 and 15.3.

Even if this view goes too far, it must be conceded that there are evaluative influences on which questions social theorists ask and on what sorts of solutions they seriously consider. Some of these influences are personal and idiosyncratic, but there are also general "ideological" influences. As Marx wrote in his Preface to *Capital*:

In the domain of Political Economy, free scientific inquiry meets not merely the same enemies as in all other domains. The peculiar nature of the material it deals with summons as foes into the field of battle the most violent, mean and malignant passions of the human breast, the Furies of private interest. (1867, p. 10)

With systematic divisions of interest and systematic differences in perspective linked to different social roles come systematic evaluative disagreements as well. It seems undeniable that ideological forces have influenced theoretical work in the social sciences (Myrdal 1955). But the extent and character of such ideological influences requires sober assessment. In any case, revulsion at the evaluative presuppositions or conclusions of a piece of social theory is never sufficient grounds for judging its purportedly factual claims to be false.

---

[29] For example, in his recent book, *Passions within Reason: The Strategic Role of the Emotions* (1988), Robert Frank wants to defend morality against objections that it is foolishly self-sacrificing. But he defines rationality as self-interest (p. 2n) and classifies morality as a kind of irrationality. His defense then turns out to be an exploration of the benefits of irrationality.

A.15   Concluding philosophical remarks

This overview of basic issues in the philosophy of science should not encourage pessimistic conclusions. There is, to be sure, a good deal of disagreement among philosophers and much to be learned about science. But much has been done, too. Although logical positivism finds few supporters today, this is not because of some change in intellectual fashion ("Clarity is OUT this year"). With their intellectual honesty and their devotion to clarity, the positivists uncovered their own mistakes. The empirically oriented philosophy of science that has succeeded them has many inadequacies, as does the emerging cognitive science perspective. But these begin with much of the knowledge that the positivists gained in the course of their efforts to capture the scientific enterprise within a formal empiricist framework.

These words are no comfort to citizens, policy-makers, economists, or other social scientists who want to know whether economics is a science, whether they should rely on particular economic theories, or how they can best contribute to economics or to some other social science. It won't do just to say that the problems are difficult, and that philosophers have discovered the mistakes of other philosophers. But, with respect to grand theories of science, philosophers cannot do better now. Unfortunately they have only criticism and *specific* insights to offer. Given how complex and diverse sciences are, it is perhaps inevitable that there is no well-founded general philosophical system to resolve the methodological difficulties of economics.

This background in the philosophy of science helps explain the peculiarities of my attempt to clarify the methodology of neoclassical economics. It is a rich background with many fruitful suggestions, insightful arguments, well-wrought concepts, and cautionary tales of philosophical work gone wrong, and I could not have written the book without studying it. But philosophy of science provides no simple algorithms. In addressing the problems of economics, one cannot use philosophy of science as a fundamentalist preacher might use the Bible in addressing the heathen. Its role is more like that which a graduate education in anthropology plays for the ethnologist. One must address the problems of economic methodology by studying economics.

Bibliography

Achinstein, P. 1983. *The Nature of Explanation.* Oxford: Oxford University Press.

Achinstein, P., ed. 1983. *The Concept of Evidence.* Oxford: Oxford University Press.

Adorno, T., ed. 1969. *Der Positivismusstreit in der Deutschen Soziologie.* Darmstadt: Hermann Luchterhand Verlag.

Ahonen, G. 1989. "On the Empirical Content of Keynes' *General Theory.*" *Richerche Economiche* 43: 256–69.

Akerlof, G. 1970. "The Market for 'Lemons': Quality Uncertainty and the Market Mechanism." *Quarterly Journal of Economics* 84: 488–500.

1980. "A Theory of Social Custom, of Which Unemployment May Be one Consequence." *Quarterly Journal of Economics* 94: 749–75.

1982. "Labor Contracts as Partial Gift Exchange." *Quarterly Journal of Economics* 97: 543–69.

1984. *An Economic Theorist's Book of Tales.* Cambridge: Cambridge University Press.

1985. "Discriminatory, Status-based Wages among Tradition-oriented, Stochastically Trading Coconut Producers." *Journal of Political Economy* 93: 265–76.

Akerlof, G. and W. Dickens. 1982. "The Economic Consequences of Cognitive Dissonance." *American Economic Review* 72: 307–19.

Akerlof, G. and J. Yellen. 1985. "Can Small Deviations from Rationality Make Significant Differences to Economic Equilibria?" *American Economic Review* 75: 708–20.

Alchian, A. 1950. "Uncertainty, Evolution and Economic Theory." *Journal of Political Economy* 57: 211–21.

Allais, M. 1947. *Economie et Intérêt.* Paris: Imprimerie Nationale.

1952. "The Foundations of a Positive Theory of Choice involving Risk and a Criticism of the Postulates and Axioms of the American School," in Allais and Hagen (1979), pp. 27–145.

Allais, M. and O. Hagen, eds. 1979. *Expected Utility Hypotheses and the Allais Paradox.* Dordrecht: Reidel.

Ando, A. and F. Modigliani. 1963. "The Life-Cycle Hypothesis of Saving: Aggregate Implications and Tests." *American Economic Review* 53: 55–84.

---

[1] For the most detailed bibliography of work in economic methodology see Redman 1989. Caldwell (1984) and Hausman (1984) also contain extensive bibliographies.

Anschutz, R. 1953. *The Philosophy of J. S. Mill.* Oxford: Clarendon Press.

Anscombe, E. 1969. *Intentionality.* Ithaca: Cornell University Press.

1981. "The Intentionality of Sensation: A Grammatical Feature," in G. Anscombe. *Metaphysics and the Philosophy of Mind.* Minneapolis: University of Minnesota Press, pp. 3–20.

Archibald, G. 1959. "The State of Economic Science." *British Journal for the Philosophy of Science* 10: 58–69.

1961. "Chamberlin *versus* Chicago." *Review of Economic Studies* 29: 2–28.

1967. "Refutation or Comparison?" *British Journal for the Philosophy of Science* 17: 279–96.

Aristotle. 1958. *Physics,* tr. R. Hardie and R. Gaye, *The Pocket Aristotle.* Repr. New York: Washington Square Press, pp. 2–47.

Aronson, E. 1979. *The Social Animal.* 3rd. edn. San Francisco: W. H. Freeman.

Arrow, K. 1963. *Social Choice and Individual Values.* New York: Wiley.

1967. "Values and Collective Decision Making." Repr. in Hahn and Hollis (1979), pp. 110–26.

1978. "Extended Sympathy and the Possibility of Social Choice." *Philosophia* 7: 223–37.

Arrow, K. and F. Hahn. 1971. *General Competitive Analysis.* San Francisco: Holden-Day.

Asimakopulos, A. 1967. "The Pure Consumption-Loan Model Once More." *Journal of Political Economy* 75: 763–4.

Ausubel, L. 1991. "The Failure of Competition in the Credit Card Market." *American Economic Review* 81: 50–81.

Ayer, A. 1936. *Language, Truth and Logic.* 2nd. edn. Repr. New York: Dover, 1946.

Ayer, A., ed. 1959. *Logical Positivism.* New York: Free Press.

Baker, C. 1975. "The Ideology of the Economic Analysis of Law." *Philosophy and Public Affairs* 5: 3–48.

Balzer, W. and B. Hamminga, eds. 1989. *Philosophy of Economics.* Dordrecht: Kluwer-Nijhoff.

Barrett, M. and D. Hausman. 1990. "Making Interpersonal Comparisons Coherently." *Economics and Philosophy* 6: 293–300.

Barro, R. 1974. "Are Government Bonds Net Wealth?" *Journal of Political Economy* 82: 1095–117.

Basmann, R. 1963. "The Causal Interpretation of Non-Triangular Systems of Economic Relations." *Econometrica* 31: 439–48.

Battalio, R. C., L. Green and J. H. Kagel. 1981. "Income-Leisure Trade-Offs of Animal Workers." *American Economic Review* 71: 621–32.

Battalio, R. C., J. H. Kagel, L. Green. 1979. "Consumer Demand Behavior with Pigeons as Subjects." *Journal of Political Economy* 89: 67–91.

Baumberger, J. 1977. "No Kuhnian Revolutions in Economics." *Journal of Economic Issues* 11: 1–20.

Bear, D. and D. Orr. 1967. "Logic and Expediency in Economic Theorizing." *Journal of Political Economy* 75: 188–96.

Beauchamp, T. and A. Rosenberg. 1981. *Hume and the Problem of Causation.* Oxford: Oxford University Press.

Becker, G. 1962. "Irrational Behavior and Economic Theory." *Journal of Political Economy* 70: 1–13.

1976. *The Economic Approach to Human Behavior*. Chicago: University of Chicago Press.

1981. *A Treatise on the Family*. Cambridge, MA.: Harvard University Press.

Becker, G., M. deGroot, and J. Marschak. 1964. "Measuring Utility by a Single-Response Sequential Method." *Behavioral Science* 9: 226–32.

Begg, D. 1982. *The Rational Expectations Revolution in Macroeconomics: Theories and Evidence*. Baltimore: Johns Hopkins University Press.

Bell, D. and I. Kristol, eds. 1981. *The Crisis in Economic Theory*. New York: Basic Books.

Bennett, J. 1984. "Counterfactuals and Temporal Direction." *Philosophical Review* 93: 57–91.

Bentham, J. 1789. *An Introduction to the Principles of Morals and Legislation*, ed. W. Harrison. Oxford: Basil Blackwell, 1967.

Berg, J., J. Dickhaut, and J. O'Brien. 1985. "Preference Reversal and Arbitrage," in V. Smith, ed. *Research in Experimental Economics*, vol. 3. Greenwich: JAI Press, pp. 31–72.

Bergmann, B. 1989. "Does the Market for Women's Labor Need Fixing?" *Journal of Economic Perspectives* 3: 43–60.

Berofsky, B. 1971. *Determinism*. Princeton: Princeton University Press.

Bicchieri, C. 1988. "Should a Scientist Abstain from Metaphor?" in Klamer *et al.* (1988), pp. 100–14.

Binmore, K. 1987. "Modeling Rational Players: Part I." *Economics and Philosophy* 3: 179–214.

1988. "Modeling Rational Players: Part II." *Economics and Philosophy* 4: 9–56.

Blaug, M. 1975. 1976. "Kuhn versus Lakatos *or* Paradigms versus Research Programmes in the History of Economics," in Latsis, ed. (1976), pp. 149–80.

1980a. *The Methodology of Economics: Or How Economists Explain*. Cambridge: Cambridge University Press.

1980b. *A Methodological Appraisal of Marxian Economics*. Amsterdam: North-Holland.

1985. "Comment on D. Wade Hand's 'Karl Popper and Economic Methodology: A New Look.'" *Economics and Philosophy* 1: 286–9.

1987. "Second Thoughts on the Keynesian Revolution," Mimeograph English version of "Ripensamenti Sulla Rivoluzione Keynesiana." *Rassegna Economica* 51: 605–34.

Blaug, M. and N. de Marchi, eds. 1991. *Appraising Modern Economics: Studies in the Methodology of Scientific Research Programs*. Edward Elgar.

Blinder, A. 1974. "The Economics of Brushing Teeth." *Journal of Political Economy* 82: 887–91.

Blinder, A. and D. Choi. 1990. "A Shred of Evidence on Theories of Wage Stickiness." *Quarterly Journal of Economics* 105: 1003–15.

Bliss, C. 1975. *Capital Theory and the Distribution of Income*. Amsterdam: North-Holland.

Böhm-Bawerk, E. 1888. *The Positive Theory of Capital*, tr. W. Smart. Repr. New York: G. E. Stechert & Co., 1923.

Boland, L. 1979. "A Critique of Friedman's Critics." *Journal of Economic Literature* 17: 503–22.

1981. "On the Futility of Criticizing the Neoclassical Maximization Hypothesis." *American Economic Review* 73: 1031–6.

1982a. "Difficulties with the Element of Time and the 'Principles' of Economics or Some Lies My Teachers Told Me." *Eastern Economic Journal* 8: 47–58.

1982b. *The Foundations of Economic Method.* London: Allen & Unwin.

1986. *Methodology for a New Microeconomics.* Boston: Allen & Unwin.

1987. "Boland on Friedman's Methodology: A Summation." *Journal of Economic Issues* 21: 380–8.

1989. *The Methodology of Economic Model Building: Methodology after Samuelson.* London: Routledge.

Booth, W. 1974. *Modern Dogma and the Rhetoric of Assent.* Chicago: University of Chicago Press.

1979. *Critical Understanding: The Powers and Limits of Pluralism.* Chicago: University of Chicago Press.

Boyd, R. 1984. "The Current Status of Scientific Realism," in J. Leplin, ed. *Scientific Realism.* Berkeley: University of California Press, pp. 41–82.

Braithwaite, R. 1953. *Scientific Explanation: A Study of the Function of Theory, Probability and Law in Science.* Cambridge: Cambridge University Press.

Bray, J. 1977. "The Logic of Scientific Method in Economics." *Journal of Economic Studies* 4: 1–28.

Braybrooke, D. 1987. *Meeting Needs.* Princeton: Princeton University Press.

Bridgman, P. 1927. *The Logic of Modern Physics.* New York: Macmillan.

1938. "Operational Analysis." *Philosophy of Science* 5: 114–31.

Brodbeck, M. 1958. "Methodological Individualism: Definition and Reduction." *Philosophy of Science* 25: 1–22.

Bromberger, S. 1966. "Why Questions," in R. Colodny, ed. *Mind and Cosmos: Essays in Contemporary Science and Philosophy.* Pittsburgh: University of Pittsburgh Press.

Bronfenbrenner, M. 1966. "A 'Middlebrow' Introduction to Economic Methodology," in S. Krupp, ed. *The Structure of Economic Science.* New York: Prentice-Hall, pp. 5–24.

1971. "The Structure of Revolutions in Economic Thought." *History of Political Economy* 3: 136–51.

Brunner, K. 1969. "'Assumptions' and the Cognitive Quality of Theories." *Synthese* 20: 501–25.

Brzeziński, J., F. Coniglione, R. Kuipers, and L. Nowak, eds. 1990. *Idealization I: General Problems. Poznań Studies in the Philosophy of the Sciences and Humanities.* 16. Amsterdam: Rodopi.

Buchanan, J. 1975. *The Limits of Liberty: Between Anarchy and the Leviathan.* Chicago: University of Chicago Press.

1979. *What Should Economists Do?* Indianapolis: Liberty Press.

Buck, R. 1963. "Reflexive Predictions." *Philosophy of Science* 30: 359–69.

Burke, K. 1950. *A Rhetoric of Motives.* Berkeley: University of California Press.

1961. *The Rhetoric of Religion: Studies in Logology.* Berkeley: University of California Press.

Cairnes, J. 1875. *The Character and Logical Method of Political Economy.* 2nd. edn. Repr. New York: A. M. Kelley, 1965.

Caldwell, B. 1980a. "A Critique of Friedman's Methodological Instrumentalism." *Southern Economic Journal* 47: 366–74.

1982. *Beyond Positivism: Economic Methodology in the Twentieth Century.* London: Allen & Unwin.

1983. "The Neoclassical Maximization Hypothesis: Comment." *American Economic Review* 75: 824–7.

1990. "Does Methodology Matter? How Should It Be Practiced?" *Finnish Economic Papers* 3: 64–71.

1991. "Clarifying Popper." *Journal of Economic Literature* 29: 1–33.

Caldwell, B., ed. 1984. *Appraisal and Criticism in Economics*. London: Allen & Unwin.

Campbell, N. 1957. *Foundations of Science* (originally titled *Physics, The Elements*). New York: Dover.

Carnap, R. 1936, 1937. "Testability and Meaning." *Philosophy of Science* 3: 420–68 and 4: 1–40.

1950. *Logical Foundations of Probability*. Chicago: University of Chicago Press.

1956. "The Methodological Character of Theoretical Concepts," in H. Feigl and M. Scriven, eds. *Minnesoata Studies in the Philosophy of Science*, vol. 1. Minneapolis: University of Minnesota Press, pp. 33–76.

Carter, M. and R. Maddock. 1984. *Rational Expectations: Macroeconomics for the 1980's?* London: Macmillan.

Cartwright, N. 1983. *How the Laws of Physics Lie*. Oxford: Clarendon Press.

1989. *Nature's Capacities and their Measurement*. Oxford: Clarendon Press.

Cass, D., M. Okuno, and I. Zilcha. 1980. "The Role of Money in Supporting the Pareto Optimality of Competitive Equilibrium in Consumption Loan Type Models," in Kareken and Wallace (1980), pp. 13–48.

Cass, D. and K. Shell. 1980. "In Defense of a Basic Approach," in Kareken and Wallace (1980), pp. 251–60.

Cass, D. and M. Yaari. 1966. "A Re-examination of the Pure Consumption Loans Model." *Journal of Political Economy* 74: 353–67.

Chisholm. R. 1957. *Perceiving*. Ithaca: Cornell University Press.

Christensen, D. 1983. "Glymour on Evidential Relevance." *Philosophy of Science* 50: 471–81.

1990. "The Irrelevance of Bootstrapping." *Philosophy of Science* 57: 644–62.

Chu, Y. and R. Chu. 1990. "The Subsidence of Preference Reversals in Simplified and Marketlike Experimental Settings: A Note." *American Economic Review* 80: 902–11.

Churchland, P. and C. Hooker, eds. 1985. *Images of Science*. Chicago: University of Chicago Press.

Coase, R. 1960. "The Problem of Social Cost." *Journal of Law and Economics* 3: 1–30.

Coats, A. 1969. "Is There a 'Structure of Scientific Revolutions' in Economics?" *Kyklos* 22: 289–94.

Coddington, A. 1972. "Positive Economics." *Canadian Journal of Economics* 5: 1–15.

1975. "The Rationale of General Equilibrium Theory." *Economic Inquiry* 13: 539–58.

1979, "Friedman's Contribution to Methodological Controversy." *British Review of Economic Issues*, 2: 1–13.

Colander, D. and A. Klamer. 1987. "The Making of An Economist." *Journal of Economic Perspectives* 1: 95–112.

Coleman, James. 1986. *Individual Interest and Collective Action: Selected Essays*. Cambridge: Cambridge University Press.

Coleman, Jules. 1984. "Economics and the Law: A Critical Review of the Foundations of the Economic Approach to Law." *Ethics* 94: 649–79.

Collingwood, R. 1940. *An Essay on Metaphysics.* Oxford: Clarendon Press.

Cooter, R. and P. Rappoport. 1984. "Were the Ordinalists Wrong About Welfare Economics?" *Journal of Economic Literature* 22: 507–30.

Copernicus, Nicholas, 1543. *On the Revolutions of the Heavenly Spheres,* tr. A. Duncan. New York: Barnes & Noble, 1976.

Cox, J. and S. Epstein. 1989. "Preference Reversals Without the Independence Axiom." *American Economic Review* 79: 408–26.

Cross, R. 1982. "The Duhem-Quine Thesis, Lakatos and the Appraisal of Theories in Macroeconomics." *Economic Journal* 92: 320–40.

Cyert, R., and E. Grunberg. 1963. "Assumption, Prediction and Explanation in Economics," in Cyert and March (1963), pp. 298–311.

Cyert, R., and J. March, eds. 1963. *A Behavioral Theory of the Firm.* Englewood Cliffs, NJ: Prentice-Hall.

Cyert, R. and G. Pottinger. 1979. "Towards a Better Micro-economic Theory." *Philosophy of Science* 46: 204–22.

Dagum, C. 1986. "Economic Model, System and Structure, Philosophy of Science and Lakatos' Methodology of Scientific Research Programs." *Rivista Internazionale di Scienze Economiche e Commerciali* 33: 859–86.

Davidson, D. 1963. "Actions, Reasons and Causes." *Journal of Philosophy* 60: 685–700.

1980. *Essays on Actions and Events.* Oxford: Oxford University Press.

De Alessi, L. 1971. "Reversals of Assumptions and Implications." *Journal of Political Economy* 79: 867–77.

Debreu, G. 1959. *Theory of Value.* New York: Wiley.

1991. "The Mathematization of Economic Theory." *American Economic Review* 81: 1–7.

de Marchi, N. 1970. "The Empirical Content and Longevity of Ricardian Economics." *Economica* 37: 257–76.

1976. "Anomaly and the Development of Economics: The Case of the Leontief Paradox," in Latsis, ed. (1976), pp. 100–28.

1986. "Discussion: Mill's Unrevised Philosophy of Economics: A Comment on Hausman." *Philosophy of Science* 53: 89–100.

de Marchi, N., ed. 1988. *The Popperian Legacy in Economics.* Cambridge: Cambridge University Press.

Dewey, J. 1939a. "Experience, Knowledge and Value: A Rejoinder," in Schilpp (1939), pp. 515–608.

1939b. *Theory of Valuation.* Chicago: University of Chicago Press.

Diamond, P. 1965. "National Debt in a Neoclassical Growth Model." *American Economic Review* 55: 1126–50.

Diesing, P. 1982. *Science and Ideology in the Policy Sciences.* New York: Aldine.

Dillard, D. 1978. "Revolutions in Economic Theory." *Southern Economic Journal* 44: 705–24.

Dolan, E., ed. 1976. *The Foundations of Modern Austrian Economics.* Kansas City: Sheed & Ward.

Dorling, J. 1972. "Bayesianism and the Rationality of Scientific Inference." *British Journal for the Philosophy of Science* 23: 181–90.

1979. "Bayesian Personalism, The Methodology of Scientific Research Programmes, and Duhem's Problem." *Studies in the History and Philosophy of Science* 10: 177–87.

Dray, W. 1957. *Laws and Explanation in History.* Oxford: Oxford University Press.

Dreyer, J. 1953. *A History of Astronomy from Thales to Kepler* (formerly titled *History of the Planetary Systems from Thales to Kepler*). New York: Dover.

Dugger, W. 1979. "Methodological Differences between Institutional and Neoclassical Economics." *Journal of Economic Issues* 13: 899–909.

Duhem, P. 1906. *The Aim and Structure of Scientific Theories,* tr. P. Wiener. Princeton: Princeton University Press, 1954.

1908. *To Save the Phenomena,* tr. S. Jaki. Chicago: University of Chicago Press, 1969.

Durkheim, D. 1951. *Suicide: A Study in Sociology,* tr. J. Spaulding and G. Simpson. New York: Free Press.

Earman, John, ed. 1983. *Testing Scientific Theories.* Minneapolis: University of Minnesota Press.

Earman, J. and C. Glymour. 1988. "What Revisions Does Bootstrap Testing Need? A Reply." *Philosophy of Science* 55: 260–4.

Edgeworth, F. 1881. *Mathematical Psychics: An Essay on the Application of Mathematics to the Moral Sciences.* London: Routledge & Kegan Paul.

Edidin, A. 1981. "Glymour on Confirmation." *Philosophy of Science* 48: 292–307.

1983. "Bootstrapping without Bootstraps," in Earman (1983), pp. 43–54.

1988. "From Relative Confirmation to Real Confirmation." *Philosophy of Science* 55: 255–71.

Eells, E. 1982. *Rational Decision and Causality.* Cambridge: Cambridge University Press.

1985. "Problems of Old Evidence." *Pacific Philosophical Quarterly* 66: 283–302.

Eichner, A. 1983. "Why Economics is not yet a Science," in A. Eichner, ed. *Why Economics is not yet a Science.* Armonk, New York: M.E. Sharpe, pp. 205–41.

Ellsberg, D. 1954. "Classic and Current Notions of 'Measurable Utility.'" *Economic Journal* 64: 528–56. Repr. in A. Page, ed. *Utility Theory: A Book of Readings.* New York: Wiley, 1968, pp. 269–96.

Elster, J. 1983. *Sour Grapes: Studies in the Subversion of Rationality.* Cambridge: Cambridge University Press.

1989a. *The Cement of Society: A Study of Social Order.* Cambridge: Cambridge University Press.

1989b. *Solomonic Judgements: Studies in the Limitations of Rationality.* Cambridge: Cambridge University Press.

Elster, J. and J. Roemer, eds. 1991. *Interpersonal Comparisons of Well-Being.* Cambridge: Cambridge University Press.

Engle, R., D. Hendry, and J. Richard. 1983. "Exogeneity." *Econometrica* 51: 277–304.

Esteban, J. 1986. "A Characterization of the Core in Overlapping-Generations Economies: An Exact Consumption-Loan Model of Interest with or without the Social Contrivance of Money." *Journal of Economic Theory* 39: 439–56.

Etzioni, A. 1986. "The Case for a Multiple-Utility Conception." *Economics and Philosophy* 2: 159–84.

1988. *The Moral Dimension. Toward a New Economics.* New York: Macmillan.

Fair, R. 1978. "A Theory of Extramarital Affairs." *Journal of Political Economy* 86: 45–61.

Fama, E. 1980. "Agency Problems and the Theory of the Firm." *Journal of Political Economy* 88: 288–307.

Feigl, H. and G. Maxwell, eds. 1962. *Minnesota Studies in the Philosophy of Science*, vol. 3. Minneapolis: University of Minnesota Press.

Feyerabend, P. 1965. "On the Meaning of Scientific Terms." *Journal of Philosophy* 62: 266–74.

   1975. *Against Method: Outline of an Anarchistic Theory of Knowledge.* London: Verso Edition.

Fish, S. 1980. *Is There a Text in This Class? The Authority of Interpretive Communities.* Cambridge, MA: Harvard University Press.

   1988. "Comments from Outside Economics," in Klamer *et al.* (1988), pp. 21–30.

Fisher, R. 1986. *The Logic of Economic Discovery: Neoclassical Economics and the Marginal Revolution.* New York: New York University Press.

Frank, R. 1988. *Passions within Reason: The Strategic Role of the Emotions.* New York: W. W. Norton.

Franklin, A. 1986. *The Neglect of Experiment.* Cambridge: Cambridge University Press.

Fraser, L. 1937. *Economic Thought and Language. A Critique of Some Fundamental Concepts.* London: A & C Black.

Frazer, W. and L. Boland. 1983. "An Essay on the Foundations of Friedman's Methodology." *American Economic Review* 73: 129–44.

Friedman, Michael. 1974. "Explanation and Scientific Understanding." *Journal of Philosophy* 71: 5–19.

   1979. "Truth and Confirmation." *Journal of Philosophy* 76: 361–82.

   unpublished. "Philosophy and the Exact Sciences: Logical Positivism as a Case Study."

Friedman, Milton. 1953a. *Essays in Positive Economics.* Chicago: University of Chicago Press.

   1953b. "The Marshallian Demand Curve," in Friedman (1953a), pp. 47–99.

   1953c. "The Methodology of Positive Economics," in Friedman (1953a), pp. 3–43.

   1957. *A Theory of the Consumption Function.* Princeton: Princeton University Press.

   1962a. *Capitalism and Freedom.* Chicago: University of Chicago Press.

   1962b. *Price Theory: A Provisional Text*, Revised edition. Chicago: Aldine.

   1970. "Leon Walras and His Economic System," in I. Rima, ed. *Readings in the History of Economic Theory.* New York: Holt, Rinehart & Winston, pp. 145–53.

Friedman, M. and L. Savage. 1952. "The Expected-Utility Hypothesis and the Measurability of Utility." *Journal of Political Economy* 60: 463–74.

Fuchs, V. 1989. "Women's Quest for Economic Equality." *Journal of Economic Perspectives* 3: 25–42.

Fulton, G. 1984. "Research Programmes in Economics." *History of Political Economy* 16: 187–206.

Gale, D. 1973. "Pure Exchange Equilibrium of Dynamic Economic Models." *Journal of Economic Theory* 6: 12–36.

Galileo Galilei. 1632. *Dialogue Concerning the Two Chief World Systems.* Berkeley: University of California Press, 1967.

1638. *Discourses Concerning Two New Sciences.* New York, 1917.

Garber, D. 1983. "Old Evidence and Logical Omniscience in Bayesian Confirmation Theory," in Earman (1983), pp. 99–131.

Gauthier, D. 1986. *Morals by Agreement.* Oxford: Oxford University Press.

Geanakoplos, J. and H. Polemarchakis. 1986. "Walrasian Indeterminacy and Keynesian Macroeconomics." *Review of Economic Studies* 53: 755–79.

Gellner, E. 1973. *Cause and Meaning in the Social Sciences,* ed. I. Jarvie and J. Agassi. London: Routledge.

Geweke, J. 1982. "Causality, Exogeneity and Inference," in W. Hildenbrand, ed. *Advances in Econometrics.* Cambridge: Cambridge University Press.

1984. "Inference and Causality in Economic Time Series Models," in Z. Griliches and M. Intriligator, eds. *Handbook of Econometrics,* vol. 2. Amsterdam: North-Holland.

Gibbard, A. and H. Varian. 1978. "Economic Models." *Journal of Philosophy* 75: 664–77.

Giere, R. 1979, 1982. *Understanding Scientific Reasoning.* New York: Holt, Rinehart & Winston. 2nd. edn. 1982.

1980. "Causal Systems and Statistical Hypotheses," in L. Cohen and M. Hesse, eds. *Applications of Inductive Logic.* Oxford: Oxford University Press, pp. 251–70.

1983. "Testing Theoretical Hypotheses," in Earman (1983), pp. 269–98.

1988. *Explaining Science: A Cognitive Approach.* Chicago: University of Chicago Press.

Glymour, C. 1980. *Theory and Evidence.* Princeton: Princeton University Press.

1983. "On Testing and Evidence," in Earman (1983), pp. 3–26.

Glymour, C., K. Kelly, R. Scheines, and P. Spirtes. 1987. *Discovering Causal Structure.* New York: Academic Press.

Goldman, A. 1986. *Epistemology and Cognition.* Cambridge, MA: Harvard University Press.

Goodman, N. 1973. *Fact, Fiction and Forecast.* 3rd. edn. Indianapolis: Bobbs-Merrill.

Gorovitz, S. 1969. "Aspects of the Pragmatics of Explanation." *Nous* 3: 61–72.

Granger, C. 1969. "Investigating Causal Relations by Econometric Models and Cross-Spectral Methods." *Econometrica* 37: 424–38.

1980. "Testing for Causality: A Personal Viewpoint." *Journal of Economic Dynamics and Control* 2: 329–52.

1985. "Causality Testing in a Decision Science." Department of Economics, University of California, San Diego Discussion Paper #85-19.

Granovetter, M. 1981. "Toward a Sociological Theory of Income Differences," in I. Berg, ed. *Sociological Perspectives on Labor Markets.* New York: Academic Press, pp. 11–47.

1985. "Economics and Social Structure: The Problem of Embeddedness." *American Journal of Sociology* 91: 481–510.

Green, E. 1981. "On the Role of Fundamental Theory in Positive Economics," in Pitt (1981), pp. 5–15.

Grether, D. and C. Plott. 1979. "Economic Theory of Choice and the Preference Reversal Phenomenon." *American Economic Review* 69: 623–38.

1982. "Economic Theory of Choice and the Preference Reversal Phenomenon: Reply." *American Economic Review* 72: 575.

Griffin, J. 1986. *Well-Being: Its Meaning, Measurement and Moral Importance.* Oxford: Clarendon Press.

Grimes, T. 1987. "The Promiscuity of Bootstrapping." *Philosophical Studies* 51: 101-7.

Gruchy, A. 1947. *Modern Economic Thought: The American Contribution.* Repr. New York: A. M. Kelley, 1967.

Grünbaum, A. 1976. "Is Falsifiability the Touchstone of Scientific Rationality? Karl Popper Versus Inductivism," in R. Cohen *et al.*, eds. *Essays in Memory of Imre Lakatos.* Dordrecht: Reidel, pp. 213-52.

Hacking, I. 1979. "Imre Lakatos's Philosophy of Science." *British Journal for the Philosophy of Science* 30: 181-202.

1983. *Representing and Intervening.* Cambridge: Cambridge University Press.

Hagen, O. 1979. "Towards a Positive Theory of Preferences Under Risk," in Allais and Hagen (1979), pp. 271-302.

Hahn, F. 1973. "The Winter of Our Discontent." *Economica* 40: 322-30.

1980. "Discussion," in Kareken and Wallace (1980), pp. 161-5.

1982. *Money and Inflation.* Oxford: Basil Blackwell.

1986. "Arjo Klamer's *Conversations with Economists: New Classical Economists and Opponents Speak out on the Current Controversy in Microeconomics.*" *Economics and Philosophy* 2: 275-81.

Hahn, F. and M. Hollis., eds. 1979. *Philosophy and Economic Theory.* Oxford: Oxford University Press.

Hall, R. and C. Hitch. 1939. "Price Theory and Business Behaviour." *Oxford Economic Papers* 2: 12-45.

Hamminga, B. forthcoming. "Comment to Wade Hands on the Meaning and Measurement of Excess Content," in Blaug and de Marchi (1991).

Händler, E. 1980. "The Logical Structure of Modern Neoclassical Static Microeconomic Equilibrium Theory." *Erkenntnis* 15: 33-53.

Hands, D. 1979. "The Methodology of Economic Research Programs." *Philosophy of the Social Sciences* 9: 292-303.

1985a. "Karl Popper and Economic Methodology." *Economics and Philosophy* 1: 83-100.

1985b. "Second Thoughts on Lakatos." *History of Political Economy* 17: 1-16.

1985c. "The Structuralist View of Economic Theories: The Case of General Equilibrium in Particular." *Economics and Philosophy* 1: 303-36.

1988. "Ad Hocness in Economics and the Popperian Tradition," in de Marchi (1988), pp. 121-39.

1990. "Second Thoughts on 'Second Thoughts': Reconsidering the Lakatosian Progress of *The General Theory.*" *Review of Political Economy* 2: 69-81.

forthcoming a. "The Problem of Excess Content: Economics, Novelty and a Long Popperian Tale," in Blaug and de Marchi (1991).

forthcoming b. "Essentialism and Novelty: Reply to Mäki and Hamminga," in Blaug and de Marchi (1991).

Hanfling, O. 1981a. *Logical Positivism.* Oxford: Basil Blackwell.

1981b. *Essential Readings in Logical Positivism.* Oxford: Basil Blackwell.

Hanson, N. 1961. "Is there A Logic of Discovery?" in H. Feigl and G. Maxwell, eds. *Current Issues in the Philosophy of Science.* New York: Holt, Rinehart & Winston, pp. 20–35.

Harburger, A. 1978. "On the Use of Distributional Weights in Social Cost-Benefit Analysis." *Journal of Political Economy* 86: s87–s120.

Hardin, R. 1988. *Morality within the Limits of Reason.* Chicago: University of Chicago Press.

Harman, G. 1973. *Thought.* Princeton: Princeton University Press.

Harsanyi, J. 1955. "Cardinal Welfare, Individualistic Ethics and Interpersonal Comparisons of Utility." *Journal of Political Economy* 63: 309–21.

  1977a. "Morality and the Theory of Rational Behavior." *Social Research* 44. Repr. Sen and Williams (1982), pp. 39–62.

  1977b. *Rational Behavior and Bargaining Equilibrium in Games and Social Situations.* Cambridge: Cambridge University Press.

Hart, H. and T. Honoré. 1985. *Causation in the Law.* 2nd. edn. Oxford: Clarendon Press.

Hausman, D. 1980. "How to Do Philosophy of Economics," in P. Asquith and R. Giere, eds. *PSA 1980.* East Lansing: Philosophy of Science Association, pp. 352–62.

  1981a. *Capital, Profits, and Prices: An Essay in the Philosophy of Economics.* New York: Columbia University Press.

  1981b. "John Stuart Mill's Philosophy of Economics." *Philosophy of Science* 48: 363–85.

  1983. "The Limits of Economic Science," in N. Rescher, ed. *The Limits of Lawfulness.* Pittsburgh: Center for Philosophy of Science, University of Pittsburgh, pp. 93–100.

  1984. "Causal Priority." *Nous* 18: 261–79.

  1986. "Causation and Experimentation." *American Philosophical Quarterly* 23: 143–54.

  1988a. "An Appraisal of Popperian Methodology," in de Marchi (1988), pp. 65–86.

  1988b. "Economic Methodology and Philosophy of Science," in Winston and Teichgraeber (1988), pp. 88–116.

  1989a. "Arbitrage Arguments." *Erkenntnis* 30: 5–22.

  1989b. "Economic Methodology in a Nutshell." *Journal of Economic Perspectives* 3: 115–28.

  1989c. "*Ceteris Paribus* Clauses and Causality in Economics," in A. Fine, ed. *PSA 1988,* vol. 2. East Lansing: Philosophy of Science Association, pp. 308–16.

  1990a. "The Deductive Method." *Midwest Studies in Philosophy* 15: 372–88.

  1990b. "Supply and Demand Explanations and their *Ceteris Paribus* Clauses." *Review of Political Economy* 2: 168–86.

Hausman, D., ed. 1984. *The Philosophy of Economics: An Anthology.* Cambridge: Cambridge University Press.

Hayek, F. 1937. "Economics and Knowledge." *Economica* 4: 33–54.

  1952. *The Counter-Revolution of Science: Studies in the Abuse of Reason.* New York: Free Press.

Helm, D. 1984. "Predictions and Causes: A Comparison of Friedman and Hicks on Method." *Oxford Economic Papers* 36 (Supplement): 118–34.

Hempel, C. 1965. *Aspects of Scientific Explanation and Other Essays in the Philosophy of Science*. New York: Free Press.

1966. *Philosophy of Natural Science*. Englewood Cliffs, NJ: Prentice-Hall.

Henderson, J. and R. Quandt. 1971. *Microeconomic Theory: A Mathematical Approach*. 2nd. edn. New York: McGraw-Hill.

Herstein, I. and J. Milnor. 1953. "An Axiomatic Approach to Measurable Utility." *Econometrica* 21: 291–7.

Hesse, M. 1974. *The Structure of Scientific Inference*. Cambridge: Cambridge University Press.

Hicks, J. 1939. "The Foundations of Welfare Economics." *Economic Journal* 49: 696–712.

1946. *Value and Capital*. 2nd. edn. Oxford: Oxford University Press.

Hicks, J. and R. Allen. 1934. "A Reconsideration of the Theory of Value." *Economica*. N.S. 1: 52–76 and 196–219.

Hirsch, A. forthcoming "John Stuart Mill on Verification and the Business of Science."

Hirsch, A. and N. de Marchi. 1986. "Making a Case When Theory is Unfalsifiable: Friedman's Monetary History." *Economics and Philosophy* 2: 1–22.

1990. *Milton Friedman: Economics in Theory and Practice*. Ann Arbor: University of Michigan Press.

Hirsch, F. 1976. *The Social Limits to Growth*. Cambridge, MA: Harvard University Press.

Hirschman, A. 1985. "Against Parsimony: Three Easy Ways of Complicating Some Categories of Economic Discourse." *Economics and Philosophy* 1: 7–22.

Hodgson, G. 1986. "Behind Methodological Individualism." *Cambridge Journal of Economics* 10: 211–24.

Holland, J., K. Holyoak, R. Nisbett, and P. Thagard. 1986. *Induction: Processes of Inference, Learning, and Discovery*. Cambridge, MA: MIT Press.

Hollander, S. 1985. *The Economics of John Stuart Mill*. vol. 1 *Theory and Method*. Toronto: University of Toronto Press.

Hollis, M. and E. Nell. 1975. *Rational Economic Man: A Philosophical Critique of Neo-Classical Economics*. London: Cambridge University Press.

Holt, C. 1986. "Preference Reversals and the Independence Axioms." *American Economic Review* 76: 508–15.

Homans, G. 1953. "The Cash Posters." *American Sociological Review* 19: 724–33.

Hoover, K. 1988. *The New Classical Macroeconomics: A Sceptical Inquiry*. Oxford: Basil Blackwell.

1990. "The Logic of Causal Inference: Econometrics and the Conditional Analysis of Causation." *Economics and Philosophy* 6: 207–34.

Horwich, P. 1978. "An Appraisal of Glymour's Confirmation Theory." *Journal of Philosophy* 75: 98–113.

1982. *Probability and Evidence*. Cambridge: Cambridge University Press.

1987. *Asymmetries in Time: Problems in the Philosophy of Science*. Cambridge, MA: MIT Press.

Houtthaker, H. 1950. "Revealed Preference and the Utility Function." *Economica* 17: 159–74.

Howson, C. and P. Urbach. 1989. *Scientific Reasoning: The Bayesian Approach*. LaSalle, IL: Open Court.

Hoyningen-Huene, P. 1987. "Context of Discovery and Context of Justification." *Studies in the History and Philosophy of Science* 18: 501-16.

Hull, D. 1988. *Science as a Process*: *An Evolutionary Account of the Social and Conceptual Development of Science.* Chicago: University of Chicago Press.

Hume, D. 1738. *A Treatise of Human Nature.* Repr. Oxford: Clarendon Press, 1966.

1748. *An Inquiry Concerning Human Understanding.* Repr. Bobbs-Merrill, Indianapolis, 1955.

Hutchison, T. 1938. *The Significance and Basic Postulates of Economic Theory.* Repr. with a new Preface. New York: A.M. Kelley, 1960.

1941. "The Significance and Basic Postulates of Economic Theory: A Reply to Professor Knight." *Journal of Political Economy* 49: 732-50.

1956. "Professor Machlup on Verification in Economics." *Southern Economic Journal* 22: 476-83.

1960. "Methodological Prescriptions in Economics: A Reply." *Economica* 27: 158-60.

1977. *Knowledge and Ignorance in Economics.* Chicago: University of Chicago Press.

1978. *On Revolutions and Progress in Economic Knowledge.* Cambridge: Cambridge University Press.

1981. *The Politics and Philosophy of Economics*: *Marxians, Keynesians and Austrians.* Oxford: Basil Blackwell.

1988. "The Case for Falsification," in de Marchi (1988), pp. 169-82.

Jalladeau, J. 1978. "Research Program versus Paradigm in the Development of Economics." *Journal of Economic Issues* 12: 583-608.

Jeffrey, R. 1983a. "Bayesianism with a Human Face," in Earman (1983), pp. 133-56.

1983b. *The Logic of Decision.* 2nd. edn. Chicago. University of Chicago Press.

Jensen, M. and W. Meckling. 1976. "Theory of the Firm: Managerial Behavior, Agency Costs and Ownership Structure." *Journal of Financial Economics* 3: 305-60.

Jensen, N. 1967. "An Introduction to Bernoullian Utility Theory: I. Utility Functions." *Swedish Journal of Economics* 69: 163-83.

Johnson, G. and L. Zerby. 1973. *What Economists Do About Values*: *Case Studies of their Answers to Questions They Don't Dare Ask.* East Lansing: Michigan State University.

Jones, E. 1977. "Positive Economics or What?" *Economic Record* 53: 350-63.

Kagel, J. and R. Battalio 1975. "Experimental Studies of Consumer Behavior Using Laboratory Animals." *Economic Inquiry* 13: 22-38.

Kahneman, D., J. Knetsch, and R. Thaler. 1986. "Fairness as a Constraint on Profit Seeking." *American Economic Review* 76: 728-41.

1990. "Experimental Tests of the Endowment Effect and the Coase Theorem." *Journal of Political Economy* 98: 1325-48.

Kahneman, D. and A. Tversky. 1979. "Prospect Theory: An Analysis of Decision Making under Risk." *Econometrica* 47: 263-91.

Kaldor, N. 1939. "Welfare Propositions of Economics and Interpersonal Comparisons of Utility." *Economic Journal* 49: 549-52.

Kant, I. 1787. *Critique of Pure Reason*, tr. N. Kemp Smith. New York: St. Martin's Press, 1965.

Kaplan, M. 1989. "Bayesianism without the Black Box." *Philosophy of Science* 56: 48-69.

Kareken, J. and N. Wallace, eds. 1980. *Models of Monetary Economies*. Minneapolis: Federal Reserve Bank of Minneapolis: 1980.

Karelis, C. 1986. "Distributive Justice and the Public Good." *Economics and Philosophy* 2: 101-26.

Karni, E. and Z. Safra. 1987. "'Preference Reversal' and the Observability of Preferences by Experimental Methods." *Econometrica* 55: 675-85.

Katz, J. 1988. "The Refutation of Indeterminacy." *Journal of Philosophy* 85: 227-52.

Kaufmann, F. 1933. "On the Subject-Matter and Method of Economic Science." *Economica* 13: 381-401.

1934. "The Concept of Law in Economic Science." *Review of Economic Studies* 1: 102-9.

1942. "On the Postulates of Economic Theory." *Social Research* 9: 379-95.

1944. *Methodology of the Social Sciences*. London: Oxford University Press.

Kelly, K. 1987. "The Logic of Discovery." *Philosophy of Science* 54: 435-52.

Kelly, K. and C. Glymour. 1989. "Convergence to the Truth and Nothing but the Truth." *Philosophy of Science* 56: 185-220.

Keynes, J. N. 1917. *The Scope and Method of Political Economy* (4th edn.) (1st edn. 1891). Repr. New York: A. M. Kelley, 1955.

Kincaid, H. 1986. "Reduction, Explanation, and Individualism." *Philosophy of Science* 53: 492-513.

1989. "Confirmation, Complexity and Social Laws," in A. Fine, ed. *PSA 1988*, vol. 2. East Lansing: Philosophy of Science Association, pp. 299-307.

Kitcher, P. 1982. *Abusing Science: The Case Against Creationism*. Cambridge, MA: MIT Press.

Kitcher, P. and W. Salmon, eds. 1989. *Scientific Explanation*. Minneapolis: University of Minnesota Press.

Klamer, A. 1984. *Conversations with Economists: New Classical Economists and Opponents Speak Out on the Current Controversy in Macroeconomics*. Totowa, NJ: Rowman and Allanheld.

Klamer, A. and D. Colander. 1990. *The Making of An Economist*. Boulder, CO: Westview Press.

Klamer, A., D. McCloskey, and R. Solow, eds. 1988. *The Consequences of Economic Rhetoric*. New York: Cambridge University Press.

Klant, J. 1984. *The Rules of the Game*. Cambridge: Cambridge University Press.

Klappholz, K. 1964. "Value Judgments and Economics." *British Journal for the Philosophy of Science* 15: 97-114.

Klappholz, K. and J. Agassi. 1959. "Methodological Prescriptions in Economics." *Economica* 26: 60-74.

1960. "Methodological Prescriptions in Economics: A Rejoinder." *Economica* 27: 160-1.

Knies, K. 1853. *Die Politische Oekonomie Vom Standpunkte der Geschichtlichen Methode*. 2nd edn. Braunschweig: C.A. Schwetschke, 1883.

Knight, F. 1921. "Traditional Economic Theory – Discussion." *American Economic Review Papers and Proceedings* 22: 143-6.

1935a. "Economics and Human Action," from Knight 1935b. Repr. in Hausman, ed. (1984), pp. 141-8.

1935b. *The Ethics of Competition and Other Essays.* New York and London: Harper and Brothers.

1940. "What is 'Truth' in Economics?" *Journal of Political Economy* 48: 1–32.

1941. "The Significance and Basic Postulates of Economic Theory: A Rejoinder." *Journal of Political Economy* 49: 750–3.

1961. "Methodology in Economics." *Southern Economic Journal* 27: 185–93, 273–82.

Koopmans, T. 1949. "Identification Problems in Economic Model Construction." *Econometrica* 17: 125–44.

1957. *Three Essays on the State of Economic Science.* New York: McGraw-Hill.

1979. "Economics Among the Sciences." *American Economic Review* 69: 1–13.

Krajewski, W. 1977. *Correspondence Principle and the Growth of Knowledge.* Dordrecht: Reidel.

Kreps, D., P. Milgrom, J. Roberts, and R. Wilson. 1982. "Rational Cooperation in the Finitely Repeated Prisoners' Dilemma." *Journal of Economic Theory* 27: 245–52.

Krupp, S., ed. 1966. *The Structure of Economic Science.* Englewood Cliffs: Prentice-Hall.

Kuenne, R. 1971. *Eugen von Böhm Bawerk.* New York: Columbia University Press.

Kuhn, T. 1957. *The Copernican Revolution.* Cambridge, MA: Harvard University Press.

1970. *The Structure of Scientific Revolutions.* 2nd edn. Chicago: University of Chicago Press.

1974. "Second Thoughts on Paradigms," in Suppe (1977), pp. 459–82.

Kuipers, T., ed. 1987. *What is Closer-to-the Truth? A Parade of Approaches to Truthlikeness. Poznań Studies in the Philosophy of the Sciences and Humanities.* 10. Amsterdam: Rodopi.

Kunin, L. and F. Weaver. 1971. "On the Structure of Scientific Revolutions in Economics." *History of Political Economy* 3: 391–7.

Kyburg, H. 1970. *Probability and Inductive Logic.* London: Macmillan.

1974. *The Logical Foundations of Statistical Inference.* Dordrecht: Reidel.

Lakatos, I. 1968. "Changes in the Problem of Inductive Logic." Repr. in Lakatos, vol. 2 (1978b), pp. 128–200.

1970. "Falsification and the Methodology of Scientific Research Programmes," in Lakatos and Musgrave (1970), pp. 91–196 and in Lakatos, vol. 1 (1978b), pp. 8–101.

1971. "History of Science and its Rational Reconstructions." Repr. in Lakatos, vol. 1 (1978b), pp. 102–38.

1974. "Popper on Demarcation and Induction," in P. Schlipp, ed. *The Philosophy of Karl Popper.* LaSalle, IL, Open Court, pp. 241–73. Repr. in Lakatos, vol. 1 (1978b), pp. 139–67.

1976. *Proofs and Refutations: The Logic of Mathematical Discovery,* eds. J. Worrall and E. Zahar. Cambridge: Cambridge University Press.

1978a. "Anomalies versus "Crucial Experiments" (a Rejoinder to Professor Grünbaum)," in Lakatos, vol. 2 (1978b), pp. 211–23.

1978b. *Philosophical Papers.* 2 vols. Cambridge: Cambridge University Press.

Lakatos, I. and A. Musgrave, eds. 1970. *Criticism and the Growth of Knowledge.* Cambridge: Cambridge University Press.

Lakatos, I. and E. Zahar. 1976. "Why Did Copernicus's Research Programme Supersede Ptolemy's?" Repr in Lakatos, vol. 1 (1978b), pp. 168–92.

Langley, P. H. Simon, G. Bradshaw and J. Zytkow. 1987. *Scientific Discovery: Computational Explorations of the Creative Process.* Cambridge, MA: MIT Press.

Latis, S. 1976. "A Research Programme in Economics," in Latsis, ed. (1976), pp. 1–42.

Latsis, S., ed. 1976. *Method and Appraisal in Economics.* Cambridge: Cambridge University Press.

Laudan, L. 1977. *Progress and its Problems.* Berkeley: University of California Press.

1981. "A Confutation of Convergent Realism." *Philosophy of Science* 48: 19–49.

1983. "The Demise of the Demarcation Problem." *Working Papers in Science and Technology* 2: 7–36. Virginia Tech. Center for the Study of Science in Society.

Leamer, E. 1984. "Vector Autoregressions for Causal Inference?" delivered at 1984 Carnegie-Rochester Conference.

Leibenstein, H. 1976. *Beyond Economic Man: A New Foundation for Economics.* Cambridge, MA: Harvard University Press.

Leijonhufvud, A. 1968. *On Keynesian Economics and the Economics of Keynes.* Oxford: Oxford University Press.

1976. "Schools, 'Revolutions' and Research Programmes in Economic Theory,." in Latsis, ed. (1976), pp. 65–100.

Leontief, W. 1971. "Theoretical Assumptions and Nonobserved Facts." *American Economic Review* 61: 1–7.

Lerner, A. 1959a. "Consumption-Loan Interest and Money." *Journal of Political Economy* 67: 512–18.

1959b. "Rejoinder." *Journal of Political Economy* 67: 523–5.

Lester, R.A. 1946. "Shortcomings of Marginal Analysis for Wage-Employment Problems." *American Economic Review* 36: 62–82.

1947. "Marginal, Minimum Wages, and Labor Markets." *American Economic Review* 37: 135–48.

Levi, I. 1967. *Gambling with Truth.* Cambridge, MA: MIT Press.

1980. *The Enterprise of Knowledge.* Cambridge, MA: MIT Press.

1986. "The Paradoxes of Allais and Ellsberg." *Economics and Philosophy* 2: 23–53.

1989. "Reply to Maher." *Economics and Philosophy* 5: 79–90.

1991. "Reply to Maher and Kashima." *Economics and Philosophy* 7.

Levi, I. and S. Morgenbesser. 1964. "Beliefs and Dispositions." *American Philosophical Quarterly* 1: 221–32.

Levine, A., E. Sober, and E. Wright. 1987. "Marxism and Methodological Individualism." *New Left Review* 162 (March/April): 67–84.

Levison, A. 1974. "Popper, Hume, and the Traditional Problem of Induction," in Schilpp (1974), pp. 322–31.

Levy, D. 1985. "The Impossibility of a Complete Methodological Individualist Reduction When Knowledge is Imperfect." *Economics and Philosophy* 1: 101–9.

Lewis, D. 1973a. "Causation." *Journal of Philosophy* 70: 556–67.

1973b. *Counterfactuals.* Cambridge: MA, Harvard University Press.

1979. "Counterfactual Dependence and Time's Arrow." *Nous* 13: 455–76.

1986. "Postscripts to 'Counterfactual Dependence and Time's Arrow,'" in *Philosophical Papers*, vol. 2. Oxford: Oxford University Press, pp. 52–66.

Lichtenstein, S. and P. Slovic. 1971. "Reversals of Preference Between Bids and Choices in Gambling Decisions." *Journal of Experimental Psychology* 89: 46–55.

1973. "Response-Induced Reversals of Preference in Gambling: An Extended Replication in Las Vegas." *Journal of Experimental Psychology* 101: 16–20.

Lieberson, J. 1982a. "Karl Popper." *Social Research* 49: 68–115.

1982b. "The Romantic Rationalist." *New York Review of Books* 29 (December 2).

Lindman, H. 1971. "Inconsistent Preferences Among Gambles." *Journal of Experimental Psychology* 89: 390–7.

Lipsey, R. 1966. *An Introduction to Positive Economics.* 2nd. edn. London: Weidenfeld and Nicholson.

Lipsey, R. and K. Lancaster. 1956–7. "The General Theory of the Second Best." *Review of Economic Studies* 24: 11–31.

Little, I. 1957. *A Critique of Welfare Economics.* 2nd. edn. Oxford: Oxford University Press.

Loomes, G. and R. Sugden. 1982. "Regret Theory: an Alternative Theory of Rational Choice under Uncertainty." *Economic Journal* 92: 805–24.

1983. "A Rationale for Preference Reversal." *American Economic Review* 73: 428–32.

Loomes, G., C. Starmer, and R. Sugden. 1989. "Preference Reversal: Information-Processing Effect or Rational Nontransitive Choice." *Economic Journal* (Conference Supplement) 99: 140–51.

Lucas, R. 1976. "Econometric Policy Evaluation: A Critique." *Journal of Monetary Economics*, Supplemental Series 1: 19–46, 62.

Luce, R. and H. Raiffa. 1957. *Games and Decisions.* New York: Wiley.

Lukes, S. 1973. "Methodological Individualism Reconsidered," in Ryan (1973), pp. 119–30.

McCallum, B. 1983. "The Role of Overlapping Generations Models in Monetary Economics," in K. Brunner and A. Meltzer, eds. *Theory, Policy and Institutions: Papers from the Carnegie-Rochester Conference Series on Public Policy.* Amsterdam: North-Holland, pp. 129–64.

McClennen, E. 1983. "Sure Thing Doubts," in B. Stigum and F. Wenstop, eds. *Foundations of Utility and Risk Theory with Applications.* Dordrecht: Reidel.

1990. *Rationality and Dynamic Choice: Foundational Explorations.* Cambridge: Cambridge University Press.

McCloskey, D. 1983. "The Rhetoric of Economics." *Journal of Economic Literature* 21: 481–517.

1985a. *The Rhetoric of Economics.* Madison: University of Wisconsin Press.

1985b. "Sartorial Epistemology in Tatters: A Reply to Martin Hollis." *Economics and Philosophy* 1: 134–8.

1987. *The Writing of Economics.* New York: Macmillan.

1988a. "Thick and Thin Methodologies in the History of Economic Thought," in de Marchi (1988), pp. 245–58.

1988b. "Towards a Rhetoric of Economics," in Winston and Teichgraeber (1988), pp. 13–29.

1988c. "Two Replies and a Dialogue on the Rhetoric of Economics: Mäki, Rappaport, Rosenberg." *Economics and Philosophy* 4: 150–66.

1989. "The Very Idea of Epistemology: A Comment on *Standards.*" *Economics and Philosophy* 5: 1–6.

1990. *If You're So Smart: The Narrative of Economic Expertise.* Chicago: University of Chicago Press.

MacCrimmon, K. and S. Larsson. 1979. "Utility Theory: Axioms versus 'Paradoxes,'" in Allais and Hagen (1979), pp. 333–409.

Macdonald, G. 1986. "Modified Methodological Individualism." *Proceedings of the Aristotelian Society* 86: 199–211.

Mach, E. 1942. *The Science of Mechanics.* La Salle, IL: Open Court.

Machina, M. 1987. "Choice under Uncertainty: Problems Solved and Unsolved." *Journal of Economic Perspectives* 1: 121–54.

Machlup, F. 1946. "Marginal Analysis and Empirical Research." *American Economic Review* 36: 519–54.

1947. "Rejoinder to an Antimarginalist." *American Economic Review* 37: 148–54.

1955. "The Problem of Verification in Economics." *Southern Economic Journal* 22: 1–21.

1956. "Rejoinder to a Reluctant Ultra-Empiricist." *Southern Economic Journal* 22: 483–93.

1960. "Operational Concepts and Mental Constructs in Model and Theory Formation." *Giornale Degli Economisti* 19: 553–82.

1963. *Essays on Economic Semantics,* ed. M. Miller. Englewood Cliffs: Prentice-Hall.

1964. "Professor Samuelson on Theory and Realism." *American Economic Review* 54: 733–6.

1969. "If Matter Could Talk." Repr. in Machlup 1978, pp. 309–32.

1978. *Methodology of Economics and Other Social Sciences.* New York: Academic Press.

MacIntyre, A. 1967. "The Idea of a Social Science." *Proceedings of the Aristotelian Society Supplementary Volume* 41: 95–114.

MacKay, A. 1980. *Arrow's Theorem: The Paradox of Social Choice. A Case Study in the Philosophy of Economics.* New Haven: Yale University Press.

1986. "Extended Sympathy and Interpersonal Utility Comparisons." *Journal of Philosophy* 83: 305–22.

McKenzie, R. 1979. "The Non-Rational Domain and the Limits of Economic Analysis." *Southern Economic Journal* 26: 145–57.

Mackie, J. 1974. *The Cement of the Universe.* Oxford: Oxford University Press.

Maher, P. 1989. "Levi on the Allais and Ellsberg Paradoxes." *Economics and Philosophy* 5: 69–78.

Maher, P. and Y. Kashima. 1991. "On the Descriptive Adequacy of Levi's Decision Theory." *Economics and Philosophy* 7.

Mäki, U. 1986. "Rhetoric and the Expense of Coherence: A Reinterpretation of Milton Friedman's Methodology." *Research in the History of Economic Thought and Methodology* 4: 127–43.

1988a. "How to Combine Rhetoric and Realism in the Methodology of Economics." *Economics and Philosophy* 4: 89–109.

1988b. "Realism, Economics, and Rhetoric: A Rejoinder to McCloskey." *Economics and Philosophy* 4: 167–9.

1990a. "Mengerian Economics in Realist Perspective." *History of Political Economy* 22: 289–310.

1990b. "Methodology of Economics: Complaints and Guidelines." *Finnish Economic Papers* 3: 77–84.

1990c. "Scientific Realism and Austrian Explanation." *Review of Political Economy* 2: 310–44.

forthcoming a. "Friedman and Realism." *Research in the History of Economic Thought and Methodology* 10:

forthcoming b. "On the Method of Isolation in Economics," in C. Dilworth, ed. *Intelligibility in Science* in *Poznan Studies in the Philosophy of the Sciences and the Humanities.* Amsterdam: Rodopi.

Malinvaud, E. 1972. *Lectures on Microeconomic Theory,* tr. A. Silvey. Amsterdam: North-Holland.

1987. "The Overlapping Generations Model in 1947." *Journal of Economic Literature* 25: 103–5.

Marschak, J. 1969. "On Econometric Tools." *Synthese* 20: 483–8.

Marshall, A. 1930. *Principles of Economics.* 8th edn. London: Macmillan.

Marx, K. 1867. *Capital,* vol. 1, tr. S. Moore and E. Aveling. New York: International Publishers, 1967.

Marwell, G. and R. Ames. 1981. "Economists Free Ride. Does Anyone Else? Experiments on the Provision of Public Goods. IV." *Journal of Public Economics* 15: 295–310.

Mas-Collell, A. 1974. "An Equilibrium Existence Theorem without Complete or Transitive Preferences." *Journal of Mathematical Economics* 1: 237–46.

Mason, W. 1980–1. "Some Negative Thoughts on Friedman's Positive Economics." *Journal of Post-Keynesian Economics* 3: 235–55.

Masterman, M. 1970. "The Nature of a Paradigm," in Lakatos and Musgrave (1970), pp. 59–90.

Mauss, M. 1954. *The Gift: Forms and Functions of Exchange in Archaic Societies,* tr. I. Cunnison. London: Cohen and West.

Maxwell, G. 1962. "The Ontological Status of Theoretical Entities," in H. Feigl and G. Maxwell, eds. (1962), pp. 3–27.

Maxwell, G. and R. Anderson, Jr., eds. 1975. *Induction, Probability and Confirmation,* Minnesota Studies in the Philosophy of Science, vol. 6. Minneapolis: University of Minnesota Press.

Meckling, W. 1960a. "An Exact Consumption-Loan Model of Interest: A Comment." *Journal of Political Economy* 68: 72–6.

1960b. "Rejoinder." *Journal of Political Economy* 68: 83–4.

Melitz, J. 1965. "Friedman and Machlup on the Significance of Testing Economic Assumptions." *Journal of Political Economy* 73: 37–60.

Menger, C. 1883. *Problems of Economics and Sociology,* ed. L. Schneider, tr. F. Nock. Urbana: University of Illinois Press, 1963.

Mill, James. 1820. *An Essay on Government,* ed. Currin V. Shields. Indianapolis: Bobbs-Merrill, 1955.

Mill, J. S. 1836. "On the Definition of Political Economy and the Method of Investigation Proper to It." Repr. in *Collected Works of John Stuart Mill,* vol. 4. Toronto: University of Toronto Press, 1967.

1843. *A System of Logic.* London: Longman, Green & Co., 1949.

1871. *Principles of Political Economy.* 7th edn., ed. W. Ashley (1909). Repr. New York: A. M. Kelley, 1976.

Miller, D. 1974. "Popper's Qualitative Theory of Verisimilitude." *British Journal for the Philosophy of Science* 25: 166–77.

1982. "Conjectural Knowledge: Popper's Solution to the Problem of Induction," in P. Levinson, ed. *In Pursuit of Truth: Essays in Honor of Karl Popper's 80th Birthday.* Hassocks: Harvester, pp. 17–49.

Miller, H. and W. Williams, eds. 1982. *The Limits of Utilitarianism.* Minneapolis: University of Minnesota Press.

Miller, R. 1978. "Methodological Individualism and Social Explanation." *Philosophy of Science* 45: 387–414.

1987. *Fact and Method: Explanation, Confirmation and Reality in the Natural and the Social Sciences.* Princeton: Princeton University Press.

Minford, P. and D. Peel. 1983. *Rational Expectations and the New Macroeconomics.* Oxford: Martin Robertson & Co.

Mirowski, P. 1989. "How Not to Do Things with Metaphors: Paul Samuelson and the Science of Neoclassical Economics." *Studies in the History and Philosophy of Science* 20: 175–91.

1990. *More Heat Than Light.* Cambridge: Cambridge University Press.

Mises, L. von. 1949. *Human Action. A Treatise on Economics.* New Haven: Yale University Press.

1978. *The Ultimate Foundation of Economic Science: An Essay on Method.* 2nd. edn. Kansas City: Sheed Andrews.

1981. *Epistemological Problems of Economics,* tr. G. Reisman. New York: New York University Press.

Mishan, E. 1971. *Cost Benefit Analysis: An Introduction.* New York: Praeger.

1981. *An Introduction to Normative Economics.* Oxford: Oxford University Press.

Modigliani, F. and R. Brumberg. 1955. "Utility Analysis and the Consumption Function," in K. Kurihara, ed. *Post-Keynesian Economics.* London: Allen & Unwin, pp. 383–436.

Mongin, P. 1986a. "Are 'All-and-Some' Statements Falsifiable After All? The Example of Utility Theory." *Economics and Philosophy* 2: 185–96.

1986b. "La Controverse sur l'Entreprise (1940–1950) et la Formation de l'Irréalisme Méthodologique." *Economies et Sociétés,* série Oeconomia 5: 91–151.

1990-1. "The Early Full-Cost Debate and the Problem of Empirically Testing Profit-Maximization." *Journal of Post-Keynesian Economics* 13: 236–81.

Morgenbesser, S. 1956. "Theories and Schemata in the Social Sciences." Dissertation, University of Pennsylvania.

1969. "The Realist-Instrumentalist Controversy," in S. Morgenbesser, P. Suppes, and M. White, eds. *Philosophy, Science, and Method Structure of Science.* New York: Harcourt, Brace & World, pp. 106–52.

1970. "Is It a Science?" in D. Emmett and A. MacIntyre, eds. *Sociological Theory and Philosophical Analysis.* New York: Macmillan, pp. 20–35.

Morris, H. undated. "Evolution, Creation and the Public Schools." *Impact* Series, #1. San Diego: Institute for Creation Research.

Mowen, J. and J. Gentry. 1980. "Investigation of the Preference-Reversal Phenomenon in a New Product Introduction Task." *Journal of Applied Psychology* 65: 715-22.

Murphy, N. 1989. "Another Look at Novel Facts." *Studies in the History and Philosophy of Science* 20: 385-8.

Musgrave, A. 1981. "'Unreal Assumptions' in Economic Theory: The F-Twist Untwisted." *Kyklos* 34: 377-87.

Muth, J. 1961. "Rational Expectations and the Theory of Price Movements." *Econometrica* 29: 315-35.

Myrdal, G. 1955. *The Political Element in the Development of Economic Thought*, tr. P. Streeten. Cambridge, MA: Harvard University Press.

Nagel, E. 1961. *The Structure of Science.* New York: Harcourt, Brace & World.

   1963. "Assumptions in Economic Theory." *American Economic Review Papers and Proceedings* 53: 211-19.

Nelson, A. 1986. "New Individualistic Foundations for Economics." *Nous* 20, 469-90.

Nelson, R. and S. Winter. 1974. "Neoclassical vs. Evolutionary Theory of Economic Growth: Critique and Prospectus." *Economic Journal* 84: 886-905.

   1982. *An Evolutionary Theory of Economic Change.* Cambridge, MA: Harvard University Press.

Neuberg, L. 1988. *Conceptual Anomalies in Economics.* Cambridge: Cambridge University Press.

Nickles, T. 1980. *Scientific Discovery, Logic and Rationality.* Dordrecht: Reidel.

Nickles, T., ed. 1980. *Scientific Discovery: Case Studies.* Dordrecht: Reidel.

Niiniluoto, I. 1983. "Novel Facts and Bayesianism." *British Journal for the Philosophy of Science* 34: 375-9.

Nisbett, R. and P. Thagard. 1982. "Variability and Confirmation." *Philosophical Studies* 42: 379-94.

Nooteboom, B. 1986. "Plausibility in Economics." *Economics and Philosophy* 2: 197-224.

North, D. 1990. *Institutions, Institutional Change and Economic Performance.* Cambridge: Cambridge University Press.

Nowak, L. 1972. "Laws of Science, Theory, Measurement." *Philosophy of Science* 39: 533-48.

   1980. *The Structure of Idealization: Towards a Systematic Interpretation of the Marxian Idea of Science.* Dordrecht: Reidel.

Nozick, R. 1974. *Anarchy, State and Utopia.* New York: Basic Books.

Okun, A. 1975. *Equality and Efficiency: the Big Tradeoff.* Washington, DC: Brookings Institution.

Okuno, M. and I. Zilcha. 1983. "Optimal Steady-State in Stationary Consumption-Loan Type Models." *Journal of Economic Theory* 31: 355-63.

Olson, M., Jr 1984. "Beyond Keynesianism and Monetarism." *Economic Inquiry* 22: 297-322.

O'Neill, J. 1973. *Modes of Individualism and Collectivism.* London: Heinemann.

Orcutt, G. 1952. "Actions, Consequences and Causal Relations." *Review of Economics and Statistics* 34: 305-13.

Papandreou, A. 1958. *Economics as a Science.* Chicago: Lippincott.

1963. "Theory Construction and Empirical Meaning in Economics." *American Economic Review Papers and Proceedings* 53: 205–10.

Pareto, V. 1909. *Manual of Political Economy*, tr. A. Schwier. New York: A. M. Kelley, 1971.

Pettit, P. and R. Sugden. 1989. "The Backward Induction Paradox." *Journal of Philosophy* 86: 169–82.

Pheby, J. 1988. *Methodology and Economics: A Critical Introduction.* London: Macmillan.

Pitt, J., ed. 1981. *Philosophy in Economics.* Dordrecht: Reidel.

Poincaré, H. 1905. *Science and Hypothesis.* Repr. New York: Dover, 1952.

Pommerehne, W., F. Schneider, and P. Zweifel. 1982. "Economic Theory of Choice and the Preference Reversal Phenomenon: A Reexamination." *American Economic Review* 72: 569–74.

Pope, D. and R. Pope. 1972. "Predictionists, Assumptionists and the Relatives of the Assumptionists." *Australian Economic Papers* 11: 224–8.

Popper, K. 1957. *The Poverty of Historicism.* New York: Harper & Row.

1966. *The Open Society and Its Enemies.* vol. II, 5th edn. Princeton: Princeton University Press, 1966.

1968. *The Logic of Scientific Discovery* (rev. edn.) London: Hutchinson & Co.

1969a. *Conjectures and Refutations; The Growth of Scientific Knowledge.* 3rd. edn. London: Routledge & Kegan-Paul.

1969b. "Die Logik der Sozialwissenschaften," in Adorno (1969), pp. 103–23.

1969c. "Truth, Rationality and the Growth of Scientific Knowledge," in Popper (1969a), pp. 215–50.

1972. *Objective Knowledge; An Evolutionary Approach.* Oxford: Clarendon Press.

1974. "Replies to my Critics," in Schilpp (1974), pp. 961–1200.

1976. *The Unended Quest.* La Salle, IL: Open Court.

1978. "Natural Selection and the Emergence of Mind." *Dialectica* 32: 339–55.

1979. *Die Beiden Grundprobleme der Erkenntnistheorie.* Tubingen: Mohr-Siebeck.

1983. *Realism and the Aim of Science; From the Postscript to the Logic of Scientific Discovery,* ed. W. Bartley, III. Totowa, NJ: Rowman and Littlefield.

Posner, R. 1972. *Economic Analysis of Law.* Boston: Little, Brown & Co.

Putnam, H. 1962. "The Analytic and the Synthetic," in Feigl and Maxwell (1962), pp. 350–97.

1974. "The 'Corroboration' of Theories," in Schilpp (1974), pp. 221–40.

Quine, W. 1953. "Two Dogmas of Empiricism," in *From a Logical Point of View.* Cambridge, MA: Harvard University Press, pp. 20–46.

1960. *Word and Object.* Cambridge, MA: MIT Press.

1969. "Epistemology Naturalized," in *Ontological Relativity and Other Essays in the Philosophy of Science.* New York: Columbia University Press, pp. 69–90.

Rachlin, H., R. Battalio, J. Kagel, and L. Green. 1981. "Maximization Theory in Behavioral Psychology." *Behavioral and Brain Sciences* 4: 371–418.

Railton, P. 1980. "Explaining Explanation: A Realist Account of Scientific Explanation." Ph.D. Dissertation, Princeton University.

Ramsey, F. 1926. "Truth and Probability," in R. Braithwaite, ed. *The Foundations of Mathematics and other Logical Essays.* London: Routledge & Kegan Paul, pp. 156–98.

Rawls, J. 1971. *A Theory of Justice.* Cambridge, MA: Harvard University Press.

1982. "Social Unity and Primary Goods," in Sen and Williams (1982), pp. 159–86.

Redman, D. 1989. *Economic Methodology: A Bibliography with References to Works in the Philosophy of Science, 1860–1988.* New York: Greenwood Press.

1990. *Economics and the Philosophy of Science.* Oxford: Oxford University Press.

Reichenbach, H. 1938. *Experience and Prediction. An Analysis of the Foundations and the Structure of Knowledge.* Chicago: University of Chicago Press.

1959. *Modern Philosophy of Science.* London: Routledge.

Reilly, R. 1982. "Preference Reversal: Further Evidence and Some Suggested Modifications in Experimental Design." *American Economic Review* 72: 576–84.

Rescher, N. 1970. *Scientific Explanation.* New York: Macmillan.

Resnik, M. 1987. *Choices: An Introduction to Decision Theory.* Minneapolis: University of Minnesota Press.

Ricardo, David 1817. *On the Principles of Political Economy and Taxation.* vol. 1 of *The Collected Works of David Ricardo,* ed. P. Sraffa and M. Dobb. Cambridge: Cambridge University Press, 1951.

Rizzo, M. 1982. "Mises and Lakatos: A Reformulation of Austrian Methodology," in I. Kirzner, ed. *Method, Process and Austrian Economics: Essays in Honour of Ludwig von Mises.* Lexington, MA: D.C. Heath.

Robbins, L. 1932, 1935. *An Essay on the Nature and Significance of Economic Science.* 2nd. edn. 1935. London: Macmillan.

1979. "On Latsis' *Method and Appraisal in Economics: A Review Essay.*" *Philosophy of the Social Sciences* 17: 996–1004.

Rorty, R. 1979. *Philosophy and the Mirror of Nature.* Princeton: Princeton University Press.

Roscher, W. 1874. *Geschichte der National-oekonomik in Deutschland.* Munich: R. Oldenbourg.

Rosenberg, A. 1976. *Microeconomic Laws: A Philosophical Analysis.* Pittsburgh: University of Pittsburgh Press.

1980. *Sociobiology and the Preemption of Social Science.* Baltimore: Johns-Hopkins University Press.

1983. "If Economics Isn't a Science: What Is It?" *Philosophical Forum* 14: 296–314.

1986. "Lakatosian Consolations for Economics." *Economics and Philosophy* 2: 127–40.

1987. "Weintraub's Aims: A Brief Rejoinder." *Economics and Philosophy* 3: 143–4.

1988a. "Economics is Too Important to Be Left to the Rhetoricians." *Economics and Philosophy* 4: 129–49.

1988b. *Philosophy of Social Science.* Boulder: Westview Press.

forthcoming. *An Essay in the Philosophy of Economics.* Chicago: University of Chicago Press.

Rosenkranz, R. 1977. *Inference, Method and Decision.* Dordrecht: Reidel.

1983. "Why Glymour *Is* a Bayesian," in Earman (1983), pp. 69–98.

Roth, A. 1987. "Bargaining Phenomena and Bargaining Theory," in Roth, ed. (1987), pp. 14–41.

1988. "Laboratory Experimentation in Economics: A Methodological Overview." *Economic Journal* 98: 974–1031.

Roth, A., ed. 1987. *Laboratory Experimentation in Economics: Six Points of View.* Cambridge: Cambridge University Press.

Rothbard, M. 1957. "In Defense of 'Extreme Apriorism.'" *Southern Economic Journal* 23: 314–20.

1976. "Praxeology: The Methodology of Austrian Economics," in Dolan (1976), pp. 19–39.

Rotwein, E. 1959. "On 'The Methodology of Positive Economics.'" *Quarterly Journal of Economics* 73: 554–75.

1962. "On 'The Methodology of Positive Economics' Reply." *Quarterly Journal of Economics* 76: 666–8.

Runciman, W. 1972. *A Critique of Max Weber's Philosophy of the Social Sciences.* Cambridge: Cambridge University Press.

Russell, B. 1905. "On Denoting." Repr. in B. Russell, *Logic and Knowledge: Essays 1901–50.* New York: G.P. Putnam & Sons, pp. 39–56.

1912. "On the Notion of Cause." Repr. in B. Russell, *Mysticism and Logic and Other Essays.* London: George Allen & Unwin, pp. 132–51.

Russell, T. and R. Thaler. 1985. "The Relevance of Quasi Rationality in Competitive Markets." *American Economic Review* 75: 1071–82.

Ryan, A., ed. 1973. *The Philosophy of Social Explanation.* Oxford: Oxford University Press.

Safra, Z., U. Segal, and A. Spivak. 1990. "Preference Reversal and Nonexpected Utility Behavior." *American Economic Review* 80: 922–30.

Sagoff, M. 1986. "Values and Preferences." *Ethics* 96: 301–16.

Salmon, W. 1971. "Statistical Explanation," in W. Salmon, ed. *Statistical Explanation and Statistical Relevance.* Pittsburgh: University of Pittsburgh Press, pp. 29–88.

1975. "Confirmation and Relevance," in G. Maxwell and R. Anderson, eds. (1975), pp. 5–36. Repr. in P. Achinstein, ed. *The Concept of Evidence.* Oxford: Oxford University Press, pp. 95–123.

1981. "Rational Prediction." *British Journal for the Philosophy of Science* 32: 115–25.

1985. *Scientific Explanation and the Causal Structure of the World.* Princeton: Princeton University Press.

1990. *Four Decades of Scientific Explanation.* Minneapolis: University of Minnesota Press.

Samuels, W. 1980. ed. *The Methodology of Economic Thought: Critical Papers from the Journal of Economic Thought [Issues].* New Brunswick: Transaction Books.

Samuelson, P. 1938. "A Note on the Pure Theory of Consumer's Behavior." *Economica* 5: 61–71.

1947. *Foundations of Economic Analysis.* Cambridge, MA: Harvard University Press.

1950. "Evaluation of Real National Income." *Oxford Economic Papers.* N.S. 2: 1–29.

354   Bibliography

1958. "An Exact Consumption-Loan Model of Interest with or without the Social Contrivance of Money." *Journal of Political Economy* 66: 467-82.

1959. "Reply." *Journal of Political Economy* 67: 518-22.

1960. "Infinity, Unanimity and Singularity: A Reply." *Journal of Political Economy* 68: 76-83.

1963. "Problems of Methodology - Discussion." *American Economic Review Papers and Proceedings* 53: 232-36.

1964. "Theory and Realism: A Reply." *American Economic Review* 54: 736-40.

1965. "Professor Samuelson on Theory and Realism: Reply." *American Economic Review* 55: 1162-72.

Sargent, T. 1987. *Dynamic Macroeconomic Theory.* Cambridge, MA: Harvard University Press.

Savage, L. 1972. *The Foundations of Statistics.* 2nd. edn. New York: Dover.

Scheffler, I. 1967. *Science and Subjectivity.* Indianapolis: Bobbs-Merrill.

Schick, F. 1986. "Money Pumps and Dutch Bookies." *Journal of Philosophy* 83: 112-19.

1987. "Rationality: A Third Dimension." *Economics and Philosophy* 3: 49-66.

Schilpp, P. ed. 1939. *The Philosophy of John Dewey.* La Salle, IL: Open Court.

1974. *The Philosophy of Karl Popper.* La Salle, IL: Open Court.

Schkade, D. and E. Johnson. 1989. "Cognitive Processes in Preference Reversals." *Organizational Behavior and Human Performance* 44: 203-31.

Schlesinger, G. 1976. *Confirmation and Confirmability.* Oxford: Clarendon Press.

Schlicht, E. 1984. "Cognitive Dissonance in Economics." *Schriften des Vereins für Sozialpolitik, Gesellschaft für Wirtschafts- und Sozialwissenschaften.* Neue Folge 141: 61-81.

Schmoller, G. 1888. *Zur Literatur-geschichte der Staats- und Sozialwissenschaften.* Leipzig: Duncker & Humblot.

1898. *Über einige Grundfragen der Sozialpolitik und der Volkswirtshaftslehre.* Leipzig: Duncker & Humblot.

Schumpeter, J. 1954. *History of Economic Analysis.* New York: Oxford University Press.

Schwartz, T. 1982. "What Welfare Is Not," in Miller and Williams (1982), pp. 195-206.

Segal, U. 1988. "Does the Preference Reversal Phenomenon Necessarily Contradict the Independence Axiom?" *American Economic Review* 78: 233-6.

Seidenfeld, T., M. Schervish, and J. Kadane. 1987. "Decisions Without Ordering." Technical Report N. 391, Department of Statistics, Carnegie Mellon University.

Sen, A. 1970. *Collective Welfare and Social Choice.* San Francisco: Holden-Day.

1971 "Choice Functions and Revealed Preference." *Review of Economic Studies* 38: 307-17.

1973 "Behaviour and the Concept of Preference." *Economica* 40: 241-59.

1977. "Rational Fools," in Hahn and Hollis (1981), pp. 87-109.

1979a "Personal Utilities and Public Judgment: or What's Wrong with Welfare Economics?" *Economic Journal* 89: 537-58.

1979b "Utilitarianism and Welfarism." *Journal of Philosophy* 76: 463-88.

Sen, A. and B. Williams, eds. 1982. *Utilitarianism and Beyond.* Cambridge: Cambridge University Press.

Senior, N. 1836. *Outline of the Science of Political Economy.* Repr. New York: A. M. Kelley, 1965.

Sensat, J. 1988. "Methodological Individualism and Marxism." *Economics and Philosophy* 4: 189–220.

Shapere, D. 1964. "The Structure of Scientific Revolutions." *Philosophical Review* 73: 383–94.

1969. "Towards a Post-positivistic Interpretation of Science," in P. Achinstein and S. Barkers, eds. *The Legacy of Logical Positivism.* Baltimore: Johns Hopkins University Press, pp. 115–60.

1974. "Scientific Theories and Their Domains," in Suppe (1977), pp. 518–65.

1984. *Reason and the Search for Knowledge.* Dordrecht: Reidel.

1985. "Objectivity, Rationality, and Scientific Change," in P. Asquith and P. Kitcher, eds. *PSA 1984,* vol. 2. East Lansing: Philosophy of Science Association, pp. 637–63.

Shell, K. 1971. "Notes on the Economics of Infinity." *Journal of Political Economy* 79: 1002–11.

Simon, H. 1953. "Causal Ordering and Identifiability." Repr. in *Models of Discovery and other Topics in the Methods of Science.* Dordrecht: Reidel, 1977, pp. 53–80.

1954. "Bandwagon and Underdog Effects of Election Predictions." *Public Opinion Quarterly* 18: 245–53.

1957. *Models of Man: Social and Rational.* New York: Wiley.

1959. "Theories of Decision-Making in Economics and Behavioral Science." *American Economic Review* 49: 253–83.

1963. "Problems of Methodology – Discussion." *American Economic Review Papers and Proceedings* 53: 229–31.

1976. "From Substantive to Procedural Rationality," in Latsis, ed. (1976), pp. 129–48.

1978. "Rationality as Process and as Product of Thought." *American Economic Review: Papers and Proceedings* 68: 1–16.

1979. "Rational Decision Making in Business Organizations." *American Economic Review* 69: 493–513.

1982. *Models of Bounded Rationality.* 2 vols. Cambridge, MA: MIT Press.

Sims, C. 1972. "Money, Income and Causality." *American Economic Review* 62: 540–52.

1977. "Exogeneity and Causal Orderings in Macroeconomic Models," in C. Sims, ed. *New Methods in Business Cycle Research.* Minneapolis: Federal Reserve Bank, pp. 23–43.

1981. "What Kind of Science is Economics? A Review Article on *Causality in Economics* by John R. Hicks." *Journal of Political Economy* 89: 578–83.

Skinner, B. 1953. *Science and Human Behavior.* New York: Free Press.

1974. *About Behaviorism.* New York: Random House.

Slovic, P., D. Griffin, and A. Tversky. 1990. "Compatibility Effects in Judgment and Choice," in R. M. Hogarth, ed. *Insights in Decision Making: Theory and Applications.* Chicago: University of Chicago Press, pp. 5–27.

Slovic, P. and S. Lichtenstein. 1968. "Relative Importance of Probabilities and Payoffs in Risk Taking." *Journal of Experimental Psychology Monograph* 78, Pt. 2: 1–18.

1983. "Preference Reversals: A Broader Perspective." *American Economic Review* 73: 596–605.

Slovic, P. and A. Tversky. 1974. "Who Accepts Savage's Axiom?" *Behavioral Science* 19: 368–73.

Smith, A. 1776. *An Inquiry into the Nature and Causes of the Wealth of Nations.* Repr. New York: Random House, 1937.

Smith, M. 1990. "What is New in 'New Structuralist' Analyses of Earnings?" *American Journal of Sociology* 55: 827–41.

Smith, V. 1982. "Microeconomic Systems as an Experimental Science." *American Economic Review* 72: 923–55.

Smith, V. ed. 1978. *Research in Experimental Economics.* Greenwich, Connecticut: JAI Press.

Sneed, J. 1971. *The Logical Structure of Mathematical Physics.* Dordrecht: Reidel.

Sober, E. 1983. "Equilibrium Explanation." *Philosophical Studies* 43: 201–10.

1985. "Review of *Sociobiology and the Preemption of the Social Sciences,*" *Philosophy of the Social Sciences* 15: 89–93.

1988. *Reconstructing the Past: Parsimony, Evolution and Inference.* Cambridge: Cambridge University Press.

Solow, R. 1971. "Science and Ideology in Economics." *The Public Interest* 23: 94–107.

Stalnaker, R. 1968. "A Theory of Conditionals." Repr. in E. Sosa, ed. *Causation and Conditionals.* Oxford: Oxford University Press, 1975, pp. 165–79.

1972. "Pragmatics," in D. Davidson and G. Harman, eds. *Semantics of Natural Language.* Dordrecht: Reidel, pp. 380–97.

Stanfield, R. 1974. "Kuhnian Revolutions and the Keynesian Revolution." *Journal of Economic Issues* 8: 97–109.

Stegmueller, W. 1976. *The Structure and Dynamics of Theories,* tr. William Wohlhueter. New York: Springer-Verlag.

1979. *The Structuralist View of Theories.* New York: Springer-Verlag.

Stegmueller, W., W. Balzer, and W. Spohn, eds. 1982. *Philosophy of Economics: Proceedings, Munich, July 1981.* New York: Springer-Verlag.

Stewart, I. 1979. *Reasoning and Method in Economics. An Introduction to Economic Methodology.* London: McGraw-Hill.

Stigler, G. J. 1947. "Professor Lester and the Marginalists." *American Economic Review,* 37: 154–7.

1959. "The Politics of Political Economists." *Quarterly Journal of Economics.* Repr. in *Essays in the History of Economics.* Chicago: University of Chicago Press, 1965, pp. 51–65.

1976. "Do Economists Matter?" *Southern Economic Journal.* Repr. in *The Economist as Preacher and Other Essays.* Chicago: University of Chicago Press, 1982, pp. 57–67.

Stiglitz, J. 1982. "Ownership, Control, and Efficient Markets: Some Paradoxes in the Theory of Capital Markets," in K. Boyer and W. Shepherd, eds. *Economic Regulation: Essays in Honor of James R. Nelson.* Ann Arbor: University of Michigan Press, pp. 311–40.

Stouffer, S., E. Suchman, L. de Vinney, S. Star, and R. Williams, Jr. 1949. *The American Soldier: Adjustment During Army Life.* Princeton: Princeton University Press.

Stouffer, S., A. Lumsdaine, M. Lumsdaine, R. Williams, M. Smith, I. Jarvis, S. Star, and L. Cottrell, Jr. 1949. *The American Soldier*: *Combat and its Aftermath*. Princeton: Princeton University Press.

Strasnick, S. 1981. "Neo-Utilitarian Ethics and the Ordinal Representation Assumption," in Pitt (1981), pp. 63-92.

Strotz, R. 1960. "Interdependence as a Specification Error." *Econometrica* 28: 428-42.

Strotz, R. and H. Wold. 1960. "Recursive vs. Non-recursive Systems: An Attempt at Synthesis." *Econometrica* 28: 417-27.

Sugden, R. 1986. "New Developments in the Theory of Choice Under Uncertainty." *Bulletin of Economic Research* 38: 1-24.

Suppe, F. 1974. "Theories and Phenomena," in W. Leinfeller and W. Kohler, eds. *Developments in the Methodology of Social Science*. Dordrecht: Reidel, pp. 45-92.

 1988. *The Semantic View of Theories*. Urbana: University of Illinois Press.

Suppe, F., ed. 1977. *The Structure of Scientific Theories*. 2nd. edn. Urbana: University of Illinois Press.

Suppes, P. 1957. *Introduction to Logic*. New York: Van Nostrand-Reinhold

Thagard, P. 1988. *Computational Philosophy of Science*. Cambridge, MA: MIT Press.

Thagard, P. and R. Nisbett. 1982. "Variability and Confirmation." *Philosophical Studies* 42: 379-94.

Thaler, R. 1980. "Toward a Positive Theory of Consumer Choice." *Journal of Economic Behavior and Organization* 1: 39-60.

 1987. "The Psychology of Choice and the Assumptions of Economics," in Roth, ed. (1987), pp. 99-130.

Thurow, L. 1975. *Generating Inequality*: *Mechanisms of Distribution in the U.S. Economy*. New York: Basic Books.

 1980. *The Zero-Sum Society*. New York: Basic Books. Repr. and cited in the Harmondsworth: Penguin, 1981 edition.

Tichy, P. 1974. "On Popper's Definition of Verisimilitude." *British Journal for the Philosophy of Science* 25: 155-60.

Titmuss, R. 1971. *The Gift Relationship*: *From Human Blood to Social Policy*. New York: Random House.

Tobin, J. 1980. "Discussion," in Kareken and Wallace (1980), pp. 83-90.

Toulmin, S. 1953. *The Philosophy of Science*: *An Introduction*. London: Hutchinson.

Toulmin, Stephen and June Goodfield. 1961. *The Fabric of the Heavens*: *The Development of Astronomy and Dynamics*. New York: Harper Torchbooks.

Tversky, A. and D. Kahneman. 1981. "The Framing of Decisions and the Psychology of Choice." *Science* 211: 453-8.

Tversky, A., P. Slovic, and D. Kahneman. 1990. "The Causes of Preference Reversal." *American Economic Review* 80: 204-17.

Tversky, A. and R. Thaler. 1990. "Preference Reversals." *Journal of Economic Perspectives* 4: 201-11.

Ullmann-Margalit, E. and S. Morgenbesser. 1977. "Picking and Choosing." *Social Research* 44: 757-85.

van Fraassen, B. 1980. *The Scientific Image*. Oxford: Oxford University Press.

 1983a. "Glymour on Evidence and Explanation," in Earman (1983), pp. 165-76.

1983b. "Theory Comparison and Relevant Evidence," in Earman (1983), pp. 27–52.

1989. *Laws and Symmetry.* Oxford: Clarendon Press.

Varian, H. 1985. "Dworkin on Equality of Resources." *Economics and Philosophy* 1: 110–27.

Veblen, T. 1898. "Why Is Economics Not an Evolutionary Science?" *Quarterly Journal of Economics* 12: 373–97.

1900. "The Preconceptions of Economic Science." *Quarterly Journal of Economics* 13 (1899): 121–50, 396–426; 14: 240–69.

1909. "The Limitations of Marginal Utility." *Journal of Political Economy* 17: 620–36.

von Neumann, J. and O. Morgenstern. 1947. *Theory of Games and Economic Behavior.* 2nd. edn. Princeton: Princeton University Press.

von Wright, G. 1971. *Explanation and Understanding.* Ithaca: Cornell University Press.

Wallace, N. 1980a. "Integrating Micro and Macroeconomics: An Application to Credit Controls." *Federal Reserve Bank of Minneapolis Quarterly Review* 4, #4 (Fall): 16–29.

1980b. "The Overlapping Generations Model of Fiat Money," in Kareken and Wallace (1980), pp. 49–82.

Walras, L. 1926. *Elements of Pure Economics,* tr. W. Jaffe. Homewood, IL: Richard D. Irwin, 1954.

Watkins, J. 1953. "Ideal Types and Historical Explanation," in H. Feigl and M. Brodbeck, eds. *Readings in the Philosophy of Science,* pp. 723–44. Repr. in Ryan (1973), pp. 82–104.

1968. "Methodological Individualism and Social Tendencies," in M. Brodbeck, ed. *Readings in the Philosophy of the Social Sciences.* New York: Macmillan, pp. 269–79.

1984. *Science and Scepticism.* Princeton: Princeton University Press.

Weber, M. 1904. "'Objectivity' in Social Science and Social Policy," in Weber (1949), pp. 49–112.

1949. *The Methodology of the Social Sciences,* tr. and ed. E. Shils and H. Finch. New York: Macmillan.

1975. *Roscher and Knies: The Logical Problem of Historical Economics,* tr. G. Oakes. New York: Macmillan.

Weintraub, E. 1985a. "Appraising General Equilibrium Analysis." *Economics and Philosophy* 1: 23–38.

1985b. *General Equilibrium Analysis: Studies in Appraisal.* Cambridge: Cambridge University Press.

1987. "Rosenberg's 'Lakatosian Consolations for Economics': Comment." *Economics and Philosophy* 3: 139–42.

1988. "The Neo-Walrasian Program is Empirically Progressive," in de Marchi (1988), pp. 213–30.

1990. *Stabilizing Economic Knowledge.* Cambridge: Cambridge University Press.

West, J. and J. Toonder. 1973. *The Case for Astrology.* Baltimore: Penguin.

Weyl, H. 1949. *Philosophy of Mathematics and Natural Science.* Princeton: Princeton University Press.

Whalley, J. 1988. "Lessons from General Equilibrium Models," in H. Aaron, H. Galper, and J. Pechman, eds. *Uneasy Compromise: Problems of a Hybrid Income-Consumption Tax.* Washington: Brookings Institution, pp. 15–57.

Whewell, W. 1840. *The Philosophy of the Inductive Sciences.* New York: Johnson Reprint, 1967.

White, M. 1956. *Toward Reunion in Philosophy.* Cambridge, MA: Harvard University Press.

Wible, J. 1987. "Criticism and the Validity of the Special-Case Interpretation of Friedman's Essay: Reply." *Journal of Economic Issues* 21: 430–40.

Wilber, C. and R. Harrison. 1978. "The Methodological Basis of Institutional Economics: Pattern Model, Storytelling and Holism." *Journal of Economic Issues* 12: 61–89.

Williams, M. 1977. *Groundless Belief.* New Haven: Yale University Press.

Williamson, O. 1985. *The Economic Institutions of Capitalism.* New York: Free Press.

Winch, P. 1958. *The Idea of a Social Science.* London: Routledge.

1964. "Understanding a Primitive Society." *American Philosophical Quarterly* 1: 307–24.

Winkler, R. 1972. *Introduction to Bayesian Inference and Decision.* New York: Holt Rinehart & Winston.

Winston, G. and R. Teichgraeber, eds. 1988. *The Boundaries of Economics.* Cambridge: Cambridge University Press.

Winter, S. 1962. "Economic 'Natural Selection' and the Theory of the Firm." *Yale Economic Essays* 4: 255–72.

Wold, H. 1954. "Causality and Econometrics." *Econometrica* 22: 162–77.

1960. "A Generalization of Causal Chain Models." *Econometrica* 28, 443–63.

Worland, S. 1972. "Radical Political Economy as a 'Scientific Revolution.'" *Southern Economic Journal* 39: 274–84.

Yeager, L. 1969. "*Methodenstreit* over Demand Curves." *Journal of Political Economy* 68: 53–64.

Zahar, E. 1983. "The Popper-Lakatos Controversy in the Light of 'Die Beiden Grundprobleme der Erkenntnistheorie.'" *British Journal for the Philosophy of Science.* 34: 149–74.

Zytkow, J. 1986. "What Revisions Does Bootstrap Testing Need?" *Philosophy of Science* 53: 101–9.

Index